Human Rights Reports
An annotated bibliography
of fact-finding missions

Compiled and edited by
Berth Verstappen

Published for the
Netherlands Institute of Human Rights—SIM

Hans Zell Publishers
an imprint of
K·G·Saur London·München·New York·Paris 1987

British Library Cataloguing in Publication Data
Verstappen, Berth
  Human rights reports: an annotated
  bibliography of fact-finding missions.
  1. Civil rights—Bibliography
  I. Title
  016.3234 Z7164.L6
  ISBN 0–905450–35–3

Hans Zell Publishers
An imprint of K. G. Saur Ltd.
Shropshire House, 2–10 Capper Street, London WC1E 6JA, England

Copyright © Netherlands Institute of Human Rights—SIM

Publication of this book has been made possible by grants from
the European Cultural Foundation and the European Human Rights
Foundation, which are gratefully acknowledged.

Printed in Great Britain
at the University Printing House, Oxford
by David Stanford
Printer to the University

ISBN 0–905450–35–3 (Zell)

CONTENTS

PREFACE

Since the second half of the seventies there has been a considerable increase in international human rights activities, including the practice of sending fact-finding missions to investigate the factual situation of human rights in a specific country. Not only intergovernmental organization (IGOs), such as the United Nations and the International Labour Organization, but also nongovernmental organizations (NGOs), such as Amnesty International, the Federation Internationale des Droits de l'Homme, the International Association of Democratic Lawyers, the International Commission of Jurists and Americas Watch have stepped up their activities to bring to light the degree to which internationally agreed norms of human rights are implemented or violated in practice. In this sense fact finding can be seen as a bridge over the information gap between "rules and reality", between "fiction and fact".

While IGOs usually have a number of basic procedures which govern the sending of fact-finding missions, nothing of the sort is true for NGOs. For IGOs fact finding is the result of a lengthy process in which strong account has to be taken of the position of the receiving government, which is, after all, a Member State of the sending organization. Only in extreme cases, when _prima facie_ evidence has been brought to the fore (and even then only when there is a political majority), do IGOs send missions publicly. The secretariat of the IGO and the members of the mission (often called Rapporteurs) have to negotiate, on the basis of existing rules and practices, their access to information sources, their meetings with government officials and the way the report will be published.

NGOs sometimes try to establish these official contacts, but don't _have_ to and their fact-finding practices are characterized as more informal and independent; independent not only from the receiving country but also from their own previous practices or those of their fellow NGOs.

These and other differences between fact finding by NGOs and IGOs do not away with their common treat: finding the facts and evaluating and presenting them in an objective manner. With the increase in number and variety of missions and their possible impact on public opinion and governments, the question has arisen whether sufficient attention is paid to the way in which fact finding is conducted. As the efficacy of fact finding rests largely on its credibility, i.e. the manifest integrity and consistency of the fact-finding process and which can only be judged from the resulting reports, human rights experts have been studying over the last years ways and means to improve fact-finding practices. One of the preconditions to do so is to know the past: which missions and how many were sent, where and when? It was with these questions in mind that the Netherlands Institute of Human Rights (SIM) organized in 1983 an

international seminar on the question of NGO fact-finding
procedures. Following this seminar it undertook a primarily
quantitative study of NGO fact-finding practices covering the
period 1970-1985. The initial research covered 187 reports,
while at a later stage another 153 reports were taken into
consideration. The resulting study, which was conducted on the
basis of the reports as published and not on interviews asser-
ting the intentions, was published in 1986 by Martinus Nijhoff
Publishers under the title "Human Rights Missions, a Study of
the Fact-finding practice of Non-governmental Organizations"
(ISBN 90-247-3364-2). It shows that, although there is a great
variety in the way NGOs conduct their missions, some general
conclusions can be drawn and that there is room for improvement
in the way reports are published. To remedy the shortcomings
is in the first place the responsibility of the individual NGOs
and their leadership who have to take procedural accounting for
their missions more seriously. That this is not an impossible
task is shown by another conclusion of the study that NGOs
which establish prior contacts with the governments concerned
or submit to them the report before publication (a standard
practice of Amnesty International) usually score much better in
the way the report is written and presented.

Finally there is one aspect which concerns the community of
NGOs as a whole rather than the individual organizations: the
frequency of fact-finding missions to specific countries. The
imbalance in geographical distribution of missions found by the
study is not surprising but even stronger than expected, e.g.
it turned out that Central America (in particular El Salvador
and Nicaragua) received on average more than 11 missions per
country during 1970-85, while the average for Central Africa
was 0,25 per country (44 times less frequent). Almost 50% of
all missions went to Latin America and the Caribbean. In
Europe, where the number of missions is already low, 11 of the
29 missions went to Turkey. This kind of geographical imbalance can be explained in general by considerations such as the
difference in the level of alleged violations or the refusal of
permission. But they cannot alone justify the degree of
imbalance found to exist, and motives of "home consumption" in
the selection of target countries cannot be disregarded in
explaining the differences. However, before jumping to the
conclusion that NGOs are good at selective indignation, it
should be considered that to a large extent the imbalance is
caused by an overlap of missions from different NGOs, rather
than bias within a particular organization. While those NGOs
which send missions regularly, distribute them more or less
evenly (at best 2 or 3 to the same country in a decade), other
NGOs, which undertake fact-finding missions only sporadically,
seem to send their first (and often only) mission to the
country in "fashion".

The authors of the study therefore recommend that NGOs achieve a balance within their own fact-finding activity as well as within the human rights community as a whole. A distinction has to be made between unintended overlap, which is usually the result of a lack of information, and indended overlap, which is based on other considerations, such as the cumulative effect of several missions or a temporarily receptive public opinion. With respect to the first situation, unintended overlap, it goes without saying that a faster and more complete circulation of recently published reports (or at least summaries of them) would be the right answer. It is therefore in the interest of the human-rights movement to strengthen the ongoing efforts to establish the conditions for a better circulation of human rights information (such as the network HURIDOCS which stands for Human Rights Information and Documentation System). Information concerning planned or current missions may better remain in the informal circuit, but also here decision-making concerning the advisability of and need for sending a mission should be based on up-to-date information acquired through a quick, informal consultation among the main actors.

With respect to the second type of overlap, conscious overlap, the need for better cooperation is also present. In-depth study of existing reports and, for planned missions, better consultation would help in dividing the work according to relative specialization and the desirability to cover different places and sources. In this context it would also be an improvement if NGOs would show in their reports that they were aware of previous missions and reports.

In the hope of contributing to improved fact finding and smoother cooperation, the Netherlands Institute of Human Rights and the Henry Dunant Institute jointly convened a Round Table on February 2, 1987 in Geneva. Representatives of human rights NGOs, United Nations bodies and the media discussed the conclusions and recommendations of the Human Rights Missions study. It was generally agreed that only if organizations and individuals concerned accept that they have a shared responsibility for the way in which their activities reach the public and have an impact on the level of human rights violations in the world, any progress will be possible.

As mentioned above the study was conducted on the basis of a large number of NGO fact-finding reports, the collection of which was far from easy as many of the NGOs (have to) publish their own mission reports. Because of lack of resources (combined sometimes with a lack of attention) the print order is often low while dissemination is equally weak. The result is that many of the reports cannot be tracked or obtained, a situation which contributes to problems discussed above such as the unintended overlap and lack of knowledge about what was done already. When the descriptions of the 340 NGO reports were

done and entered into the SIM database it occurred that one of
the main contributions that SIM could make to improving the
fact-finding practice was the publication of a well-organized
bibliography of fact-finding reports. Berth Verstappen therefore undertook to expand the scope of his research to include
now also fact-finding reports by the United Nations and other
IGOs and the previously disregarded NGO-reports of observer
missions to trials and elections. Using his persistence and
skills, honed in the previous exercise of collecting and
summarizing NGO-reports, with a great measure of cooperation by
other organizations and the staff of SIM, Berth Verstappen
managed to pull together and make accessible the most complete
collection of human rights fact-finding reports published up to
date.

The European Cultural Foundation and the European Human Rights
Foundation immediately understood the importance of the
publication and wide dissemination of this kind of bibliography
and did not hesitate to contribute to the realization of the
project. One can only hope that it will prove to be possible to
keep the collection up to date and issue regularly addenda with
the most recent mission reports.

Hans Thoolen (former Director of SIM)   Geneva, February 1987

Introduction

"Information about human rights is hard to obtain, difficult to
disseminate and essential to the protection and promotion of all
human rights." (Martin Ennals)

A relatively large amount of the relevant literature in the field
of human rights falls within the category of so-called "grey" or
"fugitive" literature, being documents which are often reproduced
in a non-commercial way through simple techniques and distributed
in relatively low print orders.

This holds also true for reports of fact-finding missions, especially for missions of non-governmental organizations.

The last decade has witnessed a considerable increase in the
practice of sending fact-finding missions to investigate specific
problems involving human-rights issues ad locum.

This annotated bibliography of reports of fact-finding missions
is published in the framework of the fact-finding project which
was carried out by the Netherlands Institute of Human Rights
(SIM) as a follow-up to its inaugural conference on Factfinding
and specialized research in the field of human rights organized
from 2-4 June 1983. One of the main characteristics of this project is that it constituted a combination of research and documentation.

The titles of relevant reports were at first instance retrieved
through checking bibliographies on human rights, such as the HU-
RIDOCS' list of NGO publications on human rights and the Human
Rights Internet Reporter, as well as lists of publications of relevant organizations. Of course, also fact-finding reports
already available at SIM were included in the project.

On the basis of the information collected in this way, more than
sixty non-governmental organizations were approached with the request to make available a listed number of fact-finding reports.

The collection of reports was further broadened through visits to
the Fdération Internationale des Droits de l'Homme in Paris,
Human Rights Internet at Harvard Law School and Professor David
Weissbrodt in the Law School of the University of Minnesota. The
last two visits resulted in copies of reports of missions by
other organizations.

On the basis of the reports thus collected, a quantitative and
descriptive research into the fact-finding practises of non-governmental organizations was conducted. The analysis focussed on
areas such as mission and the "Purpose of the mission", "The sending organization", "Government contacts", "Finding the facts",
"The report", and "Frequency of NGO fact-finding missions to specific countries and regions". Attention was paid to questions

such as: do the reports contain clear indications of the terms of reference (mandate) of the mission? Did the government cooperate with the mission? Is there a strong imbalance in the distribution of missions over countries and regions? The research resulted in the publication "Human Rights Missions: a study of the fact-finding practice of non-governmental organizations", by Hans Thoolen and Berth Verstappen, published by Martinus Nijhoff Publishers and SIM at the end of 1986.

In the course of 1986, it was decided to publish also an annotated bibliography of the reports collected in the course of the project. It was considered valuable to include within this bibliography also reports on election observation missions and trial observation missions by non-governmental organizations, as well as reports of missions by intergovernmental organizations, which were not included in the "research part" of the project.

For this purpose, over fifty organizations were approached with a request for additional reports, again with a good response rate.

The bibliographic descriptions of the reports collected were made according to the Standard Formats which have been developed by the Human Rights Information and Documentation System (HURIDOCS). These formats for the recording and exchange of information on human rights consist of a number of fixed fields for various bibliographic descriptors and a free-text section.

The descriptions thus made of the reports were entered into SIM's computerized documentation system, where they form part of a public database system with approximately 5.000 documents on human rights.

Criteria for the selection of reports

1) It will be clear that the bibliography is restricted to those reports which can be considered to be public information, which implies that reports which were written for a limited audience (like the Board and members of the organization(s) which dispatched the mission) are not included in this bibliography and is SIM's public documentation collection.

2) Another limitation is that only reports published by intergovernmental and nongovernmental organizations are included. Reports or investigations undertaken by governmental delegations, or products of "investigative journalism" were left out of the scope of the project.

3) The reports had to deal with matters in the field of human rights, be it civil and political rights and / or economic, social and cultural rights. Reports which had a wider scope, but which did contain sections on the situation of human rights in the country or region visited, were not excluded.

4) Another selection criterium was that the fact-finding activity
had to include a visit to the country of which the human-rights
situation was to be investigated, so-called field research. Additional desk research is often undertaking in preparation of the
visit, or for writing the report after the mission. This was no
reason for exclusion of certain reports. This in turn implied
that national fact-finding, i.e. the holding of commissions of
inquiry within the country where the non-governmental organization conducting such an inquiry is based was to be excluded.

5) The bibliography is confined to missions of which the reports
were published between 1970 and September 1986.

The reports are classified according to the country (countries)
or regions visited by the organizations. A look through the book
or at the country index leads to remarkable conclusions with regard to the division of fact-finding missions and their reports
over the different countries and regions.

The descriptions of the documents are reproduced here according
to fixed fields as contained in the HURIDOCS Standard Formats.
For practical purposes, the number of fixed fields included in
this bibliography has been slightly reduced. The fields for "BIB-
LIOGRAPHIES" and "STATISTICAL INFORMATION" have only been included for those reports which contain a bibliography or statistical
information.

The reports have in first instance been classified according to
the continent to which the mission took place (Africa, Latin America, Asia, Europe, and Australia and Oceania), and then alphabe-
tically according to country. Missions to more than one country
are grouped at the end of each continent-chapter. For each
country or region, the reports have been classified chronologi-
cally.

I would like to thank all organizations which provided SIM with
various fact-finding reports, and especially the institutions
mentioned above which allowed me to go through their collection
of fact-finding reports in order to select relevant material. The
contribution of Hans Thoolen, former director of SIM, especially
in providing references to relevant organizations, factfinding
missions and reports, was no less than essential. Also I would
like to thank all members of the SIM staff, and especially Chris-
ta Keller and Gert Westerveen, who where of great help during various stages of the publication of this book.

This bibliography could be produced and disseminated thanks to
financial contributions by the European Cultural Foundation and
the European Human Rights Foundation.

Note to index on publishers: This index is according to the orga-
nization(s) which published the report; this is not necessarily
the same organization as the one(s) which organized and gave
their mandate to the mission.

Berth Verstappen
Oslo, December 1986   xiii

ALGERIA

CATALOGUE SIGNATURE: 0000/0035/-3=850800
TITLE: Algerie: Ligue des Droits de l'Homme: Ali Yahia: rapport de
mission
AUTHOR: Senghor, Jean-Gabriel
PLACE OF PUBLICATION: Paris
PUBLISHER: Fédération Internationale des Droits de l'Homme - FIDH (D)
DATE OF PUBLICATION: 850800
NUMBER OF PAGES: 5 p.
LANGUAGE: FRE
INDEX: nongovernmental organizations / trials / fact-finding missions
GEOGRAPHICAL INDEX: Algeria
GEOGRAPHICAL CODE: 5311
FREE TEXT: Report of a fact-finding mission in August 1985 to
investigate the situation of the defense lawyer Ali Yahia and other
members of the recently created Algerian League of Human Rights,
which were arrested by the police. According to the authorities,
Mr Yahia was arrested because of his involvement in an illegal
organization of children of martyrs, his detention conditions are
good and the rights of the defense are respected. However,
information provided by relatives does not support these statements.

CATALOGUE SIGNATURE: 0000/0035/-3=851200
TITLE: Rapport de mission: Algerie du 15 au 19 décembre 1985: procès de
la Ligue des Droits de l'Homme: Médéa
AUTHOR: Senghor, J.C.
PLACE OF PUBLICATION: Paris
PUBLISHER: Fédération Internationale des Droits de l'Homme - FIDH (D)
DATE OF PUBLICATION: 851200
NUMBER OF PAGES: 15 p. in v.p.
LANGUAGE: FRE
INDEX: association (freedom of) / trials / fact-finding missions
GEOGRAPHICAL INDEX: Algeria
GEOGRAPHICAL CODE: 5311
FREE TEXT: Report of the trial against certain members of the Algerian
Ligue for Human Rights and members of the Association of the "Children
of Martyrs", which took place in Medéa before the State Security Court.
The report contains information on events leading to the trial, the
enrollment of the hearings and the verdict, including an analysis. With
appendices: telegrams and information on the accused.

Algeria

CATALOGUE SIGNATURE: 0000/0035/-4
TITLE: Rapport de mission sur les conditions d'incarcération des
détenus de la Ligue Algérienne des Droits de l'Homme à Lambèse:
Algerie
AUTHOR: Bouvier, Philippe
TITLE OF GENERIC ITEM: La Lettre de la FIDH
VOLUME: no. 146
PLACE OF PUBLICATION: Paris
PUBLISHER: Fédération Internationale des Droits de l'Homme - FIDH (D)
DATE OF PUBLICATION: 860211
NUMBER OF PAGES: p. 3-10
LANGUAGE: FRE
INDEX: detention / nongovernmental organizations / fact-finding missions
GEOGRAPHICAL INDEX: Algeria
GEOGRAPHICAL CODE: 5311
FREE TEXT: The author was mandated to investigate the detention
conditions and physical conditions of six persons belonging to the
Algerian League of Human Rights which are detained in the prison of
Lambèse. He visited Algeria from 24 to 26 January 1986. The report
contains information on the taking place of the mission. The delegate
himself was not allowed to visit the prisoners, but family members of
the detained persons were; the conditions of the prisoners are
considered bad.

CATALOGUE SIGNATURE: 0000/0088/-4
TITLE: Report of a mission to Medéa, Algeria
AUTHOR: Charfi, Mohamed
TITLE OF GENERIC ITEM: ICJ Newsletter
EDITION: no. 28
PLACE OF PUBLICATION: Geneva
PUBLISHER: International Commission of Jurists - ICJ (D)
DATE OF PUBLICATION: 860300
NUMBER OF PAGES: p. 29-31
LANGUAGE: ENG
STATISTICAL INFORMATION: Y
INDEX: trials / fact-finding missions
GEOGRAPHICAL INDEX: Algeria
GEOGRAPHICAL CODE: 5311
FREE TEXT: The trial of nine founder members of the Ligue Algerienne
des Droits de l'Homme took place in December 1985 in Medéa before the
"cour de securité de l'Etat" (state security court), which tries all
offences against the state and is composed of three civilian and two
military judges. The trial proceeded normally and the rights of defence
were respected. However, the case against the accused was very weak,
and the sentences were severe. With list of sentences.

ANGOLA

CATALOGUE SIGNATURE: 5412/-0=810200
TITLE: Report on a visit to Angola: February 1-10, 1981
AUTHOR: Davis, Jennifer
PLACE OF PUBLICATION: (New York)
PUBLISHER: (American Committee on Africa - ACOA) (D)
DATE OF PUBLICATION: 810200
NUMBER OF PAGES: 9 p.
LANGUAGE: ENG
INDEX: armed conflict / fact-finding missions
GEOGRAPHICAL INDEX: Angola
GEOGRAPHICAL CODE: 5412
FREE TEXT: The author participated in the International Commission of
Inquiry into the Crimes of the Racist and Apartheid Regimes in Southern
Africa, and stayed on in Angola for several days after the conclusion
of the Commission. In her report, attention is paid to the role of
mercenaries, the involvement of the United States, torture and terror,
support for the liberation struggle and perspectives for development.

BOURKINA FASO

CATALOGUE SIGNATURE: 0000/0035/-4
TITLE: Burkina Faso: compte-rendu de mission: procès CEAO contre
Diawara et autres
AUTHOR: Miaille, Michel
TITLE OF GENERIC ITEM: La Lettre de la FIDH
EDITION: no. 157
PLACE OF PUBLICATION: Paris
PUBLISHER: Fédération Internationale des Droits de l'Homme (D)
DATE OF PUBLICATION: 860527
NUMBER OF PAGES: p. 5-8
LANGUAGE: FRE
INDEX: trials / fact-finding missions
GEOGRAPHICAL INDEX: Bourkina Faso
GEOGRAPHICAL CODE: 5516
FREE TEXT: The aim of the mission was to evaluate the procedures
applied during a trial in Ouagadougou, and especially the guarantees
given to the accused. The report deals with access to the trial and to
relevant persons, the conditions of preventive detention, the rights
of the defence and the verdict.

CAMEROON

CATALOGUE SIGNATURE: 0000/0035/-3=840200
TITLE: Procès de monsieur Ahidjo et de ses deux aides de camp devant
le tribunal militaire de Yaounde
AUTHOR: Baudelot, Yves ; Pognon, Alfred
PLACE OF PUBLICATION: Paris
PUBLISHER: Fédération Internationale des Droits de l'Homme - FIDH (D)
DATE OF PUBLICATION: 840200
NUMBER OF PAGES: 21 p.
LANGUAGE: FRE
INDEX: trials / fact-finding missions
GEOGRAPHICAL INDEX: Cameroon
GEOGRAPHICAL CODE: 5118
FREE TEXT: Baudelot and Pognon were mandated by the FIDH and by the
International Movement of Catholic Lawyers Pax Romana to observe the
trial against the former chief of state of Cameroon, Mr Ahidjo, and two
of his associates, commander Ibrahim and captain Salatou. They were
accused of an attempt to commit a conspiracy to kill the President,
and a coup d'état. Attention is paid to the political background of
the trial, the accusations (including relevant legislation), the
judicial procedure, the hearings, the requisitory and the verdict. The
delegates consider the verdict (death penalty for Ahidjo, lifelong
imprisonment for Ibrahim and Salatou) extremely severe.

COMORES

CATALOGUE SIGNATURE: 0000/0035/-3=800000
TITLE: Rapport de mission effectuée en République Fédérale et
Islamique des Comores du 21 au 28 juin 1980
AUTHOR: Henry, Pierre
PLACE OF PUBLICATION: Paris
PUBLISHER: Fédération Internationale des Droits de l'Homme - FIDH (D)
DATE OF PUBLICATION: 800000
NUMBER OF PAGES: 13 p.
LANGUAGE: FRE
INDEX: detention / political prisoners / fact-finding missions
GEOGRAPHICAL INDEX: Comores
GEOGRAPHICAL CODE: 5422
FREE TEXT: The purpose of the mission was to investigate detention
conditions of political prisoners in general, as well as some specific
cases. The delegate was not allowed to have contact with the prisoners,
and was menaced with imprisonment. He received information on the legal
and penitentiary situation, especially from the authorities. With
reference to specific cases. The author concludes that fundamental
human rights are violated in the Comores.

CATALOGUE SIGNATURE: 0000/0035/-3=800000
TITLE: Rapport de la mission effectuée en République Fédérale et
Islamique des Comores du 12 au 20 décembre 1980...
AUTHOR: Zavrian, Michel
PLACE OF PUBLICATION: Paris
PUBLISHER: Fédération Internationale des Droits de l'Homme - FIDH (D)
DATE OF PUBLICATION: 800000
NUMBER OF PAGES: 7 p.
LANGUAGE: FRE
INDEX: political prisoners / trials / fact-finding missions
GEOGRAPHICAL INDEX: Comores
GEOGRAPHICAL CODE: 5422
FREE TEXT: On the Comores, partisans of the ancient regime are kept in
prison without being accused. The purpose of the mission was to
investigate the functioning of a Special Court, the possibilities for
foreign defence lawyers to plead before it, and get known to the dates
of the trial and the charges against the accused. It is concluded that
there is a lack of defence lawyers in the Comores; French lawyers are
permitted to plead, but of course this would have financial consequences
for the families of detained persons.

CATALOGUE SIGNATURE: 0000/0035/-3=850500
TITLE: Rapport de mission 4 au 8 mai 1985: les Comores: la situation
des droits de l'homme en République Islamique des Comores
AUTHOR: Fagart, Thierry
PLACE OF PUBLICATION: Paris
PUBLISHER: Fédération Internationale des Droits de l'Homme - FIDH (D)
DATE OF PUBLICATION: 850500
NUMBER OF PAGES: 23 p.
LANGUAGE: FRE
INDEX: detention / trials / fact-finding missions
GEOGRAPHICAL INDEX: Comores
GEOGRAPHICAL CODE: 5422
FREE TEXT: On 8 March 1985, certain events occurred in the Comores
which were qualified by the government as a conspiracy against the
state. Subsequently, information was received concerning procedures
followed by the government, especially dealing with the participation
of mercenaries in repressive operations, possible ill-treatment of
prisoners, detention conditions, and more generally the occurrence of
the alleged conspiracy. The author describes the enrollment of his
fact-finding mission, his observations with regard to the different
versions of the events (government, people near to the oppositionary
Democratic Front), and his personal observations with regard to the
number of detainees, the procedures used, ill-treatment, detention
conditions, and the rights of the defence. With conclusions and
recommendations.

EGYPT

CATALOGUE SIGNATURE: 0000/0138/-3=770400
TITLE: Rapport sur la mission d'information de l'AIJD en Egypte du
16 au 23 avril 1977
AUTHOR: Bentoumi, Amar ; Winter, Timo
PLACE OF PUBLICATION: Brussels
PUBLISHER: Association Internationale des Juristes Démocrates - IADL (D)
DATE OF PUBLICATION: 770400
NUMBER OF PAGES: 11 p.
LANGUAGE: FRE
INDEX: political prisoners / fact-finding missions
GEOGRAPHICAL INDEX: Egypt
GEOGRAPHICAL CODE: 5325
FREE TEXT: The aim of the mission was to collect information on the
situation of democrats imprisoned after the events of January 1977,
when manifestations occurred after prices were raised. In March, there
were still 300 to 400 people in prison. A difference is made between
three different categories of inculpations. The circumstances of the
arrestations and the detention conditions are described. One prison
was visited. Attention is paid to the rights of the detainees and to
the activities of a lawyers organization and a political party. With
conclusions.

CATALOGUE SIGNATURE: 0000/0138/-3=780000
TITLE: Mission générale d'information sur la situation juridique et
les procès en cours en République Arabe Egyptienne: 10-22 juin 1978
AUTHOR: Lagadec, Jean
PLACE OF PUBLICATION: Brussels
PUBLISHER: Association Internationale des Juristes Démocrates - IADL (D)
DATE OF PUBLICATION: 780000
NUMBER OF PAGES: 13 p.
LANGUAGE: FRE
INDEX: judicial systems / trials / fact-finding missions
GEOGRAPHICAL INDEX: Egypt
GEOGRAPHICAL CODE: 5325
FREE TEXT: The first part of the report, "Legal situation", is on the
Constitution, the jurisdiction, the (undemocratic) character of the
legislative dispositions, the exceptional character of jurisdiction,
procedures and the role of the general-attorney.
The second part is on three trials on political affairs, with a
description of the cases and hearings. Jean Lagadec assisted as a trial
observer at one of these trials. Attention is also paid to public
liberties.
With conclusion: there is a policy of repression which limits
manifestations of democratic life.

CATALOGUE SIGNATURE: 0000/0138/-3=810000
TITLE: Mission en République Arabe Egyptienne 1-7 avril 1981
AUTHOR: De Castelnau, Regis
PLACE OF PUBLICATION: Brussels
PUBLISHER: Association Internationale des Juristes Democrates - IADL (D)
DATE OF PUBLICATION: 810000
NUMBER OF PAGES: 15 p.
LANGUAGE: FRE
INDEX: arrest / trials / fact-finding missions
GEOGRAPHICAL INDEX: Egypt
GEOGRAPHICAL CODE: 5325
FREE TEXT: Originally, the three member mission wanted to observe a
trial before the High Court of State Security. However, on 29 March the
State Security Services started a campaign to arrest political and
trade union militants. The mission changed its terms of reference and
tried to obtain information on the material and legal situation of the
persons arrested. It is concluded that a multitude of repressive and
generally inconstitutional legal texts have been pronounced to suppress
oppositionary forces. With annexes: letter of Ramsey Clark, member of
the mission, to president Sadat; figures and lists of persons arrested.

CATALOGUE SIGNATURE: 0000/0138/-3=810000
TITLE: Mission en République Arabe Egyptienne: 5-10 septembre 1981
AUTHOR: Kleniec, Yves
PLACE OF PUBLICATION: Brussels
PUBLISHER: Association Internationale des Juristes Démocrates - IADL (D)
DATE OF PUBLICATION: 810000
NUMBER OF PAGES: 14 p.
LANGUAGE: FRE
INDEX: arbitrary arrest / trials / fact-finding missions
GEOGRAPHICAL INDEX: Egypt
GEOGRAPHICAL CODE: 5325
FREE TEXT: The mission consisted of Yves Kleniec and Melvin Wulf.
Originally, they intended to assist at a trial against members of the
Egyptian National Front, accused under the law for "the protection of
values against immorality" (law 95/80), and to collect information on
the dissolution of the Bar Association and the revocation of its Dean.
The members observed the trial.
The mandate of the mission was extended after the arrest of about 1.500
persons on 3 September, and the announcement of a referendum at the day
when the mission arrived. These developments, and legal and political
explanations for it are analyzed; it is stated that human rights seem
to be systematically violated. In the conclusion, the referendum is
criticized.

CATALOGUE SIGNATURE: 0000/0088/-4
TITLE: Report of a mission to Egypt: 26 February to 9 March 1983
= Rapport de mission effectuée en Egypte du 26 février au 9 mars 1983
AUTHOR: Dolgopol, Ustinia
TITLE OF GENERIC ITEM: CIJL bulletin
EDITION: no. 11
PLACE OF PUBLICATION: Geneva
PUBLISHER: Centre for the Independence of Judges and Lawyers - CIJL (D)
DATE OF PUBLICATION: 830400
NUMBER OF PAGES: p. 37-48, 39-50
LANGUAGE: ENG / FRE / SPA
INDEX: judicial systems / association (freedom of) /
fact-finding missions
GEOGRAPHICAL INDEX: Egypt
GEOGRAPHICAL CODE: 5325
FREE TEXT: The purpose of the mission was to investigate the facts
surrounding and following the dissolution of the elected Bar Council in
July 1981, and, if possible, to make attempts to resolve the situation.
For this purpose, the observer obtained information about the text of a
new law being drafted by the People's Assembly, which is intended to
govern the future organization and operation of the Bar Association. On
this matter, there are controversies between members of the dissolved
Bar Council and other lawyers on the one hand, and government
representatives and members of People's Assembly on the other hand.
Despite the opposition, the new legislation was adopted.
With conclusions.

CATALOGUE SIGNATURE: 0000/0138/-0=830500
TITLE: Mission en République Arabe Egyptienne: 30 avril - 1er mai 1983
AUTHOR: Puylagarde, Bernard
PLACE OF PUBLICATION: Brussels
PUBLISHER: Association Internationale des Juristes Démocrates - IADL (D)
DATE OF PUBLICATION: 830500
NUMBER OF PAGES: (5 p.)
AVAILABILITY: X
LANGUAGE: FRE
INDEX: lawyers / association (freedom of) / fact-finding missions
GEOGRAPHICAL INDEX: Egypt
GEOGRAPHICAL CODE: 5325
FREE TEXT: The aim of the mission was to find out on the events
occurring after the dissolution of the Council of the Egyptian Bar
Association by President Sadat in July 1981 and its replacement by a
Council which is under certain government control. The two members of
the mission met with representatives of the Arab Lawyers Union, and
with the secretary-general of the committee which organizes the
elections for a new Council. With conclusion: the dissolution of the
Council is an intolerable attack on the independence of the legal
profession.

CATALOGUE SIGNATURE: 0000/0249/-0=840000
TITLE: Egypt: update to 1983 report
AUTHOR: (Amnesty International - AI)
PLACE OF PUBLICATION: (London)
PUBLISHER: Amnesty International - AI (D)
DATE OF PUBLICATION: 840000
NUMBER OF PAGES: 15 p.
DOCUMENT SYMBOL: AI Index: MDE 12/01/84
AVAILABILITY: X
LANGUAGE: ENG
INDEX: political prisoners / legislation / fact-finding missions
GEOGRAPHICAL INDEX: Egypt
GEOGRAPHICAL CODE: 5325
FREE TEXT: The report updates AI's 1983 report Egypt: violations of
human rights, and draws on discussions and communications since then
between the organization and the government. An AI delegation went
to Egypt for talks with officials in May 1983. The report contains the
memorandum based on these talks and on fresh information received, and
the response of the government with a covering letter. Issues dealt
with are legal issues (detention procedures, legislation under which
prisoners are charged and tried, trials), prisoners of conscience,
political prisoners, allegations of torture and ill-treatment and the
death penalty. With Amnesty's recommendations to the government and
ensuing correspondence.

EQUATORIAL GUINEA

CATALOGUE SIGNATURE: 0000/1185/-3=781100
TITLE: Equatorial Guinea - Macías country: the forgotten refugees:
an International University Exchange Fund (IUEF) field study on the
Equatorial Guinea refugee situation
AUTHOR: Klinteberg, Robert af
PLACE OF PUBLICATION: Geneva
PUBLISHER: International University Exchange Fund - IUEF
DATE OF PUBLICATION: 781100
NUMBER OF PAGES: 87 p.
AVAILABILITY: O
LANGUAGE: ENG
BIBLIOGRAPHIES: Y
INDEX: refugees / fact-finding missions
GEOGRAPHICAL INDEX: Equatorial Guinea
GEOGRAPHICAL CODE: 5126
FREE TEXT: The aim of the mission was to provide information about the
situation of refugees and to make proposals for programmes of
assistance, particularly in the field of education and training; and
to provide firsthand information about the situation in Equatorial
Guinea in order to facilitate assessment of the possibilities for
repatriation. After a very risky visit to the country itself, the
author spent four months living with the refugees in Gabon, Cameroon,
Nigeria and Spain. In his report, attention is given to the background
of the country, recent developments and the present situation (the
state apparatus, economy, forced labour, law and law enforcement,
relations with foreign powers); the personality of dictator Macías;
the situation of refugees (outflux and influx), solutions and
recommendations (legal recognition, rehabilitation, education,
suggestions). With appendices.

CATALOGUE SIGNATURE: 0000/0088/-3=791100
TITLE: The trial of Macías in Equatorial Guinea: the story of a
dictatorship = El juicio contra Macías en Guinea Ecuatorial:
historia de una dictadura
AUTHOR: Artucio, Alejandro
PLACE OF PUBLICATION: Geneva
PUBLISHER: International Commission of Jurists - ICJ (D) ;
International University Exchange Fund - IUEF
DATE OF PUBLICATION: 791100
NUMBER OF PAGES: 61 p.
LANGUAGE: ENG / SPA
INDEX: dictatorship / trials / fact-finding missions
GEOGRAPHICAL INDEX: Equatorial Guinea
GEOGRAPHICAL CODE: 5126
FREE TEXT: On 3 August 1979, the Macías regime was overthrown by a
military coup. The ICJ was invited to send an observer to the trial
of the former President-for-life and several of his close associates
before the Special Military Tribunal.
In the first part of the report, the nature of the Macías regime and
the conditions prevailing in the country at the time of the trial are
described. Following is a description of the trial in detail. The
author concludes that, having regard to the chaotic conditions and the
complete absence for several years of any judicial system, the trial
given to Macías and his co-accused was reasonably fair.

CATALOGUE SIGNATURE: 0000/1079/-3=800212
TITLE: Study of the human rights situation in Equatorial Guinea...
AUTHOR: Volio Jiménez, Fernando
PLACE OF PUBLICATION: Geneva
PUBLISHER: Commission on Human Rights of the United Nations Economic and Social Council - UNCHR (D)
DATE OF PUBLICATION: 800212
NUMBER OF PAGES: 89 p. in v.p.
SERIES TITLE: Commission on Human Rights: thirty-sixth session: item 12 of the provisional agenda: question of the violation of human rights and fundamental freedoms in any part of the world, with particular reference to colonial and other dependent countries and territories
DOCUMENT SYMBOL: E/CN.4/1371
AVAILABILITY: F
LANGUAGE: ENG / FRE / SPA
INDEX: protection / legislation / fact-finding missions
GEOGRAPHICAL INDEX: Equatorial Guinea
GEOGRAPHICAL CODE: 5126
FREE TEXT: Volio Jiménez is Special Rapporteur on the situation of human rights in Equatorial Guinea, in accordance with resolution 15 (XXXV) of the Commission on Human Rights. He visited the country in November 1979. His report contains: an introduction (on mandate, consideration of the situation in Equatorial Guinea under ECOSCOC resolution 1503, and contacts with the government); background information on the country; a report on the visit to Equatorial Guinea (with attention to the programme, difficulties encountered, information gathered on the human rights situation); conclusions and recommendations. With annexes: decisions adopted by the Commission on Human Rights; maps of Equatorial Guinea and of the itinerary; text of radio communiqué; letters and questionnaires; press communiqué by the National Alliance for Democratic Restoration.

CATALOGUE SIGNATURE: 0000/1079/-3=801219
TITLE: The human rights situation in Equatorial Guinea...
AUTHOR: Volio Jiménez, Fernando
PLACE OF PUBLICATION: Geneva
PUBLISHER: Commission on Human Rights of the United Nations Economic
and Social Council - UNCHR (D)
DATE OF PUBLICATION: 801219
NUMBER OF PAGES: 48 p. in v.p.
SERIES TITLE: Commission on Human Rights: thirty-seventh session: item
13 of the provisional agenda: question of the violation of human rights
and fundamental freedoms in any part of the world, with particular
reference to colonial and other dependent countries and territories
DOCUMENT SYMBOL: E/CN.4/1439
AVAILABILITY: F
LANGUAGE: ENG / SPA
BIBLIOGRAPHIES: Y
INDEX: protection / legislation / fact-finding missions
GEOGRAPHICAL INDEX: Equatorial Guinea
GEOGRAPHICAL CODE: 5126
FREE TEXT: Volio Jiménez was appointed as expert in accordance with
resolution 33 (XXXVI) of the Commission on Human Rights. The aim of his
mission was to assist the government in taking the action necessary for
the full restoration of human rights and fundamental freedoms, keeping
in mind the recommendations of the earlier report and the economic,
political and social realities of the country.
The report contains an introduction on the relation between the
Commission and the government of Equatorial Guinea, a report of visits
paid to Spain and to Equatorial Guinea in November 1980, preliminary
observations, conclusions and recommendations.
With appendices: resolution 33 (XXXVI) of the Commission; the plan of
action of the expert; programme of work for the mission; list of
legislative instruments; correspondence between the government and
United Nations bodies; maps.

Equatorial Guinea

CATALOGUE SIGNATURE: 0000/1079/-3=850116
TITLE: Equatorial Guinea: provision of expert assistance in the field
of human rights
AUTHOR: Volio Jiménez, Fernando
PLACE OF PUBLICATION: Geneva
PUBLISHER: Commission on Human Rights of the United Nations Economic
and Social Council - UNCHR (D)
DATE OF PUBLICATION: 850116
NUMBER OF PAGES: 52 p.
SERIES TITLE: Commission on Human Rights: forty-first session: items
12 and 22 of the provisional agenda: question of the violation of
human rights and fundamental freedoms in any part of the world, with
particular reference to colonial and other dependent countries and
territories: advisory services in the field of human rights
DOCUMENT SYMBOL: E/CN.4/1985/9 ; E/CN.4/1985/9/Add.1
AVAILABILITY: F
LANGUAGE: ENG / SPA
INDEX: protection / legislation / fact-finding missions
GEOGRAPHICAL INDEX: Equatorial Guinea
GEOGRAPHICAL CODE: 5126
FREE TEXT: Pursuant to resolution 1984/36 of the Economic and Social
Council, Volio Jiménez was appointed as expert to visit Equatorial
Guinea in order to study, in conjunction with the government, the best
way of implementing the plan of action proposed by the United Nations.
He visited the country in November 1984. The report contains an
introduction, an account of the mission, conclusions and
recommendations. With annexes: text of resolution 1984/36; draft plan
of action; programme of work; four questionnaires; preliminary
observations and recommendations; itinerary; letters by Volio Jiménez
to the Minister of State for Foreign Affairs and Co-operation.
The addendum contains an introductory note to the report, dated 26
February 1985.

ETHIOPIA

CATALOGUE SIGNATURE: 5227/-0=850528
TITLE: 'Athiopien: Deportationen und Zwangsarbeitslager: fragwÜrdige
Methoden zur Bekämpfung der Hungersnot: Untersuchung von Peter
Niggli, Schweiz, im Auftrage des Berliner Missionswerkes
AUTHOR: Niggli, Peter
PLACE OF PUBLICATION: Frankfurt am Main
PUBLISHER: Haus der Evangelischen Publistik ; Evangelischer
Pressendienst - EPD (D)
DATE OF PUBLICATION: 850528
NUMBER OF PAGES: 43 p.
SERIES TITLE: EPD Dokumentation
VOLUME: no. 25/85
LANGUAGE: GER
BIBLIOGRAPHIES: Y
INDEX: migration / refugees / development cooperation /
fact-finding missions
GEOGRAPHICAL INDEX: Ethiopia
GEOGRAPHICAL CODE: 5227
FREE TEXT: This report is on the implementation of the policy of the
government of Ethiopia to resettle people living in the provinces
Tigray and Wollo in the north of the country to the south of Ethiopia.
It is based on a number of interviews with people who did not want to
participate in this project and fled to Sudan. Attention is paid to
the background of the migration policy, the practical implementation,
the forced character of the migration, the situation in the areas for
resettlement, collectivization and national integration, and the
consequences for the development organizations.

CATALOGUE SIGNATURE: 5227/-0=851011
TITLE: Statement submitted to the Committee on Foreign Affairs United
States House of Representatives, Subcommittees on Africa and on Human
Rights
AUTHOR: Collins, Joseph
PLACE OF PUBLICATION: San Francisco
PUBLISHER: Institute for Food and Development Policy (D)
DATE OF PUBLICATION: 851011
NUMBER OF PAGES: 5 p.
LANGUAGE: ENG
INDEX: food (right to) / agrarian reform /
human rights and foreign policy / fact-finding missions
GEOGRAPHICAL INDEX: Ethiopia
GEOGRAPHICAL CODE: 5227
FREE TEXT: The author visited Ethiopia in March 1985 to investigate
the famine situation and the policy of the Ethiopian government. He
concludes that the famine in Ethiopia is definitely not explained by
poor rainfall; the true cause is the vulnerability of the peasant
majority to any natural hardship. There are numerous reasons to see
this vulnerability as man-made, or more accurately, government-made.
By commission and omission, the Ethiopian government has increasingly
eroded the capacity of peasants to cope with natural adversities that
are to be periodically expected. He outlines some of the specific
policies contributing to this vulnerability.

CATALOGUE SIGNATURE: 0000/1298/-3=851200
TITLE: Politics and the Ethiopian famine 1984-1985
AUTHOR: Clay, Jason W. ; Holcomb, Bonnie K.
PLACE OF PUBLICATION: Cambridge, MA
PUBLISHER: Survival International (D)
DATE OF PUBLICATION: 851200
NUMBER OF PAGES: 250 p.
LANGUAGE: ENG
STATISTICAL INFORMATION: Y
BIBLIOGRAPHIES: Y
INDEX: food (right to) / refugees / indigenous peoples /
ethnic conflict / fact-finding missions
GEOGRAPHICAL INDEX: Ethiopia
GEOGRAPHICAL CODE: 5227
FREE TEXT: An assessment of political complications as well as research
into the causes of the famine is crucial to the delivery of appropriate
assistance. Cultural Survival conducted a research into the causes of
famine in Ethiopia in Sudan in February and March 1985; the delegates
were not allowed to enter Ethiopia and undertake independent research.
In Sudan, more than 250 people who had been displaced by the famine or
programs that the Ethiopian government claimed would alleviate it were
interviewed. In addition, they interviewed government and agency
personnel, journalists and academics, and undertook a systematic review
of the academic and popular literature on the area and this famine.
With introduction, and chapters on: the background to the current
crisis; the research design; victims of food shortages who fled
westward from Tigray into Sudan; escapees from the resettlement camps;
escapees from resettlement interviewed while in transit to Damazine
holding camp; escapees from repression and displacement interviewed in
Yabuus; victims of displacement and coercion - peoples indigenous to
the areas affected by the resettlement; the impact of resettlement on
indigenous peoples. With conclusions, recommendations, appendices
(general survey, texts of interviews), bibliography and maps.

CATALOGUE SIGNATURE: 0000/0035/-3=860400
TITLE: Torture and the violation of human rights in Tigray, Ethiopia:
interim report on the prisoners freed from Makelle prison, Tigray on
February 8th, 1986
AUTHOR: Lyon, Alex ; McColgan, Michael ; Rostoker, Christian (...et al)
PLACE OF PUBLICATION: Paris
PUBLISHER: Fédération Internationale des Droits de l'Homme - FIDH (D)
DATE OF PUBLICATION: 860400
NUMBER OF PAGES: 53 p. in v.p.
LANGUAGE: ENG
INDEX: detention / torture / fact-finding missions
GEOGRAPHICAL INDEX: Ethiopia
GEOGRAPHICAL CODE: 5227
FREE TEXT: The report is based on a fact-finding mission to Tigray in
March-April 1986. At the end of February 1986, the Tigray People's
Liberation Front (TPLF) announced that it had freed some 1,800 prisoners
from the Grand Prison in Makelle, the capital of Tigray. The TPLF
alleged that many of these prisoners had been tortured before and during
their imprisonment at the hands of the Ethiopian government, the Dergue.
The delegation interviewed 121 released prisoners. The report contains
background information on Makelle prison and the treatment of the
prisoners. With appendices: illustrations on the prison and torture
methods; testimonies of nineteen persons.
The mission team concludes that the prisoners were arbitrarily arrested
and subjected to quasi-systematic torture; they were detained without
trial and are imprisoned in bad conditions.

19

GAMBIA

CATALOGUE SIGNATURE: 0000/0249/-3=830600
TITLE: Amnesty International trial observer missions to the Republic
of the Gambia: December 1980 / January 1982
AUTHOR: (Boyle, C.K.)
PLACE OF PUBLICATION: London
PUBLISHER: Amnesty International - AI (D)
DATE OF PUBLICATION: 830600
NUMBER OF PAGES: 45 p. in v.p.
DOCUMENT SYMBOL: AI Index: AFR 27/01/83
LANGUAGE: ENG
INDEX: trials / fact-finding missions
GEOGRAPHICAL INDEX: Gambia
GEOGRAPHICAL CODE: 5466
FREE TEXT: The first trial concerned six members of a banned political
organization called the Movement for Justice in Africa MOJA, tried on
charges of "managing an unlawful society" and "possessing firearms and
ammunition". In January 1982, AI's observer attended the trials of nine
individuals who were among over 1,000 arrested and detained under
executive detention following a failed armed rebellion.
The report contains the two trial observation reports, and the comments
of the Gambian government on these. With appendices: a summary of major
points of discussion during AI's mission to the Gambia in 1982 to
discuss the trial observer's reports; excerpts from a letter dated 15
December 1982 by AI to the President of Gambia; communication from the
President of Gambia to the Minister of the Interior.

GHANA

CATALOGUE SIGNATURE: 0000/0249/-0=840700
TITLE: The public tribunals in Ghana: July 1984
AUTHOR: (Amnesty International - AI)
PLACE OF PUBLICATION: London
PUBLISHER: Amnesty International - AI (D)
DATE OF PUBLICATION: 840700
NUMBER OF PAGES: 11 p.
DOCUMENT SYMBOL: AI Index AFR 28/10/84
LANGUAGE: ENG
INDEX: judicial systems / trials / fact-finding missions
GEOGRAPHICAL INDEX: Ghana
GEOGRAPHICAL CODE: 5530
FREE TEXT: The document includes a description of the origin and
nature of the Public Tribunals, and the text of a memorandum on the
Public Tribunals sent to the Government of Ghana on 26 October 1983,
following a fact-finding mission in August 1983. The aim of the
mission was to observe the Public Tribunals and to collect information
with respect to their functioning. In this memorandum, AI made ten
specific recommendations which it called upon the Government of Ghana
to implement as steps towards bringing the structure and procedures of
the Public Tribunals into comformity with internationally recognized
standards of justice.

CATALOGUE SIGNATURE: 0000/0088/-3=850000
TITLE: Human rights in Ghana: report of a mission...
AUTHOR: Flinterman, Cees
PLACE OF PUBLICATION: Utrecht ; Geneva
PUBLISHER: Netherlands Institute of Human Rights - SIM (D) ;
International Commission of Jurists - ICJ (D)
DATE OF PUBLICATION: 850000
NUMBER OF PAGES: 47 p.
SERIES TITLE: SIM Special
VOLUME: no. 4
ISBN: 92 9037 025 4
LANGUAGE: ENG
INDEX: judicial systems / legislation / fact-finding missions
GEOGRAPHICAL INDEX: Ghana
GEOGRAPHICAL CODE: 5530
FREE TEXT: The author visited Ghana in June and July 1984 on behalf of
the Netherlands Committee for Human Rights (NJCM, the Dutch section of
the ICJ) and the International Commission of Jurists.
The first part of his report deals with the administration of justice,
in particular the system of Public Tribunals for certain criminal
cases. The second part deals with the general human rights situation.
While acknowledging that the Provisional National Defence Council
(PNDC) is making considerable efforts to improve the quality of life
of its citizens and to overcome the country's grave economic ills,
Professor Flinterman points out that economic, social and cultural
rights are being implemented to the detriment of the free exercise of
civil and political rights. The report ends with final remarks and
recommendations.

GUINEA

CATALOGUE SIGNATURE: 0000/0035/-3=790000
TITLE: Guinée: novembre 1979
AUTHOR: Jouffa, Yves
PLACE OF PUBLICATION: Paris
PUBLISHER: Fédération Internationale des Droits de l'Homme - FIDH (D)
DATE OF PUBLICATION: 790000
NUMBER OF PAGES: 8 p.
LANGUAGE: FRE
INDEX: detention / fact-finding missions
GEOGRAPHICAL INDEX: Guinea
GEOGRAPHICAL CODE: 5531
FREE TEXT: The purpose of the mission was to receive information on
the detention conditions in Boiro camp, and especially on the legal
situation of two prisoners.
The delegate was received by president Sekou Touré, had discussions
with him, and was taken on a tour through Conakry. He was allowed to
visit the Boiro camp, but not to enter the penitentiary locals. He
spoke with a prisoner, Mr. Bah, who was accused of planning an attack
on a public building and consequently to commit a coup d'état. This
prisoner was in good condition. With conclusion.

CATALOGUE SIGNATURE: 0000/0249/-3=821000
TITLE: La mission d'Amnesty International en République Populaire et
Révolutionnaire de Guinée (décembre 1981)
AUTHOR: (Zalaquett, José) ; (Elsner, Richard)
PLACE OF PUBLICATION: London
PUBLISHER: Amnesty International - AI (D)
DATE OF PUBLICATION: 821000
NUMBER OF PAGES: 23 p.
DOCUMENT SYMBOL: AI Index: AFR 29/09/82
LANGUAGE: FRE
INDEX: political prisoners / fact-finding missions
GEOGRAPHICAL INDEX: Guinea
GEOGRAPHICAL CODE: 5531
FREE TEXT: The aim of the mission was to discuss the situation of human
rights with government representatives and officials. The report
contains information on the conduct of the mission and contacts
established; information obtained on the concerns of AI (long-term
detention without trial of real or presumed opponents of the
government, political detainees "disappeared" while in prison);
political trials; torture and cruel, inhuman or degrading treatment;
the death penalty and extrajudicial executions. With conclusions. The
report was forwarded to the authorities.

GUINEA-BISSAU

CATALOGUE SIGNATURE: 0000/1068/-3=720900
TITLE: Report of the United Nations special mission to Guinea (Bissau)
AUTHOR: Löfgren, Folke ; Sevilla-Borja, Horacio ; Belkhiria, Kamel E.
EDITION: repr.
PLACE OF PUBLICATION: (New York)
PUBLISHER: United Nations Office on Public Information (D)
DATE OF PUBLICATION: 720900
NUMBER OF PAGES: 14 p.
AVAILABILITY: F
LANGUAGE: ENG
INDEX: self-determination / fact-finding missions
GEOGRAPHICAL INDEX: Guinea-Bissau
GEOGRAPHICAL CODE: 5532
FREE TEXT: The mission consisted of members of the Special Committee on
Decolonization, who were invited by the political party PAIGC to visit
the liberated areas of Guinea-Bissau. The purpose was to secure
first-hand information on conditions in the area, and to ascertain the
views and aspirations of the people regarding their future. The report
contains background information on the mission, a description of its
activities, and its findings with regard to educational conditions,
health conditions, the administration of justice, the reconstruction of
the economy, the establishment of a National Assembly. With conclusions
and recommendations.
-Reprint from Objective: Justice, vol.4(3), September 1972, with the
addition of the introduction to the report.

LESOTHO

CATALOGUE SIGNATURE: 0000/0088/-4
TITLE: Report on the treason trial in Maseru, Lesotho
AUTHOR: Sakala, Julius B.
TITLE OF GENERIC ITEM: ICJ Newsletter
EDITION: no. 22
PLACE OF PUBLICATION: Geneva
PUBLISHER: International Commission of Jurists - ICJ (D)
DATE OF PUBLICATION: 840900
NUMBER OF PAGES: p. 39-45
LANGUAGE: ENG
INDEX: association (freedom of) / trials / fact-finding missions
GEOGRAPHICAL INDEX: Lesotho
GEOGRAPHICAL CODE: 5435
FREE TEXT: Report on the observation of a trial against twelve
alleged members or symphatizers of the Lesotho Liberation Army LLA,
charged with high treason (conspiration to overthrow the government
of Lesotho by force). Attention is given to the background of the
country, the description of the trial and activities of the observer.
Information is provided on Lea Sebatana, the only woman accused, who
was discharged and released in the opening of the case. In the end,
all accused were acquitted.

CATALOGUE SIGNATURE: 0000/0018/-0=851200
TITLE: Report of AACC-WCC delegation to Lesotho
AUTHOR: Okullu, Henry; Wako, Amos; Koshy, Ninan
PLACE OF PUBLICATION: Geneva
PUBLISHER: Commission of the Churches on International Affairs of the
World Council of Churches - CCIA-WCC (D)
DATE OF PUBLICATION: 851200
NUMBER OF PAGES: 13 p. in v.p.
LANGUAGE: ENG
INDEX: church and state / fact-finding missions
GEOGRAPHICAL INDEX: Lesotho
GEOGRAPHICAL CODE: 5435
FREE TEXT: A joint delegation of five persons of the All African
Council of Churches and the World Council of Churches visited Lesotho
in December 1985. The aim of the visit was to affirm solidarity with
the churches in Lesotho, express to them the pastoral concern of the
churches represented in AACC and WCC and to learn about the general
socio-political situation in the country, especially relating to human
rights. The programme was arranged by the Christian Council of Lesotho
(CCL). The report contains background information on the country,
on recent political developments and on the situation of human rights.
Attention is also paid to the influence of South Africa, refugees and
liberation movements and the position of the churches.
With recommendations and appendices: update information on the take-
over by a military council on 20 January 1986, and a call for national
reconciliation by the CCL.

LIBERIA

CATALOGUE SIGNATURE: 5536/-0=850300
TITLE: Report on Liberia: human rights issues
AUTHOR: Hayden, Thomas
PLACE OF PUBLICATION: Washington DC
PUBLISHER: Society of African Missions - SMA - Social Concerns
Department (D)
DATE OF PUBLICATION: 850300
NUMBER OF PAGES: 12 p.
LANGUAGE: ENG
INDEX: human rights and foreign policy / fact-finding missions
GEOGRAPHICAL INDEX: Liberia
GEOGRAPHICAL CODE: 5536
FREE TEXT: The author visited Liberia from 17 January to 4 February
1985. He was especially concerned with the invasion of the University
of Liberia on 22 August 1984 and subsequent actions, and the
deterioriation of personal and political freedom within the country.
In his report, attention is given to SMA concerns for human rights in
Liberia, the invasion of the University, free elections, meetings
with US officials and the US Ambassador, report on a visit to the
State Department and contacts with the Subcommittee on Africa of the
US House of Representatives.

CATALOGUE SIGNATURE: 0000/2917/-3=860500
TITLE: Best friends: violations of human rights in Liberia, America's
closest ally in Africa
AUTHOR: Massing, Michael
PLACE OF PUBLICATION: New York
PUBLISHER: Fund for Free Expression - FFE (D)
DATE OF PUBLICATION: 860500
NUMBER OF PAGES: 54 p.
LANGUAGE: ENG
INDEX: civil and political rights / human rights and foreign policy /
trials / fact-finding missions
GEOGRAPHICAL INDEX: Liberia
GEOGRAPHICAL CODE: 5536
FREE TEXT: The report is based on visits to Liberia in August-September
1985 and in February-March 1986. It contains background information on
the country, the relation of Liberia and its President Samuel Doe to
the United States, the elections of October 1985, the coup attempt of
12 November and the treason trial following, freedom of the press,
future perspectives, and the role of the United States. It is concluded
that on 6 January 1986, when Samuel Doe was inaugurated president, the
country ostensibly returned to democracy after more than five years of
military rule; however, there are various negative indicators of
serious problems with regard to human rights and fundamental freedoms.

CATALOGUE SIGNATURE: 0000/1246/-3=860606
TITLE: Human rights in Liberia: a preliminary report based on two
trial observer missions: February - March and May 1986
AUTHOR: Schneebaum, Steven M. ; Whalen, Jeffrey
PLACE OF PUBLICATION: Washington DC
PUBLISHER: International Human Rights Law Group - IHRLG (D)
DATE OF PUBLICATION: 860606
NUMBER OF PAGES: 43 p. in v.p.
LANGUAGE: ENG
INDEX: trials / fact-finding missions
GEOGRAPHICAL INDEX: Liberia
GEOGRAPHICAL CODE: 5536
FREE TEXT: The report describes the conduct of several politically
sensitive trials that occurred between February 2 and May 31, and
comments generally on human rights in Liberia during this period.
After a summary of findings and conclusions the report is divided
into the following parts:
I) Background; II) General considerations: the constitution;
III) Arbitrary arrest and detention; IV) The holder - Philips case;
V) Ellen Johnson-Sirleaf's case; VI) Other human rights problems;
VII) United States policy. In the annexes:
1) Remarks of Steven M. Schneebaum; 2) Memorandum on human rights
in Liberia; 3) Indictment of Ellen Johnson-Sirleaf in the Republic
of Liberia; 4) Position of the Liberian National Bar Association
(LNBA); 5) Verdict; 6) House and senate resolutions on Liberia;
7) Articles: - Withhold aid to Liberia; - The analogies being drawn
in Liberia.

MAURETANIA

CATALOGUE SIGNATURE: 0000/0104/-3=820000
TITLE: Slavery in Mauretania today
AUTHOR: Mercer, John
PLACE OF PUBLICATION: Edinburgh
PUBLISHER: Human Rights Group - HRG (D)
DATE OF PUBLICATION: 820000
NUMBER OF PAGES: 38 p.
LANGUAGE: ENG
STATISTICAL INFORMATION: Y
BIBLIOGRAPHIES: Y
INDEX: slavery / fact-finding missions
GEOGRAPHICAL INDEX: Mauretania
GEOGRAPHICAL CODE: 5541
FREE TEXT: Mauretania holds a minimum of 100.000 total slaves with a
further 300.000 part-slaves and ex-slaves. The aim of the report is
to support the practical implementation of the government's decree of
5 July 1980 which abolishes slavery. With attention to background of
the country, the present situation: tributary system, the slave
community, the situation of released slaves, the emancipation
movement. With photographs and appendices: transcript of interviews
with former slaves; testimony on a revolt; Islam and slavery in
Mauretania; enforced Arabisation; population; specific cases of
recent ill-treatment of slaves.

CATALOGUE SIGNATURE: 0000/1077/-3=840702
TITLE: Report of the mission to Mauretania
AUTHOR: Bossuyt, Marc
PLACE OF PUBLICATION: Geneva
PUBLISHER: Commission on Human Rights of the United Nations Economic
and Social Council - UNCHR - Sub-Commission on Prevention of
Discrimination and Protection of Minorities (D)
DATE OF PUBLICATION: 840702
NUMBER OF PAGES: 47 p. in v.p.
SERIES TITLE: Commission on Human Rights: Sub-Commission on Prevention
of Discrimination and Protection of Minorities: thirty-seventh session:
agenda item 12(a): slavery and slavery like practices: question of
slavery and the slave trade in all their practices and manifestations,
including the slavery-like practices of apartheid and colonialism
DOCUMENT SYMBOL: E/CN.4/Sub.2/1984/23
AVAILABILITY: F
LANGUAGE: ENG / FRE
BIBLIOGRAPHIES: Y
INDEX: forced labour / slavery / fact-finding missions
GEOGRAPHICAL INDEX: Mauretania
GEOGRAPHICAL CODE: 5541
FREE TEXT: M. Bossuyt, member of the Sub-Commission, visited Mauretania
in January 1984 at the invitation of the government. The aim of the
mission was to acquaint the Sub-Commission with the situation in
Mauretania following the abolition of slavery proclaimed by the
Military Committee for National Salvation on 5 July 1980 and confirmed
by the Ordinance of 9 November 1981, and to determine what aid the
country might need from the international community to surmount the
consequences of slavery. The report contains the findings of the
mission, recommendations and annexes: note on Mauretania; information
provided by the government; texts of Declaration and Ordinance; press
release on the mission; communication submitted by the "El Hor"
movement.

MOROCCO

CATALOGUE SIGNATURE: 0000/0249/-3=770300
TITLE: The Casablanca trials January / February 1977
AUTHOR: (Hoss, Jean)
PLACE OF PUBLICATION: London
PUBLISHER: Amnesty International - AI (D)
DATE OF PUBLICATION: 770300
NUMBER OF PAGES: 4 p.
DOCUMENT SYMBOL: AI Index: AFR 43/03/77
LANGUAGE: ENG
INDEX: association (freedom of) / trials / fact-finding missions
GEOGRAPHICAL INDEX: Morocco
GEOGRAPHICAL CODE: 5344
FREE TEXT: On 3 January 1977, the trial of 178 radical socialists
(commonly known as the Frontistes) opened before the criminal court of
appeal in Casablanca. The majority of those on trial were arrested in
November 1974. The report contains background information on the
accused, and a description of the proceedings of the trial. It is
stated that the rights of the prisoners to defend their cases, and to
be defended by their lawyers, were severely restricted. With sentences,
information on the evidence of torture and conclusions.

CATALOGUE SIGNATURE: 0000/0138/-3=770000
TITLE: Maroc: situation des détenus frontistes
AUTHOR: Baudelot, Yves ; Lépany, Franceline ; Vernant, Jean-Paul
PLACE OF PUBLICATION: Brussels
PUBLISHER: Association Internationale des Juristes Démocrates - IADL (D)
DATE OF PUBLICATION: 770000
NUMBER OF PAGES: 20 p.
LANGUAGE: FRE
INDEX: prison conditions / detention / fact-finding missions
GEOGRAPHICAL INDEX: Morocco
GEOGRAPHICAL CODE: 5344
FREE TEXT: Report, based on a fact-finding mission in December 1977,
on the conditions of detained persons accused of infraction of state
security, their hunger strike, the death of one of them, and on persons
recently arrested and not yet delivered to judicial powers. The report
contains the findings of the mission, information provided by the
prosecutor and communiqué of the defence concerning the hunger strike
and the death of one person.

CATALOGUE SIGNATURE: 0000/0138/-3=810700
TITLE: La répression au Maroc après les évenements du 20 juin 1981
AUTHOR: Kleniec, Yves
PLACE OF PUBLICATION: Brussels
PUBLISHER: Association Internationale des Juristes Démocrates - IADL (D)
DATE OF PUBLICATION: 810700
NUMBER OF PAGES: 17 p.
LANGUAGE: FRE
INDEX: trade unions / peaceful assembly (right to) /
fact-finding missions
GEOGRAPHICAL INDEX: Morocco
GEOGRAPHICAL CODE: 5344
FREE TEXT: The aim of the mission was to inquire into the repression of
board and members of two trade unions, USFP and CDT. After two days,
the delegate and representatives of other organizations were forced to
leave the country. The report is on the background and consequences of
the events of 20 June (protests against the rising food prices). With
annexes: list of members of regional boards of the two trade unions;
list of activists arrested; press reports.

CATALOGUE SIGNATURE: 0000/0035/-3=810000
TITLE: Rapport de mission ... au Maroc, et plus particulièrement dans
les villes de Rabat et de Casablanca du 1er juillet au 5 juillet 1981
AUTHOR: Mignard, Jean-Pierre
PLACE OF PUBLICATION: Paris
PUBLISHER: Fédération Internationale des Droits de l'Homme - FIDH (D)
DATE OF PUBLICATION: 810000
NUMBER OF PAGES: 20 p.
LANGUAGE: FRE
INDEX: trials / fact-finding missions
GEOGRAPHICAL INDEX: Morocco
GEOGRAPHICAL CODE: 5344
FREE TEXT: The purpose of the mission was to investigate the state of
civil liberties after the general strike on 20 June. With description
of the incidents, arrests and judicial consequences. The delegate
visited the Tribunal of Casablanca. He states that the punishments
for the accused were high and the rights of the defence were ignored.
It is not possible to determine the number of victims because the
authorities refuse to provide information. The number of deaths is not
verificable, but it is likely that the authorities do everything to
hide the truth. With conclusions and recommendations, and description
of specific cases.

CATALOGUE SIGNATURE: 0000/0088/-3=810900
TITLE: Report ... on a mission in July 1981 to Morocco to attend as an
observer a trial in Rabat of a number of persons accused of "arson,
unlawful assemblies and the destruction of public property and other
crimes"
AUTHOR: Tremblay, André
PLACE OF PUBLICATION: Geneva
PUBLISHER: International Commission of Jurists - ICJ (D) ;
International Commission of Jurists,Canadian Section - ICJ-CA (D)
DATE OF PUBLICATION: 810900
NUMBER OF PAGES: 25 p.
LANGUAGE: ENG
INDEX: association (freedom of) / judicial systems / trials /
fact-finding missions
GEOGRAPHICAL INDEX: Morocco
GEOGRAPHICAL CODE: 5344
FREE TEXT: Professor Tremblay wanted to observe the trial in Rabat.
After attending the opening of the trial on 13 July, he and other
international observers were expelled from the country in the early
hours of the morning of 14 July, in a manner described in the report.
After the introduction, the report is divided in five parts.
I) the origin of the events of 20 and 21 June 1981 which gave rise to
the trial; II) the consequences of those events; III) the conduct of
the trial, with an analysis of the proceedings; IV) other matters
related to human rights in Morocco which give cause for concern; V)
the arrest and expulsion of Tremblay. With conclusions, and a
supplement by the ICJ with information on further developments in
this and other trials since Tremblay's expulsion.

CATALOGUE SIGNATURE: 0000/0035/-3=810000
TITLE: Commission internationale d'enquête sur la situation des droits
de l'homme en Maroc 13-15 décembre 1981
AUTHOR: Gifford, Antony ; Goffin, Robert-Charles ; Lazarus, Antoine
(...et al)
PLACE OF PUBLICATION: Paris
PUBLISHER: Fédération Internationale des Droits de l'Homme - FIDH (D)
DATE OF PUBLICATION: 810000
NUMBER OF PAGES: 10 p.
LANGUAGE: FRE
INDEX: armed violence / peaceful assembly (right to) /
fact-finding missions
GEOGRAPHICAL INDEX: Morocco
GEOGRAPHICAL CODE: 5344
FREE TEXT: The purpose of the mission of five members was to
investigate the violent events of June 1981, torture and ill-treatment
of prisoners, disappearances of civilians and military and repression
against students. With background information on the country.
The delegates could not fulfill their mission. They had many problems
with the Moroccan authorities, and were forced to leave the country.
The report contains a description of events and conclusions.

CATALOGUE SIGNATURE: 0000/0249/-3=820500
TITLE: Report of an Amnesty International mission to the Kingdom of
Morocco: 10-13 February 1981
AUTHOR: (Ennals, Martin)
PLACE OF PUBLICATION: London
PUBLISHER: Amnesty International - AI (D)
DATE OF PUBLICATION: 820500
NUMBER OF PAGES: 80 p. in v.p.
ISBN: 086210 046 1
DOCUMENT SYMBOL: AI Index: AFR 40/01/82
LANGUAGE: ENG
STATISTICAL INFORMATION: Y
INDEX: detention / fact-finding missions
GEOGRAPHICAL INDEX: Morocco
GEOGRAPHICAL CODE: 5344
FREE TEXT: The aim of the three member mission was to discuss with
government officials issues of concern to Amnesty International, and
especially violations of human rights during the period of garde à vue
detention, the period after arrest which often lasts several months and
sometimes more than a year.
The report contains background information on the country; the findings
of the mission, with summary of discussions concerning the practice of
garde à vue, practices under the authority of the juge d'instruction,
prisoners of conscience, prison conditions and availability of medical
care, safeguards and remedies to guarantee the fundamental human rights
of people in custody and other issues of AI concern. With review of
developments since the mission, conclusions and recommendations. With
appendices: relevant provisions of international law, cases submitted
by AI to the authorities; prison writings (testimony and letters).

CATALOGUE SIGNATURE: 0000/0138/-0=840000
TITLE: Report Morocco January February 1984: mission report on the
legal and judiciary situation after the events of January 1984
AUTHOR: International Association of Democratic Lawyers - IADL ;
International Movement of Catholic Lawyers Pax Romana - IMCL
PLACE OF PUBLICATION: (Brussels)
PUBLISHER: International Association of Democratic Lawyers - IADL (D);
International Movement of Catholic Lawyers Pax Romana - IMCL (D)
DATE OF PUBLICATION: 840000
NUMBER OF PAGES: 12 p.
LANGUAGE: ENG
INDEX: political violence / judicial systems / fact-finding missions
GEOGRAPHICAL INDEX: Morocco
GEOGRAPHICAL CODE: 5344
FREE TEXT: The aims of the mission were to enquire the functioning of
the judiciary institutions and the body of laws that were implemented
in the framework of the repression following the events (popular
revolts, leading to armed violence by government forces) that took
place in Morocco in January 1984, and the importance of this
repression, its causes and consequences. The report contains
information on the events, the way the mission was executed, the
situation of specific human rights (freedom of information and
assembly, freedom of thought and expression), political repression and
its legal means, the functioning of the police and of the judiciary.
With conclusions.

CATALOGUE SIGNATURE: 0000/0035/-3=840600
TITLE: Rapport de mission: Maroc: suite et fin: procès de Casablanca –
affaire des Baha'is
AUTHOR: Ledermann, Nicolas ; Weber, Alain
PLACE OF PUBLICATION: Paris
PUBLISHER: Fédération Internationale des Droits de l'Homme – FIDH (D)
DATE OF PUBLICATION: 840600
NUMBER OF PAGES: 6 p.
LANGUAGE: FRE
INDEX: religion (freedom of) / trials / fact-finding missions
GEOGRAPHICAL INDEX: Morocco
GEOGRAPHICAL CODE: 5344
FREE TEXT: The document contains the report by Nicolas Ledermann of a
trial observation mission to the hearings in a trial on 7 June 1984
against adherents of the Baha'i faith, and a summary and conclusions on
the trials of the Baha'is by Alain Weber.

CATALOGUE SIGNATURE: 0000/0035/-4
TITLE: Special Maroc: la situation des grévistes de la faim
AUTHOR: Cheysson, Eric ; Rostoker, Christian
TITLE OF GENERIC ITEM: La Lettre de la FIDH
EDITION: v. 77
PLACE OF PUBLICATION: Paris
PUBLISHER: Fédération Internationale des Droits de l'Homme – FIDH (D)
DATE OF PUBLICATION: 841019
NUMBER OF PAGES: p. 1-11
LANGUAGE: FRE
INDEX: detention / fact-finding missions
GEOGRAPHICAL INDEX: Morocco
GEOGRAPHICAL CODE: 5344
FREE TEXT: The aims of the mission were to obtain information on the
legal and health situation of hunger strikers detained in Marrakech,
Essaouira and Safi; investigate the contents of the agreement between
the authorities and the strikers; and to take initiatives which would
lead to a humanitarian solution and the preservation of the physical
integrity of the detainees.
The delegation was not permitted to have hearings with Moroccan
authorities, but had contacts with representatives of nongovernmental
organizations, families of the detained and their lawyers. The report
contains the findings of the mission and conclusions: a number of
articles of the Universal Declaration on Human Rights have been
violated.

CATALOGUE SIGNATURE: 0000/0035-3=850806
TITLE: Maroc: la situation des grèvistes de la faim de Marrakech: 28
juillet - 1 aôut 1985
AUTHOR: Minkowski, Alexandre ; Rostoker, Christian
PLACE OF PUBLICATION: Paris
PUBLISHER: Fédération Internationale des Droits de l'Homme - FIDH (D)
DATE OF PUBLICATION: 850806
NUMBER OF PAGES: 8 p.
LANGUAGE: FRE
INDEX: prison conditions / social and economic rights /
food (right to) / fact-finding missions
GEOGRAPHICAL INDEX: Morocco
GEOGRAPHICAL CODE: 5344
FREE TEXT: The aim of the mission was to collect information on the
health situation and the detention conditions of nine hunger strikers
who were arrested after riots in January 1984 and tried to obtain the
status of political prisoners. With descriptions of meetings with
officials and family members of the hunger strikers. The
circumstances of the nine hunger strikers remains unclear; the members
of the mission express their concern.

MOZAMBIQUE

CATALOGUE SIGNATURE: 0000/0088/-0=730000
TITLE: Report on visit to Mozambique
AUTHOR: (Niekerk, Barend van)
PLACE OF PUBLICATION: Geneva
PUBLISHER: International Commission of Jurists - ICJ (D)
DATE OF PUBLICATION: 730000
NUMBER OF PAGES: 5 p.
LANGUAGE: ENG
INDEX: political prisoners / fact-finding missions
GEOGRAPHICAL INDEX: Mozambique
GEOGRAPHICAL CODE: 5445
FREE TEXT: Report of a mission to investigate the situation of two
Spanish priests who are detained. The delegate was not allowed to
visit them, but received information that they were in good health,
despite the fact that they have been in prison for about 17 months.
He also obtained information on the fate of political prisoners in
general, and of Presbyterians in particular.

NAMIBIA

CATALOGUE SIGNATURE: 0000/0427/-3=820400
TITLE: Namibia - a national wronged: the report of a visit to Namibia by a delegation sent by the British Council of Churches at the invitation of the Council of Churches in Namibia, 16th to 28th November 1981
AUTHOR: Booth-Clibborn, Stanley ; Johansen-Berg, John ; Hughes, Catherine (...et al)
PLACE OF PUBLICATION: London
PUBLISHER: Division of International Affairs of the British Council of Churches - BCC (D)
DATE OF PUBLICATION: 820400
NUMBER OF PAGES: 38 p.
LANGUAGE: ENG
STATISTICAL INFORMATION: Y
INDEX: church and state / apartheid / fact-finding missions
GEOGRAPHICAL INDEX: Namibia
GEOGRAPHICAL CODE: 5446
FREE TEXT: The purpose of the mission was to express goodwill and fellowship, get known to the political situation, and to advise Christians and members of the BCC on an attitude and the need for actions with regard to Namibia.
The mission of four persons travelled around Namibia and met with delegates of many churches and other persons. They gathered information on the general political and social situation, specific problems and the situation and role of the churches.
With appendices: church member figures, education, cases of violations, press release, conclusions and recommendations by the British Council of Churches on basis of the mission report.

SOUTH AFRICA

CATALOGUE SIGNATURE: 5458/-0=790515
TITLE: Report of the committee to visit South Africa
AUTHOR: Pinderhughes, Charles ; Spurlock, Jeanne ; Weinberg, Jack
(et al...)
PLACE OF PUBLICATION: (Washington DC)
PUBLISHER: American Psychiatric Association - APA (D)
DATE OF PUBLICATION: 790515
NUMBER OF PAGES: 27 p.
LANGUAGE: ENG
INDEX: health / mental ill persons / discrimination /
fact-finding missions
GEOGRAPHICAL INDEX: South Africa
GEOGRAPHICAL CODE: 5458
FREE TEXT: The aim of the mission of four members was to investigate
allegations of abuse of black people in psychiatric facilities, and of
placing blacks in such facilities for political reasons. The facilities
investigated are part of a group of private facilities which, under
contract with the government of South Africa, provide racially
segregated care on a per diem basis for chronic psychiatric patients
transferred from state institutions.
The report contains a description of the methods of investigation, an
analysis of the findings with regard to allegations made and
recommendations on specific aspects.
It is concluded that there is good reason for international concern
about black psychiatric patients in South Africa; the mission found
medical practices which were unacceptable and which resulted in
needless deaths; medical and psychiatric care provided blacks was
grossly inferior to that provided whites; apartheid has a destructive
impact on blacks, their families, social institutions and mental
health.

CATALOGUE SIGNATURE: 0000/0088/-4
TITLE: The PAC trial at Bethal and the Soweto students trial at
Kempton Park
AUTHOR: Otton, Philip
TITLE OF GENERIC ITEM: ICJ Newsletter
EDITION: no. 1
PLACE OF PUBLICATION: Geneva
PUBLISHER: International Commission of Jurists - ICJ (D)
DATE OF PUBLICATION: 790600
NUMBER OF PAGES: p. 34-42
LANGUAGE: ENG
INDEX: legislation / judicial systems / trials / fact-finding missions
GEOGRAPHICAL INDEX: South Africa
GEOGRAPHICAL CODE: 5458
FREE TEXT: Eightteen black males were standing trial at Bethal in the
State of Transvaal arising out of their alleged activities on behalf
of and association with the Pan Africanist Congress PAC, which was
banned in 1960. In this report, attention is paid to the charges, the
legal representation, the trial, the judge, the evidence of detained
witnesses, the "in camera" ruling, and allegations of torture.
The author also observed a trial at Kempton Park against eleven
students, charged with sedition and incitement to violence.
He concludes that the distortion of the judicial process does not lie
in the courts, but in the system in which they operate, and especially
in the Terrorism Act of 1976.

CATALOGUE SIGNATURE: 0000/0088/-4
TITLE: Report on appeal of Peterose Mpho Makae and Jacob Tlelima to the
Supreme Court of South Africa, Orange Free State Provincal Division,
against their conviction by the Regional Magistrate's Court at
Kroonstad
AUTHOR: Melville Williams, John
TITLE OF GENERIC ITEM: ICJ Newsletter
EDITION: no. 4
PLACE OF PUBLICATION: Geneva
PUBLISHER: International Commission of Jurists - ICJ (D)
DATE OF PUBLICATION: 800300
NUMBER OF PAGES: p. 48-57
LANGUAGE: ENG
INDEX: legislation / judicial systems / trials / fact-finding missions
GEOGRAPHICAL INDEX: South Africa
GEOGRAPHICAL CODE: 5458
FREE TEXT: The appeal of Makae and Tlelima, members of the Roman
Catholic Young Christian Workers, against their conviction on charges
of conspiracy to commit sabotage was heard on 19 November 1979. The
appeal was allowed and the conviction quashed. The trial was typical of
trials under the General Law Amendment Act 1962 section 21 (sabotage)
and the Terrorism Act 1967, used by the authorities to suppress or
destroy unwelcome political, social or religious organizations amongst
black people. With description of the trial at Kroonstad and the appeal
at Bloemfontein, conclusions and a note on the judgment.

CATALOGUE SIGNATURE: 0000/1247/-3=830000
TITLE: Observation of the trial of the State v. Ramaligela and Mangaga
in the Supreme Court of Venda, South Africa, February 1983
AUTHOR: Deffenbaugh, Ralston H.
PLACE OF PUBLICATION: Washington DC
PUBLISHER: Lawyers Committee for Civil Rights Under Law - LCCRL (D)
DATE OF PUBLICATION: 830000
NUMBER OF PAGES: (37 p.)
LANGUAGE: ENG
INDEX: apartheid / trials / fact-finding missions
GEOGRAPHICAL INDEX: South Africa
GEOGRAPHICAL CODE: 5458
FREE TEXT: The case concerns one of the two prosecutions following
death in detention under the security laws; the author attended the
last two days of the trial. The report includes: the order of mission;
background to the case (the "homeland" Venda, incidents leading to the
trial, the inquest into the death of the prisoner Isaac Muofhe);
description of the trial (charges, cast of characters, the courtroom,
statements by and witnesses of the State and the defence, final
arguments); the judgment; the aftermath; evaluation of proceedings.
With conclusion. With appendices: order of mission, methodology, the
inquest judgment, the charge sheet, diagram of courtroom, newspaper
articles.

CATALOGUE SIGNATURE: 0000/0088/-4
TITLE: Report of a mission to attend the trial of Father Smangaliso
Mkhatshwa at the Regional Court in Zwelitsha, Ciskei, on 7 to 8 March
1984
AUTHOR: McNulty, A.B.
TITLE OF GENERIC ITEM: ICJ Newsletter
EDITION: no. 20
PLACE OF PUBLICATION: Geneva
PUBLISHER: International Commission of Jurists - ICJ (D)
DATE OF PUBLICATION: 840300
NUMBER OF PAGES: p. 53-65
LANGUAGE: ENG
INDEX: legislation / trials / fact-finding missions
GEOGRAPHICAL INDEX: South Africa
GEOGRAPHICAL CODE: 5458
FREE TEXT: The report contains the text of the charges, a description
of the procedures and the judgment. It is concluded that the trial by
the magistrate and counsel, both prosecution and defence, was correct,
fair and very competent. The objectional element is the Ciskei
Internal Security Act 1982, under which the accused has been arrested
and detained. The author states that the provisions providing for the
indefinite detention of a person without trial, his detention
incommunicando and his exclusion from the jurisdiction from any court
violate recognized international human rights provisions.

CATALOGUE SIGNATURE : 0000/1582/-3=860000
TITLE: The war against children: South Africa's youngest victims
AUTHOR: Cook, Helena ; Orentlicher, Diane
PLACE OF PUBLICATION: New York
PUBLISHER: Lawyers Committee for Human Rights - LCIHR (D)
DATE OF PUBLICATION: 860000
NUMBER OF PAGES: 151 p.
ISBN: 0 934243 00 5
LANGUAGE: ENG
BIBLIOGRAPHIES: Y
INDEX: children / political violence / detention / torture /
fact-finding missions
GEOGRAPHICAL INDEX: South Africa
GEOGRAPHICAL CODE: 5458
FREE TEXT: The report examines recent abuses of human rights in South
Africa against children under the age of 18 years. It is based on two
fact-finding missions by Helena Cook, in June-July and in November
1985. She met with a number of ex-detainees and victims of human
rights violations, various individuals knowledgeable on the problem
and representatives of the United States government. In gathering
information for the report, she worked closely with two leading human
rights organizations in South Africa, the Black Sash and the Detainees'
Parents Support Committee. The conclusions are based largely on
interviews, signed statements or sworn affidavits.
The report contains a foreword by Bishop Desmond Tutu, an introduction
with a summary of conclusions, and chapters on the background to the
unrest, the apparatus of control, violence in the streets, abuses
against children, security forces in the schools, arrests, assault and
torture of children in detention, deaths in detention, conditions in
detention, investigation and prosecution by the security forces, the
operation of the justice system and the role of the United States.

CATALOGUE SIGNATURE: 0000/0649/-3=860000
TITLE: Mission to South Africa: the Commonwealth report
AUTHOR: Commonwealth Eminent Persons Group
PLACE OF PUBLICATION: Harmondsworth
PUBLISHER: Penguin Books (D) ; Commonwealth Secretariat
DATE OF PUBLICATION: 860000
NUMBER OF PAGES: 176 p.
SERIES TITLE: Penguin Special
ISBN: 0 14 052384 7
AVAILABILITY: X
LANGUAGE: ENG
INDEX: apartheid / fact-finding missions
GEOGRAPHICAL INDEX: South Africa
GEOGRAPHICAL CODE: 5458
FREE TEXT: The report of the Commonwealth Eminent Persons Group,
which was appointed under the Nassau Accord on Southern Africa to
promote a process of dialogue for change, for ending apartheid and
establishing a genuine, non-racial democracy in South Africa. In
addition to its formal meetings in London, its visits to South Africa
and the front-line states, members of the group both jointly and
individually undertook a series of consultations in Southern Africa,
Nigeria and Tanzania, the United States and Europe.
The introduction contains biographical details on the members of the
Group, a note on the Commonwealth, a foreword by Secretary-General
Shridath Ramphal and the letter of transmittal.
The report itself contains chapters on background information on
apartheid, the issue of violence, the release of Nelson Mandela
and others, the establishment of political freedom, prospects for
negotiations, the proposals of the Commonwealth Group, the regional
dimensions of the conflict, and conclusions. With annexes: i.a. the
Commonwealth Accord on Southern Africa; the Group's programme.

South Africa

CATALOGUE SIGNATURE: 0000/0050/-3=860400
TITLE: Apartheid: wie lange noch?: Bericht über die Reise einer
IGFM-Gruppe nach Südafrika
AUTHOR: Martin, Ludwig ; Norberg, Brita ; Musa, Ndabezinhle
(... et al)
PLACE OF PUBLICATION: Frankfurt am Main
PUBLISHER: Internationale Gesellschaft für Menschenrechte - IGFM (D)
DATE OF PUBLICATION: 860400
NUMBER OF PAGES: 136 p.
ISBN: 3 89248 001 X
LANGUAGE: GER
STATISTICAL INFORMATION: Y
BIBLIOGRAPHIES: Y
INDEX: apartheid / peace / fact-finding missions
GEOGRAPHICAL INDEX: South Africa
GEOGRAPHICAL CODE: 5458
FREE TEXT: Report of a fact-finding mission of six members in January-
February 1986. The aim of the mission was to investigate possibilities
for a non-violent change, reconciliation, and peaceful cohabitation in
South Africa.
The report contains background information on apartheid; information
on Soweto, Crossroads, and the new settlement Khayelitsha; meetings
and interviews with representatives of a large number of Church and
nongovernmental organizations, for example with Dr. Beyers Naudé
and Allan Boesak of the South African Council of Churches; information
on the educational system; visits to a farm, factories, and prisons;
visits to government representatives, for example to Minister of
Justice H.J. Coetsee and Minister of Foreign Affairs Roelof Botha;
meetings with members of Parliament and with Chief Buthulezi; visit to
the homeland Bophuthatswana.
With summary and recommendations and appendices: the viewpoints of the
IGFM with regard to South Africa; apartheid legislation and extracts
from international conventions; newspaper articles.

CATALOGUE SIGNATURE: 0000/2121/-0=860710
TITLE: Het proces Hélène Passtoors en het Zuidafrikaanse
strafprocesrecht: verslag van een observator
AUTHOR: Wyngaert, Chris van den
PLACE OF PUBLICATION: (Gent)
PUBLISHER: Liga voor Mensenrechten (D)
DATE OF PUBLICATION: 860710
NUMBER OF PAGES: 32 p.
LANGUAGE: DUT
BIBLIOGRAPHIES: Y
INDEX: trials / fact-finding missions
GEOGRAPHICAL INDEX: South Africa
GEOGRAPHICAL CODE: 5458
FREE TEXT: In Spring 1986, the author observed the trial in Johannesburg
of the Dutch-Belgian Hélène Passtoors and studied it against the
background of the Southafrican criminal law. She also observed various
other trials and established various contacts.
The report contains a description of the proceedings at the trial and
an analysis of the significance of the trial in the framework of
Southafrican criminal law. Following, the question is answered whether
Passtoors had a fair trial (with attention to the proceedings, the
conviction to ten years imprisonment for high treason, and the penalty).
With final remarks.

CATALOGUE SIGNATURE: 0000/0069/-3=860000
TITLE: The Passtoors trial: a report to the ICJ and the NJCM on a
treason trial in South Africa: April - May 1986
AUTHOR: Manen, Willem van
PLACE OF PUBLICATION: Leiden
PUBLISHER: Nederlands Juristen Comité voor de Mensenrechten - NJCM
(D)
DATE OF PUBLICATION: 861111
NUMBER OF PAGES: 162 p.
LANGUAGE: ENG
INDEX: trials / fact-finding missions
GEOGRAPHICAL INDEX: South Africa
GEOGRAPHICAL CODE: 5458
FREE TEXT: In April 1986 the trial of Ms Passtoors and Mr De Jonge,
accused of high treason and terrorism, started before the Rand Supreme
Court in Johannesburg. On 15 May 1986, Ms Passtoors was convicted of
high treason after having been found guilty, inter alia, of having been
a member of the banned African National Congress and having been
involved in the estalishment of one arms cache for the ANC.
The author attended the trial as an observer for the International
Commission of Jurists and its Dutch section, the NJCM.
The report on the trial of Ms Passtoors is preceded by extracts from
reports on violence and other apartheid related items, and is followed
by accounts of other trials attended by the observer. It ends with
three pages of personal comments.

SUDAN

CATALOGUE SIGNATURE: 0000/0088/-3=860500
TITLE: The return to democracy in Sudan: report of a mission on behalf
of the International Commission of Jurists
AUTHOR: Hasala, Adib ; Cook, John D. ; Dolgopol, Ustinia
PLACE OF PUBLICATION: Geneva
PUBLISHER: International Commission of Jurists - ICJ (D)
DATE OF PUBLICATION: 860500
NUMBER OF PAGES: 103 p.
LANGUAGE: ENG
INDEX: legislation / judicial systems / fact-finding missions
GEOGRAPHICAL INDEX: Sudan
GEOGRAPHICAL CODE: 5259
FREE TEXT: The aim of the mission from 17 September to 6 October 1985
was to enquire into and report on the legal system and the
administration of justice in Sudan, with particular reference to: the
guarantees for the protection of human rights to be contained in the
transitional constitution; the functioning of the judicial system and
guarantees for its independence; the status of the "September laws"
enacted by former President Gaafar Mohamed Nimeiri, ostensibly to create
an Islamic legal system; the revisions being made to the National
Security Act, the Penal Code and the Code of Criminal Procedure; the
status of the negotiations with those representing the interests of the
south; and the ability of lawyers to exercise freely their profession.
The report contains: information on the preliminary report; responses
of the government; comments by the mission; a historical overview;
problems facing the new government; the southern conflict; legislation
affecting human rights; other constitutional and human rights issues;
summary of further recommendations. With appendices: detention order
form; convening order of the State Security Court.

TUNESIA

CATALOGUE SIGNATURE: 0000/0035/-3=780000
TITLE: La répression anti syndicale et les violations des droits de
l'homme en Tunisie: les procès de Sfax et de Sousse
AUTHOR: Goffin, Robert Charles
PLACE OF PUBLICATION: Brussels
PUBLISHER: Fédération Internationale des Droits de l'Homme - FIDH (D) ;
Ligue Belge pour la Défense des Droits de l'Homme - LBDDH (D)
DATE OF PUBLICATION: 780000
NUMBER OF PAGES: 22 p.
LANGUAGE: FRE
INDEX: trade unions / trials / civil and political rights /
fact-finding missions
GEOGRAPHICAL INDEX: Tunisia
GEOGRAPHICAL CODE: 5362
FREE TEXT: Tensions between the government and the UGTT trade union
escalated into violence on 26 January 1978, after which the trade
union was dismantled.
In the report, attention is paid to preparations for the mission and
the position of the government (based on interviews with government
representatives). The report contains a description of observations
made at the trials of Sfax and Soussa, with information received by
barristers and text of questions posed by a President of a tribunal.
Included is also information on torture (based on testimonies of
witnesses), freedom of association, freedom of the press, forced
labour and human rights organizations. With conclusions.

CATALOGUE SIGNATURE: 0000/0138/-3=780200
TITLE: Rapports de missions en Tunisie
AUTHOR: Auffray-Milesy, Marigrine ; Guillemot, J.
PLACE OF PUBLICATION: Brussels
PUBLISHER: Association Internationale des Juristes Démocrates - IADL (D)
DATE OF PUBLICATION: 780200
NUMBER OF PAGES: 18 p.
LANGUAGE: FRE
INDEX: trade unions / trials / fact-finding missions
GEOGRAPHICAL INDEX: Tunisia
GEOGRAPHICAL CODE: 5362
FREE TEXT: Auffray was trial observer at the process of twenty students,
accused after a conflict occurred between them and officially appointed
University supervisors. Her report contains background information and
a description of the hearings and the verdict. The second part is a
description of her experiences in Tunis: one of the leaders of the trade
union UGTT was arrested; a democratic lawyer, Mohamed Rafai, is not
allowed to perform his profession; on 26 January, a massacre occurred.
The third part is on detention conditions in Tunisian prisons, the
fourth contains information received after her return.
The report of J. Guillemot is on the trade union UGTT, of which many
members have been arrested and detained.

Tunesia

CATALOGUE SIGNATURE: 0000/0138/-3=780600
TITLE: Rapport de mission en Tunisie: 18-21 juin 1978
AUTHOR: Mabille, Catharine Danielle
PLACE OF PUBLICATION: Brussels
PUBLISHER: Association Internationale des Juristes Démocrates - IADL (D)
DATE OF PUBLICATION: 780600
NUMBER OF PAGES: 6 p.
LANGUAGE: FRE
INDEX: detention / trials / fact-finding missions
GEOGRAPHICAL INDEX: Tunisia
GEOGRAPHICAL CODE: 5362
FREE TEXT: The mission had two aims: to assist at the trial of the
lawyer Mohamed Rafai, and to investigate the detention conditions of
arrested trade union activists, and the charges made against them.
Rafai was accused of criticism on the government and partiality in
defending a client. The trial was delayed once more; intimidation and
pressure continue.
The second part starts with an outline of the political situation.
Special attention is paid to forced labour for young unemployed, the
(bad) detention conditions and the trials of trade union members.

CATALOGUE SIGNATURE: 0000/0138/-3=780700
TITLE: Tunisie: rapport de mission: 2-5 juillet 1978
AUTHOR: Yakovlev, Basile
PLACE OF PUBLICATION: Brussels
PUBLISHER: Association Internationale des Juristes Démocrates - IADL (D)
DATE OF PUBLICATION: 780700
NUMBER OF PAGES: 8 p.
LANGUAGE: FRE
INDEX: detention / trade unions / trials / fact-finding missions
GEOGRAPHICAL INDEX: Tunisia
GEOGRAPHICAL CODE: 5362
FREE TEXT: The mandate of the mission was to observe at the trial of
the lawyer Mohamed Rafai, and to investigate the detention conditions
of members of the trade union UGTT, and the charges against them.
The trial was postponed sine die. The detention conditions of trade
union members were bad; some were seriously ill. The trials of Soussa,
Sfax and Gafsa are described in short. The document also gives
information on the general situation of the trade unions. With
conclusions.

CATALOGUE SIGNATURE: 0000/0249/-3=781024
TITLE: Interview with researcher concerning recent trial of trade
unionist leaders in Tunis
AUTHOR: (Amnesty International - AI)
PLACE OF PUBLICATION: London
PUBLISHER: Amnesty International - AI (D)
DATE OF PUBLICATION: 781024
NUMBER OF PAGES: 4 p.
DOCUMENT SYMBOL: AI Index: AFR 58/05/78
LANGUAGE: ENG
INDEX: trials / fact-finding missions
GEOGRAPHICAL INDEX: Tunisia
GEOGRAPHICAL CODE: 5362
FREE TEXT: On 30 September, AI researcher June Ray landed at Tunis
airport; her mission was to observe the trial of 20 trade union leaders
facing charges before the State Security Court. In the interview, she
explains AI's concern of human rights violations in Tunisia and tells
what happened during her ten day stay in Tunis. The observer was not
allowed to attend the trial, but received information indicating that
the rights of the defence were gravely violated.

CATALOGUE SIGNATURE: 0000/0249/-3=790200
TITLE: Tunisia: imprisonment of trade unionists in 1978
AUTHOR: Amnesty International
PLACE OF PUBLICATION: London
PUBLISHER: Amnesty International - AI (D)
DATE OF PUBLICATION: 790200
NUMBER OF PAGES: 24 p.
DOCUMENT SYMBOL: AI Index: AFR 58/03/79
LANGUAGE: ENG
INDEX: trade unions / association (freedom of) / trials /
fact-finding missions
GEOGRAPHICAL INDEX: Tunisia
GEOGRAPHICAL CODE: 5362
FREE TEXT: In January 1978, when a general strike took place in
Tunisia, many hundreds of Tunisian trade unionists were arrested
throughout the country. The document outlines the circumstances of
their arrest, treatment and trials.
The trials in Sfax, July 1978 and Sousse, commencing July 1978, were
observed by an AI delegate. An AI observer was refused entry at the
trial at the State Security Court in Tunis, September / October 1978.
The report also deals with allegations of torture and prison
conditions. With conclusions and appendix: information on five
political prisoners, all trade unionists.

CATALOGUE SIGNATURE: 0000/0249/-3=790907
TITLE: Arrest, trial and imprisonment of Ech-Chaab group of prisoners
AUTHOR: Amnesty International - AI
PLACE OF PUBLICATION: London
PUBLISHER: Amnesty International - AI (D)
DATE OF PUBLICATION: 790907
NUMBER OF PAGES: 5 p.
DOCUMENT SYMBOL: AI Index: AFR 58/13/79
LANGUAGE: ENG
INDEX: political prisoners / detention / trials /
fact-finding missions
GEOGRAPHICAL INDEX: Tunisia
GEOGRAPHICAL CODE: 5362
FREE TEXT: During November 1978, 49 people were arrested in connection
with the publication and distribution of a clandestine version of
Ech-Chaab (The People), the name of the official organ of the General
Union of Tunisian Workers (UGTT), which until the general strike of 26
January 1978 had been critical on the government's policies. The 49
people were held incommunicando in police custody (so-called garde à
vue), and the majority claim to have been subjected to torture.
The report contains information on arrest and pre-trial detention,
prison conditions and the trial in July-August before the Criminal
Court of Tunis.

CATALOGUE SIGNATURE: 0000/0138/-0=840800
TITLE: Rapport d'observation: voyage en Tunesie du 12 au 15 juillet
1984
AUTHOR: Comte, Antoine
PLACE OF PUBLICATION: Brussels
PUBLISHER: Association Internationale des Juristes Démocrates - IADL (D)
DATE OF PUBLICATION: 840800
NUMBER OF PAGES: 6 p.
LANGUAGE: FRE
INDEX: political violence / judicial systems / fact-finding missions
GEOGRAPHICAL INDEX: Tunisia
GEOGRAPHICAL CODE: 5362
FREE TEXT: The aim of the mission was to obtain information on the
legal consequences of events (demonstrations against the raising of
prices for cereal, leading to violent acts by armed forces) occurring
in Tunisia at the end of December 1983 and the beginning of January
1984. In his report, the author tries the evaluate the consequences of
these events, and the functioning of the legal system. With
conclusions.

CATALOGUE SIGNATURE: 0000/0035/-3=860604
TITLE: Rapport de mission: Tunis le 4 juin 1986: procès de Mr. Ahmed
Mestiri, Secrétaire Général du Mouvement des Démocrates Socialistes
(MDS)
AUTHOR: Sidem-Poulain, Odile
PLACE OF PUBLICATION: Paris
PUBLISHER: Fédération Internationale des Droits de l'Homme - FIDH (D)
DATE OF PUBLICATION: 860604
NUMBER OF PAGES: 19 p.
LANGUAGE: FRE
INDEX: trials / fact-finding missions
GEOGRAPHICAL INDEX: Tunesia
GEOGRAPHICAL CODE: 5362
FREE TEXT: The aim of the mission was to observe the trial against
Ahmed Mestiri, secretary general of the Movement of Social Democrats
(RSP) before a tribunal in Tunis. The report contains background
information, and a description of the trial (legal background,
procedures, detention, and hearings). The report also contains
information on the trials of Moncef Ben Slimane, secretary general
of the National Syndicat of Higher Education and Scientific Research,
and of Fahren Mouldi, secretary general of the Office of Cereals and
member of the RSP.

CATALOGUE SIGNATURE: 0000/0035/-3=860700
TITLE: Rapport de mission: Tunis les 7-10 juillet 1986: mission
d'observation judiciaire: Rassemblement Socialiste Progressiste
(RSP) Mouvement de la Tendance Islamique (MTI)
AUTHOR: Sidem-Poulain, Odile
PLACE OF PUBLICATION: Paris
PUBLISHER: Fédération Internationale des Droits de l'Homme - FIDH (D)
DATE OF PUBLICATION: 860700
NUMBER OF PAGES: 14 p.
LANGUAGE: FRE
INDEX: trials / fact-finding missions
GEOGRAPHICAL INDEX: Tunisia
GEOGRAPHICAL CODE: 5362
FREE TEXT: The aim of the mission was to observe the trial against
activists of the opposition movements RSP and MTI. The report
contains information on the RSP, the MTI and the Union Générale
des Travailleurs Tunisiens UGTT. The report deals with trials which
took place earlier in 1986, and trials observed: the trial of 14
persons on 9 July at the Tribunal of First Instance in Tunis; the
trial of 26 persons on 4-9 July before the Military Tribunal.
Information is provided on repercussions against journalists and
detention conditions. With conclusions.

UGANDA

CATALOGUE SIGNATURE: 0000/0249/-3=820730
TITLE: Memorandum to the government of the Republic of Uganda on a mission by Amnesty International to Uganda in January 1982 and ensuing correspondence
AUTHOR: (Oosting, Dick) ; (Posner, Michael H.)
PLACE OF PUBLICATION: London
PUBLISHER: Amnesty International - AI (D)
DATE OF PUBLICATION: 820730
NUMBER OF PAGES: 26 p.
DOCUMENT SYMBOL: AI Index: AFR 59/23/82
LANGUAGE: ENG
INDEX: civil and political rights / political prisoners / fact-finding missions
GEOGRAPHICAL INDEX: Uganda
GEOGRAPHICAL CODE: 5263
FREE TEXT: The aim of the mission was to express AI's concern about allegations of serious violations of fundamental human rights by security forces in Uganda during 1981 to the government, and seek its response. The report contains information on the protection of human rights in Uganda, political imprisonment (arrest and detention by the army, indefinite detention without trial, criminal proceedings, political prisoners, the detention of former members of ex-President Amin's security forces); torture; prison conditions; "disappearances" and deaths in detention; extrajudicial executions. With conclusions and summary of main recommendations.

ZAIRE

CATALOGUE SIGNATURE: 0000/0249/-3=810700
TITLE: Memorandum to the (Zairian) Head of State following a mission
by Amnesty International to Zaire in July 1981
AUTHOR: Amnesty International - AI
PLACE OF PUBLICATION: London
PUBLISHER: Amnesty International - AI (D)
DATE OF PUBLICATION: 810700
NUMBER OF PAGES: 41 p. in v.p.
DOCUMENT SYMBOL: AI Index: AFR 62/33/81
LANGUAGE: ENG / FRE
INDEX: penal systems / judicial systems / political prisoners /
fact-finding missions
GEOGRAPHICAL INDEX: Zaire
GEOGRAPHICAL CODE: 5165
FREE TEXT: Two AI delegates visited Zaire in July 1981 at the
invitation of the Executive Council (the government), following an
exchange of views between AI and the government authorities during
1980. The delegates met with government officials and visited places
of detention.
The memorandum attempts to set out both the explanation of the penal
system which officials made during the mission and AI's analysis of
the way in which the penal system works. It also deals with AI's major
concerns in Zaire: detention without trial, administrative banishment,
torture and deaths in detention, and the death penalty, as well as
reports of harsh prison conditions and the continuing imprisonment of
alleged opponents of the government sentenced after fair trials. With
information on specific cases, conclusions and appendices: list of
meetings with officials; comments by the Zairian authorities on the
memorandum, with copies of the original letters.

CATALOGUE SIGNATURE: 0000/0035/-0=820700
TITLE: Une mission de la FIDH au Zaire
AUTHOR: Toutain, Jacques
PLACE OF PUBLICATION: Paris
PUBLISHER: Fédération Internationale des Droits de l'Homme - FIDH (D)
DATE OF PUBLICATION: 820700
NUMBER OF PAGES: 20 p.
LANGUAGE: FRE
INDEX: association (freedom of) / prison conditions / trials /
fact-finding missions
GEOGRAPHICAL INDEX: Zaire
GEOGRAPHICAL CODE: 5165
FREE TEXT: The aim of the mission was to investigate into the situation
and detention conditions of persons appearing before the State Security
Court. It concerns specifically 13 members of parliament firstly
arrested after sending a letter to the President and once again after
trying to establish a new political party. The author observed the
second part of the trial; in his report, he provides a description of
events in 1980-1982 leading to the arrests, the procedure before the
Court, the trial itself, and the human rights aspects of the case. With
recommendations.

ZIMBABWE

CATALOGUE SIGNATURE: 0000/1234/-2=800000
TITLE: Elections in Zimbabwe Rhodesia
AUTHOR: Drummond, Roscoe; Rustin, Bayard; Sussman, Leonard R.
TITLE OF GENERIC ITEM: Freedom in the world: political rights and civil
liberties
PLACE OF PUBLICATION: New York
PUBLISHER: Freedom House - FH (D)
DATE OF PUBLICATION: 800000
NUMBER OF PAGES: p.157-189
LANGUAGE: ENG
BIBLIOGRAPHIES: Y
INDEX: elections   fact-finding missions
GEOGRAPHICAL INDEX: Zimbabwe
GEOGRAPHICAL CODE: 5467
FREE TEXT: Freedom House sent a nine member delegation to observe the
common roll election in April 1979. While, given the context, the
delegation judged the election to be not fully democratic, it thought
it was a step toward democracy. The report consists of an introduction,
a description of the goals and activities of the observer mission, the
context of the common roll election, issues of primary significance in
the evaluation of the election, and conclusions.
With annexes: the results of the common roll election; political,
ethnic and geographic aspects of the nationalist struggle in Zimbabwe
Rhodesia.

CATALOGUE SIGNATURE: 0000/0249/-3=800100
TITLE: Report of an Amnesty International mission to Rhodesia: 3-12
January 1980
AUTHOR: (Oosting, Dick) ; (Smart, Malcolm)
PLACE OF PUBLICATION: London
PUBLISHER: Amnesty International - AI (D)
DATE OF PUBLICATION: 800100
NUMBER OF PAGES: 10 p.
DOCUMENT SYMBOL: AI Index: AFR 46/03/80
LANGUAGE: ENG
INDEX: detention   civil and political rights   fact-finding missions
GEOGRAPHICAL INDEX: Zimbabwe
GEOGRAPHICAL CODE: 5467
FREE TEXT: The aim of the mission was to assess the human rights
situation, and to make further representations to the Governor of
South Rhodesia, Lord Soames, and his administration concerning AI's
outstanding concerns. The report contains the findings of the mission
with regard to detention without trial, especially under martial law;
restriction orders; convicted political prisoners; torture; the death
penalty; and other issues.

CATALOGUE SIGNATURE: 5467/-0=800319
TITLE: The Zimbabwe miracle: an observer's report on the Rhodesian
elections February 27-29, 1980
AUTHOR: Houser, George M.
PLACE OF PUBLICATION: New York
PUBLISHER: American Committee on Africa - ACOA (D)
DATE OF PUBLICATION: 800319
NUMBER OF PAGES: 11 p.
LANGUAGE: ENG
INDEX: elections / fact-finding missions
GEOGRAPHICAL INDEX: Zimbabwe
GEOGRAPHICAL CODE: 5467
FREE TEXT: The author was member of a delegation of the American
Committee on Africa. In his report, he tries to convey something of
the atmosphere in the period leading up to the elections, and to assess
how free and fair the elections under the British administration were.
Attention is paid to the activities of the mission, intimidation, the
detention of the observer group, the victory of the Patriotic Front
ZANU-PF and future perspectives. With conclusions: there were many
voting irregularities, but contrasted to the intimidation leading up to
the actual voting, the election was remarkably peaceful.

CATALOGUE SIGNATURE: 5467/-0=800300
TITLE: The independence of Zimbabwe: a responsibility for all of us:
the report of the Quebec delegation to Zimbabwe submitted to the
Quebec Human Rights League and the International Federation of Human
Rights (Paris)
AUTHOR: Campbell, Bonnie ; Poirier, Roger ; Charbonneau, Yvon
(et al...)
EDITION: repr.
PLACE OF PUBLICATION: Trenton
PUBLISHER: Africa Research & Publications Project (D)
DATE OF PUBLICATION: 800300
NUMBER OF PAGES: 8 p.
LANGUAGE: ENG
INDEX: self-determination / elections / fact-finding missions
GEOGRAPHICAL INDEX: Zimbabwe
GEOGRAPHICAL CODE: 5467
FREE TEXT: Report of a four-member mission sponsored by the Quebec
Human Rights League to observe the transition towards independence in
Zimbabwe, which was to become independent on 18 April 1980. The report
deals with events leading to independence, the Lancaster House
Agreement, the ceasefire, the highly militarized elections, the use of
intimidation as political weapon and systematic obstruction by the
Rhodesian government against the Patriotic Front party, the level of
political consciousness, problems for the new government and the need
for international support, with recommendations.

CATALOGUE SIGNATURE: 0000/0088/-4
TITLE: Report on the trial of Dumiso Dabengwa, Lookout Masuku and five
others in Harare, Zimbabwe: 7 February - 27 April 1983
AUTHOR: Sakala, Julius B.
TITLE OF GENERIC ITEM: ICJ Newsletter
EDITION: no. 17
PLACE OF PUBLICATION: Geneva
PUBLISHER: International Commission of Jurists - ICJ (D)
DATE OF PUBLICATION: 830600
NUMBER OF PAGES: p. 21-33
LANGUAGE: ENG
INDEX: legislation / trials / fact-finding missions
GEOGRAPHICAL INDEX: Zimbabwe
GEOGRAPHICAL CODE: 5467
FREE TEXT: The basic allegation in the trial, as the State put it, was
that the accused were actively engaged in preparations to overthrow the
lawful government by armed rebellion. The report contains information
on the background of the trial, a review of the charges and a
description of the hearings. With general comments (conclusions) with
regard to the press, defence and prosecution lawyers, the judge and his
assessors, and disturbing features.

CATALOGUE SIGNATURE: 0000/1246/-3=860200
TITLE: Zimbabwe: report on the 1985 elections based on a mission of
the election observer project of the IHRLG
AUTHOR: Arnold, Millard W. ; Garber, Larry ; Wrobel, Brian
PLACE OF PUBLICATION: Washington D.C.
PUBLISHER: International Human Rights Law Group - IHRLG (D)
DATE OF PUBLICATION: 860200
NUMBER OF PAGES: (150 p.)
LANGUAGE: ENG
INDEX: elections / fact-finding missions
GEOGRAPHICAL INDEX: Zimbabwe
GEOGRAPHICAL CODE: 5467
FREE TEXT: The International Human Rights Law Group organized a
delegation to observe Zimbabwe's first post-independence elections.
The three members of the delegation were in Zimbabwe between 21 June
and 6 July. The report is divided into three parts:
I) Zimbabwe's 1985 elections, by Larry Garber;
in this part, attention is paid to the background of the elections;
the electoral conditions; the framework of the electoral process;
the parties participating in the electoral process; the electoral
campaign; the administration of the elections; the election results;
concluding observations;
II) Intimidation, political freedom, and the common roll, by Brian
Wrobel; with attention to the enquiry: its methods and background;
the "indicators" occurring during the election year; conclusions;
III) The Zimbabwe general election of 1985: an analysis and
appraisal, by Millard Arnold; with an overview, and attention to:
independent Zimbabwe; competing personalities; black political
developments; the liberation struggle; and, the political strike
1981-1985.
In the appendices: terms of reference; biographies of members of
the delegation; summary of University of Zimbabwe election project;
post-election statement issued by the Catholic Commission on Justice
and Peace; results of 1985 white roll elections; results of 1985
common roll elections.

CATALOGUE SIGNATURE: 0000/1582/-3=860000
TITLE: Zimbabwe: wages of war: a report on human rights
AUTHOR: Berkeley, Bill ; Schrage, Elliot
PLACE OF PUBLICATION: New York
PUBLISHER: Lawyers Committee for Human Rights - LCIHR (D)
DATE OF PUBLICATION: 860000
NUMBER OF PAGES: 171 p.
ISBN: 0 934143 07 2
LANGUAGE: ENG
BIBLIOGRAPHIES: Y
INDEX: ethnic conflict / civil and political rights /
fact-finding missions
GEOGRAPHICAL INDEX: Zimbabwe
GEOGRAPHICAL CODE: 5467
FREE TEXT: The report is based on two visits to Zimbabwe, in late 1985
and in January 1986. The LCIHR representatives met with victims of
human rights violations and their relatives, persons who could provide
an overview of such abuses, government authorities and officials, and
representatives of the United States government. The report contains
an introduction with a summary of conclusions, and chapters on: the
conflict in Matabeleland; the apparatus of state security; political
kidnappings; political detentions; torture; political intimidation;
the 1984 curfew; and the legal context.
With appendices: correspondence between Deputy Prime Minister S.V.
Muzenda and the LCIHR.
The first of nine conclusions is that although human rights conditions
have improved for most Zimbabweans since independence from white rule
in 1980, the government's campaign to suppress armed dissidents in
Matabeleland has resulted in grave and persistent abuses of human
rights against the minority Ndebele population.

DJIBOUTI / ETHIOPIA

CATALOGUE SIGNATURE: 0000/0050/-3=830817
TITLE: Die nicht ganz freiwillige Repatriierung äthiopischer
Flüchtlinge aus Djibouti: fact-finding mission Djibouti
AUTHOR: Niggli, Peter
PLACE OF PUBLICATION: Frankfurt am Main
PUBLISHER: Internationale Gesellschaft für Menschenrechte Deutsche
Sektion - IGFM (D)
DATE OF PUBLICATION: 830817
NUMBER OF PAGES: 21 p.
LANGUAGE: GER
INDEX: refugees / fact-finding missions
GEOGRAPHICAL INDEX: Djibouti / Ethiopia
GEOGRAPHICAL CODE: 5224 / 5227
FREE TEXT: About forty thousand Ethiopians fled to the small republic
of Djibouti in the period 1977-1983. For the Djibouti government, it
is not possible to integrate the refugees, because of the limited
economic resources of the country. In 1983, a Tripartite Commission
of the Djibouti and Ethiopian governments and the United Nations High
Commissioner for Refugees UNHCR worked out a program for "voluntary
repatriation", starting 15 August 1983. The refugees are not willing
to return, and seem to be deported by force. The findings in the
report are based on talks with dozens of refugees and members of
official bodies concerned.

EAST AFRICA / WEST AFRICA

CATALOGUE SIGNATURE: 5000/-0=830400
TITLE: Women, health and development in East and West Africa: a personal view
AUTHOR: Hosken, Fran P.
TITLE OF GENERIC ITEM: WIN News
EDITION: v.9(2)
PLACE OF PUBLICATION: Lexington
PUBLISHER: Women's International Network - WIN (D)
DATE OF PUBLICATION: 830400
NUMBER OF PAGES: p. 1-12
LANGUAGE: ENG
INDEX: female circumcision / women / health / fact-finding missions
GEOGRAPHICAL INDEX: East Africa / West Africa
GEOGRAPHICAL CODE: 5200 / 5500
FREE TEXT: The aim of the visit in February - March 1983 was to find out if recommendations to abolish traditional sexual operations and to strengthen health education and training made at the World Health Organization-sponsored seminar on "Traditional practices affecting the health of women and children" had been implemented. More specifically, the trip was concerned with introducing "The universal childbirth picture book" and education program with the preventive "Additions on excision / infibulation".
The author paid visits to Egypt, Sudan, Ethiopia, Somalia, Kenya, Nigeria, Niger, Upper Volta, Mali, Senegal, Sierra Leone and France. With description of findings, and summary.

EQUATORIAL GUINEA / GABON

CATALOGUE SIGNATURE: 0000/0035/-3=740000
TITLE: Mission concernant la Guinée Equatoriale: août 1974
AUTHOR: Mignon, Thierry
PLACE OF PUBLICATION: Paris
PUBLISHER: Fédération Internationale des Droits de l'Homme - FIDH (D)
DATE OF PUBLICATION: 740000
NUMBER OF PAGES: 11 p.
LANGUAGE: FRE
INDEX: detention / political prisoners / fact-finding missions
GEOGRAPHICAL INDEX: Equatorial Guinea / Gabon
GEOGRAPHICAL CODE: 5126 / 5128
FREE TEXT: The purpose of the mission was to gather information on
the detention conditions of Gabonese political prisoners, and on
the general human rights situation in Equatorial Guinea; this report
covers the second part of the mandate. The author decided not to
visit Equatorial Guinea for safety reasons, and bases his report on
information received in Gabon, mainly from refugees from Equatorial
Guinea. Attention is paid to the general situation in the country,
and relations with Gabon. With testimonies of refugees and
conclusions.

HORN OF AFRICA

CATALOGUE SIGNATURE: 0000/0018/-0=780400
TITLE: The Horn of Africa: travel report: first reflections
AUTHOR: Koshy, Ninan
PLACE OF PUBLICATION: Geneva
PUBLISHER: Commission of the Churches on International Affairs of the
World Council of Churches - CCIA-WCC (D)
DATE OF PUBLICATION: 780400
NUMBER OF PAGES: 30 p.
SERIES TITLE: Background information
VOLUME: v. 1978/3
LANGUAGE: ENG
INDEX: ethnic conflict / armed conflict / church and state /
fact-finding missions
GEOGRAPHICAL INDEX: Horn of Africa
GEOGRAPHICAL CODE: 5001
FREE TEXT: In January-February 1978, Leopoldo J. Niilus and Ninan Koshy
visited Kenya, Ethiopia and the Sudan, at the request of the National
Christian Council of Kenya. The visit was undertaken with a view to
assisting the churches in the area and outside in understanding and
interpreting the factors underlying the conflicts in the Horn of
Africa. The delegates were able to make a series of contacts with
several people in the political, diplomatic and academic fields. In
the report, most attention is given to the conflicts in the region.
It contains chapters on the Somalia-Ethiopia conflict, the Ethiopian
revolution, the question of Eritrea, Djibouti, the relations between
Somalia and Kenya, the roles of the United States and other Western
powers, the Soviet Union, Cuba, the Middle East countries, and the
relation between Sudan and Ethiopia. With conclusion: the issues of
ethnic groups, nationalisms and territorial integrity of countries in
the region are unfortunately today intertwined with expressions of the
interests of many countries in the neighbourhood and outside the region.

SAHARA / ALGERIA

CATALOGUE SIGNATURE: 5551/-0=790000
TITLE: Report on a visit to the Democratic Arab Saharawi Republic and
Algeria
AUTHOR: Knight, Richard
PLACE OF PUBLICATION: New York
PUBLISHER: American Committee on Africa - ACOA (D)
DATE OF PUBLICATION: 790000
NUMBER OF PAGES: 9 p.
LANGUAGE: ENG
INDEX: self-determination / armed conflict / fact-finding missions
GEOGRAPHICAL INDEX: Saharan Arab Democratic Republic / Algeria
GEOGRAPHICAL CODE: 5551 / 5311
FREE TEXT: The purpose of the visit from 24 February to 17 March 1979
was to study the military, political and refugee situation of the
Western Sahara, where a political movement, the Polisario, is engaged
in an armed struggle to ensure self-determination for its country. The
author also represented the American Committee on Africa at the Third
Anniversary Celebrations of the proclamation of the Saharan Arab
Democratic Republic. In the report, attention is paid to the history of
the struggle, the Celebrations, the situation of refugees, health and
education, the situation in the Western Sahara. With short report on
the visit to Algeria.

SENEGAL / NIGERIA

CATALOGUE SIGNATURE: 0000/0001/-4
TITLE: Visit to West Africa
AUTHOR: Scoble, Harry M.
TITLE OF GENERIC ITEM: Human Rights Internet Newsletter
EDITION: v. 5(8-9)
PLACE OF PUBLICATION: Washington DC
PUBLISHER: Human Rights Internet - HRI (D)
DATE OF PUBLICATION: 800700
NUMBER OF PAGES: p.56-61
LANGUAGE: ENG
INDEX: nongovernmental organizations / fact-finding missions
GEOGRAPHICAL INDEX: Senegal / Nigeria
GEOGRAPHICAL CODE: 5554 / 5548
FREE TEXT: The author was in Senegal and in Nigeria from 18 May to
1 June 1980. He attended the Organizing Congress of the proposed new
Inter-African Union of Lawyers in Dakar, Senegal, and met with human
rights organizations in Nigeria, which are working in the context of
a return to civilian rule after thirteen years of military regime,
and of the shift from the British parliamentary to the American
constitutional system. The report contains an analysis of the Dakar
congress, including texts of resolutions adopted, and information on
political developments and the work of human rights organizations in
Nigeria.

SOUTH AFRICA / ZIMBABWE

CATALOGUE SIGNATURE: 0000/2921/-3=830300
TITLE: South Africa and Zimbabwe: the freest press in Africa?: a report
by the Committee to Protect Journalists
AUTHOR: Nadel, Laurie ; Neier, Aryeh
PLACE OF PUBLICATION: New York
PUBLISHER: Committee to Protect Journalists - CPJ (D)
DATE OF PUBLICATION: 830300
NUMBER OF PAGES: 98 p.
LANGUAGE: ENG
INDEX: journalists (protection of) / censorship / fact-finding missions
GEOGRAPHICAL INDEX: South Africa / Zimbabwe
GEOGRAPHICAL CODE: 5458 / 5467
FREE TEXT: The CPJ decided to sent a delegation to South Africa because
of its concern with the increasing threats to press freedom in that
country. In its ten-day visit, the members of the delegation met with a
broad spectrum of South Africans working in, or concerned with local
media. Zimbabwe was chosen as a second country because of its obvious
contrasts with South Africa. It is concluded that words such as "free"
or "freest" are inappropriate in describing the press in either South
Africa or Zimbabwe.
The report contains: an introduction on the background of the mission,
a summary and conclusions; a part on South Africa, with attention to
detentions, banning, harassment, legislation, prosecutions, planned and
organized self-censorship, alternate media, the South African
Broadcasting Corporation SABC, trade unions, discrimination in
connection with employment and editorial decisions, the freedom of the
press and the role of the United States; a part on Zimbabwe, with
attention to detentions, media ownership, the Zimbabwe Broadcasting
Company ZBC, and the foreign press.

SOUTHERN AFRICA

CATALOGUE SIGNATURE: 0000/0138/-0=780800
TITLE: IADL fact finding mission to Southern Africa (26th July -
17th August 1978)
AUTHOR: Pierson-Mathy, Paulette ; Schware, Rudolph ; Harvey, Richard
(et al...)
PLACE OF PUBLICATION: Brussels
PUBLISHER: Association Internationale des Juristes Démocrates - IADL (D)
DATE OF PUBLICATION: 780800
NUMBER OF PAGES: 31 p. in v.p.
LANGUAGE: ENG
INDEX: armed violence / self-determination / fact-finding missions
GEOGRAPHICAL INDEX: Southern Africa
GEOGRAPHICAL CODE: 5400
FREE TEXT: The aim of the four member fact-finding mission was to
study, with the assistance of authorities of the countries visited and
of the liberation movements, the crimes committed against the peoples
of Southern Africa by the minority regimes of South Africa and Rhodesia
in pursuance of their policy of racist and colonialist oppression. The
mission also investigated the armed attacks launched by these regimes
against the front line states. The countries visited were the People's
Republic of Angola, the Republic of Zambia and the People's Republic of
Mozambique. The report contains a description of activities of the
mission, general observations, and testimonies of witnesses and victims
of violence.

CATALOGUE SIGNATURE: 0000/0035/-3=830600
TITLE: La situation des réfugiés sud-africains au Lesotho et au
Botswana: mission d'enquête effectuée au mois de juin 1983
AUTHOR: Laurin, Yves
PLACE OF PUBLICATION: Paris
PUBLISHER: Fédération Internationale des Droits de l'Homme - FIDH (D)
DATE OF PUBLICATION: 830600
NUMBER OF PAGES: 27 p.
LANGUAGE: FRE
STATISTICAL INFORMATION: Y
INDEX: refugees / fact-finding missions
GEOGRAPHICAL INDEX: Southern Africa
GEOGRAPHICAL CODE: 5400
FREE TEXT: The delegate outlines the institutions of apartheid, which
justify the provision of the refugee status to all people in exile,
and describes the situation of refugees in Lesotho and Botswana.
Attention is given to the South African raid of 12 December 1982 and
the reception and security of the refugees. With conclusions: the
delegate denounces South African interventions and calls for
international measures. With annexes: maps, list of victims of the
December 1982 raid, schedule and description of buildings damaged.

WEST AFRICA

CATALOGUE SIGNATURE: 0000/1212/-0=810000
TITLE: Human rights in Africa: report of a visit to Nigeria, Ghana,
Ivory Coast, Senegal and Upper Volta
AUTHOR: Kannyo, Edward
PLACE OF PUBLICATION: New York
PUBLISHER: International League for Human Rigths - ILHR (D)
DATE OF PUBLICATION: 810100
NUMBER OF PAGES: 42 p.
LANGUAGE: ENG
INDEX: nongovernmental organizations / association (freedom of) /
fact-finding missions
GEOGRAPHICAL INDEX: West Africa
GEOGRAPHICAL CODE: 5500
FREE TEXT: The aims of the mission were to study and assess human
rights activities and organizations in Nigeria, Ghana, Ivory Coast,
Senegal and Upper Volta (now named Bourkina Fasso) and to establish
contacts with them. The author also used the opportunity to study the
socio-economic and political life in these countries - at least what
could be ascertained in their capital cities.
The report consists of a summary on the general situation in the
countries visited and the situation of the human rights organizations,
and descriptions of the findings on each country. In these sections,
attention is paid to the political and socio-economic situation, and
the character and work of nongovernmental organizations. With
conclusions on each country.

AFGHANISTAN

CATALOGUE SIGNATURE: 0000/0249/-3=790900
TITLE: Violations of human rights and fundamental freedoms in the
Democratic Republic of Afghanistan: an Amnesty International report
AUTHOR: (Soysal, Mümtaz)
PLACE OF PUBLICATION: London
PUBLISHER: Amnesty International - AI (D)
DATE OF PUBLICATION: 790900
NUMBER OF PAGES: 34 p.
DOCUMENT SYMBOL: AI Index: ASA 11/04/79
LANGUAGE: ENG
INDEX: political prisoners / political killings / fact-finding missions
GEOGRAPHICAL INDEX: Afghanistan
GEOGRAPHICAL CODE: 7411
FREE TEXT: The report covers the period of one year after the People's
Democratic Party (PDP) government, led by President Noor Mohammad
Taraki, came to power through a military takeover in April 1978. In
October 1978, an AI mission discussed allegations of human rights
violations with government representatives. The delegation was not
allowed to visit political prisoners. The report deals with political
imprisonment, maltreatment and torture, the rights and safety of
political prisoners and the right not to be arbitrarily deprived of
one's life. Attention is also paid to legal provisions and the right
to a fair trial.
With appendices: memorandum to the government; list of well known
Afghan citizens and officials arrested after 27 April 1978; list of
persons arrested after 27 April and reported to have been killed while
in the custody of the PDP government.

CATALOGUE SIGNATURE: 0000/0035/-3=800000
TITLE: Afghanistan 1978-1980: répression et guerre Soviétiques
AUTHOR: Barry, Michael
PLACE OF PUBLICATION: Paris
PUBLISHER: Fédération Internationale des Droits de l'Homme - FIDH (D)
DATE OF PUBLICATION: 800000
NUMBER OF PAGES: 32 p. in v.p.
LANGUAGE: FRE
INDEX: refugees / armed conflict / military / fact-finding missions
GEOGRAPHICAL INDEX: Afghanistan
GEOGRAPHICAL CODE: 7411
FREE TEXT: The author is a specialist in Moslim civilisation. During
his fact-finding mission in February-March 1980, he interviewed
refugees in the area around Peshawar in Pakistan, and in different
camps situated near the border between Pakistan and Afghanistan. The
report contains background information and testimonies, which can be
divided in two groups: those on urban repression and those on rural,
military repression. With description of the background of the country,
and complete texts of testimonies.

CATALOGUE SIGNATURE: 7411/-4
TITLE: Gamble in Panjsher
AUTHOR: Issot-Sergent, Pierre
TITLE OF GENERIC ITEM: The letter from the BIA
EDITION: v. 6
PLACE OF PUBLICATION: Paris
PUBLISHER: Bureau International Afghanistan - BIA (D)
DATE OF PUBLICATION: 830600
NUMBER OF PAGES: p. 3-9
LANGUAGE: ENG
INDEX: armed conflict / fact-finding missions
GEOGRAPHICAL INDEX: Afghanistan
GEOGRAPHICAL CODE: 7411
FREE TEXT: Report dated May 1983 on a secret visit to the Panjsher
region in Afghanistan, where military encounters between Soviet
troups and resistance fighters take place. The report contains
impressions on the situation and information on the attitude of the
population towards the Soviet occupation forces and the resistance
movement, based on interviews with resistance fighters.

CATALOGUE SIGNATURE: 7411/-4
TITLE: Dossier: mission dans le Kunar
AUTHOR: Delpuech, Bernard ; Parret, Camile ; De Bures, Alain
TITLE OF GENERIC ITEM: Défis Afghans
EDITION: no. 1
PLACE OF PUBLICATION: Paris
PUBLISHER: Bureau International Afghanistan - BIA (D)
DATE OF PUBLICATION: 841200
NUMBER OF PAGES: p. 18-25
LANGUAGE: FRE
INDEX: development cooperation / armed conflict /
fact-finding missions
GEOGRAPHICAL INDEX: Afghanistan
GEOGRAPHICAL CODE: 7411
FREE TEXT: The dossier consists of three articles, by each of the
members of a BIA mission which visited the border region between
Afghanistan and Pakistan in July 1984. The aim of the mission was to
study problems in agriculture and possibilities for effective aid.
Attention is paid to the ongoing struggle and the strenght and
weaknesses of the resistance movement. There is an interview with
Walid Madjrouh, a commander of resistance forces, and an article on
the impact of the guerilla war on the development of the agriculture
and the situation of farmers.

CATALOGUE SIGNATURE: 0000/1245/-3=841200
TITLE: "Tears, blood and cries": human rights in Afghanistan since
the invasion: 1979-1984
AUTHOR: Laber, Jeri ; Rubin, Barnett
PLACE OF PUBLICATION: New York
PUBLISHER: Helsinki Watch - HW (D)
DATE OF PUBLICATION: 841200
NUMBER OF PAGES: 210 p.
LANGUAGE: ENG
BIBLIOGRAPHIES: Y
INDEX: armed conflict / fact-finding missions
GEOGRAPHICAL INDEX: Afghanistan
GEOGRAPHICAL CODE: 7411
FREE TEXT: Report on the human rights situation in Afghanistan, partly
based on a fact-finding mission in September to Peshawar and Quetto
in Pakistan, where refugees were interviewed. The report contains an
introduction, and chapters on: the background of the country; mass
destruction in the countryside (crimes against the rural population
and destruction of the rural economy); mass repression in the cities
(suppression of civil liberties and independent institutions, and
repression of the individual); other violations of international
agreements (the killing of prisoners of war, the prevention of medical
and humanitarian assistance, restrictions and attacks on journalists,
the training of children as spies, prevention of international
inspection), and human rights violations by the Afghan resistance
(treatment of prisoners of war and other prisoners, attacks on
civilian targets).

CATALOGUE SIGNATURE: 0000/1079/-3=850219
TITLE: Report on the situation of human rights in Afghanistan...
AUTHOR: Ermacora, Felix
PLACE OF PUBLICATION: Geneva
PUBLISHER: Commission on Human Rights of the United Nations Economic and Social Council - UNCHR (D)
DATE OF PUBLICATION: 850219
NUMBER OF PAGES: 60 p. in v.p.
SERIES TITLE: Commission on Human Rights: forty-first session: agenda item 12: question of the violation of human rights and fundamental freedoms in any part of the world, with particular reference to colonial and other dependent countries and territories
DOCUMENT SYMBOL: E/CN.4/1985/21
AVAILABILITY: F
LANGUAGE: ENG / FRE
STATISTICAL INFORMATION: Y
INDEX: armed conflict / refugees / fact-finding missions
GEOGRAPHICAL INDEX: Afghanistan
GEOGRAPHICAL CODE: 7411
FREE TEXT: Felix Ermacora is Special Rapporteur on the situation of human rights in Afghanistan in accordance with Commission on Human Rights resolution 1984/55. In December 1984, he went to Pakistan to collect information from the many Afghan refugees in that country. His report contains a general introduction, and chapters on: his mandate; the background of the country (survey of recent events; the question of refugees); information on the situation with regard to respect for human rights; relevant constitutional and international legal framework in regard to human rights. With conclusions and recommendations, and annex: Fundamental Principles of the Democratic Republic of Afghanistan.

CATALOGUE SIGNATURE: 0000/0035/-3=850000
TITLE: Commission d'enquête humanitaire internationale sur les
personnes deplacées en Afghanistan: rapport de mission en Afghanistan
et au Pakistan: septembre-octobre-novembre 1985
AUTHOR: Barry, Michael ; Lagerfelt, Johan ; Terrenoire, Marie-Odile
(...et al)
PLACE OF PUBLICATION: Paris
PUBLISHER: Fédération Internationale des Droits de l'Homme - FIDH (D)
DATE OF PUBLICATION: 850000
NUMBER OF PAGES: 49 p.
LANGUAGE: FRE
STATISTICAL INFORMATION: Y
BIBLIOGRAPHIES: Y
INDEX: refugees / fact-finding missions
GEOGRAPHICAL INDEX: Afghanistan
GEOGRAPHICAL CODE: 7411
FREE TEXT: An International Investigating Commission was established to
raise the issue of refugees from Afghanistan. In the period September-
November 1985, a fact-finding mission was conducted in Afghanistan and
Pakistan.
The report contains:
-an introduction with background information and a bibliography;
-a section on the findings of the first group, which paid an illegal
visit to Afghanistan. Attention is paid to the methods of investigation
used; statistics on the degree of depopulation; the situation of the
agriculture; refugees; displaced persons within Afghanistan; and
atrocities.
- a section on the findings of the second group, which visited refugee
camps in Pakistan in order to obtain testimonies of refugees which
recently arrived. Attention is paid to the methods of investigation,
problems for obtaining statistical information, and testimonies of
refugees. With conclusions and appendix: notes on testimonies.

Afghanistan

CATALOGUE SIGNATURE: 0000/1079/-3=860217
DATE OF ENTRY: 861005
TITLE: Report on the situation of human rights in Afghanistan...
AUTHOR: Ermacora, Felix
PLACE OF PUBLICATION: Geneva
PUBLISHER: Commission on Human Rights of the United Nations Economic
and Social Council - UNCHR (D)
DATE OF PUBLICATION: 860217
NUMBER OF PAGES: 27 p.
SERIES TITLE: Commission on Human Rights: forty-second session: agenda
item 12: question of the violation of human rights and fundamental
freedoms in any part of the world, with particular reference to
colonial and other dependent countries and territories
DOCUMENT SYMBOL: E/CN.4/1986/24
AVAILABILITY: F
LANGUAGE: ENG / FRE
STATISTICAL INFORMATION: Y
INDEX: armed conflict / refugees / fact-finding missions
GEOGRAPHICAL INDEX: Afghanistan
GEOGRAPHICAL CODE: 7411
FREE TEXT: Felix Ermacora is Special Rapporteur on the situation of
human rights in Afghanistan, in accordance with Commission on Human
Rights resolution 1985/38. He did not receive permission to visit
Afghanistan, and heard the testimony of witnesses in refugee camps in
Baluchistan and in the North-West Frontier Province of Pakistan in July
- August 1985. In his report, attention is given to the mandate, the
political background and the development of the human rights situation
in Afghanistan, the situation of refugees, and information concerning
respect for human rights in Afghanistan (before and since the
intervention of foreign troups on 27 December 1979). With conclusions
and recommendations, and annex: figures on civilian deaths caused by
the conflict in 1985.

BANGLADESH

CATALOGUE SIGNATURE: 0000/0249/-3=780200
TITLE: Report of an Amnesty International mission to Bangladesh (4-12 April 1977)
AUTHOR: (Ennals, Martin)
PLACE OF PUBLICATION: London
PUBLISHER: Amnesty International - AI (D)
DATE OF PUBLICATION: 780200
NUMBER OF PAGES: 28 p. in v.p.
DOCUMENT SYMBOL: AI Index: ASA 13/03/78
LANGUAGE: ENG
STATISTICAL INFORMATION: Y
INDEX: political prisoners / fact-finding missions
GEOGRAPHICAL INDEX: Bangladesh
GEOGRAPHICAL CODE: 7413
FREE TEXT: Amnesty International was gravely concerned about the execution of at least 130, and perhaps several hundred, military men, following trials by military tribunals, for alleged involvement in abortive military uprisings in September/October 1977. The aim of the mission was to discuss the executions with the government, and to take the opportunity of discussing the implementation of the main recommendations made in the AI report of April 1977.
The report contains conclusions and recommendations; background information on the country; and chapters on political imprisonment; the legal position of political prisoners (laws, trials, releases); the judiciary and detention conditions; and treatment of political prisoners.
With appendices: members of oppositionary party allegedly killed by government forces in 1976; letter of Bangladesh Ministry of Home Affairs to AI.

CHINA, PEOPLE'S REPUBLIC

CATALOGUE SIGNATURE: 0000/0018/-0=841200
TITLE: Impressions of a visit to China
AUTHOR: Koshy, Ninan
PLACE OF PUBLICATION: Geneva
PUBLISHER: Commission of the Churches on International Affairs of the
World Council of Churches - CCIA-WCC (D)
DATE OF PUBLICATION: 841200
NUMBER OF PAGES: 15 p.
LANGUAGE: ENG
INDEX: church and state / religion (freedom of) /
fact-finding missions
GEOGRAPHICAL INDEX: China, People's Republic
GEOGRAPHICAL CODE: 7117
FREE TEXT: Philip Potter, General Secretary of the WCC, and the author
visited the People's Republic of China in October 1984, at the
invitation of the China Christian Council; it was the first official
WCC visit to China. The report contains information on the position of
the church in Bejing: the worship in houses and the policy of religious
freedom, the impact of the Cultural Revolution on Christians, the
Institute for the Study of World Religions, the position of Roman
Catholics and the Eastern Orthodox Church. The delegation also visited
Xian, Nanjing and Shanghai, where there was a meeting with the Chinese
People's Political Consultative Conference. With conclusions regarding
ecumenical relations, the relation with North Korea, the economic
system, and the future of Hong Kong.

CATALOGUE SIGNATURE: 0000/2917/-3=850700
TITLE: Intellectual freedom in China: an update
AUTHOR: Liang Heng ; Shapiro, Judith
PLACE OF PUBLICATION: New York
PUBLISHER: Asia Watch Committee (D); Fund for Free Expression - FFE (D)
DATE OF PUBLICATION: 850700
NUMBER OF PAGES: 55 p.
LANGUAGE: ENG
INDEX: freedom of expression / press (freedom of the) /
cultural rights / fact-finding missions
GEOGRAPHICAL INDEX: China, People's Republic
GEOGRAPHICAL CODE: 7117
FREE TEXT: This report updates the earlier report published in June
1984 by the Fund for Free Expression. The authors travelled through
seven central provinces of China in the period January-March 1985.
In their report, attention is paid to the current reform movement;
intellectual freedom and its relation to the economic reforms; freedom
of belief, speech, and religion; freedom of the press; and artistic
freedom. It is concluded that astonishingly original intellectual and
personal freedoms are developing in China; although basic personal
freedoms and human rights are still very limited by Western standards,
when compared with the still recent Cultural Revolution, the "warmer"
climate is remarkable.

DEMOCRATIC KAMPUCHEA

CATALOGUE SIGNATURE: 7520/-0=810505
TITLE: Religion in Kampuchea today
AUTHOR: Hawk, David R.
PLACE OF PUBLICATION: New York
PUBLISHER: World Conference on Religion and Peace - WCRP - Khmer
Project (D)
DATE OF PUBLICATION: 810505
NUMBER OF PAGES: 10 p.
SERIES TITLE: WCRP Report on Kampuchea
DOCUMENT SYMBOL: HR 26
LANGUAGE: ENG
BIBLIOGRAPHIES: Y
INDEX: refugees / religion (freedom of) / fact-finding missions
GEOGRAPHICAL INDEX: Democratic Kampuchea
GEOGRAPHICAL CODE: 7520
FREE TEXT: The purposes of the visit to Kampuchea in April 1981 were:
to review the documentation of the atrocities committed by the Khmer
Rouge; to observe the food and agricultural situation; to obtain the
perspective of the Phnom Penh authorities on the political situation
in Kampuchea and South East Asia; and to observe the state of the
revival of religion under the regime of Heng Samrin. Attention is paid
to Buddhism (monkhood, literature and education, Theravada Buddhism in
the People's Republic of Kampuchea, priorities and prospects), Khmer
Islam and Christianity. With appendix on the Angkor temple complex.

CATALOGUE SIGNATURE: 0000/1202/-0=830400
TITLE: The land in between: Cambodia ten years later
AUTHOR: Swank, Emory C. ; Leonard, James F.
PLACE OF PUBLICATION: (Washington DC)
PUBLISHER: Center for International Policy - CIP - Indochina Project
(D)
DATE OF PUBLICATION: 830400
NUMBER OF PAGES: 7 p.
SERIES TITLE: Indochina issues
VOLUME: v. 36
LANGUAGE: ENG
INDEX: development / fact-finding missions
GEOGRAPHICAL INDEX: Democratic Kampuchea
GEOGRAPHICAL CODE: 7520
FREE TEXT: The authors were members of an unofficial study mission of
retired US diplomats who visited Kampuchea, Vietnam and Thailand from
22 January to 12 February 1983. The report deals with general
developments since the war and the regime of Pol Pot, the presence and
influence of Vietnam and the international position of the country.

CATALOGUE SIGNATURE: 0000/1202/-0=850400
TITLE: Cambodia: the rough road to recovery
AUTHOR: Panaritis, Andrea
PLACE OF PUBLICATION: (Washington DC)
PUBLISHER: Center for International Policy - CIP - Indochina Project
(D)
DATE OF PUBLICATION: 850400
NUMBER OF PAGES: 7 p.
SERIES TITLE: Indochina issues
VOLUME: v. 56
LANGUAGE: ENG
INDEX: development / fact-finding missions
GEOGRAPHICAL INDEX: Democratic Kampuchea
GEOGRAPHICAL CODE: 7520
FREE TEXT: The author visited Kampuchea in January 1985. Her report
deals with the general developments of the country (infrastructure,
agriculture, health care, education) and outside development aid.
Private voluntary associations face personnel shortages, technical
problems and licensing problems. Attention is also given to possible
food shortages.

DEMOCRATIC PEOPLE'S REPUBLIC OF KOREA

CATALOGUE SIGNATURE: 0000/1192/-0=800900
TITLE: Report of the American Friends Service Committee delegation
to North Korea: September 2-13, 1980
AUTHOR: Easter, Maud ; Easter, David ; Thiermann, Steve
PLACE OF PUBLICATION: (Philadelphia)
PUBLISHER: American Friends Service Committee - AFSC (D)
DATE OF PUBLICATION: 800900
NUMBER OF PAGES: 12 p.
LANGUAGE: ENG
INDEX: social and economic rights / fact-finding missions
GEOGRAPHICAL INDEX: Democratic People's Republic of Korea
GEOGRAPHICAL CODE: 7121
FREE TEXT: The AFSC delegation visited North Korea at the invitation
of the Korean Society for Cultural Relations with Foreign Countries;
it was probably the first visit of a nongovernmental organization
based in the United States to this country. The report contains an
outline of the purpose of the mission, an itinerary, the political
background of the country, findings on social and economic aspects of
life (daily life, the position of women, social organization, city
planning, standard of living, recreation, education, health care,
anti-social behaviour, self-reliant economy), international aspects
and the relation with the United States. With recommendations.

INDIA

CATALOGUE SIGNATURE: 0000/0249/-3=790110
TITLE: Report of an Amnesty International mission to India: 31 December 1977 - 18 January 1978
AUTHOR: (Fawcett, James) ; (Terlingen, Yvonne)
PLACE OF PUBLICATION: London
PUBLISHER: Amnesty International - AI (D)
DATE OF PUBLICATION: 790110
NUMBER OF PAGES: 87 p. in v.p.
DOCUMENT SYMBOL: AI Index: ASA 20/3/78
LANGUAGE: ENG
STATISTICAL INFORMATION: Y
INDEX: political prisoners / legislation / fact-finding missions
GEOGRAPHICAL INDEX: India
GEOGRAPHICAL CODE: 7425
FREE TEXT: AI received many allegations of large-scale imprisonment of prisoners of conscience and curtailment of human rights in the period between the declaration of emergency on 26 June 1975 and the installation of a new government in March 1977. The aim of the AI mission was to obtain a first hand account of the many and serious human rights violations during the Emergency period, to acquaint itself with the measures announced by the new government for the restoration of the rule of law, and to study problems still of concern to AI.
The report contains background information and a memorandum presented to the Indian government in September 1978. This memorandum contains chapters on the restoration of the rule of law and the protection of fundamental rights in India, detention in Indian law, the current position of political prisoners, torture of political prisoners and deaths in police custody, killings of political prisoners and prison conditions.
With appendices: names and places of detention; prisoners interviewed by AI; texts of Draft Code of Conduct for Law Enforcement Officials and Declaration of The Hague; statement on oath before commission of inquiry; note on some of the main points in the memorandum.

CATALOGUE SIGNATURE: 0000/0002/-3=850700
TITLE: The trade union report on Bhopal: the report of the ICFTU-ICEF
mission to study the causes and effects of the methyl isocyanate gas
leak at the Union Carbide pesticide plant in Bhopal, India on December
2, 1984
AUTHOR: Aro, Pekka O. ; Carlsen, Johan-Ludvik ; Rice, Annie
(...et al)
PLACE OF PUBLICATION: Geneva
PUBLISHER: International Confederation of Free Trade Unions - ICFTU
(D) ; International Federation of Chemical, Energy and General
Workers' Unions - ICEF (D)
DATE OF PUBLICATION: 850700
NUMBER OF PAGES: 18 p.
LANGUAGE: ENG
INDEX: TNCs (transnational corporations) / environmental quality /
health / fact-finding missions
GEOGRAPHICAL INDEX: India
GEOGRAPHICAL CODE: 7425
FREE TEXT: The ICFTU and the ICEF have closely monitored the situation
in Bhopal since 3 December 1984. They sent a mission, in response to
requests from their Indian affiliates, to study the causes and effects
of the accidental gas leak, and to make recommendations to help prevent
similar accidents from occurring in India or anywhere else. The mission
consisted of twelve members, a number of whom had considerable
experience with the technical aspects of the process and the accident.
The report contains an introduction, conclusions, and information on
Union Carbide in Bhopal, the accident, the causes of the release,
contributing factors, non-causes, effects and implications. With
recommendations. With appendix: ILO resolution concerning dangerous
substances and processes in industry.

IRAN

CATALOGUE SIGNATURE: 0000/0138/-0=720300
DATE OF ENTRY: 860911
TITLE: La répression en Iran: rapport de Me Christian Bourguet... sur sa mission à Teheran du 21 au 28 février 1972
AUTHOR: Bourguet, Christian
PLACE OF PUBLICATION: Brussels
PUBLISHER: Association Internationale des Juristes Démocrates - IADL (D)
DATE OF PUBLICATION: 720300
NUMBER OF PAGES: 7 p.
LANGUAGE: FRE
INDEX: trials / fact-finding missions
GEOGRAPHICAL INDEX: Iran
GEOGRAPHICAL CODE: 7327
FREE TEXT: The aims of the mission were to collect information on ongoing political trials, and to inform the Iranian authorities of the international disapproval in case verdicts to death penalties would be carried out. The report contains a description of findings, the text of an interview held with a representative of the governmental Iranian Committee for Human Rights and descriptions of meetings with government representatives. The delegate was not allowed to observe trials or to see detained persons; after his departure, the first executions were carried out.

CATALOGUE SIGNATURE: 0000/0088/-3=760300
TITLE: Human rights and the legal system in Iran: two reports...
AUTHOR: Butler, William J. ; Levasseur, Georges
PLACE OF PUBLICATION: Geneva
PUBLISHER: International Commission of Jurists - ICJ (D)
DATE OF PUBLICATION: 760300
NUMBER OF PAGES: 72 p.
LANGUAGE: ENG
STATISTICAL INFORMATION: Y
BIBLIOGRAPHIES: Y
INDEX: judicial systems / fact-finding missions
GEOGRAPHICAL INDEX: Iran
GEOGRAPHICAL CODE: 7327
FREE TEXT: Reports on two fact-finding missions undertaken in 1975. The first part, by W. Butler, deals with the general human rights situation, with attention to the background of the country; the suppression of the political opposition and political trials; and the general situation of human rights and fundamental freedoms (economic and social rights, civil and political rights, the system of internal security). With conclusions and recommendations, and appendices: law on the SAVAK (secret police); achievements of the White Revolution. The second part, by G. Levasseur, deals with the legal system. With attention to the organization of the judicial system, criminal law, criminal procedure in ordinary courts and in military courts, and the prison system. With conclusions.

CATALOGUE SIGNATURE: 7327/-0=771200
TITLE: Rapport préliminaire de maître Lafue-Veron sur la mission
accomplie en Iran du 28/11/1977 au 11/12/1977
AUTHOR: Lafue-Veron, Madeleine
PLACE OF PUBLICATION: Frankfurt am Main
PUBLISHER: Confédération des Etudiants Iraniens (Union Nationale)
- CISNU (D)
DATE OF PUBLICATION: 771200
NUMBER OF PAGES: 38 p.
LANGUAGE: FRE
INDEX: dictatorship / fact-finding missions
GEOGRAPHICAL INDEX: Iran
GEOGRAPHICAL CODE: 7327
FREE TEXT: The delegate visited Iran on behalf of the International
Movement of Catholic Lawyers Pax Romana to investigate "the repression,
oppression and terror imposed on the country by the Shah" (introduction
by CISNU); she had contacts with families of political prisoners and
opposition leaders. She was not allowed to establish contacts with
political prisoners.
The report contains an introduction, information on the conduct of the
mission, and chapters on the terror, freedom of expression, new aspects
of the repression, the judicial system, the role of para-military
groups, freedom of religion, and the atmosphere of fear.
Also included are short biographies of a number of political prisoners,
and information on the press conference of 24 December in Paris.

CATALOGUE SIGNATURE: 0000/0138/-3=780000
TITLE: Mission en Iran: 24 février - 4 mars 1978
AUTHOR: Albala, Nuri
PLACE OF PUBLICATION: Brussels
PUBLISHER: Association Internationale des Juristes Démocrates - IADL (D)
DATE OF PUBLICATION: 780000
NUMBER OF PAGES: 20 p.
LANGUAGE: FRE
INDEX: detention / trials / fact-finding missions
GEOGRAPHICAL INDEX: Iran
GEOGRAPHICAL CODE: 7327
FREE TEXT: The mission to Iran was conducted by the author and
Marjorie Cohn. Permission to be present at political trials before the
Military Tribunals was denied, as was permission to visit detainees.
The mission had contacts with various organizations: the "Committee of
Human Rights", the "Iranian Committee for the Defense of Liberties and
Human Rights", the "Iranian Association of Jurists", and the "Union of
Writers". It is stated that, although officially censorship does not
exist, in practice it is severe. The mission also met with professors,
students, clergymen and former prisoners. It gathered information on
events in Tabriz on 28 February. It is concluded that the situation
is getting worse; this is stimulating the development of a movement
which tries to regain certain liberties.

CATALOGUE SIGNATURE: 0000/0138/-3=780000
TITLE: Iran: rapport de mission: 6-14 décembre 1978
AUTHORS: Mertens, Pierre ; Albala, Nuri ; Lagadec, Jean
PLACE OF PUBLICATION: Brussels
PUBLISHER: Association Internationale des Juristes Démocrates - IADL (D)
DATE OF PUBLICATION: 780000
NUMBER OF PAGES: 11 p.
LANGUAGE: FRE
INDEX: civil and political rights / nongovernmental organizations /
trials / fact-finding missions
GEOGRAPHICAL INDEX: Iran
GEOGRAPHICAL CODE: 7327
FREE TEXT: The mission was organized by the IADL and the International
Movement of Catholic Lawyers IMCL. It was held in the framework of the
celebration of the 30th anniversary of the Universal Declaration in
Teheran by Iranian nongovernmental organizations. The members spoke
with representatives of nongovernmental organizations on the situation
of detainees and persons liberated. Under the martial law, many people
are arrested without a reason. Attention is also paid to the freedoms
of expression and of speech, and the right to strike. The members
observed the trial at the military court in Teheran against Mme.
Mansouriniah, accused of possessing texts of a forbidden marxist
organization. With annex: press release of the mission.

CATALOGUE SIGNATURE: 0000/0249/-0=790000
TITLE: Torture in Iran 1971-1976
AUTHOR: (Emil, David)
PLACE OF PUBLICATION: London
PUBLISHER: Amnesty International - AI (D)
DATE OF PUBLICATION: 790000
NUMBER OF PAGES: 9 p.
DOCUMENT SYMBOL: AI Index: MDE 13/01/79
LANGUAGE: ENG
INDEX: political prisoners / torture / fact-finding missions
GEOGRAPHICAL INDEX: Iran
GEOGRAPHICAL CODE: 7327
FREE TEXT: An Amnesty International mission of two members went to
Iran from 11 to 24 November 1978, visited six cities and towns and
interviewed more than 60 people - released prisoners, relatives of
prisoners and lawyers. The interviews covered all aspects of political
imprisonment in Iran from arrest to release, including treatment of
former prisoners after release. Much of the material collected relates
to incidents of torture before 1977 and corroborates previous AI
statements on the subject. Attention is paid to methods of torture;
the report contains short description of case histories based on
individual testimonies.

CATALOGUE SIGNATURE: 0000/0035/-3=790100
TITLE: Rapport des maîtres Schmidlin et Fagart sur la mission
accomplie en Iran du 1/11/1978 au 15/11/1978
AUTHOR: Fagart, Thierry ; Schmidlin, France
PLACE OF PUBLICATION: Paris
PUBLISHER: Confédération des Etudiants Iraniens ; Fédération
Internationale des Droits de l'Homme - FIDH (D)
DATE OF PUBLICATION: 790100
NUMBER OF PAGES: 159 p.
LANGUAGE: FRE
INDEX: political prisoners / prison conditions / fact-finding missions
GEOGRAPHICAL INDEX: Iran
GEOGRAPHICAL CODE: 7327
FREE TEXT: The first part of the report is on political prisoners, the
release of a number of them, and detention conditions. Attention is
paid to the intentions of the government with regard to prisoners still
in detention, numbers of prisoners, detention conditions and torture.
The second part is on the prohibition to visit prisoners.
The third part is on political trials: general description, procedures,
a specific case.
With conclusions: human rights are violated systematically; the
resistance movement is becoming stronger.

CATALOGUE SIGNATURE: 0000/0237/-3=790000
TITLE: Iran: Folter und Inhaftierung während des Shah-Regimes
AUTHOR: Alizadeh, Homayoun
PLACE OF PUBLICATION: Vienna
PUBLISHER: Amnesty International, Austrian section - AI-AT (D)
DATE OF PUBLICATION: 790000
NUMBER OF PAGES: 32 p.
LANGUAGE: GER
STATISTICAL INFORMATION: Y
INDEX: political prisoners / fact-finding missions
GEOGRAPHICAL INDEX: Iran
GEOGRAPHICAL CODE: 7327
FREE TEXT: The report on political imprisonment, torture methods and
executions in Iran during the period of the Shah regime is based on a
fact-finding mission to Iran in February 1979. It does not concern the
official policy of AI, but a private documentation of the editor. The
report contains information collected during visits to the towns of
Tabris, Teheran, Isfahan, Shahreza and Semirom, and interviews with
former political prisoners, representatives of people's armies and
others. With recommendations and annex: list of political prisoners
adopted by AI.

CATALOGUE SIGNATURE: 0000/0138/-3=790500
TITLE: Commission internationale d'enquête en Iran...
AUTHOR: Albala, Nuri ; Dossou, Robert ; Dreyfus, Nicole (...et al)
PLACE OF PUBLICATION: Paris
PUBLISHER: Association Internationale des Juristes Démocrates - IADL ;
Albala, Nuri (D)
DATE OF PUBLICATION: 790500
NUMBER OF PAGES: 51 p.
LANGUAGE: FRE
INDEX: elections / civil and political rights / fact-finding missions
GEOGRAPHICAL INDEX: Iran
GEOGRAPHICAL CODE: 7327
FREE TEXT: A four member delegation visited Iran from 28 March to 4
April 1979. The report begins with a description of the political
background and a chronology of events from 1906 until 1979. The
members firstly investigated the preparation and execution of a
referendum to justify the change of regime after the coup d'état, and
provide points of criticism and conclusions. The second chapter is on
human rights in general, with attention to the freedom of opinion,
manifestation, and expression; trials; a visit to the prison of Ghasr;
the political forces in power; the elaboration of a constitution and
the functioning of the institutions. With annex: newspaper articles.
The third chapter is on the crimes of the ancient regime, including
testimonies of victims, the Ghasr prison under the Shah regime, the
archives of the secret police SAVAK (with copies of photographs).

CATALOGUE SIGNATURE: 0000/0249/-3=800200
TITLE: Law and human rights in the Islamic Republic of Iran: a report
covering events within the seven months period following the revolution
of February 1979
AUTHOR: Amnesty International - AI
PLACE OF PUBLICATION: London
PUBLISHER: Amnesty International - AI (D)
DATE OF PUBLICATION: 800200
NUMBER OF PAGES: 216 p.
DOCUMENT SYMBOL: AI Index: MDE 13/03/80
LANGUAGE: ENG
STATISTICAL INFORMATION: Y
BIBLIOGRAPHIES: Y
INDEX: judicial systems / trials / fact-finding missions
GEOGRAPHICAL INDEX: Iran
GEOGRAPHICAL CODE: 7327
FREE TEXT: AI had repeatedly received reports that the legal procedures
employed by the Islamic Revolutionary Tribunals are such that accused
persons have not received fair trials, that the charges upon which they
have been arranged are often extremely broad and that sentences of
death have been frequently passed. The aim of the mission from 12 April
to 1 May 1979 was to study these matters at first hand.
The report contains conclusions and recommendations, an introduction,
and chapters on the practice and procedure of arrest; the practice and
procedure of the Revolutionary Tribunals; offences and penalties; an
examination of laws adopted and proposed creating further new offences,
courts and procedures; each chapter contains conclusions.
With appendices: lists of post-revolutionary executions and non-capital
sentences until 12 August 1979; update 13 August - 14 September 1979;
international human rights standards; AI statements on human rights in
Iran before the revolution; glossary.

CATALOGUE SIGNATURE: 0000/0035/-3=830000
TITLE: Rapport: la situation des droits de l'homme en Iran: mission
d'enquête au Kurdistan iranien (9 août - 8 septembre 1983)
AUTHOR: Rostoker, Christian
PLACE OF PUBLICATION: Paris
PUBLISHER: Fédération Internationale des Droits de l'Homme - FIDH (D)
DATE OF PUBLICATION: 830000
NUMBER OF PAGES: 40 p.
LANGUAGE: FRE
INDEX: executions / right to fair trial / prison conditions /
fact-finding missions
GEOGRAPHICAL INDEX: Iran
GEOGRAPHICAL CODE: 7327
FREE TEXT: The purpose of the mission was to investigate the way in
which the Universal Declaration of Human Rights is applied by the
Iranian government and by the Democratic Party of Iranian Kurdistan
DPIK, which is controlling part of the country.
The delegate received testimonies from witnesses from the town of
Mahabad. They reported on detention conditions, torture and refugees.
The report contains abstracts from their testimonies. They also gave
information on the execution of 59 presumably innocent young
inhabitants of Mahabad by government authorities after a very short
trial, attacks by Iranian troups and families in exile.
The delegate also visited two prisons of the DPIK, where he had
contacts with many prisoners. He concludes that detention conditions
in these prisons were good. With texts of testimonies.

IRAQ

CATALOGUE SIGNATURE: 0000/0018/-0=750605
TITLE: WCC team's visit to Iraq
AUTHOR: Koshy, Ninan ; Mitton, Stanley
TITLE OF GENERIC ITEM: CCIA Newsletter
EDITION: no. 5
PLACE OF PUBLICATION: Geneva
PUBLISHER: Commission of the Churches on International Affairs of the
World Council of Churches - CCIA-WCC (D)
DATE OF PUBLICATION: 750605
NUMBER OF PAGES: 14 p.
LANGUAGE: ENG
INDEX: minorities / fact-finding missions
GEOGRAPHICAL INDEX: Iraq
GEOGRAPHICAL CODE: 7328
FREE TEXT: Report of a mission undertaken at the invitation of the
government of Iraq, with the aim to assess the situation in Kurdistan
after the declaration of an amnesty decree. The report contains
information on the background of the visit, a description of contacts
with the authorities and findings and impressions of visits to the
Kurdic areas in the north of Iraq. The general impression gained is
that the government is keen to transform the cessation of fighting
in Kurdistan into genuine peace. It has to be challenged, and also
encouraged, to continue to adhere honestly to its declarations
regarding Kurds and other minorities.

CATALOGUE SIGNATURE: 0000/0249/-3=831000
TITLE: Report and recommendations of an Amnesty International mission
to the government of the Republic of Iraq: 22-28 January 1983:
including the government's response and Amnesty International comments
AUTHOR: (Hammarberg, Thomas)
PLACE OF PUBLICATION: London
PUBLISHER: Amnesty International - AI (D)
DATE OF PUBLICATION: 831000
NUMBER OF PAGES: 74 p.
ISBN: 0 86210 061 5
DOCUMENT SYMBOL: AI Index: MDE 14/06/83
LANGUAGE: ENG
STATISTICAL INFORMATION: Y
INDEX: torture / judicial systems / death penalty /
fact-finding missions
GEOGRAPHICAL INDEX: Iraq
GEOGRAPHICAL CODE: 7328
FREE TEXT: The aim of the three member delegation was to discuss with
government representatives AI's concerns, which include allegations of
torture, lack of basic legal safeguards in special courts and the use
of the death penalty. In May 1983, AI sent a memorandum based on its
findings and research to the government; the government replied on 28
June 1983.
The report contains the text of the memorandum, with chapters on
torture and cruel, inhuman or degrading punishment, special courts and
the death penalty. Each chapter contains AI's concern, the response of
Iraqi officials, conclusions and recommendations. With information on
Iraq's international obligations and summary of recommendations.
The second part is the reply of the government, including comments on
the recommendations made in the AI memorandum and conclusions.
The third part is AI's comments on this reply, including
recommendations.
With appendices: relevant passages in letters of AI; extract from list
of people reported to have died under torture; list of people whose
legal position and whereabouts are still not known.

ISRAEL

CATALOGUE SIGNATURE: 0000/1291/-0=780000
TITLE: Report by Ernest Goodman to the National Lawyers Guild as
observer at the trial of Sami Esmail in Israel
AUTHOR: Goodman, Ernest
PLACE OF PUBLICATION: (New York)
PUBLISHER: (National Lawyers Guild - NLG) (D)
DATE OF PUBLICATION: 780000
NUMBER OF PAGES: 32 p. in v.p.
LANGUAGE: ENG
INDEX: trials / fact-finding missions
GEOGRAPHICAL INDEX: Israel
GEOGRAPHICAL CODE: 7329
FREE TEXT: The author attended the first days of the trial of Sami
Esmail, and obtained English translations of the protocols for the
subsequent trial dates at which testimony was taken. His report deals
with the entire trial. Attention is given to the background of the
defendant; the events leading up to his arrest; the detention and
interrogation of the defendant and the signing of the confessions;
the indictment; and the trial. The author makes comments on the
issues raised by the trial with regard to the role of the FBI and
Israel's extraterritorial law. With appendices: indictment of Sami
Esmail; letter of United States Department of Justice; letter of
Ernest Goodman as a reaction on comments and criticisms by Howard
Dickstein on his report.

Israel

CATALOGUE SIGNATURE: 0000/0249/-3=800000
TITLE: Report and recommendations of an Amnesty International mission
to the government of the state of Israel: 3-7 June 1979: including
the government's response and Amnesty International comments
AUTHOR: Amnesty International - AI
PLACE OF PUBLICATION: London
PUBLISHER: Amnesty International - AI (D)
DATE OF PUBLICATION: 800000
NUMBER OF PAGES: 78 p. in v.p.
ISBN: 86210 018 6
DOCUMENT SYMBOL: AI Index: MDE 15/02/80
LANGUAGE: ENG
INDEX: cruel, inhuman or degrading treatment / political prisoners /
legislation / fact-finding missions
GEOGRAPHICAL INDEX: Israel
GEOGRAPHICAL CODE: 7329
FREE TEXT: The aim of the mission was to discuss persistent allegations
of ill-treatment of prisoners in Israel and the territories occupied
by it since the 1967 Six Days' War. Following the mission, AI submitted
to the Israeli Attorney-General a memorandum, dated October 1979. In
this memorandum, AI's concerns were summarized, and areas where
administrative and legal procedures should be amended where suggested.
AI urged that the authorities initiate a full-scale investigation of
the entire subject of alleged ill-treatment, including relevant
administrative and legal procedures, and that the results be made
public.
The first part of the report is the text of the memorandum, with
amendments made in footnotes. It contains chapters on arrests and
allegations of ill-treatment, critique of legal and administrative
procedures and practices applied to security suspects in the occupied
territories, conclusions and recommendations. The second part is the
reply of the Attorney-General of Israel, and AI's comments on it.

CATALOGUE SIGNATURE: 0000/0088/-4
TITLE: Report on the hearing in the Supreme Court of Israel on 6 July
1980 concerning the petition for the rescission of the deportation
orders against the Mayors of Hebron and Halhoul and the President of
the Islamic Shara'wi Court in Hebron
AUTHOR: Werner, Auguste-Raynald
TITLE OF GENERIC ITEM: ICJ Newsletter
EDITION: no. 6
PLACE OF PUBLICATION: Geneva
PUBLISHER: International Commission of Jurists - ICJ (D)
DATE OF PUBLICATION: 800900
NUMBER OF PAGES: p. 46-48
LANGUAGE: ENG
INDEX: legislation / trials / fact-finding missions
GEOGRAPHICAL INDEX: Israel
GEOGRAPHICAL CODE: 7329
FREE TEXT: Three prominent Palestinians were abducted from their homes
by the military authorities with great haste and flown by helicopter
to southern Lebanon, following the killing of six Jewish settlers in
a Palestinian ambush. The three men were not informed of their rights,
nor given an opportunity to appeal against their deportations before a
military review board.

CATALOGUE SIGNATURE: 0000/0035/-3=800000
TITLE: Rapport sur une mission d'enquête de la Fédération
Internationale des Droits de l'Homme qui à été effectuée en Israel
et en Cisjordanie du 18 au 25 décembre 1980
AUTHOR: Blum, Michel ; Rostoker, Christian ; Dumont, Georges
PLACE OF PUBLICATION: Paris
PUBLISHER: Fédération Internationale des Droits de l'Homme - FIDH (D)
DATE OF PUBLICATION: 800000
NUMBER OF PAGES: 42 p.
LANGUAGE: FRE
STATISTICAL INFORMATION: Y
INDEX: political prisoners / prison conditions / torture /
fact-finding missions
GEOGRAPHICAL INDEX: Israel
GEOGRAPHICAL CODE: 7329
FREE TEXT: The purpose of the mission was to investigate whether
Israelian authorities are practising torture of political prisoners.
The delegates received names of twelve detainees from lawyers; seven
of them were examined by doctor Dumont.
The examination took place during visits to prisons, which enabled
the delegates to investigate general detention conditions as well.
With analysis of legal procedures and administrative measures applied
to inhabitants of the Occupied Territories, description of facts
established in the prisons, medical-legal report, reports of cases
examined and conclusions.

JAPAN

CATALOGUE SIGNATURE: 0000/0249/-3=831000
TITLE: The death penalty in Japan: report of an Amnesty International
mission to Japan: 21 February - 3 March 1983
AUTHOR: (Singvi, L.M.)
PLACE OF PUBLICATION: London
PUBLISHER: Amnesty International - AI (D)
DATE OF PUBLICATION: 831000
NUMBER OF PAGES: 31 p.
ISBN: 0 86210 060 7
DOCUMENT SYMBOL: AI Index: ASA 22/02/83
LANGUAGE: ENG
STATISTICAL INFORMATION: Y
BIBLIOGRAPHIES: Y
INDEX: death penalty / penal systems / fact-finding missions
GEOGRAPHICAL INDEX: Japan
GEOGRAPHICAL CODE: 7130
FREE TEXT: In recent years, Japanese courts have imposed death
sentences for three offences: murder, causing death in the course of
robbery and causing death by explosives. A revision of the Japanese
Penal Code has been under discussion for many years. The purposes of
the two member mission were to convey AI's concerns about the death
penalty and to gather information and Japanese views on its abolition.
The report contains background information, and chapters on the legal
aspects of the death penalty, death sentences and executions (with
tables), arrangements for executions, retrials (with specific cases)
and the ongoing discussion. With conclusions and recommendations, and
appendices: contacts of the mission; numbers of executions; resolution
on physician participation in capital punishment.

CATALOGUE SIGNATURE: 0000/0088/-3=860000
TITLE: Human rights and mental patients in Japan: report of a
mission on behalf of the International Commission of Jurists and
the International Commission of Health Professionals
AUTHOR: Harding, T.W. ; Schneider, J. ; Visotsky, H.M.
PLACE OF PUBLICATION: Geneva
PUBLISHER : International Commission of Jurists - ICJ (D) ;
International Commission of Health Professionals - ICHP (D)
DATE OF PUBLICATION: 860000
NUMBER OF PAGES : 94 p.
ISBN: 92 9037 032 7
LANGUAGE: ENG
BIBLIOGRAPHIES: Y
INDEX : mental ill persons / health / fact-finding missions
GEOGRAPHICAL INDEX : Japan
GEOGRAPHICAL CODE: 7130
FREE TEXT : Reports of serious human rights violations in mental
hospitals in Japan prompted the ICJ and the ICHP to send a mission,
with the aim to review and make recommendations on the legislation
and practices for the treatment of mental patients.
The report contains an introductory chapter, and chapters on the
current situation of mental health services with special reference
to human rights, mental health services in a modern industrialized
society, and legal protection of mentally disordered persons.
The report ends with 18 conclusions and recommendations which
identify the major areas of concern as a lack of legal protection
for patients during admission procedures and during hospitalization,
and a system of care characterized by a preponderance of long-term
institutional treatment and a relative lack of community treatment
and rehabilitation.

CATALOGUE SIGNATURE: 0000/1246/-3=860800
TITLE: Legal treatment of Koreans in Japan: the impact of international
human rights law on Japanese law
AUTHOR: Iwasawa, Yuji
PLACE OF PUBLICATION: Washington
PUBLISHER: International Human Rights Law Group - IHRLG (D)
DATE OF PUBLICATION: 860800
NUMBER OF PAGES: 146 p. in v.p.
AVAILABILITY: X
LANGUAGE: ENG
BIBLIOGRAPHY: Y
INDEX: international law / minorities / fact-finding missions
GEOGRAPHICAL INDEX: Japan
GEOGRAPHICAL CODE: 7130
FREE TEXT: The purpose of this study is to analyze the present
situation of Koreans in Japan from the viewpoint of international
human rights law, to depict what has been done to bring Japanese law
into conformity with international law, and to point out the areas
which still need improvement. Prior to publishing the study of
Professor Iwasawa, Amy Young went on a mission to Japan to confirm his
documentation and to provide any additional, relevant information.
The study is divided into the following parts:
I) Introduction; with the purpose of the study; and historical
background;
II) International law and Japan: a) Status of international law in
Japan; b) Universal Declaration of Human Rights; c) International
covenants on human rights;
III) Nationality of Koreans in Japan;
IV) Immigration controle;
V) Alien registration;
VI) Substantive rights: a) Freedom to choose profession and business;
b) Social rights; c) Education;
VII) Conclusions.
In the appendices: 1) Itinerary of a fact-finding mission to Japan,
January 1986; 2) Comments of the government of Japan.

LEBANON

CATALOGUE SIGNATURE: 0000/0035/-3=840124
TITLE: Lebanon
AUTHOR: Filiu, Jean Pierre
PLACE OF PUBLICATION: Paris
PUBLISHER: Fédération Internationale des Droits de l'Homme - FIDH (D)
DATE OF PUBLICATION: 840124
NUMBER OF PAGES: 20 p.
LANGUAGE: ENG / FRE
INDEX: disappearances / fact-finding missions
GEOGRAPHICAL INDEX: Lebanon
GEOGRAPHICAL CODE: 7334
FREE TEXT: The purpose of the mission from 26 December 1983 to 16
January 1984 was to receive information and undertake initiatives
concerning kidnapped Lebanese citizens who have disappeared and
whose detention is not the subject of a regular judicial decision.
The context of the problem of the disappeared is described. Since
June 1982, hundreds of people have disappeared at the hands of the
"Lebanese Forces". Reaction against this practice is organized in
the "Committee of the Disappeared People's Parents", which handed
over a list of disappeared to the FIDH. The list is not exhaustive.
With conclusions. With appendices: identification form of a
disappeared person; testimony; answer of the Lebanese Forces.

MALAYSIA

CATALOGUE SIGNATURE: 0000/0249/-3=790700
TITLE: Report of an Amnesty International mission to the Federation
of Malaysia: 18 November - 30 November 1978
AUTHOR: (Jones, Thomas C.) ; (Williams, Michael C.)
PLACE OF PUBLICATION: London
PUBLISHER: Amnesty International, British section - AI-UK (D)
DATE OF PUBLICATION: 790700
NUMBER OF PAGES: 67 p.
DOCUMENT SYMBOL: AI Index: ASA 28/04/79
LANGUAGE: ENG
STATISTICAL INFORMATION: Y
INDEX: detention / association (freedom of) / fact-finding missions
GEOGRAPHICAL INDEX: Malaysia
GEOGRAPHICAL CODE: 7536
FREE TEXT: Amnesty's main concern in Malaysia remains the use by the
government of preventive detention under the Internal Security Act of
1960. The report contains an introduction with background information
on the country and the mission, recommendations and chapters dealing
with harassment of political parties and trade unions; the legislation;
arrest and interrogation, preliminary interrogation and torture;
long-term detention; individual case histories of detention; and the
death penalty.
With appendices: report by ex-Minister on his detention; the Internal
Security Rules; list of political detainees in special detention camp;
health conditions of some political detainees; report on the death of
a political detainee.

CATALOGUE SIGNATURE: 7536/-3=830000
TITLE: The report of the International Mission of Lawyers to Malaysia
AUTHOR: Calvert, Barbara ; Hannum, Hurst ; Jacoby, David (...et al)
EDITION: rev.
PLACE OF PUBLICATION: London
PUBLISHER: International Mission of Lawyers ; Marram Books (D)
DATE OF PUBLICATION: 830000
NUMBER OF PAGES: 67 p.
ISBN: 0 906968 04 6
LANGUAGE: ENG
STATISTICAL INFORMATION: Y
INDEX: legislation / death penalty / trials / fact-finding missions
GEOGRAPHICAL INDEX: Malaysia
GEOGRAPHICAL CODE: 7536
FREE TEXT: In Malaysia, a great number of persons were condemned to
death. An international seven member mission visited the country in
August 1982. The aim of the mission was primarily to examine the
working of the national security legislation as it is related to
those charged with offences under the Internal Security Act 1960
(ISA), the mandatory nature of the death sentences for certain of
those offences and the trial procedures in security cases which lead
to the mandatory death sentence, and other sentences (the Essential
(Security Cases) (Amendment) Regulations 1975 - ESCAR). The mission
also investigated the position of those detained without trial under
the ISA. The report also contains the chronology of the visit and
information on the background of the country. With conclusions and
recommendations, tables and appendices.

CATALOGUE SIGNATURE: 7000/0198/-0=860500
TITLE: Param Cumaraswamy acquitted of sedition
AUTHOR: Malcolm, David K.
TITLE OF GENERIC ITEM: Newsletter
EDITION: v. 1(8)
PLACE OF PUBLICATION: Sydney
PUBLISHER: Law Association for Asia and the Western Pacific -
LAWASIA (D)
DATE OF PUBLICATION: 860500
NUMBER OF PAGES: p. 1-2
LANGUAGE: ENG
INDEX: trials / fact-finding missions
GEOGRAPHICAL INDEX: Malaysia
GEOGRAPHICAL CODE: 7536
FREE TEXT: Cumaraswamy, a former Vice-President of the Malaysian Bar
Association and Co-Chairman of Lawasia's Human Rights Standing
Committee. In September 1985, he was charged under the Sedition Act;
his trial was held in Kuala Lumpur from 26-30 November and on 2
December. Cumaraswamy was not found guilty of sedition. The report
contains a description of the hearings and relevant legislation.
A full report on the proceedings has been delivered to Lawasia.

PAKISTAN

CATALOGUE SIGNATURE: 0000/0249/-3=770500
TITLE: Islamic Republic of Pakistan: an Amnesty International report including the findings of a mission to Pakistan: 23 April - 12 May 1976
AUTHOR: (Soysal, Mümtaz) ; (Terlingen, Yvonne)
PLACE OF PUBLICATION: London
PUBLISHER: Amnesty International - AI (D)
DATE OF PUBLICATION: 770500
NUMBER OF PAGES: 92 p.
ISBN: 0 900058 57 9
DOCUMENT SYMBOL: AI Index: PUB 71/00/77
LANGUAGE: ENG
INDEX: civil and political rights / association (freedom of) / legislation / fact-finding missions
GEOGRAPHICAL INDEX: Pakistan
GEOGRAPHICAL CODE: 7441
FREE TEXT: The report is based on the findings of the mission and on subsequent research covering the period up to 31 January 1977. The aims of the mission were to discuss with members of the government the implementation of those articles of the Universal Declaration on Human Rights within AI's mandate, and to obtain information on the legal procedures applying to the detention and trial of political prisoners in Pakistan, under special and emergency legislation.
The report contains recommendations, an introduction with the main findings, and chapters on the constitution and fundamental rights, the legal profession and the erosion of fundamental rights, detention and trial of political prisoners, the banning of the National Awami Party and the trial of its leaders and other members of the opposition in Hyderabad, and other human rights issues. With appendices, including list of prisoners of conscience adopted by AI.

CATALOGUE SIGNATURE: 0000/0249/-3=780400
TITLE: Short report of an Amnesty International mission to the Islamic
Republic of Pakistan (20-25 January 1978)
AUTHOR: (Soysal, Mümtaz) ; (Terlingen, Yvonne)
PLACE OF PUBLICATION: London
PUBLISHER: Amnesty International - AI (D)
DATE OF PUBLICATION: 780400
NUMBER OF PAGES: 29 p. in v.p.
DOCUMENT SYMBOL: AI Index: ASA 33/03/78
LANGUAGE: ENG
INDEX: legislation / trials / fact-finding missions
GEOGRAPHICAL INDEX: Pakistan
GEOGRAPHICAL CODE: 7441
FREE TEXT: The aim of the mission was to discuss with authorities the
recommendations made to the previous government, and areas of concern
to AI. These relate mainly to the introduction of a set of martial law
provisions which curtail fundamental freedoms, and the infliction of
harsh punishments by military courts on civilians which exercise their
right to freedom of speech and expression.
The report contains an introduction on recent developments, conclusions
and recommendations, and chapters concerning: steps taken by the
government concerning recommendations made to the previous government;
the position of fundamental rights and the powers of the judiciary
under the martial law regime; application of martial law provisions to
political imprisonment; arrest and trial of leaders of the Pakistan
People's Party. With appendix: arrest and trial of Mr. Z.A. Bhutto in
the Nawab Ahmed Khan murder case.

CATALOGUE SIGNATURE: 7000/0198/-3=830331
TITLE: Report to the Lawasia Council on "the independence and freedom
of lawyers in Pakistan"
AUTHOR: Nicholson, R.D.
PLACE OF PUBLICATION: Sydney
PUBLISHER: Law Association for Asia and the Western Pacific - LAWASIA
(D)
DATE OF PUBLICATION: 830331
NUMBER OF PAGES: 199 p.
LANGUAGE: ENG
INDEX: lawyers / judicial systems / fact-finding missions
GEOGRAPHICAL INDEX: Pakistan
GEOGRAPHICAL CODE: 7441
FREE TEXT: The author visited Pakistan in January 1983. His report is
mainly based on documentary evidence collected from bar associations,
judges and law officers of the government. He reports on the motives
and criteria for the mission, the background of the country, the
political and constitutional context, Islamisation, martial law, the
position of the judiciary, the legal profession, and independence and
freedom of the profession to fullfil its professional duties and to
engage in social action ("political activity"). With conclusions,
recommendations and appendices: information on Lawasia, press cuttings,
resolutions of bar associations, sample orders.

CATALOGUE SIGNATURE: 0000/1582/-3=830700
TITLE: Justice in Pakistan: a report of a mission of enquiry
AUTHOR: Greenberg, Deborah M. ; Orentlicher, Diane
PLACE OF PUBLICATION: New York
PUBLISHER: Lawyers Committee for International Human Rights - LCIHR
(D) ; Committee on International Human Rights of the Association of
the Bar of the City of New York - ABNY
DATE OF PUBLICATION: 830700
NUMBER OF PAGES: 46 p.
LANGUAGE: ENG
INDEX: lawyers / judicial systems / fact-finding missions
GEOGRAPHICAL INDEX: Pakistan
GEOGRAPHICAL CODE: 7441
FREE TEXT: The purpose of the mission in January 1983 was to inquire
into the administration of justice and the independence of judges and
lawyers in Pakistan. The report shows that in an environmental rife
with fundamental violations of basic human rights, the independent
civilian judicial system has virtually collapsed and an extraordinarily
courageous bar has been subjected to harsh and unremitting harassment.
With: introduction; conclusions and recommendations, and background:
United States aid to Pakistan. Chapter one is on political arrests,
detention without trial and torture. The second chapter deals with the
expanding role of military courts and erosion of judicial independence.
The third chapter is on harassment and persecution of lawyers.

CATALOGUE SIGNATURE: 0000/0035/-3=840000
TITLE: Pakistan: rapport de mission
AUTHOR: Dodson, Joanna ; Jacoby, Daniel ; Jaudel, Etienne
PLACE OF PUBLICATION: Paris
PUBLISHER: Fédération Internationale des Droits de l'Homme - FIDH (D)
DATE OF PUBLICATION: 840000
NUMBER OF PAGES: (48 p.)
LANGUAGE: FRE
INDEX: political prisoners / dictatorship / fact-finding missions
GEOGRAPHICAL INDEX: Pakistan
GEOGRAPHICAL CODE: 7441
FREE TEXT: Report of a fact-finding mission to Pakistan in April-May
1984, to investigate the situation of human rights under martial law.
The report contains: a press release; chronology of activities of the
mission; the regime of martial law in general; the situation of
political prisoners: detention conditions, torture.
With conclusions and recommendations, testimonies of witnesses and
annexes: legislation; resolutions of bar associations; lists of
prisoners.

CATALOGUE SIGNATURE: 0000/1582/-3=850700
TITLE: Zia's law: human rights under military rule in Pakistan
AUTHOR: Newberg, Paula
PLACE OF PUBLICATION: New York
PUBLISHER: Lawyers Committee for International Human Rights - LCIHR (D)
DATE OF PUBLICATION: 850700
NUMBER OF PAGES: 121 p. in v.p.
LANGUAGE: ENG
BIBLIOGRAPHIES: Y
INDEX: legislation / judicial systems / detention /
expression (freedom of) / religion (freedom of) / women /
fact-finding missions
GEOGRAPHICAL INDEX: Pakistan
GEOGRAPHICAL CODE: 7441
FREE TEXT: The report is based on a fact-finding mission in November
1984, and continued interviews and other evidence obtained in the
United States in the first six months of 1985. It is concluded that
serious human rights violations are a widespread and important
characteristic of life in Pakistan. The report contains chapters on:
the recent history of Pakistan (political background, constitutional
framework, 1984 referendum and 1985 elections), the breakdown of the
judicial system (military and Islamic courts; illustrative special
military court trials in 1984 and 1985; government control of the
bar); detention (arbitrary detention, number of prisoners, prison
conditions); other continuing violations (death penalty, internal
surveillance, civilian-military clashes); denials of the freedom of
expression (censorship, academic freedom, freedom of movement);
denials of religious freedom (including minority religions) and the
rights of women. With appendix: selected martial law regulations and
ordinances.

CATALOGUE SIGNATURE: 0000/0249/-0=851100
TITLE: The trial and treatment of political prisoners convicted by
special military courts in Pakistan
AUTHOR: (Amnesty International - AI)
PLACE OF PUBLICATION: London
PUBLISHER: Amnesty International - AI (D)
DATE OF PUBLICATION: 851100
NUMBER OF PAGES: 56 p.
DOCUMENT SYMBOL: AI Index ASA 33/51/85
LANGUAGE: ENG
INDEX: political prisoners / trials / fact-finding missions
GEOGRAPHICAL INDEX: Pakistan
GEOGRAPHICAL CODE: 7441
FREE TEXT: Over 130 prisoners convicted by special military courts
of political or politically motivated criminal offences are currently
imprisoned in Pakistan. As of early September 1985, at least 38 other
political prisoners recently tried by these courts are awaiting the
announcement of the verdict in their cases. Amnesty International
believes that these prisoners have been deprived of the right to a
fair trial and have no opportunity to seek legal redress. The trials
and treatment of these prisoners are the subject of the report, which
contains a memorandum sent to the government of Pakistan, and
appendices: the text of the Criminal Law Amendment Order of 1982 and
details of prisoners tried by special military courts. The information
contained in the report was partly gathered during a mission to
Pakistan by Peter Duffy in November 1984.

PHILIPPINES

CATALOGUE SIGNATURE: 0000/0249/-3=760900
TITLE: Report of an Amnesty International mission to the Republic of
the Philippines: 22 November - 5 December 1975
AUTHOR: (Jones, Thomas C.) ; (Wen-hsien Huang)
PLACE OF PUBLICATION: London
PUBLISHER: Amnesty International - AI (D)
DATE OF PUBLICATION: 760900
NUMBER OF PAGES: 60 p.
ISBN: 0 900058 36 6
DOCUMENT SYMBOL: AI Index: PUB 64/00/77
LANGUAGE: ENG
INDEX: political prisoners / torture / fact-finding missions
GEOGRAPHICAL INDEX: Philippines
GEOGRAPHICAL CODE: 7542
FREE TEXT: The aims of the mission were to seek the support of members
of the government for the development of regional institutions for the
protection of human rights in South East Asia and to discuss with
members of the government, and with concerned Filipinos, problems
relating to imprisonment under martial law, the treatment of prisoners
and procedures for the release of prisoners. The mission found that
the detailed accounts given by the prisoners of brutal treatment were
convincing, and was deeply concerned about the extent to which the
prisoners interviewed had been subjected to torture.
The report contains conclusions and recommendations, information on
interviews with prisoners, incidences of torture (with references to
a large number of specific cases and testimonies), martial law and the
rule of law.
With appendices: letter by AI; statement released by the consulate of
the Philippines in San Francisco; a recent example of arrest and
detention; correspondence between the Solicitor General and AI on the
publication of the report.

CATALOGUE SIGNATURE: 0000/0088/-3=770800
TITLE: The decline of democracy in the Philippines: a report of
missions...
AUTHOR: Butler, William J. ; Humphrey, John P. ; Bisson, G.E.
PLACE OF PUBLICATION: Geneva
PUBLISHER: International Commission of Jurists - ICJ (D)
DATE OF PUBLICATION: 770800
NUMBER OF PAGES: 97 p.
LANGUAGE: ENG
STATISTICAL INFORMATION: Y
INDEX: dictatorship / martial law / fact-finding missions
GEOGRAPHICAL INDEX: Philippines
GEOGRAPHICAL CODE: 7542
FREE TEXT: Report on the situation of human rights, based on three
missions during the period May 1975 - February 1977. The aim of the
missions was to study the operation of martial law from the point
of view of both the legal system and of the allegations which have
been made of serious violations of human rights. The report deals
with: the background of the country; the Constitution of 1935; the
proclamation and perputation of martial law; the use of referenda
to legitimize and perpetuate government by presidential decree; the
situation of human rights under martial law, and the judicial system.
With conclusions and recommendations, and appendices: administration
of justice under martial law; jurisdiction of military tribunals;
charge sheets of the government with lists of people accused.

CATALOGUE SIGNATURE: 7542/-0=770000
TITLE: Human rights and martial law in the Philippines: a report of an
investigating mission to the Philippines sponsored by the Anti-Martial
Law Coalition and the Friends of the Filipino People, August 14-27,
1977
AUTHOR: Caughlan, John ; Weiss, Peter ; Luce, Don (...et al)
PLACE OF PUBLICATION: Oakland
PUBLISHER: National Resource Center on Political Prisoners in the
Philippines (D)
DATE OF PUBLICATION: 770000
NUMBER OF PAGES: 35 p.
LANGUAGE: ENG
INDEX: civil and political rights / trials / fact-finding missions
GEOGRAPHICAL INDEX: Philippines
GEOGRAPHICAL CODE: 7542
FREE TEXT: Report of a six member delegation from the United States,
headed by former Attorney General Ramsey Clark. The mission took place
at the time the World Peace Through Law Center organized her eight
congress in the Philippines, thereby supporting the so-called human
rights policy of the Marcos regime.
The report contains an introduction, and chapters contributed by
members of the mission:
Caughlan, John - Torturers on trial, on the trial of the accused
torturers of Trinidad Herrera, a widely respected organizer of Manila's
urban poor;
Weiss, Peter - World peace through martial law?;
Luce, Don - Life and death in prison;
Kaufman, Deborah - Tondo: human rights and Manila's urban poor;
Miller, Tom - Manila, August 25, 1977, on an alternative conference
organized by the Association of Major Religious Superiors Women.

CATALOGUE SIGNATURE: 0000/0249/-3=820900
TITLE: Report of an Amnesty International mission to the Republic of
the Philippines: 11-28 November 1981
AUTHOR: (Whitney Ellsworth, A.) ; (Posner, Michael)
PLACE OF PUBLICATION: London
PUBLISHER: Amnesty International - AI (D)
DATE OF PUBLICATION: 820900
NUMBER OF PAGES: 129 p. in v.p.
ISBN: 0 862310 050 X
DOCUMENT SYMBOL: AI Index: ASA 35/25/82
LANGUAGE: ENG
INDEX: disappearances / executions / judicial systems /
fact-finding missions
GEOGRAPHICAL INDEX: Philippines
GEOGRAPHICAL CODE: 7542
FREE TEXT: The terms of reference of the three member mission included:
the investigation of alleged violations of human rights within AI's
mandate, particularly those violations, such as "disappearances" and
extrajudicial executions, which were reported to have been becoming
increasingly prevalent; the effectiveness of domestic legal and other
remedies for such alleged violations; and an assessment of the impact
on human rights of the decision of the government to lift martial law
in 1981.
The report contains an introduction, conclusions and recommendations,
and chapters on the security forces and human rights violations; the
legal background; arrests, detention and trials (with illustrative
cases); investigations and complaints. With appendices: summary of
cases presented to the delegation; statements; relevant instruments of
international law; and a glossary.

CATALOGUE SIGNATURE: 0000/0088/-4
TITLE: The Philippines = Philippines
AUTHOR: Dolgopol, Tina
TITLE OF GENERIC ITEM: CIJL bulletin
EDITION: v. 12
PLACE OF PUBLICATION: Geneva
PUBLISHER: Center for the Independence of Lawyers and Judges - CIJL
(D)
DATE OF PUBLICATION: 831000
NUMBER OF PAGES: p. 8-12
LANGUAGE: ENG / FRE
INDEX: judicial systems / legal aid / fact-finding missions
GEOGRAPHICAL INDEX: Philippines
GEOGRAPHICAL CODE: 7542
FREE TEXT: The Secretary of the CIJL visited the Philippines from 1
to 14 September 1983. She had numerous opportunities to speak with
and interview lawyers and judges about the status of the judiciary
and legal profession; her report is based on those interviews and
the documentation provided by those interviewed. It is concluded
that serious threats exist to the independence of the judiciary and
the legal profession. Despite the harassment directed at them, many
members of the Bar continue to undertake the representation of all
those in need of legal services, and lawyers' associations have
continued to speak out on human rights issues.

CATALOGUE SIGNATURE: 0000/1582/-3=831200
TITLE: The Philippines: a country in crisis
AUTHOR: Frankel, Marvin E. ; Greenberg, Jack ; Orentlicher, Diane F.
PLACE OF PUBLICATION: New York
PUBLISHER: Lawyers Committee for International Human Rights - LCIHR (D)
DATE OF PUBLICATION: 831200
NUMBER OF PAGES: 142 p.
LANGUAGE: ENG
BIBLIOGRAPHIES: Y
INDEX: dictatorship / fact-finding missions
GEOGRAPHICAL INDEX: Philippines
GEOGRAPHICAL CODE: 7542
FREE TEXT: The report is based on a fact-finding mission in September
1983, and reflects both the direct observations of the delegates and
information which they gathered from others in the Philippines, whose
accounts they have judged to be reliable. The report begins with an
introduction, and conclusions and recommendations. Attention is paid
to the military rule since the lifting of martial law in 1981, abuses
of the military, other human rights violations like arbitrary arrest
and preventive detention, and targets of military abuses. There are
also descriptions of strategic hamletting, the problems of the
operation of the judicial system, the freedom of the press and the
role of the United States (including recommendations).

CATALOGUE SIGNATURE: 0000/0138/-0=840000
TITLE: Informations on the situation in the Philippines: 18 December
1983 - 16 January 1984
AUTHOR: Bridel, Renée
PLACE OF PUBLICATION: Brussels
PUBLISHER: International Association of Democratic Lawyers - IADL (D)
DATE OF PUBLICATION: 840000
NUMBER OF PAGES: (7 p.)
LANGUAGE: ENG / FRE
INDEX: political prisoners / nongovernmental organizations /
fact-finding missions
GEOGRAPHICAL INDEX: Philippines
GEOGRAPHICAL CODE: 7542
FREE TEXT: The report contains information on the general situation of
human rights in the Philippines. The author visited the detention camp
for political prisoners Bagu Bantay, and met with some political
prisoners. She also met with other human rights activists; her report
contains information provided by Senator Jose W. Diokno on repression
by the Marcos regime and the work of oppositionary groups.

Philippines

CATALOGUE SIGNATURE: 0000/1193/-0=840400
TITLE: Report of a fact-finding mission to the Philippines: 28 November - 17 December 1983
AUTHOR: Fine, Jonathan ; Lawrence, Robert ; Stover, Eric
PLACE OF PUBLICATION: Washington DC
PUBLISHER: Clearinghouse on Science and Human Rights of the Committee on Scientific Freedom and Responsibility of the American Association for the Advancement of Science - AAAS (D)
DATE OF PUBLICATION: 840400
NUMBER OF PAGES: 13 p.
LANGUAGE: ENG
INDEX: health / political prisoners / torture / fact-finding missions
GEOGRAPHICAL INDEX: Philippines
GEOGRAPHICAL CODE: 7542
FREE TEXT: The aim of the mission was to observe health and human rights conditions in the Philippines. The mission team investigated reports of human rights abuses directed against health personnel and others, particularly in rural areas of the country. It also looked for evidence on torture, and health conditions and medical care facilities for political detainees. It visited seven detention centers, as well as hospitals, psychiatric wards, and health centers and interviewed past and present political detainees and their families.
With background information on the country and the mission, summary of findings and conclusions, and sections on: the current situation of human rights; health and human rights; torture; health conditions and medical care for political detainees; and information on the sending organizations.

CATALOGUE SIGNATURE: 0000/0088/-3=840000
TITLE: The Philippines: human rights after martial law: report of a mission...
AUTHOR: Leary, Virginia ; Ellis, A.A. ; Madlener, Kurt
PLACE OF PUBLICATION: Geneva
PUBLISHER: International Commission of Jurists - ICJ (D)
DATE OF PUBLICATION: 840000
NUMBER OF PAGES: 123 p.
ISBN: 92 9037 023 8
LANGUAGE: ENG
INDEX: martial law / legislation / judicial systems / trade unions / fact-finding missions
GEOGRAPHICAL INDEX: Philippines
GEOGRAPHICAL CODE: 7542
FREE TEXT: In the Philippines, martial law was nominally lifted in 1981, but many of its worst aspects have been retained, including indefinite detention without charge or trial by Presedential order. In addition, widespread human rights abuses are taking place, like systematic extra-judicial killings by the armed forces in rural areas, known as "salvaging". The report, based on a fact-finding mission in January 1984, provides an overview of these human rights violations and gives a detailed analysis of the relevant legal provisions in force in the Philippines. Attention is also paid to the independence of the judiciary and the bar and the situation of economic and social rights (trade union rights, land reform, health, tribal lands). With conclusions and recommendations.

CATALOGUE SIGNATURE: 0000/0088/-4
TITLE: Report on trial of "negros nine"
AUTHOR: Kinlen, Dermot
TITLE OF GENERIC ITEM: ICJ Newsletter
EDITION: no. 24
PLACE OF PUBLICATION: Geneva
PUBLISHER: International Commission of Jurists - ICJ (D)
DATE OF PUBLICATION: 850100
NUMBER OF PAGES: p. 34-45
LANGUAGE: ENG
INDEX: jurisdiction / trials / fact-finding missions
GEOGRAPHICAL INDEX: Philippines
GEOGRAPHICAL CODE: 7542
FREE TEXT: Report of a trial observation mission in February 1984,
with attention to: the background of the case against nine church
workers charged with the ambush and murder of a town mayor; the
arrest, charges and bail application; appointment of observers; the
expedition of the trial; description of the trial; motion to dismiss;
aftermath. With conclusions and comments. The author concludes that
the accused are innocent, the evidence was fabricated, and they
should never have been brought to trial.

CATALOGUE SIGNATURE: 7000/0198/-0=850800
TITLE: The state of human rights advocacy in the Philippines
AUTHOR: Silajaru, Chanchai
PLACE OF PUBLICATION: (Sydney)
PUBLISHER: Law Association for Asia and the Western Pacific - LAWASIA
(D)
DATE OF PUBLICATION: 850800
NUMBER OF PAGES: 47 p.
LANGUAGE: ENG
INDEX: legal aid / nongovernmental organizations / military /
fact-finding missions
GEOGRAPHICAL INDEX: Philippines
GEOGRAPHICAL CODE: 7542
FREE TEXT: The author participated in the international fact-finding
mission from 17 to 28 August 1985, which took place at the invitation
of the Free Legal Assistance Group FLAG. The report contains background
information on recent developments in the Philippines and examples of
the response of the military and the government to FLAG activities:
instances of disappearance and murder, specific cases, relevant
legislation like proclamation no. 2045 and the Preventive Detention
Act, evidence of the military, civil disobedience, supremacy of rules
of law. With conclusions: the role of human rights lawyers in the
Philippines is being threatened and endangered as a consequence of the
improper enforcement of powers by the military, and recommendations.

CATALOGUE SIGNATURE: 7542/-0=850800
TITLE: Human rights advocacy in the Philippines: a report of a mission
of inquiry of the Association of the Bar of the City of New York
AUTHOR: Greathead, R. Scott
PLACE OF PUBLICATION: (New York)
PUBLISHER: Association of the Bar of the City of New York - ABNY (D)
DATE OF PUBLICATION: 850800
NUMBER OF PAGES: 53 p.
LANGUAGE: ENG
INDEX: legal aid / nongovernmental organizations / homicide /
fact-finding missions
GEOGRAPHICAL INDEX: Philippines
GEOGRAPHICAL CODE: 7542
FREE TEXT: The aim of the five member international mission in August
1985 was to investigate into the treatment of lawyers engaged in human
rights advocacy. The mission was invited by the Free Legal Assistance
Group FLAG.
In the report, attention is paid to the general situation of human
rights, the state of human rights advocacy and legal aid, specific
cases of murdered lawyers and detained lawyers, other incidents of
harassment and intimidation, the position of the government, the role
of the bar and judiciary. With conclusions.

CATALOGUE SIGNATURE: 0000/1234/-0=860216
TITLE: Election in the Philippines
AUTHOR: Gastil, R.D.
PLACE OF PUBLICATION: (New York)
PUBLISHER: Freedom House (D)
DATE OF PUBLICATION: 860216
NUMBER OF PAGES: 41 p.
LANGUAGE: ENG
BIBLIOGRAPHIES: Y
INDEX: elections / fact-finding missions
GEOGRAPHICAL INDEX: Philippines
GEOGRAPHICAL CODE: 7542
FREE TEXT: The National Democratic and National Republican Institutes
for International Affairs sent a team of about 40 international
observers to the Philippines to observe the "snap" presidential
election called by president Marcos; Gastil was member of this team.
In his report, attention is paid to the background of the country, the
election process and criticism on it, the National Citizens' Movement
for Free Elections NAMFREL, the UNIDO party of Cory Aquino and the
role of the New Peoples' Army. With conclusions and recommendations,
and appendices: report of the observer trip to Negros Occidentale;
evaluation form completed by Raymond Gastil.

CATALOGUE SIGNATURE: 7542/-3=860000
TITLE: "A path to democratic renewal": a report on the February 7 presidential election in the Philippines by the international observer delegation: based on a January 26 to February 19, 1986 observer mission to the Philippines by forty-four delegates from nineteen nations
AUTHOR: National Democratic Institute for International Affairs ; National Republican Institute for International Affairs
PLACE OF PUBLICATION: Washington DC
PUBLISHER: National Democratic Institute for International Affairs (D) ; National Republican Institute for International Affairs (D)
DATE OF PUBLICATION: 860000
NUMBER OF PAGES: 333 p.
LANGUAGE: ENG
STATISTICAL INFORMATION: Y
INDEX: democracy / elections / fact-finding missions
GEOGRAPHICAL INDEX: Philippines
GEOGRAPHICAL CODE: 7542
FREE TEXT: Extensive report based on the observation of the presidential elections on 7 February 1986. The report contains: an executive summary; an introduction on the delegation's activities and fact-finding methodology; chapters on: the institutional setting of the elections; an evaluation of the electoral process; administration of the elections and the pre-election phase; the observations on the day of the election; the counting phase; the presence of foreign observers; concluding observations.
With 54 annexes, including: list of members of the international observer mission; summary of report on the feasibility of an international observer mission; transcripts of press conferences; briefing schedule; terms of reference of the mission; deployment schedule; evaluation form; documents of the official election commission COMELEC and the NAMFREL commission; letters, statements and reports and affidavits concerning the elections; and figures.

CATALOGUE SIGNATURE: 0000/0018/-0=860505
TITLE: Press communiquè: delegation of the World Council of Churches
and the Christian Conference of Asia: Manila, 5. May 1986
AUTHOR: Paulos Mar Gregorios; Park Sang Jung; Chinniah, Malar
(...et al)
PLACE OF PUBLICATION: (Geneva)
PUBLISHER: Commission of the Churches on International Affairs of the
World Council of Churches - CCIA-WCC (D)
DATE OF PUBLICATION: 860505
NUMBER OF PAGES: 5 p.
LANGUAGE: ENG
INDEX: church and state / fact-finding missions
GEOGRAPHICAL INDEX: Philippines
GEOGRAPHICAL CODE: 7542
FREE TEXT: At the invitation of the National Council of Churches in the
Philippines, a delegation of thirteen persons, mainly church leaders,
representing the World Council of Churches and the Christian Conference
on Asia visited Manila from 30 April to 5 May 1986. The purpose of the
visit was to hear, understand and dialogue with the Philippine people
regarding their assessment of the present situation, to meet church
leaders and government officials to express solidarity with the
Philippine people, and to interpret the recent political events for the
benefit of the constituency of the WCC and CCIA.

REPUBLIC OF KOREA

CATALOGUE SIGNATURE: 0000/0249/-0=740000
TITLE: Political repression in South Korea: report of commission to South Korea for Amnesty International
AUTHOR: Butler, William J.
PLACE OF PUBLICATION: London
PUBLISHER: Amnesty International - AI (D)
DATE OF PUBLICATION: 740000
NUMBER OF PAGES: 11 p.
LANGUAGE: ENG
INDEX: trials / political prisoners / fact-finding missions
GEOGRAPHICAL INDEX: Republic of Korea
GEOGRAPHICAL CODE: 7144
FREE TEXT: The aims of the mission were to observe the trial of 54 South Koreans arrested under Emergency Regulations No.4, to examine the entire situation of amnesty, to make recommendations about the continuing viability of the Korean section under President Park's new regulations since January 1974, and to provide up-to-date information about political prisoners. The report contains background information on the country, the Yushin Constitution of 1972, protests for changes in the constitution and the emergency decrees, the trials, torture of political prisoners and the response of the government (including critique). With conclusions and recommendations.
With appendices: lists of completed trials and sentences and pending trials, presidential decrees, chronology of events in the period July-September 1974.

Republic of Korea

CATALOGUE SIGNATURE: 0000/0249/-3=770600
TITLE: Report of an Amnesty International mission to the Republic of
Korea: 27 March - 9 April 1975
AUTHOR: (Pedersen, Eric Karup) ; (Wrobel, Brian)
EDITION: 2nd ed.
PLACE OF PUBLICATION: London
PUBLISHER: Amnesty International - AI (D)
DATE OF PUBLICATION: 770600
NUMBER OF PAGES: 45 p.
ISBN: 0 900058 45 5
DOCUMENT SYMBOL: AI Index: PUB 49/00/76
LANGUAGE: ENG
INDEX: judicial systems / political prisoners / trials /
fact-finding missions
GEOGRAPHICAL INDEX: Republic of Korea
GEOGRAPHICAL CODE: 7144
FREE TEXT: The aims of the mission were: to carry out a medical
examination of people allegedly tortured or ill-treated while in the
custody of the main law enforcement agencies; to collect evidence on
prison conditions; to investigate the conduct of trial proceedings;
and to discuss certain findings with the Korean Minister of Justice.
The report begins with a preface, including information on recent
developments in a trial against political prisoners, followed by a
summary of the mission's report and recommendations.
The mission report contains sections on the law and civil rights,
intimidation of the legal profession, irregularities in trials,
harassment and torture, prison conditions, a case study on the
People's Revolutionary Party, and information on harassment of the
mission.

114

CATALOGUE SIGNATURE: 0000/0088/-3=790000
TITLE: Persecution of defence lawyers in South Korea: report of a
mission to South Korea in May 1979
AUTHOR: DeWind, Adrian W. ; Woodhouse, John
PLACE OF PUBLICATION: Geneva
PUBLISHER: International Commission of Jurists - ICJ (D)
DATE OF PUBLICATION: 790000
NUMBER OF PAGES: 68 p.
AVAILABILITY: X
LANGUAGE: ENG
INDEX: / judicial systems / lawyers / fact-finding missions
GEOGRAPHICAL INDEX: Republic of Korea
GEOGRAPHICAL CODE: 7144
FREE TEXT: The report consists of a preface by Niall MacDermot and
four parts.
The first part, "the nature of repression in South Korea", is a
description of the constitutional and legal framework, the extra-
legal methods of repression and aspects of the judicial process
(search, arrest, interrogation, treatment of prisoners, rights of
the defense, trial procedures). The second part, "the harassment of
defense lawyers", contains general findings, specific cases, and
information on the position of the goverment and the Korean Bar
Association. Part three contains conclusions and recommendations.
With appendix: extract from the defence speech by advocate Kang
Shin Ok.

CATALOGUE SIGNATURE: 0000/1192/-0=800700
TITLE: Two months after Kwangju: what next for South Korea?
AUTHOR: Easter, Maud ; Easter, David
PLACE OF PUBLICATION: Tokyo
PUBLISHER: Quaker International Affairs Program - East Asia (D) ;
American Friends Service Committee - AFSC
DATE OF PUBLICATION: 800700
NUMBER OF PAGES: 8 p.
LANGUAGE: ENG
INDEX: peaceful assembly (right to) / fact-finding missions
GEOGRAPHICAL INDEX: Republic of Korea
GEOGRAPHICAL CODE: 7144
FREE TEXT: Report of a visit to Kwangju and Seoul in July 1980, in
order to investigate acts of violence which occurred in May. People in
Kwangju are convinced that 1.000 to 2.000 people were killed by the
military during the resistance after demonstrations against the coup of
Chun Doo Hwan. Thousands have been detained, and recent arrests include
people who took food out to the demonstrators, as well as 17 professors
of Chonnam University. There is deep concern about the coming trial of
Kim Dae Jung and eight others. With analysis of attitudes towards North
Korea and the United States, and of the position of the United States
towards the recent events.

CATALOGUE SIGNATURE: 0000/1212/-3=850400
TITLE: Democracy in South Korea: a promise unfulfilled: a report
on human rights in the Republic of Korea 1980-1985
AUTHOR: Clark, Roger ; Shea, Nina ; Baker, Edward J.
PLACE OF PUBLICATION: New York
PUBLISHER: International League for Human Rights - ILHR (D) ;
International Human Rights Law Group - IHRLG
DATE OF PUBLICATION: 850400
NUMBER OF PAGES: 193 p. in v.p.
LANGUAGE: ENG
INDEX: democracy / civil and political rights /
press (freedom of the) / fact-finding missions
GEOGRAPHICAL INDEX: Republic of Korea
GEOGRAPHICAL CODE: 7144
FREE TEXT: The report is partly based on a mission in October 1983 by
Hurst Hannum and Steven Schneebaum. It discusses human rights and
democratic developments in the Republic of Korea since president Chun
Doo Hwan came into power in 1980. It begins with a summary of findings
and recommendations.
The first chapter provides a brief introduction to Korean history and
government. Chapter two, by Edward J. Baker, reviews the political
developments during the period of transition from the Park to the Chun
regime. Chapter three describes the international obligations with
regard to human rights. Chapter four examines the restrictions on the
press taken by the government. Chapter five covers restrictions on
labour unions and workers' rights. Chapter six is on the mechanisms
which are being used to curb political dissent, particularly those
affecting the politically active South Korean universities. Chapter
seven examines the National Assembly election process. Chapter eight
reviews United States policy toward South Korea, particularly with
respect to the implementation of the human rights provisions of the
United States. The final chapter of this report (the second part of the
paper by Edward J. Baker) provides an overview which considers in a
general manner a number of issues pertaining to respect for human
rights in the Republic of Korea during the last years. With appendices:
list of political prisoners; list of names of 683 journalists reported
to be banned from being published in South Korea since the military
coup of 1980.

SINGAPORE

CATALOGUE SIGNATURE: 0000/0249/-3=800100
TITLE: Report of an Amnesty International mission to Singapore: 30
November to 5 December 1978
AUTHOR: (Jones, Thomas C.) ; (Williams, Michael C.)
PLACE OF PUBLICATION: London
PUBLISHER: Amnesty International - AI (D)
DATE OF PUBLICATION: 800100
NUMBER OF PAGES: 60 p.
ISBN: 0 86210 002 X
DOCUMENT SYMBOL: AI Index: ASA 36/10/79
LANGUAGE: ENG
INDEX: detention / political prisoners / fact-finding missions
GEOGRAPHICAL INDEX: Singapore
GEOGRAPHICAL CODE: 7546
FREE TEXT: Amnesty International was especially concerned with
preventive detention under the Internal Security Act ISA (1960)
and the Banishment Act (1959), the systematic use of these Acts as
a means to detain political opponents of the government for long
periods of time without charge or trial, and the ill-treatment of
political prisoners during the 30-day interrogation period which
the ISA allows prior to the serving of a detention order.
The Singapore authorities refused all contact with the delegation;
requests to visit detention facilities and interview prisoners were
also denied.
The report contains recommendations, and chapters on the political
and on the legal background; arrest and interrogation; long term
detention; the position of journalists and of the legal profession;
the death penalty; and prisoner case histories. With appendices:
relevant international and domestic law.

SRI LANKA

CATALOGUE SIGNATURE: 0000/0249/-3=761200
TITLE: Report of an Amnesty International mission to Sri Lanka: 9-15
January 1975
AUTHOR: (Blom-Cooper, Louis) ; (Terlingen, Yvonne)
EDITION: 2nd ed.
PLACE OF PUBLICATION: London
PUBLISHER: Amnesty International - AI (D)
DATE OF PUBLICATION: 761200
NUMBER OF PAGES: 51 p.
DOCUMENT SYMBOL: AI Index: PUB 75/00/77
ISBN: 0 900058 40 4
LANGUAGE: ENG
INDEX: detention / fact-finding missions
GEOGRAPHICAL INDEX: Sri Lanka
GEOGRAPHICAL CODE: 7447
FREE TEXT: The report describes the judicial process and conditions of
detention applying to the estimated 2000 prisoners held at the time of
the mission in connection with the 1971 insurgency. It also describes
the circumstances of arrest and detention of a small number of young
Tamils, who are kept under the emergency regulations for different
reasons, but have not been tried and charged.
The report contains a foreword which reviews some positive steps taken
by the Sri Lankan government which follow, in part, the recommendations
made in the report.
With appendices: information on the situation of political prisoners
(trials, detention without trial, death penalty, detention conditions)
and ill-treatment during police custody.

CATALOGUE SIGNATURE: 0000/0088/-4
TITLE: Prelimary report to the International Commission of Jurists on
the trial of Mr S Nadesan, QC, in the Supreme Court of Sri Lanka on
12 to 15 May 1980 by the observer
AUTHOR: Lord Hooson
TITLE OF GENERIC ITEM: ICJ Newsletter
EDITION: no. 5
PLACE OF PUBLICATION: Geneva
PUBLISHER: International Commission of Jurists - ICJ (D)
DATE OF PUBLICATION: 800600
NUMBER OF PAGES: p. 51-54
LANGUAGE: ENG
INDEX: press (freedom of the) / judicial systems / trials /
fact-finding missions
GEOGRAPHICAL INDEX: Sri Lanka
GEOGRAPHICAL CODE: 7447
FREE TEXT: Mr Nadesan was charged for criticizing events in the
National State Assembly of Sri Lanka on 2 February 1978 with regard
to the publication of a photograph in a daily. A complaint about the
written reaction of Nadesan was raised in Parliament, and the matter
was referred to the Committee of Privileges and the Attorney-General.
With description of the trial and conclusions.

CATALOGUE SIGNATURE: 0000/0088/-3=810000
TITLE: Ethnic conflict and violence in Sri Lanka: report of a mission
to Sri Lanka in July - August 1981 on behalf of the International
Commission of Jurists
AUTHOR: Leary, Virginia A.
PLACE OF PUBLICATION: Geneva
PUBLISHER: International Commission of Jurists - ICJ (D)
DATE OF PUBLICATION: 810000
NUMBER OF PAGES: 87 p.
ISBN: 92 9037 011 9
LANGUAGE: ENG
BIBLIOGRAPHIES: Y
INDEX: ethnic conflict / armed violence / fact-finding missions
GEOGRAPHICAL INDEX: Sri Lanka
GEOGRAPHICAL CODE: 7447
FREE TEXT: The purpose of the mission was to undertake a study of
the human rights aspects of the Prevention of Terrorism Act and
events related to its adoption and application. The report provides
an elaborate background to the situation in Sri Lanka, the ethnic
conflict and violence, and efforts undertaken by the government to
cope with it. Attention is given to the relation of the Terrorism
Act to international human rights law.
With summary (conclusions), recommendations and epilogue.

CATALOGUE SIGNATURE: 0000/0249/-3=830700
TITLE: Report of an Amnesty International mission to Sri Lanka: 31
January - 9 February 1982
AUTHOR: (Schell, Orville) ; (Terlingen, Yvonne)
PLACE OF PUBLICATION: London
PUBLISHER: Amnesty International - AI (D)
DATE OF PUBLICATION: 830700
NUMBER OF PAGES: 72 p.
ISBN: 0 86210 054 2
DOCUMENT SYMBOL: AI Index: ASA 37/01/83
LANGUAGE: ENG
INDEX: detention / torture / fact-finding missions
GEOGRAPHICAL INDEX: Sri Lanka
GEOGRAPHICAL CODE: 7447
FREE TEXT: The purpose of the mission was to collect information
relating to human rights violations alleged to have been committed in
the north of the country by the security forces under the provisions
of the Prevention of Terrorism Act. With background: Amnesty's human
rights concerns in Sri Lanka, and summary of findings. Following, the
report contains chapters on the legal background, arrest and detention
practices under the Prevention of Terrorism Act and torture and
killings by the security forces.
With conclusions and recommendations. With appendices: testimonies on
torture, memorandum to President J.R. Jayewardene, letter by the High
Commissioner of Sri Lanka, schedule regarding detention conditions.

CATALOGUE SIGNATURE: 0000/0902/-3=850200
TITLE: Ethnic and communal violence: the independence of the judiciary:
protection of "fundamental rights" and the rule of law in Sri Lanka:
fragile freedoms?: report of a mission to Sri Lanka in June 1983 on
behalf of the International Commission of Jurists...
AUTHOR: Moore, Timothy J.
EDITION: 4th print
PLACE OF PUBLICATION: Sydney
PUBLISHER: International Commission of Jurists, Australian section -
ICJ-AU (D)
DATE OF PUBLICATION: 850200
NUMBER OF PAGES: 104 p.
LANGUAGE: ENG
INDEX: judicial systems / ethnic violence / fact-finding missions
GEOGRAPHICAL INDEX: Sri Lanka
GEOGRAPHICAL CODE: 7447
FREE TEXT: The author's original mission was to attend as the observer
on behalf of the ICJ a trial in the High Court of Sri Lanka, which was
to have commenced on 6 June 1983. As the case did not proceed, his
attention was turned to other issues related to the rule of law which,
coincidentally, emerged significantly during his visit. The report
traverses the current position with respect to tensions and conflict
between the Tamil and Sinhalese communities in Sri Lanka and a range of
rule of law issues. With chapters on recent political developments, the
current position of ethnic conflict, grievances of the Tamil minority,
rule of law issues (independence of the judiciary, the Prevention of
Terrorism Act, abolition of inquests, fundamental rights cases), the
position of plantation Tamils and "stateless persons", the Sri Lanka
Foundation. With summary, recommendations and appendices: article on
sovereignty; study on plantation Tamils.

CATALOGUE SIGNATURE: 7000/0198/-3=840000
TITLE: The communal violence in Sri Lanka, July 1983
AUTHOR: Hyndman, Patricia
PLACE OF PUBLICATION: Sydney
PUBLISHER: Law Association for Asia and the Western Pacific - LAWASIA
(D)
DATE OF PUBLICATION: 840000
NUMBER OF PAGES: 288 p.
LANGUAGE: ENG
STATISTICAL INFORMATION: Y
INDEX: ethnic conflict / minorities / political violence /
fact-finding missions
GEOGRAPHICAL INDEX: Sri Lanka
GEOGRAPHICAL CODE: 7447
FREE TEXT: In the last week of July 1983, there was violence directed
against the Tamil population of the country. Hundreds were killed,
thousands were displaced and lost their property. The report is based
on a fact-finding mission in late August 1983. It provides a detailed
and clear description of facts established on the events in the last
week of July, the circumstances of displaced persons, constitutional
justification for the state of emergency, assessment of the actions of
governmental authorities and the behaviour of non-governmental groups,
and breaches of human rights. With conclusions and recommendations.
With appendices: Lawasia guidelines, maps, lists of persons killed,
testimony of the massacres in Welikade prison, speeches by members of
the government, government statements, legislation, documents of
NGO's, newspaper articles.

CATALOGUE SIGNATURE: 0000/0381/-3=840300
TITLE: Sri Lanka: a mounting tragedy of errors: report of a mission to
Sri Lanka in January 1984 on behalf of the International Commission of
Jurists and its British section, Justice
AUTHOR: Sieghart, Paul
PLACE OF PUBLICATION: Geneva ; London
PUBLISHER: International Commission of Jurists - ICJ ; Justice -
JUSTICE-UK (D)
DATE OF PUBLICATION: 840300
NUMBER OF PAGES: 95 p.
ISBN: 0 907247 04 0
LANGUAGE: ENG
INDEX: judicial systems / legislation / fact-finding missions
GEOGRAPHICAL INDEX: Sri Lanka
GEOGRAPHICAL CODE: 7447
FREE TEXT: After an introduction and background information, the
report contains an elaborate section on law and institutions.
Attention is paid to the legal protection of human rights, emergency
legislation and the Prevention of Terrorism Act, the independence of
the judiciary, the Sixth Amendment, freedom of expression, and the
role of the armed forces and the police. Certain police powers under
the Prevention of Terrorism Act are shown to be serious violations
of the Rule of Law and Sri Lanka's obligations under the International
Covenant on Civil and Political Rights. The report also contains a
section on perspectives for the future, a summary and an appendix:
holders of public office interviewed during the mission.

CATALOGUE SIGNATURE: 7447/-3=841100
TITLE: Rückkehr nach Sri Lanka
AUTHOR: Projektgruppe "Tamilen"
PLACE OF PUBLICATION: Zurich
PUBLISHER: Projektgruppe "Tamilen" (D)
DATE OF PUBLICATION: 841100
NUMBER OF PAGES: 95 p. in v.p.
SERIES TITLE: Auf der Suche nach Zukunft: Tamilische Flüchtlinge aus
Sri Lanka: Analysen und Handlungsvorschläge
VOLUME: no. 2
LANGUAGE: GER
INDEX: refugees / asylum / ethnic conflict / fact-finding missions
GEOGRAPHICAL INDEX: Sri Lanka
GEOGRAPHICAL CODE: 7447
FREE TEXT: The second volume of the report on Tamil refugees from Sri
Lanka deals with the situation in Sri Lanka (based on a fact-finding
mission), the rejection of requests for asylum, and the possibilities
of refugees to return to their home country. With many appendices:
articles from newspapers and magazines; testimonies of witnesses of
violence; information from Sri Lankan nongovernmental organizations;
analysis of and letters and newspaper articles on a fact-finding
mission by Swiss federal police; information on unemployment in Sri
Lanka.

CATALOGUE SIGNATURE: 7447/-0=850300
TITLE: Some notes on Sri Lanka
AUTHOR: Koshy, Ninan
PLACE OF PUBLICATION: Madras
PUBLISHER: Centre for Human Development and Social Change (D) ; World Council of Churches - WCC
DATE OF PUBLICATION: 850300
NUMBER OF PAGES: 6 p.
LANGUAGE: ENG
INDEX: minorities / ethnic conflict / fact-finding missions
GEOGRAPHICAL INDEX: Sri Lanka
GEOGRAPHICAL CODE: 7447
FREE TEXT: Report on a mission of five delegates of the World Council of Churches WCC and the Christian Conference on Asia in February 1985. The report deals with the situation in the north of Sri Lanka, Sri Lanka as a "national security state", the settlement policy of the government, the plantation Tamils, the All Party Talks and other talks, the role of India, the responsibilities of the government and the role of the Churches.

CATALOGUE SIGNATURE: 7000/0198/-3=850321
TITLE: Sri Lanka: escalating violence and erosions of democracy
AUTHOR: Hyndman, Patricia
PLACE OF PUBLICATION: Sydney
PUBLISHER: Law Association for Asia and the Western Pacific - LAWASIA (D)
DATE OF PUBLICATION: 850321
NUMBER OF PAGES: 15 p.
LANGUAGE: ENG
INDEX: ethnic violence / democracy / fact-finding missions
GEOGRAPHICAL INDEX: Sri Lanka
GEOGRAPHICAL CODE: 7447
FREE TEXT: In view of the rapidly deteriorating situation in Sri Lanka, the LAWASIA Human Rights Standing Committee requested and received government permission for Ms Hyndman to return to the country to update the report of her fact-finding mission in August 1983. The five day visit took place on February 17-22, 1985. This report is an interim appraisal based upon the material acquired from interviews held during the mission and documentation obtained both whilst in Sri Lanka and abroad. The report is concerned with two inter-related phenomena, firstly the escalating violence and, secondly, erosions of democracy and the rule of law.

CATALOGUE SIGNATURE: 7447/-0=850630
TITLE: Report on Sri Lanka and the state of communal violence
AUTHOR: Missen, Alan
PLACE OF PUBLICATION: Melbourne
PUBLISHER: (Missen, Alan)
DATE OF PUBLICATION: 850630
NUMBER OF PAGES: 5 p.
LANGUAGE: ENG
INDEX: fact-finding missions
GEOGRAPHICAL INDEX: Sri Lanka
GEOGRAPHICAL CODE: 7447
FREE TEXT: The report is based on a visit of three days to Sri Lanka,
and meetings with among others representatives of the government and
the opposition, and representatives of nongovernmental organizations.
Next, Senator Mission paid a visit of one day to Madras, for talks
with leaders of the Tamil United Liberation Front TULF.
The report contains a general statement on attitudes towards recent
developments in Sri Lanka based upon interviews made, and conclusions
and recommendations with regard to action to be undertaken at the
international level.
The report was delivered to the Rome meeting, in July 1985, of the
Emergency Committee on Sri Lanka formed under the auspices of the
Standing International Forum on Ethnic Conflict (SIFEC) (later named
International Alert), of which Senator Missen was a member.

TAIWAN, REPUBLIC OF CHINA

CATALOGUE SIGNATURE: 7149/-0=780700
TITLE: "Made in Taiwan": a human rights investigation
AUTHOR: Cantwell, Becky ; Luce, Don ; Weinglass, Leonard
PLACE OF PUBLICATION: New York
PUBLISHER: Asian Center (D)
DATE OF PUBLICATION: 780700
NUMBER OF PAGES: 20 p.
LANGUAGE: ENG
INDEX: religion (freedom of) / labour / expression (freedom of) /
fact-finding missions
GEOGRAPHICAL INDEX: Taiwan, Republic of China
GEOGRAPHICAL CODE: 7149
FREE TEXT: Report on a visit to Taiwan in July 1978, with attention
to: the political background of the country (relation to mainland
China, political power, legislation, aspirations), the position of
the Presbyterian Church, the conditions of women workers and trade
unions, the indiction of an opposition politician, information on
and a story by one of Taiwan's folk writers.

CATALOGUE SIGNATURE: 0000/0249/-3=810800
TITLE: Memorandum submitted to the government of the Republic of China
by Amnesty International (including the government's reply and Amnesty
International's response)
AUTHOR: (Rüter, C.F.) ; (Vandale, Françoise)
PLACE OF PUBLICATION: London
PUBLISHER: Amnesty International - AI (D)
DATE OF PUBLICATION: 810800
NUMBER OF PAGES: 30 p.
DOCUMENT SYMBOL: AI Index: ASA 38/03/81
LANGUAGE: ENG
INDEX: peaceful assembly (right to) / trials / fact-finding missions
GEOGRAPHICAL INDEX: Taiwan, Republic of China
GEOGRAPHICAL CODE: 7149
FREE TEXT: The aim of the mission of February 1980 was to gather
information on matters of AI's concern, and the discuss them with
government officials. It concerns especially the arrest of a number of
people following a demonstration organized by an opposition magazine
in Kaohsiung in December 1979, which ended in violent clashes with the
police. In March 1980, AI sent an observer to the trial by a military
court of eight of those arrested, who had been charged with "sedition".
The report contains the text of a memorandum submitted to the
government on 27 February 1981, the government's comments forwarded to
AI on 13 May 1981, and the text of a letter sent by AI on 1 July 1981
in response to the government's comments.

VIET NAM

CATALOGUE SIGNATURE: 0000/0249/-3=810600
TITLE: Report of an Amnesty International mission to the Socialist
Republic of Viet Nam: 10-21 December 1979: including memoranda
exchanged between the government and Amnesty International
AUTHOR: (Hammarberg, Thomas) ; (Wickremasinghe, Suriya) ;
(Williams, Michael)
PLACE OF PUBLICATION: London
PUBLISHER: Amnesty International - AI (D)
DATE OF PUBLICATION: 810600
NUMBER OF PAGES: 44 p. in v.p.
ISBN: 0 86210 033 X
DOCUMENT SYMBOL: AI Index: ASA 41/05/81
LANGUAGE: ENG
INDEX: detention / fact-finding missions
GEOGRAPHICAL INDEX: Viet Nam
GEOGRAPHICAL CODE: 7553
FREE TEXT: The report is the result of a mission to discuss with the
government of Viet Nam reports of detention without charge or trial
for "re-education", arrest on political grounds of individuals and
the lack of legal safeguards for those detained on such grounds.
The report contains the memorandum submitted to the government in
May 1980, the written reply of the government of September 1980,
an aide-mémoire submitted to the government in December 1980, and
comments of the government on the aide-memoire, March 1981.

CATALOGUE SIGNATURE: 0000/1202/-0=830600
TITLE: "So many enemies": the view from Hanoi
AUTHOR: Kattenberg, Paul M. ; Ranard, Donald L.
PLACE OF PUBLICATION: Washington DC
PUBLISHER: Center for International Policy - CIP (D)
DATE OF PUBLICATION: 830600
NUMBER OF PAGES: 8 p.
SERIES TITLE: Indochina issues
VOLUME: v. 38
LANGUAGE: ENG
STATISTICAL INFORMATION: Y
INDEX: detention / fact-finding missions
GEOGRAPHICAL INDEX: Viet Nam
GEOGRAPHICAL CODE: 7553
FREE TEXT: The unofficial study mission consisted of four retired
U.S. diplomats. They investigated the economical and political
situation in Vietnam, the Vietnamese foreign policy and the human
rights situation.The members travelled around the country and had
conversations with government representatives. In the section on
human rights, it is stated that they were not allowed to visit a
reeducation camp. The discussions produced few new insights
concerning the status of human rights and the reeducation camps.

AFGHANISTAN / PAKISTAN

CATALOGUE SIGNATURE: 0000/0138/-0=800300
TITLE: Mission d'information en Afghanistan et au Pakistan: 4-20 mars 1980
AUTHOR: Al Shaer, Mohammed Ibrahim ; Bentoumi, Amar ; Bhagwat, Niloufer (...et al)
PLACE OF PUBLICATION: Brussels
PUBLISHER: Association Internationale des Juristes Démocrates - IADL (D)
DATE OF PUBLICATION: 800300
NUMBER OF PAGES: 11 p.
LANGUAGE: FRE
INDEX: armed conflict / military / fact-finding missions
GEOGRAPHICAL INDEX: Afghanistan / Pakistan
GEOGRAPHICAL CODE: 7411 / 7441
FREE TEXT: The eight members of the international mission had contacts with the Chiefs of State and authorities in both countries, as well as with citizens and journalists. The report begins with information on the enrollment of the mission and a review of the positions of the two Chiefs of State on the situation in Afghanistan. It also contains a description of the general situation in Kabul and the situation of human rights in Afghanistan (on freedom of religion and freedom of information), the question of the presence of Soviet military forces in Afghanistan and the humanitarian aspects of the refugee problem. With conclusions.

ASIA

CATALOGUE SIGNATURE: 0000/0001/-4
TITLE: Travels in Asia - 1979: visits to three "developing nations":
Korea, Taiwan, Philippines
AUTHOR: Wiseberg, Laurie S.
TITLE OF GENERIC ITEM: Human Rights Internet Newsletter
EDITION: v. 5(4-5)
PLACE OF PUBLICATION: Washington DC
PUBLISHER: Human Rights Internet - HRI (D)
DATE OF PUBLICATION: 800100
NUMBER OF PAGES: p.71-76
LANGUAGE: ENG
INDEX: nongovernmental organizations / fact-finding missions
GEOGRAPHICAL INDEX: Asia
GEOGRAPHICAL CODE: 7000
FREE TEXT: The aim of the mission to the Republic of Korea, Taiwan and
the Philippines was to make contact with human rights organizations
and scholars concerned with human rights. The report contains personal
reflections of the author, with background information on the
countries visited, and descriptions of activities of organizations
contacted, like factory workers organizations, church organizations
and organizations working for political prisoners.

DEMOCRATIC KAMPUCHEA / THAILAND

CATALOGUE SIGNATURE: 0000/0035/-3=770000
TITLE: Thaïlande: rapport a la Fédération Internationale des Droits
de l'Homme
AUTHOR: Mignon, Thierry
PLACE OF PUBLICATION: Paris
PUBLISHER: Fédération Internationale des Droits de l'Homme - FIDH (D)
DATE OF PUBLICATION: 770000
NUMBER OF PAGES: 16 p.
LANGUAGE: FRE
INDEX: refugees / political violence / fact-finding missions
GEOGRAPHICAL INDEX: Democratic Kampuchea / Thailand
GEOGRAPHICAL CODE: 7520 / 7550
FREE TEXT: The purpose of the mission was to investigate the situation
of Cambodian refugees in Thailand, and the situation in Cambodia
itself. The report contains a description of refugee camps, some of
which were visited by the delegate, and of the background of refugees
spoken with. With complete texts of testimonies.

CATALOGUE SIGNATURE: 7520/-0=791119
TITLE: Report to the Citizens Commission on Indochinese Refugees on the
public health and medical care needs of the Khmer refugees in Thailand
and an estimate of the needs of the millions of displaced Khmer within
Kampuchea
AUTHOR: Lee, Philip R. ; Cherne, Leo ; Rustin, Bayard (et al...)
PLACE OF PUBLICATION: Washington D.C. ; New York
PUBLISHER: Indochina Refugee Action Center (D) ; Citizens Commission on
Indochinese Refugees ; International Rescue Committee (D)
DATE OF PUBLICATION: 791119
NUMBER OF PAGES: 31 p. in v.p.
SERIES TITLE: Cambodian Action Update
VOLUME: v. 1(3)
LANGUAGE: ENG
INDEX: refugees / health / fact-finding missions
GEOGRAPHICAL INDEX: Democratic Kampuchea / Thailand
GEOGRAPHICAL CODE: 7520 / 7550
FREE TEXT: This document contains:
-an overview of the situation of refugees in the Cambodian refugee camps
situated in Thailand along the Cambodian border, with attention to
relief efforts, the work of the United Nations High Commissioner for
Refugees and medical personnel;
-statement and recommendations on Cambodia / Kampuchea and Indochinese
refugees, by representatives of the Citizens Committee who visited the
region, with general background information and sections on the
lifesaving potential inside Cambodia and inside Thailand, and
resettlement opportunities for all Indochinese refugees;
-report on the public health and medical care needs, also based on the
mission. The author states that food is the most urgent and important
need;
-a description of the International Rescue Committee and the Cambodian
refugee emergency.

CATALOGUE SIGNATURE: 7550/-0=801125
TITLE: Along the Thailand - Kampuchea border, November 1980: the situation of the Khmer refugees in the holding centers
AUTHOR: Hawk, David R.
PLACE OF PUBLICATION: New York
PUBLISHER: World Conference on Religion and Peace - WCRP - Khmer Project (D)
DATE OF PUBLICATION: 801125
NUMBER OF PAGES: 18 p.
SERIES TITLE: WCRP Report on Kampuchea
DOCUMENT SYMBOL: HR 21
LANGUAGE: ENG
STATISTICAL INFORMATION: Y
BIBLIOGRAPHIES: Y
INDEX: refugees / fact-finding missions
GEOGRAPHICAL INDEX: Democratic Kampuchea / Thailand
GEOGRAPHICAL CODE: 7520 / 7550
FREE TEXT: This report examines recent developments in the situation of refugees from Kampuchea in Thailand and their prospects for the future. It is based on visits and interviews with UNHCR and voluntary agency refugee workers at the new holding centres, discussions with officials in Bangkok, and materials and data from the UNHCR in Bangkok. With: background information on the refugees, descriptions of holding centres and perspectives for the durable refugees: settlement in Thailand, third country resettlement or repatriation to Kampuchea.

CATALOGUE SIGNATURE: 0000/1245/-3=850800
TITLE: Kampuchea: after the worst: a report on current violations
of human rights
AUTHOR: Abrams, Floyd ; Orentlicher, Diane ; Heder, Stephen
PLACE OF PUBLICATION: New York ; Washington
PUBLISHER: Lawyers Committee for International Human Rights - LCIHR
(D)
DATE OF PUBLICATION: 850800
NUMBER OF PAGES: 264 p. in v.p.
LANGUAGE: ENG
INDEX: armed conflict / fact-finding missions
GEOGRAPHICAL INDEX: Democratic Kampuchea / Thailand
GEOGRAPHICAL CODE: 7520 / 7550
FREE TEXT: The report is based on two fact-finding missions by the
Lawyers Committee for International Human Rights to areas on both
sides of the Thai-Kampuchean border. The first mission visited
areas on both sides of the border from 30 October until 14 November
1984; the second mission visited refugee camps in Thailand from 28
January until 6 February 1985.
The report is divided into three sections:
I) Human-rights conditions in the People's Republic of Kampuchea.
With attention to: arbitrary arrest, detention and torture; the
extent of political persecution; trials; and, forced labour;
II) Human-rights conditions in areas administered by the guerrilla
forces of Democratic Kampuchea ("Khmer Rouge"). With: background
information on the Pol Pot era and the administrative and command
structure of Kampuchean forces; arrest and detention; physical
integrity;
III) Human-rights conditions in areas administered by the Khmer
People's National Liberation Front. With background information;
the early years; current conditions of physical integrity; and
current adjudicatory procedures: committees for the provision of
justice.

DEMOCRATIC KAMPUCHEA / VIET NAM

CATALOGUE SIGNATURE: 0000/0138/-3=790000
TITLE: Vietnam - Kampuchea: report of mission: 25 April - 5 May 1979
= Vietnam - Kampuchea: rapport de mission: 25 avril - 5 mai 1979
AUTHOR: Agnoletti, Enzo Enrique ; Chemillier-Gendreau, Monique ;
Crown, Joe (...et al)
PLACE OF PUBLICATION: Brussels
PUBLISHER: International Association of Democratic Lawyers - IADL (D)
DATE OF PUBLICATION: 790000
NUMBER OF PAGES: 38 p. in v.p.
LANGUAGE: ENG / FRE
INDEX: armed conflict / international law / fact-finding missions
GEOGRAPHICAL INDEX: Democratic Kampuchea / Viet Nam
GEOGRAPHICAL CODE: 7520 / 7553
FREE TEXT: The mission was established to inquire into the facts and
the events relating to the Chinese aggression against Vietnam.
The first part of the report is a chronological account of the mission.
The facts and the personal testimonies which the eight members gathered
are grouped under five headings: 1) Lang Son and the Chinese invasion
of 17 February 1979; 2) Ho Chi Minh City; 3) the information obtained
on the Kampuchean frontier; 4) the situation in Kampuchea; 5) contacts
in Hanoi and information obtained.
The second part of the report is an analysis of the legal position,
divided into: 1) the frontier incidents; 2) Chinese military action on
17 February 1979 and after; 3) the situation in Kampuchea.
With annexes: chronology of events relating to the Vietnamo-Cambodian
frontier; proposals of delegations of Vietnam and China; communiqué of
the Kampuchean government.

DEMOCRATIC PEOPLE'S REPUBLIC OF KOREA / REPUBLIC OF KOREA

CATALOGUE SIGNATURE: 0000/0138/-0=740900
TITLE: Memorandum on the question of the peaceful and independent
reunification of Korea: a document prepared by a delegation of
inquiry of the International Association of Democratic Lawyers
AUTHOR: Mosston, Leora ; Okudaira, Yasuhiro ; Ferrucci, Romeo
(et al...)
PLACE OF PUBLICATION: Brussels
PUBLISHER: Association Internationale des Juristes Démocrates - IADL (D)
DATE OF PUBLICATION: 740900
NUMBER OF PAGES: 12 p.
LANGUAGE: ENG
INDEX: self-determination / fact-finding missions
GEOGRAPHICAL INDEX: Democratic People's Republic of Korea /
Republic of Korea
GEOGRAPHICAL CODE: 7121 / 7144
FREE TEXT: Report of a fact-finding mission of four members to the
Democratic People's Republic of Korea in September 1974. Attention is
paid to Korea as a nation, obstacles to reunification, systematic
violations of the Panmunjum Armistice Agreement of 1953 by the United
States, the regime of Park Chung Hee in the Republic of Korea and its
attempts to maintain the permanent division of Korea. With proposals
for a solution to the Korean problem and conclusions.

CATALOGUE SIGNATURE: 0000/0018/-0=851200
TITLE: The Tozanso process: an ecumenical contribution to the struggle
for peace and justice in North-East Asia
AUTHOR: Weingaertner, Erich
PLACE OF PUBLICATION: Geneva
PUBLISHER: Commission of the Churches on International Affairs of the
World Council of Churches - CCIA-WCC (D)
DATE OF PUBLICATION: 851200
NUMBER OF PAGES: 20 p.
LANGUAGE: ENG
INDEX: church and state / peace / fact-finding missions
GEOGRAPHICAL INDEX: Democratic People's Republic of Korea /
Republic of Korea
GEOGRAPHICAL CODE: 7121 / 7144
FREE TEXT: The CCIA organized a consultation on the situation of the
Korean peninsula, "Peace and justice in North-East Asia: prospects for
peaceful resolution of conflicts", which was held in Tozanso, near
Tokyo, from 29 October to 2 November 1984.
This document contains conclusions and recommendations of this
consultation, and the follow-up, including a visit to the Democratic
People's Republic of Korea, which is described in the report. The
reports contains also elements of an evaluation, principles for
ecumenical contact with the DPRK, ecumenical responsibilities of
churches in the United States and Canada and conclusions.

CATALOGUE SIGNATURE: 7000/2269/-3=860100
TITLE: Human rights in Korea
AUTHOR: DeWind, Adrian ; Palais, James ; Cumings, Bruce (...et al)
PLACE OF PUBLICATION: New York
PUBLISHER: Asia Watch Committee (D)
DATE OF PUBLICATION: 860100
NUMBER OF PAGES: 364 p.
LANGUAGE: ENG
BIBLIOGRAPHIES: Y
INDEX: civil and political rights / legislation /
fact-finding missions
GEOGRAPHICAL INDEX: Democratic People's Republic of Korea /
Republic of Korea
GEOGRAPHICAL CODE: 7121 / 7144
FREE TEXT: A delegation of Asia Watch visited the Republic of Korea in
June 1985 to investigate the human rights situation; permission to
visit the Democratic People's Republic of Korea was not obtained.
In the part on the Republic of Korea, special attention is paid to the
political and legal background and the elections of February 1985; the
position of students; labour, the position of workers and trade unions
(including case studies); and freedom of expression (including freedom
of religion and treatment of political prisoners). With conclusion and
analysis of the foreign policy of the United States.
The part on the Democratic People's Republic of Korea is based on desk
research; attention is paid to the political system and the situation
of political and civil rights. With conclusion.

EAST TIMOR / INDONESIA

CATALOGUE SIGNATURE: 0000/1031/-3=841000
TITLE: A visit to East Timor: hunger: under Indonesia, Timor remains
a land of misery
AUTHOR: Nordland, Rod
TITLE OF GENERIC ITEM: IWGIA Document: East Timor: the struggle
continues
EDITION: no. 50
PLACE OF PUBLICATION: Copenhagen
PUBLISHER: International Work Group for Indigenous Affairs - IWGIA (D)
DATE OF PUBLICATION: 841000
NUMBER OF PAGES: p. 59-80
LANGUAGE: ENG
BIBLIOGRAPHIES: Y
INDEX: indigenous peoples / social and economic rights /
fact-finding missions
GEOGRAPHICAL INDEX: East Timor / Indonesia
GEOGRAPHICAL CODE: 7523 / 7526
FREE TEXT: Report of a visit in 1982 to East Timor, the former
Portuguese colony that was forcibly annexed by Indonesia in 1976.
Sometimes, the author met independently with clergy of the Roman
Catholic Church in the mostly Catholic province and with average
Timorese from many walks of life. The report contains a compilation
of findings during on-site visits and interviews. It is concluded
that the land is beset by widespread malnutrition and hunger, and
that the medical care is inadequate. Thousands of people are
political prisoners, hundreds of thousands have been relocated in a
policy to depopulate the countryside and deprive FRETILIN guerillas
of civilian support.

EAST TIMOR / PORTUGAL

CATALOGUE SIGNATURE: 7523/-0=770000
TITLE: The East Timor situation: report on talks with Timorese
refugees in Portugal
AUTHOR: Dunn, J.S.
PLACE OF PUBLICATION: (Australia)
PUBLISHER: Australian Catholic Relief and Community Aid Abroad (D)
DATE OF PUBLICATION: 770000
NUMBER OF PAGES: 17 p.
LANGUAGE: ENG
INDEX: refugees / military / armed violence / fact-finding missions
GEOGRAPHICAL INDEX: East Timor / Portugal
GEOGRAPHICAL CODE: 7523 / 8242
FREE TEXT: The report is based on the findings of a visit to Portugal
in January 1977. The purpose of the visit was to obtain information
on the plight of the Timorese refugee community in Portugal, and some
information about the humanitarian situation in East Timor itself.
The author also tried to obtain a clearer picture of what transpired
in East Timor after the Indonesian invasion of Dili on 7 December 1975.
The report contains information on the (depressing) living situations
of the refugees, their accounts of the situation in East Timor and the
killing and disappearance of Australian journalists in East Timor. With
conclusions.

ISRAEL / LEBANON

CATALOGUE SIGNATURE: 8000/1072/-0=820630
TITLE: Report on the Lebanese crisis = Rapport sur la crise libanaise
AUTHOR: Eekelen, W. van
PLACE OF PUBLICATION: Strasbourg
PUBLISHER: Council of Europe - CoE - Parliamentary Assembly (D)
DATE OF PUBLICATION: 820630
NUMBER OF PAGES: 8 p.
DOCUMENT SYMBOL: Doc. 4933
AVAILABILITY: X
LANGUAGE: ENG / FRE
INDEX: armed violence / peace / fact-finding missions
GEOGRAPHICAL INDEX: Israel / Lebanon
GEOGRAPHICAL CODE: 7329 / 7334
FREE TEXT: Report by the rapporteur of the Political Affairs Committee,
partly based on a visit to Israel by the sub-committee on the Middle
East from 18 to 20 May 1982. The report contains the draft resolution
presented by the Political Affairs Committee, an explanatory memorandum,
with as an appendix the conclusions of the visit to Israel. The
delegation had contacts with Israeli leaders; the report deals with
Israel's security, the search for peace, Palestinian autonomy,
relations with Saudi Arabia, the situation in the Lebanon, the status
of Jerusalem, the economy, and suggestions for the role of Europe.

CATALOGUE SIGNATURE: 0000/1192/-0=820700
TITLE: Report of special mission to assess relief needs in Lebanon:
July 1982
AUTHOR: Mendelsohn, Everett ; Essoyan, Catherine
PLACE OF PUBLICATION: Philadelphia
PUBLISHER: American Friends Service Committee - AFSC - International
Division Middle East Program (D)
DATE OF PUBLICATION: 820700
NUMBER OF PAGES: 19 p.
LANGUAGE: ENG
INDEX: development cooperation / armed conflict / fact-finding missions
GEOGRAPHICAL INDEX: Israel / Lebanon
GEOGRAPHICAL CODE: 7329 / 7334
FREE TEXT: In July 1982, one month after the Israeli invasion of
Lebanon, the AFSC sent the two person fact-finding mission to Lebanon.
The aim was to provide a first-hand report of what was happening, on
the ground of relief needs and of prospects for service in the
immediate future. The report contains descriptions of: the impact of
the Israeli invasion; emergency relief efforts and next steps in
relief and reconstruction; the position of the Palestinian minority
in Lebanon; the emerging political situation, with Israeli and
Palestinian responses. With conclusions with regard to the American
foreign policy towards the Middle East, and itinerary.

CATALOGUE SIGNATURE: 0000/1192/-0=820800
TITLE: Human rights and the IV Geneva Convention in Israeli-occupied
South Lebanon: an initial inquiry
AUTHOR: Fine, James
PLACE OF PUBLICATION: (Philadelphia)
PUBLISHER: (American Friends Service Committee - AFSC) (D)
DATE OF PUBLICATION: 820800
NUMBER OF PAGES: 12 p.
LANGUAGE: ENG
INDEX: detention / foreign occupation / fact-finding missions
GEOGRAPHICAL INDEX: Israel / Lebanon
GEOGRAPHICAL CODE: 7329 / 7334
FREE TEXT: The aim of the mission was to get an impression of the
general welfare and safety of Lebanese and Palestinian civilians in
Israeli-occupied South Lebanon, and to identify problems with
implications for their human rights. It also tried to ascertain to
what extent Israeli treatment of the general population and of those
under detention conformed with the standards required by the Fourth
Geneva Convention of 1949 Concerning the Protection of Civilians in
Time of War and other international agreements. Attention is paid to
the situation of Israeli occupation forces, the situation of the
civilian population and the different armed forces, the situation of
detained prisoners and the degree of conformity to the Fourth Geneva
Convention. With conclusion.

CATALOGUE SIGNATURE: 0000/0028/-0=830329
TITLE: Approches du Moyen-Orient: rapport de mission au Liban, en
Israel et en Cisjordanie
AUTHOR: Bourel, Élisabeth ; Toulat, Pierre
PLACE OF PUBLICATION: Paris
PUBLISHER: Commission Française Justice et Paix - CFJP (D)
DATE OF PUBLICATION: 830329
NUMBER OF PAGES: 34 p.
LANGUAGE: FRE
INDEX: political conflicts / fact-finding missions
GEOGRAPHICAL INDEX: Israel / Lebanon
GEOGRAPHICAL CODE: 7329 / 7334
FREE TEXT: Report of a mission to Lebanon, Israel and the Occupied
Territories from 6 to 18 January 1983.
In the section on Lebanon, attention is paid to the viewpoints of
different groups: religious authorities of the catholic maronite
community, orthodoxes, Jesuits, Franciscan Sisters, phalangists,
Palestinians; the main problems: Israel as seen from Lebanon, the
future of the Palestinians, the role of France, political
perspectives, negotiations. With conclusion.
In the section on Israel and the Occupied Territories, attention
is paid to the context of the problems, the Palestinians, the Arabs
in Israel. The report contains a description of meetings which took
place with various institutions and organizations. With future
perspectives and conclusions.

ISRAEL / OCCUPIED TERRITORIES

CATALOGUE SIGNATURE: 0000/1291/-3=780000
TITLE: Treatment of Palestinians in Israeli-occupied West Bank and
Gaza: report of the National Lawyers Guild 1977 Middle East delegation
AUTHOR: Greenfield, Marsha ; Hormachea, Nancy ; Jabara, Abdeen
(...et al)
PLACE OF PUBLICATION: New York
PUBLISHER: National Lawyers Guild - NLG (D)
DATE OF PUBLICATION: 780000
NUMBER OF PAGES: 159 p. in v.p.
ISBN: 0 9602188 1 5
LANGUAGE: ENG
STATISTICAL INFORMATION: Y
BIBLIOGRAPHIES: Y
INDEX: civil and political rights / self-determination/ detention /
fact-finding missions
GEOGRAPHICAL INDEX: Israel / Occupied Territories
GEOGRAPHICAL CODE: 7329 / 7354
FREE TEXT: A NLG delegation of ten members visited Lebanon, Jordan,
Israel, the West Bank and Gaza in July 1977 in order to explore the
situation of the Palestinian people and to investigate the allegations
of violation of their rights. The report deals exclusively with the
delegation's examination of the conditions of the Palestinian people
living under Israeli military occupation. It contains an introduction,
and chapters on:
-territorial deprivation (Israeli settlements, involuntary resettlement
of the Gaza population, refusal to permit return of Palestinians
displaced in 1967);
-suppression of efforts at self-determination (development of a
colonial economy, restrictions on local institutions, restrictions on
political activities);
-suppression of resistance (collective penalties, expulsion,
administrative detention);
-mistreatment of detainees (denial of procedural rights, prison
conditions, torture).
With conclusion and appendices: list of persons interviewed; petitions
by Palestinian mayors; Working Paper of Union of Jordanian Doctors;
resolutions of the National Lawyers Guild.

CATALOGUE SIGNATURE: 0000/1291/-0=780800
TITLE: Minority report of the National Lawyers Guild Middle East
delegation on treatment of Palestinians in Israeli occupied
territories
AUTHOR: Dickstein, Howard
PLACE OF PUBLICATION: (New York)
PUBLISHER: (National Lawyers Guild - NLG) (D)
DATE OF PUBLICATION: 780800
NUMBER OF PAGES: 28 p.
LANGUAGE: ENG
INDEX: civil and political rights / fact-finding missions
GEOGRAPHICAL INDEX: Israel / Occupied Territories
GEOGRAPHICAL CODE: 7329 / 7354
FREE TEXT: As the author did not agree with the contents of a second
draft of the report by the majority of members on mission to the
Middle East, he decided to visit Israel in order to obtain information
from sources not available in the United States, to interview persons
with specific information and to visit institutions not seen by the
delegation. His minority report contains a critique of the majority
report in general, and specific with regard to Israeli settlements,
resettlement of the Gaza population, return of Palestinians displaced
in 1967, restriction on local institutions, economic conditions in the
Occupied Territories, political activity, punishment for security
offenses, prison conditions, procedural rights, allegations of torture
(including an analysis of the methodology and credibility of the
findings as contained in the majority report and findings of other
organizations).

CATALOGUE SIGNATURE: 0000/0966/-0=790000
TITLE: Report of the mission sent by the Director-General to examine
the situation of workers of the Occupied Arab Territories
AUTHOR: Blanchard, Francis ; (Valticos, N.) ; (Rossilion, C.)
(...et al)
TITLE OF GENERIC ITEM: International Labour Conference 65th session
1979: report of the Director-General: appendices
PLACE OF PUBLICATION: Geneva
PUBLISHER: International Labour Office - ILO (D)
DATE OF PUBLICATION: 790000
NUMBER OF PAGES: p. 22-53
LANGUAGE: ENG
STATISTICAL INFORMATION: Y
BIBLIOGRAPHIES: Y
INDEX: labour / fact-finding missions
GEOGRAPHICAL INDEX: Israel / Occupied Territories
GEOGRAPHICAL CODE: 7329 / 7354
FREE TEXT: An ILO mission of three members visited Israel and the
occupied Arab territories in Palestine, the Golan and the Sinai from
25 February to 10 March 1979. The aim was to continue and intensify
the examination of the situation of Arab workers of these territories,
whether employed in the territories themselves or in Israel. Talks
were held with civil and military authorities, employers' and workers'
organizations, and other people from Israeli and from Palestinian
side.
The report contains an introduction, on general population and
employment data from the occupied Arab territories, and sections on
employment in Israel of Arab workers of the occupied Arab territories
and employment in these territories. The report is focused on the
various aspects of equality of opportunity and treatment as regards
employment, conditions of work and social benefits and trade union
activities.

CATALOGUE SIGNATURE: 0000/0966/-0=800000
TITLE: Report on the situation of workers of the occupied Arab
territories
AUTHOR: Blanchard, Francis
TITLE OF GENERIC ITEM: International Labour Conference 66th session
1980: report of the Director-General: appendices
PLACE OF PUBLICATION: Geneva
PUBLISHER: International Labour Office - ILO (D)
DATE OF PUBLICATION: 800000
NUMBER OF PAGES: p. 131-158
ISBN: 92 2 102084 3
LANGUAGE: ENG
STATISTICAL INFORMATION: Y
BIBLIOGRAPHIES: Y
INDEX: work (right to) / labour / fact-finding missions
GEOGRAPHICAL INDEX: Israel / Occupied Territories
GEOGRAPHICAL CODE: 7329 / 7354
FREE TEXT: On the basis of information received from the governments
of Israel, Jordan and the Syrian Arab Republic and from the PLO, a
two member delegation was sent to Israel and the occupied territories
in March 1980. The aims of the mission were to complete and bring up
to date their information, and to examine on the spot the situation
of the workers concerned in general, and more especially the measures
taken in the field covered by ILO recommendations.
The report begins with a general outline of economic and social
developments, followed by a consideration of the points on which
recommendations were made in the 1979 report (the campaign against
"irregular" employment of Arab workers from the occupied territories;
employment conditions; enhancement of the occupational status; social
security; working conditions and cultural identity; trade union
rights; legislation for equality of opportunity and treatment;
vocational training; employment and development; labour regulations
and medical care; settlements in occupied Arab territories. With
conclusions.

CATALOGUE SIGNATURE: 0000/0001/-4
TITLE: The Middle East: report of a visit to Israel & the Occupied
Territories
AUTHOR: Wiseberg, Laurie S.
TITLE OF GENERIC ITEM: Human Rights Internet Newsletter
EDITION: v. 5(8-9)
PLACE OF PUBLICATION: Washington DC
PUBLISHER: Human Rights Internet - HRI (D)
DATE OF PUBLICATION: 800700
NUMBER OF PAGES: p.77-80
LANGUAGE: ENG
INDEX: nongovernmental organizations / fact-finding missions
GEOGRAPHICAL INDEX: Israel / Occupied Territories
GEOGRAPHICAL CODE: 7329 / 7354
FREE TEXT: The author visited Israel and made brief trips to East
Jerusalem and Ramallah from 25 April to 2 May 1980. The purpose of the
trip was not to assess the human rights situation, but to learn about,
and make contact with, organizations in the region actively concerned
about human rights. Her report contains background information on
Israel, and a description of activities of human rights organizations
like the Israel Civil Rights Association, the Nazareth Society for the
Support of the Political Prisoner, and Law in the Service of Man.

CATALOGUE SIGNATURE: 0000/0138/-3=800000
TITLE: Mission to the territories occupied by Israel: 13-20 October
1980: introductory report and legal conclusions
AUTHOR: Chemillier-Gendreau, Monique ; Ferrucci, Romeo ; MacCartan,
Patrick
PLACE OF PUBLICATION: Brussels
PUBLISHER: Association Internationale des Juristes Démocrates - IADL (D)
DATE OF PUBLICATION: 800000
NUMBER OF PAGES: 53 p.
LANGUAGE: ENG
INDEX: legislation / international law / self-determination /
fact-finding missions
GEOGRAPHICAL INDEX: Israel / Occupied Territories
GEOGRAPHICAL CODE: 7329 / 7354
FREE TEXT: The report gives a detailed description of the life in the
occupied territory of the West Bank. Attention is paid to civil and
democratic life, and social and cultural life. The part on "legal
conclusions" provides an analysis of the situation as a whole in the
light of present-day international law, based on various written and
documentary information. The delegation concludes that the argument
that Israel is administering the occupied territories does not take
account of the facts as they exist; it is stated that the presence of
the military is in the pursuit of the expansionist policies of zionism.
The task of the Israeli armed forces is the systematic harassment and
disruption of Palestinian life. With appendices: military orders;
correspondence of authorities.

CATALOGUE SIGNATURE: 0000/0966/-0=820000
TITLE: Report on the situation of workers of the occupied Arab
territories
AUTHOR: Blanchard, Francis ; (Béguin, A.)
TITLE OF GENERIC ITEM: International Labour Conference 68th session
1982: report of the Director-General: appendices
PLACE OF PUBLICATION: Geneva
PUBLISHER: International Labour Office - ILO (D)
DATE OF PUBLICATION: 820000
NUMBER OF PAGES: p. 107-133
ISBN: 92 2 102783 X
LANGUAGE: ENG
STATISTICAL INFORMATION: Y
BIBLIOGRAPHIES: Y
INDEX: work (right to) / trade unions / labour / fact-finding missions
GEOGRAPHICAL INDEX: Israel / Occupied Territories
GEOGRAPHICAL CODE: 7329 / 7354
FREE TEXT: In November-December 1981, consultations were held with
authorities, employers' and workers' organizations in the Syrian Arab
Republic and Jordan, and with Palestine bodies. The government of Egypt
was consulted in February 1982. From 9 to 18 February, a three member
delegation visited Israel and the occupied Arab territories, and had
contacts with Israeli and Palestinian authorities, and representatives
of various organizations. The report deals with the general employment
and development situation, implications of Israeli settlements,
vocational training, trade union rights, and other questions relating
to the regulation of employment, medical care and problems of cultural
identity. Attention is also paid to the employment in Israel of workers
from the occupied Arab territories and to technical cooperation.

CATALOGUE SIGNATURE: 0000/0138/-3=820000
TITLE: Mission dans les territoires occupés par Israel: 22-28 mai
1982
AUTHOR: David, Eric ; De Brie, Christian ; Schaller, Rudolf
PLACE OF PUBLICATION: Brussels
PUBLISHER: Association Internationale des Juristes Démocrates - IADL (D)
DATE OF PUBLICATION: 820000
NUMBER OF PAGES: 54 p.
LANGUAGE: FRE
INDEX: arrest / civil and political rights / fact-finding missions
GEOGRAPHICAL INDEX: Israel / Occupied Territories
GEOGRAPHICAL CODE: 7329 / 7354
FREE TEXT: The aim of the mission was to investigate the actual
situation of persons and properties in view of the Israeli occupation
and the measures adopted by the Begin government during the last six
months. The report begins with a chronological list of events between
November 1980 and May 1982. The facts established by the mission are
analyzed in the framework of international law applicable, especially
humanitarian law and the international instruments for the protection
of human rights. The situation in Cisjordania is described in detail,
with attention to the situation of specific human rights. The situation
in Golan is described in short. With general conclusions and annex:
testimonies on arrests.

CATALOGUE SIGNATURE: 0000/0966/-0=830000
TITLE: Report on the situation of workers of the occupied Arab
territories
AUTHOR: Blanchard, Francis ; (Lagergren, Ian)
TITLE OF GENERIC ITEM: International Labour Conference 69th session
1983: report of the Director-General: appendices
PLACE OF PUBLICATION: Geneva
PUBLISHER: International Labour Office - ILO (D)
DATE OF PUBLICATION: 830000
NUMBER OF PAGES: p. 15-50
ISBN: 92 2 103122 5
LANGUAGE: ENC
STATISTICAL INFORMATION: Y
BIBLIOGRAPHIES: Y
INDEX: labour / work (right to) / fact-finding missions
GEOGRAPHICAL INDEX: Israel / Occupied Territories
GEOGRAPHICAL CODE: 7329 / 7354
FREE TEXT: In order to prepare the report, an ILO delegation was
firstly sent to Jordan and the Syrian Arab Republic and subsequently to
Egypt, to hold consultations with authorities, employers' and workers'
organizations, and Palestinian bodies. A three member mission visited
Israel and the occupied territories in March 1983, and had contacts
with Israeli and Palestinian authorities, and employers' and workers'
organizations.
The report deals with the specific context (the state of occupation
and establishment of settlements) in which the problems of Arab workers
in the occupied territories have to be examined. Next, attention is
paid to population, manpower and employment; the situation of workers
employed in Israel, including recommendations; economic and social
conditions, employment, vocational training and trade union rights in
the occupied Arab territories, including recommendations; technical
assistance.

CATALOGUE SIGNATURE: 0000/0966/-0=840000
TITLE: Report on the situation of workers of the occupied Arab
territories
AUTHOR: Blanchard, Francis ; (Arlès, J.P.) ; (Minet, J.P.)
TITLE OF GENERIC ITEM: International Labour Conference 70th session
1984: report of the Director-General: appendices
PLACE OF PUBLICATION: Geneva
PUBLISHER: International Labour Office - ILO (D)
DATE OF PUBLICATION: 840000
NUMBER OF PAGES: p. 17-51
ISBN: 92 2 103434 8
LANGUAGE: ENG
STATISTICAL INFORMATION: Y
BIBLIOGRAPHIES: Y
INDEX: labour / work (right to) / fact-finding missions
GEOGRAPHICAL INDEX: Israel / Occupied Territories
GEOGRAPHICAL CODE: 7329 / 7354
FREE TEXT: Firstly, a mission visited the Syrian Arab Republic and
Jordan to hold consultations with the governmental, employers' and
workers' circles; subsequently, consultations took place in Egypt.
The mission to Israel and the occupied Arab territories took place from
23 February to 4 March 1984; contacts were made with the authorities,
employers' and workers' associations. The report deals with the state
of occupation and establishment of settlements, manpower and employment
in the occupied territories, vocational training, trade union rights,
labour regulations and medical care and technical assistance to the
population. Special attention is paid to the employment in Israel of
Arab workers from the occupied territories (irregular employment,
employment and labour conditions, the right to social security, the
trade union situation. With review of main recommendations.

146

CATALOGUE SIGNATURE: 0000/0088-3=841100
TITLE: Academic freedom under Israeli military occupation: report
of WUS/ICJ mission of enquiry into higher education in the West
Bank and Gaza
AUTHOR: Roberts, Adam ; Joergensen, Boel ; Newman, Frank
PLACE OF PUBLICATION: London ; Geneva
PUBLISHER: World University Service - WUS-UK (D) ; International
Commission of Jurists - ICJ (D)
DATE OF PUBLICATION: 841100
NUMBER OF PAGES: 87 p.
ISBN: 0 906405 20 3
LANGUAGE: ENG
BIBLIOGRAPHIES: Y
INDEX: academic freedom / political conflict / fact-finding missions
GEOGRAPHICAL INDEX: Israel / Occupied Territories
GEOGRAPHICAL CODE: 7329 / 7354
FREE TEXT: In late 1983, World University Service UK and the ICJ sent
a mission of enquiry to investigate academic freedom in the Israeli
occupied territories of the West Bank and the Gaza Strip, with
particular reference to higher education.
The report is divided into the following parts: I) Terms of reference
of the mission; II) Basic facts and figures (map, population figures,
checklist of the six principal institutions; III) An approach to the
problems; IV) The Occupied Territories: historical and legal framework;
V) A view of the universities; VI) The problems regarding academic
freedom; VII) Conclusions and recommendations.
In the appendices: Israeli legal statement, and select list of sources.

CATALOGUE SIGNATURE: 0000/0138/-3=841000
TITLE: Territories occupied by Israel (West Bank): IADL mission of
inquiry: International Standing Committee of Lawyers on Palestine
and Peace in the Middle East = Territorios occupados por Israel:
Cisjordania: misión de encuesta de la AIJD (Comité Permanente
Internacional de Juristas sobre la Palestina y la Paz en el Medio
Oriente)
AUTHOR: Schaller, Rudolf ; Charvin, Robert
PLACE OF PUBLICATION: Brussels
PUBLISHER: International Association of Democratic Lawyers - IADL (D)
DATE OF PUBLICATION: 841000
NUMBER OF PAGES: 26 p.
LANGUAGE: ENG / SPA
BIBLIOGRAPHIES: Y
INDEX: self-determination / fact-finding missions
GEOGRAPHICAL INDEX: Israel / Occupied Territories
GEOGRAPHICAL CODE: 7329 / 7354
FREE TEXT: The delegation spent the week from 8 to 15 October 1984 in
East Jerusalem and the West Bank territories. The report contains
chapters dealing with: the international law applicable in the occupied
territories; the law in force inside the occupied territories; the
infringements of the right to ownership and the denial of the right to
development; the systematic attempt to liquidate a nation; the direct
repression exerted against national opposition forces.

147

CATALOGUE SIGNATURE: 0000/0494/-0=850000
TITLE: Journalism and the press in the Arab Territories occupied by
Israel: report of a factfinding mission... = Les journalistes et la
presse dans les territoires occupès par Israel: rapport de la mission
d'enquête...
AUTHOR: Doornaert, Mia ; Moe, Trygve ; Larsen, Hans
TITLE OF GENERIC ITEM: IFJ Information = IFJ Informations
EDITION: v.34(1984-1985)
PLACE OF PUBLICATION: Brussels
PUBLISHER: International Federation of Journalists - IFJ (D)
DATE OF PUBLICATION: 850000
NUMBER OF PAGES: p. 3-36
LANGUAGE: ENG / FRE
INDEX: journalists / press (freedom of the) / censorship /
fact-finding missions
GEOGRAPHICAL INDEX: Israel / Occupied Territories
GEOGRAPHICAL CODE: 7329 / 7354
FREE TEXT: The IFJ mission visited Israel and the Occupied Territories
from 26 August to 2 September 1984. After an introduction about the
purpose of the mission, the report is divided into the following parts:
I) the Palestinian press in the Occupied Territories; II) the legal
system; III) interviews with Israeli authorities, and Palestinian
journalists and editors of newspapers; IV) conclusions.
With appendices: statement by Arab Journalists' Association; statistics
sheet used by weekly Al Fajr English to keep record of censored items,
and example of published breakdown of findings; censored article (in Al
Fajr English) on the visit by the IFJ fact-finding mission; list of
examples of articles censored.

CATALOGUE SIGNATURE: 0000/0966/-0=850000
TITLE: Report on the situation of workers of the occupied Arab
territories
AUTHOR: Blanchard, Francis ; (Rossilion, Claude) ; (Minet, Georges)
(...et al)
TITLE OF GENERIC ITEM: International Labour Conference 71st session
1985: report of the Director-General: appendices
PLACE OF PUBLICATION: Geneva
PUBLISHER: International Labour Office - ILO (D)
DATE OF PUBLICATION: 850000
NUMBER OF PAGES: p.23-60
ISBN: 92 2 103720 7
LANGUAGE: ENG
STATISTICAL INFORMATION: Y
BIBLIOGRAPHIES: Y
INDEX: labour / work (right to) / fact-finding missions
GEOGRAPHICAL INDEX: Israel / Occupied Territories
GEOGRAPHICAL CODE: 7329 / 7354
FREE TEXT: The three-member mission to Israel and the occupied Arab
territories took place from 2 to 12 March. The delegation had talks
with the Israeli authorities, employers' and workers' organizations,
and Palestinian authorities and trade unions. As in previous years,
a mission had first been undertaken to the Syrian Arab Republic,
Jordan and Tunis, to hold consultations with authorities, employers'
and workers' organizations, trade union federations and the PLO.
During a subsequent visit to Cairo, consultations were held with
Egyptian authorities.
The mission examined the situation of Arab workers living on the West
Bank (including East Jerusalem), in Gaza and in the Golan. The report
deals with the impact of settlements on the occupied Arab territories;
employment in the occupied territories; vocational training; wages,
conditions of work and welfare benefits; trade union rights; the
employment in Israel of Arab workers from the occupied territories
(irregular employment, employment and labour conditions, social
security, the trade union situation and technical assistance to the
population. With review of main recommendations.

CATALOGUE SIGNATURE: 0000/0966/-0=860000
TITLE: Report on the situation of workers of the occupied Arab
territories
AUTHOR: Blanchard, Francis
TITLE OF GENERIC ITEM: International Labour Conference 72nd session
1986: report of the Director-General: appendices
PLACE OF PUBLICATION: Geneva
PUBLISHER: International Labour Office - ILO (D)
DATE OF PUBLICATION: 860000
NUMBER OF PAGES: p.17-72
ISBN: 92 2 105186 2
LANGUAGE: ENG
STATISTICAL INFORMATION: Y
BIBLIOGRAPHIES: Y
INDEX: labour / trade unions / fact-finding missions
GEOGRAPHICAL INDEX: Israel / Occupied Territories
GEOGRAPHICAL CODE: 7329 / 7354
FREE TEXT: In January 1986, the Director-General sent two ILO officials
to the Syrian Arab Republic and Jordan, to hold consultations with the
authorities and employers' and workers' organizations, trade union
federations and the PLO. Consultations with the Egyptian authorities
were held during a subsequent visit to Cairo. A mission composed of
three ILO officials visited Israel and the Palestine territories from
8 to 18 February 1986. Talks were held with employers' and workers'
organizations, Israeli and Palestinian authorities. The report provides
an account of the information gathered and the observations made by the
last mission. It contains sections on the programme of the mission, the
overall employment and development situation, conditions of work and
welfare benefits and the situation of trade unions.
With appendices: technical cooperation to assists the population in the
occupied Arab territories during the period 1985-1986; a compendium of
documentation received from Arab countries and organizations visited
in January; communications received from the Israeli government.

ISRAEL / SYRIAN ARAB REPUBLIC

CATALOGUE SIGNATURE: 0000/0249/-3=750400
TITLE: Report of an Amnesty International mission to Israel and the
Syrian Arabic Republic to investigate allegations of ill-treatment and
torture: 10-24 October 1974
AUTHOR: (Eide, Asbjørn) ; (Nobel, Peter) ; (Vuuren, Kees van)
PLACE OF PUBLICATION: London
PUBLISHER: Amnesty International - AI (D)
DATE OF PUBLICATION: 750400
NUMBER OF PAGES: 34 p.
ISBN: 0 900058 06 4
DOCUMENT SYMBOL: AI Index: PUB 35/00/75
LANGUAGE: ENG
INDEX: torture / detention / fact-finding missions
GEOGRAPHICAL INDEX: Israel / Syrian Arab Republic
GEOGRAPHICAL CODE: 7329 / 7348
FREE TEXT: In the context of its Campaign for the Abolition of Torture,
AI decided to send a mission to Israel and Syria, to investigate
allegations of ill-treatment and torture during 1973-1974, arising out
of the October 1973 war in the Middle East.
The report contains an introduction, information on the activities of
the mission, and sections on problems of investigation with regard to
prisoners of war and civilian (political) prisoners; problems of
evidence; case histories of Israeli prisoners of war in Syria and of
Syrian prisoners of war in Israel; the application of safeguards;
conclusions and recommendations. The consistency of many of the
testimonies received and corroboration with the findings of the medical
examination leave little doubt that abuses have been committed by both
parties concerned.

MIDDLE EAST

CATALOGUE SIGNATURE: 7300/-0=811000
TITLE: The path to peace: Arab-Israeli peace and the United States:
report of a study mission to the Middle East
AUTHOR: Greene, Joseph N.; Klutznick, Philip M.; Saunders, Harold H.
(...et al.)
PLACE OF PUBLICATION: Mount Cisco (New York)
PUBLISHER: Seven Springs Center (D)
DATE OF PUBLICATION: 811000
NUMBER OF PAGES: 50 p.
LANGUAGE: ENG
INDEX: peace / fact-finding missions
GEOGRAPHICAL INDEX: Middle East
GEOGRAPHICAL CODE: 7300
FREE TEXT: In August 1981, a four-member private study group traveled
to the Middle East to re-examine the prospects for a negotiated Arab-
Israeli peace. The delegation hoped to sharpen its understanding of
what the process of making peace requires. It visited Israel, the
West Bank, Jordan, Syria, Saudi Arabia, and Egypt. The report consists
of a summary with principal conclusions and reflections on the choices
to be made if the Arab - Israeli peace process is to move forward, and
separate chapters with background information and findings on the
different areas visited: Israel, the Palestinians, Saudi Arabia,
Jordan, Syria, Egypt and Jerusalem. With recommendations, and some
information on the members of the mission.

CATALOGUE SIGNATURE: 0000/0427/-3=820600
TITLE: Towards understanding the Arab-Israeli conflict: the report
of a British Council of Churches delegation to the Middle East
AUTHOR: Bleakley, David W. ; Habgood, John S. ; Hopkins, Gillian E.
(... et al)
PLACE OF PUBLICATION: London
PUBLISHER: British Council of Churches - BCC (D)
DATE OF PUBLICATION: 820600
NUMBER OF PAGES: 130 p.
LANGUAGE: ENG
INDEX: church and state / peace / fact-finding missions
GEOGRAPHICAL INDEX: Middle East
GEOGRAPHICAL CODE: 7300
FREE TEXT: A group of seven representatives appointed by the British
Council of Churches held a goodwill and fact-finding tour in the Middle
East from 7 to 26 September 1981. They visited Lebanon, Syria, Jordan,
Israel, the West Bank, Gaza and Egypt, and were received by Church
leaders of the Christian and Islamic communities and political leaders.
The report consists of a detailed travel diary, a detailed evaluation
of findings with regard to the political and religious situation, and
recommendations accepted by the BCC Assembly. With appendices: maps,
resolutions of the United Nations, statements.

152

CATALOGUE SIGNATURE: 0000/0035/-3=820000
TITLE: Rapport de mission du 26 août au 7 septembre 1982 en
Cisjordanie, Gaza, Israel et Liban
AUTHOR: Coche, Serge ; Tubiana, Michel
PLACE OF PUBLICATION: Paris
PUBLISHER: Fédération Internationale des Droits de l'Homme - FIDH (D) ;
Ligue Française pour la Défense des Droits de l'Homme et du Citoyen (D)
DATE OF PUBLICATION: 820000
NUMBER OF PAGES: 68 p.
LANGUAGE: FRE
INDEX: fact-finding missions
GEOGRAPHICAL INDEX: Middle East
GEOGRAPHICAL CODE: 7300
FREE TEXT: The purpose of the mission was to investigate the general
human rights situation of the Israeli, Libanese and Palestinian people
in Cisjordania, Gaza, Golan, Israel, Jordania and Syria. The report
contains a description of preparations made for the mission, and a day-
to-day account of the activities and findings of the team. Attention is
paid to refugees, detained persons, applicable legislation, the judicial
system, civil and political rights and social and economic rights. With
conclusions and annexes: correspondence with embassies of the countries
concerned.

AUSTRIA

CATALOGUE SIGNATURE: 0000/2242/-3=850300
TITLE: Gemeinsam oder getrennt?: die Situation der slowenischen
Minderheit in Karnten am Beispiel der Schulfrage: Bericht einer
internationalen Beobachterkommission
AUTHOR: Bommer, Heiner van ; Heinhold-Klichowski, Kristina ;
Meyer, Michelle (...et al)
PLACE OF PUBLICATION: Basle
PUBLISHER: European Committee for the Defence of Refugees and
Immigrants - CEDRI (D)
DATE OF PUBLICATION: 850300
NUMBER OF PAGES: 98 p.
LANGUAGE: GER
BIBLIOGRAPHIES: Y
INDEX: minorities / education / fact-finding missions
GEOGRAPHICAL INDEX: Austria
GEOGRAPHICAL CODE: 8213
FREE TEXT: In the Austrian republic of Karinthia lives a minority of
Slovenian speaking people which has been strongly persecuted during the
Second World War. The desire is expressed in German-nationalist circles
that the education of German and Slovenian children should be separated.
An international delegation on behalf of CEDRI visited Karinthia in
September 1984 to investigate especially the pedagogical and legal
aspects of this problem, and the discrimination of a group because of
its language and ethnic origins.
The report contains a description of a visit to a bilingual school, the
educational system in Karinthia, the school as a means of assimilation
or a guarantee of bilinguality, the call for segregation, the minority
school question against the political background of Karinthia.
With conclusions, press release, newspaper articles, letter to the
Head of State and resolution of nongovernmental organizations with
consultative status in the Council of Europe.

BULGARIA

CATALOGUE SIGNATURE: 0000/1245/-3=860600
TITLE: Destroying ethnic identity: the Turks of Bulgaria
AUTHOR: Laber, Jeri
PLACE OF PUBLICATION: New York
PUBLISHER: Helsinki Watch - HW (D)
DATE OF PUBLICATION: 860600
NUMBER OF PAGES: 39 p.
LANGUAGE: ENG
BIBLIOGRAPHIES: Y
INDEX: minorities / fact-finding missions
GEOGRAPHICAL INDEX: Bulgaria
GEOGRAPHICAL CODE: 8115
FREE TEXT: The author was not allowed to investigate the situation of
ethnic Turks in Bulgaria, but managed to obtain direct evidence during
a visit to Istanbul in December 1985. Chapter I of her report contains
summaries of the oral testimonies obtained during interviews made in
Istanbul; Chapter II summarizes the documentary evidence available to
Helsinki Watch concerning the name-changing campaign (the official
version, the evidence, destroying the Turkish national identity, anti-
Moslem campaign, and day-to-day discrimination); Chapter III examines
documents on the subject that have been submitted to the United
Nations.
With appendices: 1) Some prisoners on Belene Island; 2) Petition to
change one's name; 3) Citation for speaking Turkish; 4) Declaration
against circumcision; 5) Some media reports on the campaign by the
Bulgarian Government to assimilate its ethnic Turkish minority.

CYPRUS

CATALOGUE SIGNATURE: 0000/0088/-0=740000
TITLE: Report ... on a visit to Cyprus from 22 to 29 August to
enquire into the situation regarding the rule of law in Cyprus, and
in particular the abduction of the Minister of Justice, and numerous
allegations of ill-treatment of detained persons
AUTHOR: Garrett, Geoffrey
PLACE OF PUBLICATION: Geneva
PUBLISHER: International Commission of Jurists - ICJ (D)
DATE OF PUBLICATION: 740000
NUMBER OF PAGES: 12 p.
LANGUAGE: ENG
INDEX: detention / political violence / fact-finding missions
GEOGRAPHICAL INDEX: Cyprus
GEOGRAPHICAL CODE: 8218
FREE TEXT: Report on the situation in Cyprus, with attention to the
background of the country, the use of violence for political ends,
brutal violence by para-military auxiliary police forces, lack of
official initiative in respect of complaints of malpractices,
weaknesses in the legislation, physical and economic intimidation
and interference with the freedom of the press. With conclusions
and recommendations.

CATALOGUE SIGNATURE: 0000/0035/-3=750000
TITLE: Mission à Chypre du 16 au 20 juillet 1975: rapport à la
Fédération Internationale des Droits de l'Homme sur la situation des
droits de l'homme
AUTHOR: Aisenstein, Leopold
PLACE OF PUBLICATION: Paris
PUBLISHER: Fédération Internationale des Droits de l'Homme - FIDH (D)
DATE OF PUBLICATION: 750000
NUMBER OF PAGES: 25 p.
LANGUAGE: FRE
INDEX: refugees / ethnic conflict / minorities / fact-finding missions
GEOGRAPHICAL INDEX: Cyprus
GEOGRAPHICAL CODE: 8218
FREE TEXT: The purpose of the four member mission was to receive
information on the situation of refugees and political prisoners, and
on the general human rights situation. With attention to background
of the country, tensions between the Greek and Turkish populations
and the situation of minorities in both zones. After the invasion of
the Turkish army in the North in July-August 1974, Greeks were treated
badly; about 150.000 people were deplaced, many were deprivated.
With conclusions.

CZECHOSLOVAKIA

CATALOGUE SIGNATURE: 0000/0249/-3=800115
TITLE: Trials of members of the Committee for the Defence of the
Unjustly Persecuted (VONS) in Czechoslovakia
AUTHOR: (Goldman, Henry)
PLACE OF PUBLICATION: London
PUBLISHER: Amnesty International - AI (D)
DATE OF PUBLICATION: 800115
NUMBER OF PAGES: 13 p.
DOCUMENT SYMBOL: AI Index: EUR 16/04/80
LANGUAGE: ENG
INDEX: expression (freedom of) / trials / fact-finding missions
GEOGRAPHICAL INDEX: Czechoslovakia
GEOGRAPHICAL CODE: 8119
FREE TEXT: The trial of six members of the VONS took place on 22 and
23 October 1979. The report is based on the text of the indictment,
the transcript of the trial reconstructed from memory by members of
the accused's families who were present at the trial, the text of the
verdict and information provided by the observer. Goldman was denied
admission to the court room, but was able to interview members of the
families who were present at the trial and others. Attention is given
to the indictment, the examination of the accused, closing speeches of
the prosecutor, the defence lawyers and the accused, the verdict,
international response to the trial and the appeal hearing. With
assessment, short information on other trials and AI actions at
international level.

CATALOGUE SIGNATURE: 0000/2242/-3=830700
TITLE: Political asylum in West Germany: law and practice = La
situation du droit d'asile en Allemagne Federale
AUTHOR: Brodal, Sissel ; Busch, Nicholas ; Goldschmied, Hans
(...et al)
PLACE OF PUBLICATION: Basel
PUBLISHER: European Committee for the Defence of Refugees and
Immigrants - CEDRI (D)
DATE OF PUBLICATION: 830700
NUMBER OF PAGES: 63 p.
LANGUAGE: ENG / FRE
INDEX: asylum / refugees / fact-finding missions
GEOGRAPHICAL INDEX: FRG
GEOGRAPHICAL CODE: 8225
FREE TEXT: The purpose of the mission in November 1982 was to obtain
information on the treatment of people seeking policital asylum, in
view of the fact that the German government had been criticised,
sometimes sharply, by humanitarian and church organizations. The
delegation consisted of eleven members.
In the report, attention is paid to the German policy of asylum and
its economic and political background; recent developments in the
practice of asylum; the policy of deterrence in practice:
observations of the delegation in Bavaria and Baden-Wurttemberg.
With conclusions and annexes.

GERMAN DEMOCRATIC REPUBLIC

CATALOGUE SIGNATURE: 0000/0249/-3=810402
TITLE: Observation of the trial of Reiner Hoefer, a prisoner of
conscience in the German Democratic Republic (GDR)
AUTHOR: (Frisch, Alfred)
PLACE OF PUBLICATION: London
PUBLISHER: Amnesty International - AI (D)
DATE OF PUBLICATION: 810402
NUMBER OF PAGES: 3 p.
DOCUMENT SYMBOL: AI Index: EUR 22/05/81
LANGUAGE: ENG
INDEX: political prisoners / opinion (freedom of) / trials /
fact-finding missions
GEOGRAPHICAL INDEX: German Democratic Republic
GEOGRAPHICAL CODE: 8124
FREE TEXT: The accused sent letters to the Chairman of the State
Council, Mr Honecker, in which he criticized a number of aspects of
the economic and political system of the country. He was accused of
"incitement hostile to the state". His trial took place on 15 November
1979 in the regional court in Erfurt. The report contains a description
of the trial proceedings. The observer was allowed to explain his
position in the courtroom. Afterwards, the court decided that the
public, including the observer, would be excluded from the trial.

GREECE

CATALOGUE SIGNATURE: 0000/1291/-0=700700
TITLE: Report of Greek military trial: July 6-8, 1970
AUTHOR: Goodman, Ernest
PLACE OF PUBLICATION: (New York)
PUBLISHER: (National Lawyers Guild - NLG) (D)
DATE OF PUBLICATION: 700700
NUMBER OF PAGES: 11 p. in v.p.
LANGUAGE: ENG
INDEX: trials / fact-finding missions
GEOGRAPHICAL INDEX: Greece
GEOGRAPHICAL CODE: 8227
FREE TEXT: Ernest Goodman, attorney of Detroit, was requested by
American friends of Nick Kaloudis, who had once been resident of the
United States, to attend a military trial at Athens, beginning on
July 6, 1970, before a military court where Kaloudis and ten other
defendants were charged with conspiracy to overthrow the social order
of Greece by force. His report contains a detailed description of the
hearings. An appendix contains a copy of an article in The Nation of
October 19, 1970, in which the report was published in full.

CATALOGUE SIGNATURE: 0000/0088/-3=730000
TITLE: Report of an international commission of inquiry into the
detention of... practicing Greek lawyers arrested without warrant by
military police and being held incommunicando at a military prison
in Athens without charges on bail since March 3, 1973
AUTHOR: Abram, Morris B. ; Butler, William J. ; Humphrey, John P.
PLACE OF PUBLICATION: Geneva
PUBLISHER: International Commission of Jurists - ICJ (D) ;
International League for the Rights of Man - FIDH (D) ;
International Law Section, American Bar Association - ABA ;
Association of the Bar of the City of New York - ABNY (D)
DATE OF PUBLICATION: 730000
NUMBER OF PAGES: 32 p.
LANGUAGE: ENG
INDEX: detention / martial law / fact-finding missions
GEOGRAPHICAL INDEX: Greece
GEOGRAPHICAL CODE: 8227
FREE TEXT: Report of a mission in April 1973 to investigate into the
detention of six practicing lawyers arrested without warrant by
military police and being held incommunicando since 3 March 1973.
The report contains a chronology of events during the mission,
background and description of facts (historical, position of the Greek
government, arrest and detention), report of meetings with embassy of
the United States and the Athens Bar Association, general comment on
applicable Greek martial and constitutional law since the coup of
1968, erosion of the judiciary. With conclusions and recommendations.

HUNGARY

CATALOGUE SIGNATURE: 0000/0966/-3=840000
TITLE: The trade union situation and industrial relations in Hungary:
report of an ILO mission
AUTHOR: Lagergren, Ian ; Schregle, Johannes ; Monat, Jacques
(...et al)
PLACE OF PUBLICATION: Geneva
PUBLISHER: International Labour Office - ILO (D)
DATE OF PUBLICATION: 840000
NUMBER OF PAGES: 100 p.
ISBN: 92 2 103894 7
LANGUAGE: ENG
INDEX: association (freedom of) / trade unions / fact-finding missions
GEOGRAPHICAL INDEX: Hungary
GEOGRAPHICAL CODE: 8129
FREE TEXT: Report based on a fact-finding mission in October-November
1982, to study the trade union situation and the industrial relations
system. Contacts were established with government representatives, the
trade union movement, the management of enterprises, the political
party and research institutes; visits were paid to industrial and
agricultural enterprises. The report contains chapters on the
background of the country, trade union organization, organizations of
heads of enterprises, the fixing of renumeration, labour relations
within the enterprise, disputes, final remarks. With appendices
containing discussion on the report: report of a meeting of the
Working Party on the Trade Union Situation and Labour Relations
Systems in European Countries; extracts of minutes of the 225th
Session of the Governing Body.

CATALOGUE SIGNATURE: 0000/0035/-3=840000
TITLE: Rapport de mission en Hongrie: procès Demszky Gabor: 22 mai 1984
AUTHOR: Coche, Serge
PLACE OF PUBLICATION: Paris
PUBLISHER: Fédération Internationale des Droits de l'Homme - FIDH (D)
DATE OF PUBLICATION: 840000
NUMBER OF PAGES: 15 p.
LANGUAGE: FRE
INDEX: trials / fact-finding missions
GEOGRAPHICAL INDEX: Hungary
GEOGRAPHICAL CODE: 8129
FREE TEXT: The author assisted as legal observer in a trial at the Court of Buda against Gabor Demszky, accused of violence against policemen. With: description of procedures; the background and position of the accused, an intellectual who published illegally; description of the hearings. With conclusion and appendices: mandate; correspondence.
The observer could assist at the trial without difficulties. He concludes that the procedures were very strict, and the political character of the trial was rejected by the Court. Publicity on the debates was controlled.

IRELAND

CATALOGUE SIGNATURE: 0000/0249/-3=771229
TITLE: Report of an Amnesty International mission to the Republic of
Ireland in June 1977
AUTHOR: (Korff, Douwe) ; (Wright, Angela)
PLACE OF PUBLICATION: London
PUBLISHER: Amnesty International - AI (D)
DATE OF PUBLICATION: 771229
NUMBER OF PAGES: 10 p.
DOCUMENT SYMBOL: AI Index: EUR 29/03/77
LANGUAGE: ENG
INDEX: law enforcement personnel / police / detention / legislation /
fact-finding missions
GEOGRAPHICAL INDEX: Ireland
GEOGRAPHICAL CODE: 8231
FREE TEXT: The aim of the mission was to inquire into allegations of
police brutality to detained suspects, focusing on the nature of, and
evidence for, the allegations themselves; the possible contribution
of the emergency and other anti-terrorist legislation to the incidence
of such brutality; the possible judicial consequences, with particular
regard to the admissibility of statements made in police stations. The
report contains the findings of the mission, and a statement of AI's
concerns.

MALTA

CATALOGUE SIGNATURE: 8000/2251/-0=830530
TITLE: Verslag van de Politieke Commissie over de situatie op Malta
AUTHOR: Heuvel, I. van den
PLACE OF PUBLICATION: (Brussels)
PUBLISHER: European Parliament - EP (D)
DATE OF PUBLICATION: 830530
NUMBER OF PAGES: 25 p.
SERIES TITLE: Zittingsdocumenten = Working Documents
DOCUMENT SYMBOL: 1-368/83 ; PE 77.866
LANGUAGE: DUT / ENG
INDEX: democracy / fact-finding missions
GEOGRAPHICAL INDEX: Malta
GEOGRAPHICAL CODE: 8236
FREE TEXT: The report contains a motion for a resolution and an
explanatory statement. The rapporteur visited Malta on 23 and 24
February 1983. The report contains a list of contacts established,
background information on the situation in Malta, the political
situation after the elections of 1981, and a number of recent
events which would require some activity of the European Parliament.
It concerns i.a. the Foreign Interference Act, the judicial system,
radio and television, and the foreign policy. With conclusions: the
political situation is polarized, normal democratic functioning of
all political parties is difficult.
With additional statement: the Nationalist Party has taken its seats
in Parliament; all other problems are negotiable.
With annexes: draft resolutions.

CATALOGUE SIGNATURE: 8000/1072/-0=841219
TITLE: Report on the Foreign Interference Act and the human rights
situation in Malta
AUTHOR: Schwarz
PLACE OF PUBLICATION: Strasbourg
PUBLISHER: Council of Europe - CoE - Parliamentary Assembly (D)
DATE OF PUBLICATION: 841219
NUMBER OF PAGES: 25 p. in v.p.
DOCUMENT SYMBOL: Doc. 5325
LANGUAGE: ENG
INDEX: legislation / fact-finding missions
GEOGRAPHICAL INDEX: Malta
GEOGRAPHICAL CODE: 8236
FREE TEXT: The report contains the draft resolution presented by the
Legal Affairs Committee, a draft order and an explanatory memorandum.
Many members of the Parliamentary Assembly are concerned about the
deterioration of the way human rights are respected and the rule of
law is being applied in Malta, as well as the worsening of the
political climate. The delegate visited Malta from 31 October to 2
November 1984, and had contacts with representatives of the government
and the opposition, and with trade unions, human rights organizations,
the Church etc. He also consulted written material.
The report deals with the Foreign Interference Act, representation of
Malta in the Parliamentary Assembly, and the application of the rule
of law and human rights in general. With conclusions and appendices:
Declaration on the Freedom of Expression and Information, adopted by
the Committee of Ministers of the CoE; motion for a resolution on the
enactment of the Foreign Interference Act; resolutions of the European
Parliament on aspects of the situation in Malta; text of a telex by
the Permanent Representative of Malta.

CATALOGUE SIGNATURE: 8000/1072/-0=850121
TITLE: Provisional opinion on the "Foreign Interference Act" of Malta
presented by the Political Affairs Committee
AUTHOR: Amadei, Giuseppe
PLACE OF PUBLICATION: Strasbourg
PUBLISHER: Council of Europe - CoE - Parliamentary Assembly (D)
DATE OF PUBLICATION: 850121
NUMBER OF PAGES: 9 p.
DOCUMENT SYMBOL: Doc. 5337 provisional
LANGUAGE: ENG
INDEX: legislation / fact-finding missions
GEOGRAPHICAL INDEX: Malta
GEOGRAPHICAL CODE: 8236
FREE TEXT: The task of the rapporteur was to draw up an opinion on the
compatibility of the "Foreign Interference Act" with the principles
upon which the Council of Europe is founded. He conducted a mission to
Malta. His report deals with Malta's participation in the main organs
of the CoE, main observations on the Act, and the relation of the Act
to the European Convention of Human Rights. With conclusions, and
proposals to the draft resolution and order adopted by the Legal
Affairs Committee on 17 December 1984.

CATALOGUE SIGNATURE: 0000/2999/-3=850500
TITLE: Human rights violations in Malta: a report from the
International Helsinki Federation for Human Rights
AUTHOR: Mattson, Lisa ; Alexandersson, Birgitta ; Nagler, Gerald
PLACE OF PUBLICATION: Vienna
PUBLISHER: International Helsinki Federation for Human Rights - IHFHR
(D)
DATE OF PUBLICATION: 850500
NUMBER OF PAGES: 63 p.
LANGUAGE: ENG
BIBLIOGRAPHIES: Y
INDEX: democracy / civil and political rights / legislation /
Helsinki agreements / fact-finding missions
CEOGRAPHICAL INDEX: Malta
GEOGRAPHICAL CODE: 8236
FREE TEXT: Report of a fact-finding mission in March 1985, to
investigate the general situation of human rights. The report contains
a description of the general political background of the country, and
the findings of the mission on various aspects of rights and freedoms.
Attention is paid to: political violence; the "Foreign Interference"
Act of 1982; trade union rights and strikes; the independence of the
judiciary; freedom of religion and freedom of education; freedom of
the press; broadcasting; prisons; freedom of speech, assembly and
associations.
Conclusions: institutions characteristic of a democratic society on
the Western model exist in Malta and function in a way which would
ensure full respect for human rights. There are free elections, and
the freedom of movement, of speech, of religion, of assembly and of
the press are exercised with only minor restrictions. On the other
hand, the institutions established and safeguarded by the Maltese
constitution do not function all the time and in all aspects, and
there exist serious violations of human rights which need to be
remedied.
With annexes: list of persons interviewed, selected list of recent
press articles, part of the "Foreign Interference" Act of 1982.

NETHERLANDS

CATALOGUE SIGNATURE: 0000/0966/-0=840000
TITLE: Report on direct contacts with the government of the Netherlands regarding the implementation of the Freedom of Association and Protection of the Right to Organise Convention, 1948 (no. 87)
AUTHOR: Windmuller, John P.
TITLE OF GENERIC ITEM: International Labour Conference 70th session 1984: report of the Committee of Experts on the Application of Conventions and Recommendations: general report and observations concerning particular countries: annex
EDITION: report III, part 4a
PLACE OF PUBLICATION: Geneva
PUBLISHER: International Labour Office - ILO (D)
DATE OF PUBLICATION: 840000
NUMBER OF PAGES: annex, p. 1-19
LANGUAGE: ENG
INDEX: association (freedom of) / trade unions / fact-finding missions
GEOGRAPHICAL INDEX: Netherlands
GEOGRAPHICAL CODE: 8238
FREE TEXT: John P. Windmuller, representative of the Director-General, and Jane Hodges conducted a direct contacts mission in the Netherlands in January 1984. The report contains information on the conduct of the mission, the imposition of wage measures by the government (background of current measures; receivability under Convention no. 87; recent developments in government policies; the government's income note of 8 December 1983; the views of workers' and employers' organizations, and of the government); and trend followers. With concluding observations.

NORTHERN IRELAND

CATALOGUE SIGNATURE: 0000/0249/-3=780600
TITLE: Report of an Amnesty International mission to Northern Ireland
(28 November - 6 December 1977)
AUTHOR: Amnesty International - AI
PLACE OF PUBLICATION: London
PUBLISHER: Amnesty International - AI (D)
DATE OF PUBLICATION: 780600
NUMBER OF PAGES: 72 p.
DOCUMENT SYMBOL: AI Index: EUR 45/01/78
LANGUAGE: ENG
INDEX: cruel, inhuman or degrading treatment / detention /
law enforcement / fact-finding missions
GEOGRAPHICAL INDEX: Northern Ireland
GEOGRAPHICAL CODE: 8239
FREE TEXT: During 1976, AI received a number of allegations of
ill-treatment by security forces in Northern Ireland. The four member
delegation obtained direct testimony from 52 persons who alleged that
they had been maltreated while in police custody. The team examined
medical reports relating to 13 to the 52 cases; 5 persons where
examined in detail. Medical reports and other data in relation to a
further 26 cases were obtained.
The report contains background information on the situation in Northern
Ireland, a short description of the activities of the mission. Chapter
three contains the case studies of alleged maltreatment; chapter four
deals with relevant legislation. With conclusions and recommendations,
and glossary.

CATALOGUE SIGNATURE: 0000/0249/-0=850306
TITLE: Northern Ireland: alleged torture and ill-treatment of Paul
Caruana
AUTHOR: (Kelstrup, Jørgen) ; (Oosting, Dick)
PLACE OF PUBLICATION: London
PUBLISHER: Amnesty International - AI (D)
DATE OF PUBLICATION: 850306
NUMBER OF PAGES: 14 p. in v.p.
DOCUMENT SYMBOL: AI Index: EUR 45/02/85
LANGUAGE: ENG
INDEX: prison conditions / torture / fact-finding missions
GEOGRAPHICAL INDEX: Northern Ireland
GEOGRAPHICAL CODE: 8239
FREE TEXT: In September 1984, AI received reports that Paul Caruana
had been subjected to torture during his interrogation by the Royal
Ulster Constabulary (RUC) in Belfast. Subsequently, two AI delegates
went to Northern Ireland to interview Paul Caruana, his lawyer and
medical personnel. The document contains correspondence between AI
and the United Kingdom Secretary of State for Northern Ireland,
including the abridged medical report of the mission.

NORWAY

CATALOGUE SIGNATURE: 0000/0966/-3=840000
TITLE: The trade union situation and industrial relations in Norway:
report of an ILO mission
AUTHOR: Lagergren, Ian ; Schregle, Johannes ; Monat, Jacques
(...et al)
PLACE OF PUBLICATION: Geneva
PUBLISHER: International Labour Office - ILO (D)
DATE OF PUBLICATION: 840000
NUMBER OF PAGES: 90 p.
ISBN: 92 2 103893 9
LANGUAGE: ENG
INDEX: association (freedom of) / trade unions / fact-finding missions
GEOGRAPHICAL INDEX: Norway
GEOGRAPHICAL CODE: 8240
FREE TEXT: Report based on a fact-finding mission in September-October
1982, to study the trade union situation and the industrial relations
system. The delegation met with representatives of the government, the
trade unions and employers' associations, and other persons familiar
with trade union and industrial relations problems, and visited
industrial enterprises. The aim of the report is to describe as
faithfully as possible the major features of a particular industrial
relations system, with special emphasis with the trade union situation.
It contains chapters on the background of the country, trade unions
and employers' associations, the functioning of employers and workers'
organizations, remunerations and collective bargaining, the various
forms of participation in decisions, labour disputes and settlement
procedures, final remarks. With appendices containing discussion on
the report: report of a meeting of the Working Party on the Trade
Union Situation and Labour Relations Systems in European Countries;
extracts of minutes of the 225th Session of the Governing Body.

POLAND

CATALOGUE SIGNATURE: 0000/0088/-4
TITLE: Report on the case of Alicja Wesolowska
AUTHOR: Hadding, Carl F.
TITLE OF GENERIC ITEM: ICJ Newsletter
EDITION: no. 4
PLACE OF PUBLICATION: Geneva
PUBLISHER: International Commission of Jurists - ICJ (D)
DATE OF PUBLICATION: 800300
NUMBER OF PAGES: p. 58-60
LANGUAGE: ENG
INDEX: legislation / judicial systems / trials / fact-finding missions
GEOGRAPHICAL INDEX: Poland
GEOGRAPHICAL CODE: 8141
FREE TEXT: Alicja Wesolowska is of Polish nationality and employed by
the United Nations since 1971. She was arrested during a visit to
Poland for "anti-state activities" and "acts against friendly states".
The observer was not allowed to enter the country; Wesolowska was
sentenced to seven years imprisonment. The Polish authorities have not
given an assurance that her immunity as UN staff member has not been
violated, and refused to let UN officials or representatives visit
Wesolowska or let the UN appoint a defence lawyer.

CATALOGUE SIGNATURE: 0000/0966/-3=820000
TITLE: Case No. 1097: complaints presented by the International
Confederation of Free Trade Unions and the World Confederation of
Labour against the government of Poland
AUTHOR: International Labour Office - ILO - Committee on Freedom of
Association ; Valticos, Nicolas
TITLE OF GENERIC ITEM: Official Bulletin: reports of the
Committee on Freedom of Association (217th and 218th)
EDITION: vol. LXV, series B no. 2
PLACE OF PUBLICATION: Geneva
PUBLISHER: International Labour Office - ILO (D)
DATE OF PUBLICATION: 820000
NUMBER OF PAGES: p. 149-186
LANGUAGE: ENG
INDEX: association (freedom of) / trade unions / fact-finding missions
GEOGRAPHICAL INDEX: Poland
GEOGRAPHICAL CODE: 8141
FREE TEXT: Following the declaration of martial law in Poland on 13
December 1981 and the measures taken by the authorities against the
trade union Solidarity and its militants and leaders, the ICFTU and
the WCL had submitted to the ILO complaints of violation of trade union
rights. With the consent of the government, Nicolas Valticos and
Bernard Gernigon visited Poland from 10 to 16 May 1982.
The report contains information on previous examination of the case
by the Committee, a communication provided by the government on 8 May
1982, the visit to the country (with an analysis of the facts prior to
13 December 1981, the present situation and prospects for the future).
With conclusions and recommendations of the Committee, and annexes:
information provided by the government on persons released, arrested
or interned; report of Valticos to the Director-General of the ILO on
his visit to Poland (with general indications about the trade union
situation, statements of government representatives and of various
trade union representatives, the meeting with Lech Walesa, conclusions
and final suggestions).

CATALOGUE SIGNATURE: 0000/1079/-3=840301
TITLE: Report on the situation in Poland presented by Under-Secretary-
General Patricio Ruedas
AUTHOR: Ruedas, Patricio
PLACE OF PUBLICATION: Geneva
PUBLISHER: Commission on Human Rights of the United Nations Economic
and Social Council - UNCHR (D)
DATE OF PUBLICATION: 840301
NUMBER OF PAGES: 20 p. in v.p.
SERIES TITLE: Commission on Human Rights: fortieth session: item 12 of
the agenda: question of the violation of human rights and fundamental
freedoms in any part of the world, with particular reference to
colonial and other dependent territories
DOCUMENT SYMBOL: E/CN.4/1984/26
AVAILABILITY: F
LANGUAGE: ENG
INDEX: martial law / legislation / fact-finding missions
GEOGRAPHICAL INDEX: Poland
GEOGRAPHICAL CODE: 8141
FREE TEXT: The report on the situation of human rights in Poland begins
with an introduction on the contacts between the government and the
Commission on Human Rights (including the text of a questionnaire to
the government). Two UN officials visited Poland recently: Emilio de
Olivares in 1982 and Patricio Ruedas in 1983.
In his report, Ruedas attempts to provide a double perspective to the
situation, by submitting factual information on developments during the
last twelve months and by measuring the evolution of the situation.
Attention is paid to legislative developments and other developments.
With conclusions and annexes: resolution of the Council of State of 20
July 1983 on lifting martial law; law of 21 July 1983 on amnesty; law
of 20 July 1983 on amending the constitution of the Polish People's
Republic.

CATALOGUE SIGNATURE: 0000/1245/-3=840327
TITLE: Polish lawyers under attack
AUTHOR: Neier, Aryeh
PLACE OF PUBLICATION: New York
PUBLISHER: Helsinki Watch - HW (D)
DATE OF PUBLICATION: 840327
NUMBER OF PAGES: 10 p.
LANGUAGE: ENG
INDEX: lawyers / fact-finding missions
GEOGRAPHICAL INDEX: Poland
GEPGRAPHICAL CODE: 8141
FREE TEXT: Some of the information was gathered during a visit to
Warsaw in March 1984. The lawyers under attack are defending
political prisoners. With accounts of some of the political cases
handled by specific lawyers, the courts, the attitude of the
government and measures taken against the lawyers. With appendix:
recommendations for action.

PORTUGAL

CATALOGUE SIGNATURE: 0000/2121/-3=750000
TITLE: Mission d'observation au Portugal: 31 mai - 8 juin 1975
AUTHOR: Kock, Marc de
PLACE OF PUBLICATION: Brussels
PUBLISHER: Ligue Belge pour la Défense des Droits de l'Homme - LBDDH
(D)
DATE OF PUBLICATION: 750000
NUMBER OF PAGES: 45 p. in v.p.
LANGUAGE: FRE
INDEX: political prisoners / civil and political rights /
fact-finding missions
GEOGRAPHICAL INDEX: Portugal
GEOGRAPHICAL CODE: 8242
FREE TEXT: The report is on the human rights situation after the
change of government on April 25, 1974. Attention is paid to the
background of the country, state institutions and the general situation
of human rights: freedom of speech and individual expression, freedom
of association, freedom of the press. The report mainly deals with
detention conditions of political prisoners, based on personal
observations and interviews. Legal guarantees and the rights of the
defence are analyzed. Special attention is given to the military
tribunals and the archives of the PIDE secret police. With conclusions
and annex: visit to Caxias prison for political prisoners.

CATALOGUE SIGNATURE: 8242/-0=851000
TITLE: Bericht über den Prozess gegen Otelo de Carvalho am 22. Juli
1985 in Lissabon
AUTHOR: Rottman, Verena S.
TITLE OF GENERIC ITEM: Informationsbrief
EDITION: v.33
PLACE OF PUBLICATION: Hannover
PUBLISHER: Republikanischer Anwaltsverein - RAV (D)
DATE OF PUBLICATION: 851000
NUMBER OF PAGES: p.32-37
LANGUAGE: GER
INDEX: trials / fact-finding missions
GEOGRAPHICAL INDEX: Portugal
GEOGRAPHICAL CODE: 8242
FREE TEXT: The author attended the trial of Otelo de Carvalho and
member of his left-wing organization FUP on behalf of the RAV and
CEDRI, and assisted in the defence. She describes and criticizes
the conditions under which the trial took place.

CATALOGUE SIGNATURE: 8242/-0=851000
TITLE: Rapport d'un observateur au procès d'Otelo Saraiva de Carvalho et d'autres membres du FUP: le 6 octobre 1985 à Lisbonne
AUTHOR: Müller, Ingo
PLACE OF PUBLICATION: Bremen
PUBLISHER: Republikanischer Anwaltsverein - RAV (D) ; European Committee for the Defence of Refugees and Immigrants - CEDRI (D)
DATE OF PUBLICATION: 851000
NUMBER OF PAGES: 4 p.
LANGUAGE: FRE
INDEX: trials / fact-finding missions
GEOGRAPHICAL INDEX: Portugal
GEOGRAPHICAL CODE: 8242
FREE TEXT: The author attended the trial on behalf of the RAV and CEDRI. The report contains a description of the trial (accusation and enrollment of the trial) and a summary in which the author points to the importance of the presence of international trial observers for the accused, the tribunal and the public opinion.

CATALOGUE SIGNATURE: 0000/0138/-3=850125
TITLE: Rapport de mission Otelo de Carvalho: 1. Lisbonne 24/08 au 27/08/84: 2. Lisbonne 9/12 au 10/12/84
AUTHOR: Bourgaux, Jacques
PLACE OF PUBLICATION: Brussels
PUBLISHER: International Association of Democratic Lawyers - IADL (D)
DATE OF PUBLICATION: 850125
NUMBER OF PAGES: (20 p.)
LANGUAGE: FRE
INDEX: trials / fact-finding missions
GEOGRAPHICAL INDEX: Portugal
GEOGRAPHICAL CODE: 8242
FREE TEXT: The aim of the first mission was to investigate the reasons for which lieutenant-colonel Otelo de Carvalho was arrested. The first part of the report describes the background of the case, the legal grounds for the arrest and detention and the rights of the defence, and contains preliminary conclusions. During the second mission, the author met with de Carvalho in the military prison of Caxias. With annexes: newspaper articles, relevant legislation.

SPAIN

CATALOGUE SIGNATURE: 0000/0249/-3=750000
TITLE: Report of an Amnesty International mission to Spain: July 1975
AUTHOR: (Jones, Thomas) ; (Wisser, Burkhard)
PLACE OF PUBLICATION: London
PUBLISHER: Amnesty International - AI (D)
DATE OF PUBLICATION: 750000
NUMBER OF PAGES: 24 p.
ISBN: 0 900058 14 5
DOCUMENT SYMBOL: AI Index: PUB 37/00/75
LANGUAGE: ENG
INDEX: torture / death penalty / fact-finding missions
GEOGRAPHICAL INDEX: Spain
GEOGRAPHICAL CODE: 8245
FREE TEXT: In July 1975, Amnesty International sent a mission to Spain
to investigate allegations of torture reported to have occurred during
the three month state of exception (estado de excepcion) in the Basque
provinces of Vizcaya and Guipuzcoa, from 25 April to 25 July 1975. In
addition, the mission was to seek clarification of the government's
intentions regarding the renewed use of the death penalty both in civil
and political cases throughout Spain.
The delegation was not allowed to interview specific prisoners. The
report contains chapters on the nature of the evidence, the findings of
the mission, the methods of torture, intimidation, and legislation with
regard to torture. With conclusion and recommendations, and appendices:
testimonies of torture; torture elsewhere in Spain; the death penalty.

CATALOGUE SIGNATURE: 0000/0088/-4
TITLE: Spain
AUTHOR: International Commission of Jurists - ICJ
TITLE OF GENERIC ITEM: ICJ Review
EDITION: no. 15
PLACE OF PUBLICATION: Geneva
PUBLISHER: International Commission of Jurists - ICJ (D)
DATE OF PUBLICATION: 751200
NUMBER OF PAGES: p. 25-32
LANGUAGE: ENG
INDEX: trials / fact-finding missions
GEOGRAPHICAL INDEX: Spain
GEOGRAPHICAL CODE: 8245
FREE TEXT: During 1974, there was a significant increase in activity
of opposition groups in Spain. Some has taken the form of violent armed
confrontations, but much of it has been peaceful political and trade
union action. The Spanish government has reacted to these "offensives"
with severe repressive measures, giving rise to still further violence,
and a number of right-wing groups have appeared which have been
responsible for attacks on militant Basque separatists and their
sympathizers. Arising out of those events there have been a number of
important political trials, as well as new decrees, which are of
interest from the standpoint of the principles of the Rule of Law.
This article contains analyses of trials of trade unionists, repression
of terrorism in the Basque provinces, the Decree Law concerning the
Repression of Terrorism and death sentences and executions of five
Spaniards. The report contains descriptions of trials, among which the
trial in Burgos observed by ICJ representative Edmond Martin-Achard.

CATALOGUE SIGNATURE: 0000/0018/-0=760400
TITLE: Impressions on a visit to Spain
AUTHOR: Villalpando, Waldo L.
TITLE OF GENERIC ITEM: CCIA Newsletter
EDITION: no. 2
PLACE OF PUBLICATION: Geneva
PUBLISHER: Commission of the Churches on International Affairs of the
World Council of Churches - CCIA-WCC (D)
DATE OF PUBLICATION: 760400
NUMBER OF PAGES: 15 p.
LANGUAGE: ENG
INDEX: religion (freedom of) / church and state / fact-finding missions
GEOGRAPHICAL INDEX: Spain
GEOGRAPHICAL CODE: 8245
FREE TEXT: Report of a fact-finding mission, the aim of which was to
make an assessment of the general situation in the country, especially
from an ecumenical angle and concern. In the report, attention is paid
to the general situation of the country (problems of the "overture"),
regionalism, repression, the situation of the church (relationship with
the state, ecumenism, education and other social activities, economic
conditions, isolation). With recommendations.

CATALOGUE SIGNATURE: 8000/1072/-0=771001
TITLE: Report on the situation in Spain = Rapport sur la situation en
Espagne
AUTHOR: Channon
PLACE OF PUBLICATION: Strasbourg
PUBLISHER: Council of Europe - CoE - Parliamentary Assembly (D)
DATE OF PUBLICATION: 771001
NUMBER OF PAGES: 26 p.
DOCUMENT SYMBOL: Doc. 4037
LANGUAGE: ENG / FRE
INDEX: democracy / fact-finding missions
GEOGRAPHICAL INDEX: Spain
GEOGRAPHICAL CODE: 8245
FREE TEXT: Report by the rapporteur of the Committee on European
Non-Member Countries, based on a fact-finding mission to Spain from 12
to 15 September 1977. The report contains a draft resolution by the
Committee, and an explanatory statement. The three member delegation
visited Madrid, and had contacts with the authorities, members of
parliament and representatives of political parties. It followed the
first real debate to be held in the new Cortés.
The report contains chapters on: the new democratic institutions and
political activity since the elections (the parliament, the judiciary,
government action and the attitude of the opposition); the timing and
substance of the constitution; trade unions and the economy; the
regions (Catalonia, the Basque country), and by way of conclusion,
Spain's European vocation. With appendix: Declaration of 8 October,
adressed to the Assembly and signed by the spokesmen of all political
groups in the Cortés.

CATALOGUE SIGNATURE: 0000/0249/-3=801100
TITLE: Report of an Amnesty International mission to Spain: 3-28
October 1979
AUTHOR: Amnesty International - AI
PLACE OF PUBLICATION: London
PUBLISHER: Amnesty International - AI (D)
DATE OF PUBLICATION: 801100
NUMBER OF PAGES: 64 p.
ISBN: 0 86210 022 4
DOCUMENT SYMBOL: AI Index: EUR 41/03/80
LANGUAGE: ENG / SPA
INDEX: cruel, inhuman or degrading treatment / detention / police /
law enforcement personnel / legislation / fact-finding missions
GEOGRAPHICAL INDEX: Spain
GEOGRAPHICAL CODE: 8245
FREE TEXT: The report deals with the legal and medical aspects of the
treatment of people detained in Spanish police stations.
The first part is on the legislation regarding detention; the second
part is a report on medical examinations, with a description of
methods used, a summary of findings, conclusions and a description of
14 individual case histories. With conclusions and recommendations;
it is concluded that recent reforms in the legal and constitutional
provisions affecting detainees have led to important improvements.
However, it would be incorrect to say that the present situation of
detained people is without major faults.
With appendices: relevant domestic legislation (in spanish) and
glossary.

Spain

CATALOGUE SIGNATURE: 0000/0966/-3=840000
TITLE: The trade union situation and labour relations in Spain: ILO
mission report
AUTHOR: Lagergren, Ian ; Cordova, Efren ; Servais, Jean-Michel
(...et al)
PLACE OF PUBLICATION: Geneva
PUBLISHER: International Labour Office - ILO (D)
DATE OF PUBLICATION: 840000
NUMBER OF PAGES: 114 p.
LANGUAGE: ENG
STATISTICAL INFORMATION: Y
BIBLIOGRAPHIES: Y
INDEX: association (freedom of) / trade unions / fact-finding missions
GEOGRAPHICAL INDEX: Spain
GEOGRAPHICAL CODE: 8245
FREE TEXT: Report of a fact-finding mission in November-December 1983,
to study the trade union situation and the industrial relations system.
Contacts were established with the authorities, employers' and workers'
organizations and researchers; several undertakings were visited.
The report contains chapters on the background of the country, the
situation of employers and trade unions (including the right to
association), the functioning of occupational organizations, collective
bargaining, other forms of workers' participation, labour disputes:
peaceful settlement and direct action, and industrial relations in the
public sector. With closing remarks.

CATALOGUE SIGNATURE: 0000/0035/-4
TITLE: Espagne: rapport de mission
AUTHOR: Jacoby, D.
TITLE OF GENERIC ITEM: La Lettre de la FIDH
EDITION: no. 138
PLACE OF PUBLICATION: Paris
PUBLISHER: Fédération Internationale des Droits de l'Homme - FIDH (D)
DATE OF PUBLICATION: 851231
NUMBER OF PAGES: p. 7-10
LANGUAGE: FRE
INDEX: trials / fact-finding missions
GEOGRAPHICAL INDEX: Spain
GEOGRAPHICAL CODE: 8245
FREE TEXT: The author assisted as observer at the trial of José Carlos
García Ramirez, held on November 27 before the Audiencia Nacional in
Madrid. Garcia Ramirez is one of the three Basque militants which were
extradited by the French government in 1984. The report contains a
description of the trial, which is considered fair.

CATALOGUE SIGNATURE: 0000/2242/-0=860402
TITLE: Andalucian day labourers "jornaleros" report
AUTHOR: Watkinson, David
PLACE OF PUBLICATION: London
PUBLISHER: Agricultural Allied Workers National Trade Group / Transport and General Workers Union ; Haldane Society of Socialist Lawyers ; European Committee for the Defence of Refugees and Immigrants - CEDRI (D)
DATE OF PUBLICATION: 860402
NUMBER OF PAGES: 5 p.
LANGUAGE: ENG
INDEX: labour / trials / fact-finding missions
GEOGRAPHICAL INDEX: Spain
GEOGRAPHICAL CODE: 8245
FREE TEXT: Report on the trial of eight day labourers, accused of causing public disorder contrary to article 246 of the Penal Code, held in the Audiencia Provincial of Seville on 12 and 13 February 1986; judgment was delivered on February 21. The report contains background information on the case (the defendants protested after they had been refused payment for two weeks work under the Community Works Scheme) and the conduct of the trial. The author concludes that imprisonment for any length of time is completely inappropriate on the facts of this case.

SWITZERLAND

CATALOGUE SIGNATURE: 0000/2242/-3=841000
TITLE: Asile ou dissuasion?: l'exemple de Fribourg: la politique
d'asile suisse, 40 ans après
AUTHOR: Busch, Nicholas ; Caloz-Tschopp, Marie-Claire ; Klinger,
Gotthard (ed.) (...et al)
PLACE OF PUBLICATION: Basle
PUBLISHER: European Committee for the Defence of Refugees and
Immigrants - CEDRI (D)
DATE OF PUBLICATION: 841000
NUMBER OF PAGES: 66 p.
LANGUAGE: FRE
BIBLIOGRAPHIES: Y
INDEX: asylum / refugees / fact-finding missions
GEOGRAPHICAL INDEX: Switzerland
GEOGRAPHICAL CODE: 8247
FREE TEXT: On 19 June 1984, over sixty asylum seekers were arrested
in Fribourg after they protested against the way in which they were
treated by the authorities. CEDRI, the Swiss Committee for the Defence
of the Right to Asylum and the Swiss League for Human Rights decided
to constitute a delegation with persons from different cantons to
investigate the events in Fribourg, their origins and consequences
for those asylum seekers directly engaged and the Swiss policy with
regard to asylum.
Besides an introduction, the report consists of two parts, on the
policy of dissuasion in the canton of Fribourg and on the general
asylum policy in Switzerland.

182

TURKEY

CATALOGUE SIGNATURE: 0000/0088/-4
TITLE: The trial of the Turkiye Emerkci Partisi (Turkish Workers'
Party) before the Constitutional Court of Turkey
AUTHOR: Simon, Manfred
TITLE OF GENERIC ITEM: ICJ Review
EDITION: no. 24
PLACE OF PUBLICATION: Geneva
PUBLISHER: International Commission of Jurists - ICJ (D)
DATE OF PUBLICATION: 800600
NUMBER OF PAGES: p. 53-64
LANGUAGE: ENG
INDEX: trials / fact-finding missions
GEOGRAPHICAL INDEX: Turkey
GEOGRAPHICAL CODE: 8248
FREE TEXT: The report of the mission contains an introduction on the
political, economic, social and judicial situation in Turkey and
sections on the Turkish Workers' Party (TEP) and its leader Mihri
Belli, the different stages of the trial against leaders of the TEP,
comments and conclusions, the trial before the Constitutional Court.
The author concludes that this trial was fair, but that the
constitutional provisions and legal enactments applicable, and
strictly interpreted by the Court, are in several respects contrary
to essential human rights.

CATALOGUE SIGNATURE: 0000/0138/-3=800000
TITLE: Mission d'enquête en Turquie: 31 mars - 4 avril 1980
AUTHOR: Vandernoot, Pierre ; Wartel, Jean Claude
PLACE OF PUBLICATION: Brussels
PUBLISHER: Association Internationale des Juristes Démocrates - IADL (D)
DATE OF PUBLICATION: 800000
NUMBER OF PAGES: 8 p.
LANGUAGE: FRE
INDEX: trade unions / civil and political rights /
fact-finding missions
GEOGRAPHICAL INDEX: Turkey
GEOGRAPHICAL CODE: 8248
FREE TEXT: The aim of the mission was to investigate the human rights
situation in general, and the freedom of association for trade unions
in particular.
The findings of the mission are described under the headings: Bar -
rights of the defence; the right to work; detentions and inculpations;
freedoms of assembly, expression, association; violent acts of the
police and repression; freedom of the press; torture and detention
conditions; liberties of trade unions. With conclusion.

CATALOGUE SIGNATURE: 0000/0035/-3=800000
TITLE: Mission d'enquête effectuée en Turquie du 8 au 18 mai 1980
AUTHOR: Verdier, Robert ; Rostoker, Christian ; Terrasson, Madeleine
PLACE OF PUBLICATION: Paris
PUBLISHER: Fédération Internationale des Droits de l'Homme - FIDH (D)
DATE OF PUBLICATION: 800000
NUMBER OF PAGES: 12 p.
LANGUAGE: FRE
INDEX: civil and political rights / fact-finding missions
GEOGRAPHICAL INDEX: Turkey
GEOGRAPHICAL CODE: 8248
FREE TEXT: The purpose of the mission was to investigate the general
human rights situation in Turkey. It is stated that the functioning
of democratic institutions is menaced by violence and repression,
and by the announcement of the state of siege. Attention is given to
political prisoners, and to the situation of the Kurdic minority.

CATALOGUE SIGNATURE: 8000/1072/-0=810127
TITLE: Report on the situation in Turkey = Rapport sur la situation en
Turquie
AUTHOR: Steiner, Ludwig
PLACE OF PUBLICATION: Strasbourg
PUBLISHER: Council of Europe - CoE - Parliamentary Assembly (D)
DATE OF PUBLICATION: 810127
NUMBER OF PAGES: 18 p.
DOCUMENT SYMBOL: Doc. 4657
LANGUAGE: ENG / FRE
INDEX: democracy / fact-finding missions
GEOGRAPHICAL INDEX: Turkey
GEOGRAPHICAL CODE: 8248
FREE TEXT: Report by the rapporteur of the Political Affairs Committee
on the situation in Turkey, based on a fact-finding mission to Turkey
from 5 to 8 January 1981. The report contains a draft resolution by the
Political Affairs Committee and an explanatory memorandum. The
memorandum contains an introduction on the mission, and sections on:
the situation preceding the military take-over of 12 September 1980,
and the causes of the military intervention; various aspects of the
current situation (return to democracy, the Constitution, allegations
of torture, executions, trade unions and the press); Turkey as a member
of the Council of Europe. It is stated that both the government and
other persons met expect the Council of Europe to show understanding,
and at the same time to help Turkey to achieve the full restoration of
democracy.

CATALOGUE SIGNATURE: 0000/0138/-3=810000
TITLE: Mission d'enquête et d'observation en Turquie: 12-17 mai 1981
AUTHOR: Vandernoot, Pierre
PLACE OF PUBLICATION: Brussels
PUBLISHER: Association Internationale des Juristes Démocrates - IADL (D)
DATE OF PUBLICATION: 810000
NUMBER OF PAGES: 5 p.
LANGUAGE: FRE
INDEX: trade unions / trials / fact-finding missions
GEOGRAPHICAL INDEX: Turkey
GEOGRAPHICAL CODE: 8248
FREE TEXT: Vandernoot assisted at two trials against the president
and members of the executive committee of the DISK trade union. He
obtained information on their detention conditions and describes
the trial procedures.
Vandernoot and A. Davidson took part in the congress of the Union
of Bars of Turkey, where they received information on the political
situation and the freedom of the press.

CATALOGUE SIGNATURE: 0000/0084/-3=810000
TITLE: WCC delegation visit to Turkey: November 30 - December 4, 1981
AUTHOR: Appel, André ; Wessels, Antoine ; Butler, J. Richard
(...et al)
PLACE OF PUBLICATION: Geneva
PUBLISHER: World Council of Churches - WCC (D)
DATE OF PUBLICATION: 810000
NUMBER OF PAGES: 9 p.
LANGUAGE: ENG
INDEX: religion (freedom of) / minorities / fact-finding missions
GEOGRAPHICAL INDEX: Turkey
GEOGRAPHICAL CODE: 8248
FREE TEXT: The mission team consisted of seven ecumenical delegates,
chosen to reflect the European close involvement in the problem of
the situation of the Christian minorities in Turkey, and especially
the Souryanis. The report consist of a description of the living
conditions of the Souryanis, and of the position of the Armenian and
Greek communities in Turkey. The delegates met with two officials to
get known to the government view on the Souryanis problem. With
extract of evaluation session, and conclusions.

CATALOGUE SIGNATURE: 0000/0138/-3=811200
TITLE: Mission en Turquie: 19-26 décembre 1981
AUTHOR: Weyl, Frédéric
PLACE OF PUBLICATION: Brussels
PUBLISHER: Association Internationale des Juristes Démocrates - IADL (D)
DATE OF PUBLICATION: 811200
NUMBER OF PAGES: 12 p.
LANGUAGE: FRE
INDEX: association (freedom of) / judicial systems / trials /
fact-finding missions
GEOGRAPHICAL INDEX: Turkey
GEOGRAPHICAL CODE: 8248
FREE TEXT: The aim of the mission was to collect information on the
large number of trials of groups accused of terrorist activities in
the period before the military took over on 12 September 1980, and
to assist in the trials before the Tribunal of the State of Siege in
Golcuk against 280 persons accused of belonging to the clandestine
communist party TKP and before the Tribunal of the State of Siege in
Istanbul against the leadership and members of the trade union DISK.
The report contains background information on these trials, as well
as on other trials in preparation. With preliminary conclusions.

CATALOGUE SIGNATURE: 8000/1072/-0=820126
TITLE: Report on the situation in Turkey = Rapport sur la situation en
Turquie
AUTHOR: Urwin, Tom ; Steiner, Ludwig
PLACE OF PUBLICATION: Strasbourg
PUBLISHER: Council of Europe - CoE - Parliamentary Assembly (D)
DATE OF PUBLICATION: 820126
NUMBER OF PAGES: 12 p.
DOCUMENT SYMBOL: Doc. 4841
LANGUAGE: ENG / FRE
INDEX: democracy / fact-finding missions
GEOGRAPHICAL INDEX: Turkey
GEOGRAPHICAL CODE: 8248
FREE TEXT: Report by the rapporteurs of the Political Affairs Committee
on the situation in Turkey, based on a fact-finding mission by a
delegation of the Parliamentary Assembly from 7 to 14 January 1982. The
report contains a draft resolution presented by the Political Affairs
Committee, a draft recommendation, a draft order and explanatory
memoranda by the rapporteurs, with recommendations with regard to the
policy to be followed by the Parliamentary Assembly. With appendices:
list of parliamentarians who took part in the mission; programme of the
mission in Ankara and Istanbul.

CATALOGUE SIGNATURE: 8000/1072/-0=820127
TITLE: Opinion of the legal aspects of the situation in Turkey
presented by the Legal Affairs Committee = Avis sur les aspects
juridiques de la situation en Turquie présenté par la commission
des questions juridiques
AUTHOR: Bardens, Hans
PLACE OF PUBLICATION: Strasbourg
PUBLISHER: Council of Europe - CoE - Parliamentary Assembly (D)
DATE OF PUBLICATION: 820127
NUMBER OF PAGES: 32 p.
DOCUMENT SYMBOL: Doc. 4849
LANGUAGE: ENG / FRE
BIBLIOGRAPHIES: Y
INDEX: legislation / judicial systems / democracy /
fact-finding missions
GEOGRAPHICAL INDEX: Turkey
GEOGRAPHICAL CODE: 8248
FREE TEXT: A delegation of the Parliamentary Assembly visited Turkey
from 7 to 14 January 1982. The report of the Legal Affairs Committee
deals with the constitutional situation after the military intervention
on 12 September 1980, the return to democracy and the preparation of a
Constitution, other legislative activities, independence of the courts,
a number of important trials, torture, the death penalty and Turkey's
compliance with the European Convention on Human Rights.
With conclusions and appendices: law no. 2485 on a Constituent Assembly
adopted on 29 June 1981 by the National Security Council; list of
organizations and institutions consulted by the Committee on the
Constitution and the Consultative Assembly; some important articles of
the Turkish Criminal Code.
It is concluded that several human rights are still not respected,
and the situation in Turkey is not compatible with the Statute of the
Council of Europe. However, measures have been taken to restore
democracy and the rule of law.

CATALOGUE SIGNATURE: 0000/0010/-3=820128
TITLE: Legal report on the trial of the 52 Turkish trade unionists
AUTHOR: Drooghenbroeck, François van
PLACE OF PUBLICATION: Brussels
PUBLISHER: World Confederation of Labour - WCL (D)
DATE OF PUBLICATION: 820128
NUMBER OF PAGES: 27 p.
DOCUMENT SYMBOL: 8/82
LANGUAGE: ENG
INDEX: trade unions / political prisoners / trials /
fact-finding missions
GEOGRAPHICAL INDEX: Turkey
GEOGRAPHICAL CODE: 8248
FREE TEXT: The author was sent to the trial of 52 leaders of the DISK
trade union as a legal observer. The trial took place on 24 and 25
December 1981 before the military tribunal in Istanbul.
After some historical background information, the document contains
the following parts: (I) the bill of indictment, in particular
articles 141, 142, 146 of the penal code, and a brief summary of the
bill; (II) before the hearing: information about the period that the
52 leaders of the DISK had spent under close watch; many of them were
tortured and ill-treated; (III) the hearings; (IV) (provisional)
conclusions.

CATALOGUE SIGNATURE: 0000/0138/-3=820400
TITLE: Mission en Turquie: 17-24 avril 1982
AUTHOR: Larzul, Claude
PLACE OF PUBLICATION: Brussels
PUBLISHER: Association Internationale des Juristes Démocrates - IADL (D)
DATE OF PUBLICATION: 820400
NUMBER OF PAGES: 15 p.
LANGUAGE: FRE
INDEX: judicial systems / detention / trials / fact-finding missions
GEOGRAPHICAL INDEX: Turkey
GEOGRAPHICAL CODE: 8248
FREE TEXT: During his mission, the delegate assisted in two hearings of
the trial against the DISK trade union in Istanbul, and in a hearing of
the trial against the Workers Party of Turkey TIP. His report contains
a description of his findings with regard to the hearings, information
on other trials and on the situation of defence lawyers and arrested
persons.

CATALOGUE SIGNATURE: 0000/0966/-3=821100
TITLE: Cases No. 997, 999 and 1029: complaints presented by the
World Confederation of Labour, the World Federation of Trade Unions,
the International Confederation of Free Trade Unions and several
other trade union organisations against the government of Turkey
AUTHOR: International Labour Office - ILO - Committee on Freedom of
Association ; Lagergren, Ian
TITLE OF GENERIC ITEM: Official Bulletin: reports of the
Committee on Freedom of Association (219th, 220th and 221st)
EDITION: v. LXV, series B no. 3
PLACE OF PUBLICATION: Geneva
PUBLISHER: International Labour Office - ILO (D)
DATE OF PUBLICATION: 821100
NUMBER OF PAGES: p. 226-281
LANGUAGE: ENG
INDEX: association (freedom of) / trade unions / legislation /
detention / fact-finding missions
GEOGRAPHICAL INDEX: Turkey
GEOGRAPHICAL CODE: 8248
FREE TEXT: The Committee had before it various complaints of
infringements of trade union rights in Turkey presented by a number of
trade union organizations. The report contains information on previous
examination of the cases by the Committee, further communications from
the complainants, the observations of the government, and the direct
contacts mission to Turkey in July 1982 by Ian Lagergren.
The analysis of the mission report deals with the situation prior to
12 September 1980; the suspension of DISK, MISK and other organizations
and of trade union activities; the Supreme Arbitration Board; the draft
constitution and the future labour legislation; questions concerning
detained trade unionists; the DISK trial; allegations of torture and
other violations.
The report continues with further developments, and conclusions and
recommendations of the Committee.
With annex: text of the report of the direct contacts mission, with
headings mentioned above and concluding remarks.

CATALOGUE SIGNATURE: 0000/0035/-3=830100
TITLE: Bericht einer Untersuchungskommission der Fédération
Internationale des Droits de l'Homme über die Türkei
AUTHOR: Aebersold, Peter ; Dubois, Jean-Alain ; Oberdiek, Helmut
PLACE OF PUBLICATION: Geneva
PUBLISHER: Fédération Internationale des Droits de l'Homme - FIDH -
représentation permanente auprès de l'ONU
DISTRIBUTOR: Koordinationsstelle Türkei
DATE OF PUBLICATION: 830100
NUMBER OF PAGES: 47 p.
LANGUAGE: GER
STATISTICAL INFORMATION: Y
INDEX: prison conditions / military / trials / fact-finding missions
GEOGRAPHICAL INDEX: Turkey
GEOGRAPHICAL CODE: 8248
FREE TEXT: Report of a fact-finding mission to Turkey from 8 to 27
November 1982. The first aim of the mission were to visit prisons
and especially military prisons, to investigate the possibilities
for future missions to prisons, and to collect information on
prison conditions. The second aim was to obtain information on
criminal proceedings and to observe trials.
The report deals with the enrollment of the mission, the general
situation in Turkey, criminal proceedings in military courts and
prison conditions. The visit to the military prison Mamak in Ankara
and the observations made at trials are described in detail. With
appendices.

CATALOGUE SIGNATURE: 0000/0035/-3=830600
TITLE: Rapport sur la mission effectuée les 19, 20 et 21 juin...
AUTHOR: Charrière-Bournazel, Christian ; Stasi, Mario
PLACE OF PUBLICATION: Paris
PUBLISHER: Fédération Internationale des Droits de l'Homme - FIDH (D)
DATE OF PUBLICATION: 830600
NUMBER OF PAGES: 4 p.
LANGUAGE: FRE
INDEX: trials / fact-finding missions
GEOGRAPHICAL INDEX: Turkey
GEOGRAPHICAL CODE: 8248
FREE TEXT: The aim of the mission was to observe the trial of the
dean of the Bar Apaydin before the Military Tribunal in Istanbul. The
report contains information on the mission, the hearings attended and
the accusations, and information on the detention of Apaydin and
others. With conclusions and recommendations for international bar
associations.

CATALOGUE SIGNATURE: 0000/2242/-4
TITLE: Text of the press conference held in Basle on July 5 1983 by
the first delegation of European mayors and city councillors after
its return from Fatsa (Turkey)
AUTHOR: Bourchardeau, François; Higgins, Michael; Diaz, Mario
(...et al)
TITLE OF GENERIC ITEM: CEDRI Bulletin
EDITION: v. 3
PLACE OF PUBLICATION: Basle
PUBLISHER: European Committee for the Defence of Refugees and
Immigrants - CEDRI (D)
DATE OF PUBLICATION: 830810
NUMBER OF PAGES: 8 p.
LANGUAGE: ENG
INDEX: trials / fact-finding missions
GEOGRAPHICAL INDEX: Turkey
GEOGRAPHICAL CODE: 8248
FREE TEXT: CEDRI aims to protect immigrants and refugees in European
countries. It sent a delegation of four persons to observe a trial
against 759 inhabitants of Fatsa. The report consists of the written
text of a press conference held by CEDRI and the delegation after the
mission; attention is paid to contacts with the authorities, a
description of the trial, the general atmosphere, meetings with the
police, the accused and inhabitants of Fatsa and the experiment of
self-management in Fatsa.

CATALOGUE SIGNATURE: 0000/0002/-3=830000
TITLE: Report of an assignment in Turkey 12/7 - 21/7/83 on behalf of
the Norwegian National Union of General Workers
AUTHOR: Johansen, Thor-Erik
PLACE OF PUBLICATION: Brussels
PUBLISHER: Norwegian National Union of General Workers ; International
Confederation of Free Trade Unions - ICFTU (D)
DATE OF PUBLICATION: 830000
NUMBER OF PAGES: 9 p.
LANGUAGE: ENG
INDEX: trade unions / trials / fact-finding missions
GEOGRAPHICAL INDEX: Turkey
GEOGRAPHICAL CODE: 8248
FREE TEXT: The purpose of the mission was to contact representatives
from mine workers' unions and to attend the trial against these unions,
as well as to get better known to the current situation for organized
workers. Special attention is paid to arrests, torture, detention,
working conditions of lawyers and legislation. With conclusions and
recommendations. With appendix: trade union trials.

CATALOGUE SIGNATURE: 0000/0966/-3=831100
TITLE: Cases No. 997, 999 and 1029: complaints presented by the
World Confederation of Labour, the World Federation of Trade Unions,
the International Confederation of Free Trade Unions and several
other trade union organisations against the government of Turkey
AUTHOR: International Labour Office - ILO - Committee on Freedom of
Association ; Lagergren, Ian
TITLE OF GENERIC ITEM: Official Bulletin: reports of the
Committee on Freedom of Association (230th, 231st and 232nd)
EDITION: v. LXVI, series B no. 3
PLACE OF PUBLICATION: Geneva
PUBLISHER: International Labour Office - ILO (D)
DATE OF PUBLICATION: 831100
NUMBER OF PAGES: p. 239-283
LANGUAGE: ENG
INDEX: association (freedom of) / trade unions / legislation /
detention / fact-finding missions
GEOGRAPHICAL INDEX: Turkey
GEOGRAPHICAL CODE: 8248
FREE TEXT: The Committee had before various complaints of infringements
of trade union rights in Turkey presented by various trade union
organizations. The report contains information on prior consideration
of the cases, new developments, new allegations by the complainants
and information gathered by representative of the Director-General Ian
Lagergren during his direct contacts mission in September 1983.
The analysis of the mission report deals with questions relating to
the detention of trade union officials (with information provided by
authorities and DISK detainees), questions concerning the new trade
union legislation and written information by the government. With
conclusions and recommendations of the Committee.
With annex: text of the report on the direct contacts mission, with
introduction, description of findings related to the detention of trade
unionists and the new trade union legislation, and concluding remarks.

CATALOGUE SIGNATURE: 0000/1245/-3=831103
TITLE: Human rights in Turkey's "transition to democracy": a Helsinki
Watch report
AUTHOR: Algrant, Roland ; Gieringer, Deborah ; Laber, Jeri
PLACE OF PUBLICATION: New York
PUBLISHER: Helsinki Watch - HW (D)
DATE OF PUBLICATION: 831103
NUMBER OF PAGES: 117 p.
LANGUAGE: ENG
BIBLIOGRAPHIES: Y
INDEX: democracy / civil and political rights / fact-finding missions
GEOGRAPHICAL INDEX: Turkey
GEOGRAPHICAL CODE: 8248
FREE TEXT: The report is partially based on information gathered by
Roland Algrant and Jeri Laber during a fact-finding mission to Turkey
in late September, 1983, partially on desk research. The fact finders
met with over fifty people representing a variety of professions and
attitudes. The report is divided in four sections: abuse of
individuals and their rights; destruction of independent institutions;
the legal basis for repression; the role of the United States in
Turkey. With recommendations, bibliography, appendices: appeals by
prisoners and family members; official court transcript of the
Kurtulus trial in Diyarbakir, 7 September 1983.

CATALOGUE SIGNATURE: 0000/0494/-0=831200
TITLE: Report on IFJ factfinding mission to Turkey
AUTHOR: Larsen, Hans
PLACE OF PUBLICATION: Brussels
PUBLISHER: International Federation of Journalists - IFJ (D)
DATE OF PUBLICATION: 831200
NUMBER OF PAGES: 5 p.
LANGUAGE: ENG
INDEX: press (freedom of the) / censorship / fact-finding missions
GEOGRAPHICAL INDEX: Turkey
GEOGRAPHICAL CODE: 8248
FREE TEXT: Report of a mission to Turkey from 18 to 26 October 1983.
Larsen investigated the existence of the freedom of press in Turkey,
and concludes that it does not exist at the moment. The military
authorities control the press by a number of measures, among which
the closing down of newspapers. Journalists are threatened and often
freely admit that they practice self-censorship. From time to time
indirect criticism is practised between the lines. The new Turkish
press laws make conditions worse. The Turkish Union of Journalists
is at present functioning under very strict limitations.

CATALOGUE SIGNATURE: 0000/0002/-3=840105
TITLE: ICFTU mission to Turkey
AUTHOR: Vanderveken, John ; Kluncker, Heinz ; Petterson, Björn
(...et al)
PLACE OF PUBLICATION: Brussels
PUBLISHER: International Confederation of Free Trade Unions - ICFTU
(D)
DATE OF PUBLICATION: 840105
NUMBER OF PAGES: 8 p. in v.p.
LANGUAGE: ENG
INDEX: trade unions / political prisoners / trials /
fact-finding missions
GEOGRAPHICAL INDEX: Turkey
GEOGRAPHICAL CODE: 8248
FREE TEXT: The mission of seven members met with leadership of the
Turk-Is trade union and discussed the reorganization of the trade
union movement in accordance with the new labour legislation. The
delegates observed the trial of the DISK trade union, accused of
marxist-leninist allegations; the trial only slowly takes its course.
The delegates also visited the Metris military prison, where the trade
union prisoners are kept. The (bad) detention conditions are described,
as well as a session with the prisoners. With annexes: circular of
General Secretary Vanderveken on Turkey; letter to the Prime Minister
of Turkey, Özal.

CATALOGUE SIGNATURE: 8000/1072/-0=840507
TITLE: Report on the situation in Turkey (I)
AUTHOR: Steiner, Ludwig
PLACE OF PUBLICATION: Strasbourg
PUBLISHER: Council of Europe - CoE - Parliamentary Assembly (D)
DATE OF PUBLICATION: 840507
NUMBER OF PAGES: 12 p. in v.p.
DOCUMENT SYMBOL: Doc. 5208
LANGUAGE: ENG
INDEX: democracy / fact-finding missions
GEOGRAPHICAL INDEX: Turkey
GEOGRAPHICAL CODE: 8248
FREE TEXT: Report by the rapporteur of the Political Affairs Committee
on the situation in Turkey, based on a fact-finding mission from 25 to
28 April 1984. The report contains a draft resolution by the Political
Affairs Committee, and an explanatory memorandum with conclusions on
the human rights situation in Turkey. With as an appendix the report
of the visit of the delegations of the Sub-committees on the situation
in Turkey of the Political Affairs and Legal Affairs Committees to the
military prisons in Mamak (Ankara) and Diyarbakir. The conduct of the
visits and the findings are described in detail.

CATALOGUE SIGNATURE: 8000/1072/-0=840508
TITLE: Opinion on the situation in Turkey presented by the Legal
Affairs Committee = Avis sur la situation en Turquie présenté par la
commission des questions juridiques
AUTHOR: Stoffelen, P.
PLACE OF PUBLICATION: Strasbourg
PUBLISHER: Council of Europe - CoE - Parliamentary Assembly (D)
DATE OF PUBLICATION: 840508
NUMBER OF PAGES: 9 p.
DOCUMENT SYMBOL: Doc. 5216
LANGUAGE: ENG / FRE
INDEX: democracy / fact-finding missions
GEOGRAPHICAL INDEX: Turkey
GEOGRAPHICAL CODE: 8248
FREE TEXT: Report by the rapporteur of the Legal Affairs Committee on
the situation in Turkey, based on a fact-finding mission from 26 to 28
28 April 1984. The report contains an introduction on the mission, and
information on the position of the Grand National Assembly, elections,
martial law, amnesty for political prisoners, and further respect for
human rights (the situation in prisons, freedom for lawyers and the
defence, freedom for political parties and trade unions, freedom of
the press, freedom of education and universities). With conclusions.

CATALOGUE SIGNATURE: 0000/0088/-4
TITLE: Report of a mission to Ankara in October 1984
AUTHOR: Truckenbrodt, Walter
TITLE OF GENERIC ITEM: ICJ Newsletter
EDITION: no. 24
PLACE OF PUBLICATION: Geneva
PUBLISHER: International Commission of Jurists - ICJ (D)
DATE OF PUBLICATION: 850100
NUMBER OF PAGES: p. 46-51
LANGUAGE: ENG
INDEX: association (freedom of) / trials / fact-finding missions
GEOGRAPHICAL INDEX: Turkey
GEOGRAPHICAL CODE: 8248
FREE TEXT: Report of a trial observation in the appeal of the TIKP
(Workers Peasants Party of Turkey) case before the Military Supreme
Court in Ankara. The defendants were charged with with having founded
the TIKP in January 1978 with the aim of establishing the domination
of one social class over other social classes and overthrowing the
existing social and economic order. With description of the case and
observations made during the hearings.

CATALOGUE SIGNATURE: 8000/1072/-0=850325
TITLE: Report on the situation in Turkey = Rapport sur la situation en Turquie
AUTHOR: Steiner, Ludwig
PLACE OF PUBLICATION: Strasbourg
PUBLISHER: Council of Europe - CoE - Parliamentary Assembly (D)
DATE OF PUBLICATION: 850325
NUMBER OF PAGES: 11 p.
DOCUMENT SYMBOL: Doc. 5378
LANGUAGE: ENG / FRE
INDEX: democracy / fact-finding missions
GEOGRAPHICAL INDEX: Turkey
GEOGRAPHICAL CODE: 8248
FREE TEXT: Report by the rapporteur of the Political Affairs Committee
on the situation in Turkey, based on a fact-finding mission to Turkey
from 5 to 9 March 1985. The report contains a draft resolution by the
Political Affairs Committee and an explanatory memorandum, based on
information of Turkish authorities and representatives of various
organizations and institutions. The report contains findings with
regard to the political and human-rights situation, and conclusions
with regard to the policy to be followed by the Council of Europe.
It is stated that some progress towards democracy has been made in
Turkey, but there still is much to be done. The Council of Europe has
the duty to persevere in its action to safeguard human rights and
freedoms, and campaign for their extension.
With appendices: articles of the Turkish constitution of 1982, in
connection with a possible amnesty; article of the constitution
dealing with institutions of higher education.

CATALOGUE SIGNATURE: 8000/1072/-0=850418
TITLE: Opinion on the situation in Turkey presented by the Legal
Affairs Committee
AUTHOR: Stoffelen, P.
PLACE OF PUBLICATION: Strasbourg
PUBLISHER: Council of Europe - CoE - Parliamentary Assembly (D)
DATE OF PUBLICATION: 850417
NUMBER OF PAGES: 15 p.
DOCUMENT SYMBOL: Doc. 5391
AVAILABILITY: X
LANGUAGE: ENG / FRE
INDEX: democracy / fact-finding missions
GEOGRAPHICAL INDEX: Turkey
GEOGRAPHICAL CODE: 8248
FREE TEXT: Opinion by the rapporteur of the Legal Affairs Committee on
the situation in Turkey, based on a fact-finding mission from 5 to 9
March 1985. The starting point of his evaluation was to see whether
or not the conclusions reached so far, concerning the Constitution,
important legislation and the position of the Grand National Assembly
are still valid. The report deals with martial law; amnesty for those
prosecuted or convicted for their opinions; the rights of the defence;
the situation in prisons, torture and degrading treatment; death
penalties; and other human rights issues. With conclusions: progress
can be noticed towards the full restoration of a normal parliamentary
democracy and complete respect of human rights, although a long way has
to be gone. With appendix: resolution 822 (1984) of the Parliamentary
Assembly on the situation in Turkey.

CATALOGUE SIGNATURE: 8000/2251/-3=851009
TITLE: Report drawn up on behalf of the Political Affairs Committee
on the human rights situation in Turkey = Verslag namens de Politieke
Commissie over de situatie van de mensenrechten in Turkije
AUTHOR: Balfe, R.
PLACE OF PUBLICATION: (Brussels)
PUBLISHER: European Parliament - EP (D)
DATE OF PUBLICATION: 851009
NUMBER OF PAGES: 47 p.
SERIES TITLE: Working Documents
DOCUMENT SYMBOL: A 2-117/85; PE 98.572/fin.
LANGUAGE: ENG / DUT
INDEX: democracy / fact-finding missions
GEOGRAPHICAL INDEX: Turkey
GEOGRAPHICAL CODE: 8248
FREE TEXT: The report on the situation of human rights in Turkey is
based on a fact-finding mission from 13 to 17 May 1985. Meetings were
held with representatives of five political parties, trade union
leaders, lawyers, journalists, civil servants, members of diplomatic
missions, ex-prisoners, relatives of prisoners and numerous other
witnesses. The report contains a motion for a resolution, and an
explanatory statement. This statement contains an introduction on the
background of the report, the method of enquiry and criteria used,
and chapters on: the right to life; the right to fair treatment and
security of the person; the right to a fair trial by independent
courts; the right to freedom of expression; the right to freedom of
association and assembly. The rapporteur concludes that, while there
has been some improvement in respect for human rights in Turkey, it
has been by no means dramatic; the views expressed were that respect
for human rights in Turkey is still a long way short of complying
with the most elementary standards. The rapporteur regrets that he
cannot recommend resumption of the parliamentary relations which
existed between the European and Turkish Parliaments before the
military intervention in 1980 resulted in the abolition of the
Turkish Parliament. With annexes: nine motions for a resolution.

CATALOGUE SIGNATURE: 0000/2921/-3=851100
TITLE: Turkey: "civilized" censorship under the sword of Damocles
AUTHOR: Kramer, Jane ; Randal, Jonathan
PLACE OF PUBLICATION: New York
PUBLISHER: Committee to Protect Journalists - CPJ (D)
DATE OF PUBLICATION: 851100
NUMBER OF PAGES: 32 p.
LANGUAGE: ENG
INDEX: censorship / press (freedom of the) / fact-finding missions
GEOGRAPHICAL INDEX: Turkey
GEOGRAPHICAL CODE: 8248
FREE TEXT: The report is based on a mission to Turkey in November 1984,
more than 50 interviews, and regular updates. The aim of the report is
to record changes in the situation of the Turkish press since a
parliamentary government was restored by the military regime, and with
it a small measure of press freedom. Attention is paid to the general
situation in Turkey, the way censorship works, and cases that
specifically involve press freedom.

CATALOGUE SIGNATURE: 0000/1245/-3=860300
TITLE: Freedom and fear: human rights in Turkey
AUTHOR: Laber, Jeri ; Henkin, Alice A.
PLACE OF PUBLICATION: New York ; Washington
PUBLISHER: Helsinki Watch - HW (D)
DATE OF PUBLICATION: 860300
NUMBER OF PAGES: 122 p.
LANGUAGE: ENG
INDEX: torture / civil and political rights / political prisoners /
fact-finding missions
GEOGRAPHICAL INDEX: Turkey
GEOGRAPHICAL CODE: 8248
FREE TEXT: This report is based on information gathered by the authors
during a fact-finding mission to Turkey in December 1985. It is divided
into four parts:
I) Freedom of expression and association: legal safeguards; freedom of
speech; freedom of the press; freedom to publish; academic freedom;
intellectual freedom; political freedom; freedom of assembly; freedom
of association; trade unions: the DISK trial;
II) Torture: recent cases of torture; police detention; punishment of
torturers;
III) The prisons: political prisoners, with attention to the Turkish
Peace Association, and Jehovah's witnesses; prison conditions; the
parliamentary report on prison conditions; the repentance law; amnesty;
rehabilitation of prisoners;
IV) The role of the United States, and some recommendations.

CATALOGUE SIGNATURE: 8000/1072/-0=860407
TITLE: Report on the situation in Turkey
AUTHOR: Steiner, Ludwig
PLACE OF PUBLICATION: Strasbourg
PUBLISHER: Council of Europe - CoE - Parliamentary Assembly (D)
DATE OF PUBLICATION: 860407
NUMBER OF PAGES: 6 p.
DOCUMENT SYMBOL: Doc. 5546
LANGUAGE: ENG / FRE
INDEX: democracy / fact-finding missions
GEOGRAPHICAL INDEX: Turkey
GEOGRAPHICAL CODE: 8248
FREE TEXT: Report by the rapporteur of the Political Affairs Committee
on the situation in Turkey, based on a fact-finding mission to Turkey
from 10 to 15 March 1986. The report contains a draft resolution by
the Political Affairs Committee and an explanatory memorandum, based
on information of Turkish authorities, the Turkish press, parties and
organizations inside and outside Turkey, and Amnesty International.
With findings of the mission and conclusions: "without any doubt, the
situation in Turkey has continued to improve over the last year...
The Parliamentary Assembly cannot but express approval if a European
state has the inner strength to find its way back to democracy."

CATALOGUE SIGNATURE: 0000/0138/-3=860800
TITLE: Rapport de mission en Turquie: Istanbul, 26-30 juillet 1986
AUTHOR: Salmon, Mireille
PLACE OF PUBLICATION: Brussels
PUBLISHER: Association Internationale des Juristes Démocrates - IADL (D)
DATE OF PUBLICATION: 860800
NUMBER OF PAGES: 6 p.
AVAILABILITY: X
LANGUAGE: FRE
INDEX: association (freedom of) / trials / fact-finding missions
GEOGRAPHICAL INDEX: Turkey
GEOGRAPHICAL CODE: 8248
FREE TEXT: The delegate went to Turkey to observe the part of a trial
against the Communist Party of Turkey during which the verdict was
pronounced. Her report contains background information on ongoing trials
in Turkey, the hearings and the verdict, and conclusions with regard to
future developments in Turkey.

UNITED KINGDOM

CATALOGUE SIGNATURE: 0000/0138/-0=840200
TITLE: Rapport de mission en Grande Bretagne sur les poursuites dont
sont l'objet les femmes de Greenham: 20-24 février 1984
AUTHOR: Picard-Weyl, Monique
PLACE OF PUBLICATION: Brussels
PUBLISHER: Association Internationale des Juristes Démocrates - IADL (D)
DATE OF PUBLICATION: 840200
NUMBER OF PAGES: 9 p.
LANGUAGE: FRE
INDEX: peace / peaceful assembly (right to) / trials /
fact-finding missions
GEOGRAPHICAL INDEX: United Kingdom
GEOGRAPHICAL CODE: 8251
FREE TEXT: In order to protest against the placement of US missiles in
the United Kingdom, a number of British women have established a camp
near the first basis where the missiles were to be installed. The
establishment of this peace camp and actions undertaken by the women
have been considered illegal by the authorities, and a number of them
has been arrested. During her mission, the delegate met with defense
lawyers of Greenham women; she also observed the hearings of 23
February at Newbury.
The report contains information on the alleged repression used against
the women, and impressions from the hearings. With appendices: relevant
legislation; Genocide Act; list of accused; newspaper article.

YUGOSLAVIA

CATALOGUE SIGNATURE: 0000/2856/-4
TITLE: The criminal trial of Yugoslav poet Vlado Gotovac: an
eyewitness account
AUTHOR: Kolb, Charles E.M.
TITLE OF GENERIC ITEM: Human Rights Quarterly: a comparative and
international journal of the social sciences, philosophy, and law
EDITION: v. 4(2)
PLACE OF PUBLICATION: Baltimore
PUBLISHER: Urban Morgan Institute for Human Rights - UMIHR ; John
Hopkins University Press (D)
DATE OF PUBLICATION: 820500
NUMBER OF PAGES: p. 184-211
LANGUAGE: ENG
BIBLIOGRAPHIES: Y
INDEX: expression (freedom of) / trials / fact-finding missions
GEOGRAPHICAL INDEX: Yugoslavia
GEOGRAPHICAL CODE: 8153
FREE TEXT: After the 1971 uprising, Gotovac was charged with
disseminating hostile propaganda, convicted and sentenced, and served
three years in prison. His sentence and also included a three-year
prohibition on public appearance and expression after completion of
his prison term. In 1981, he was charged again for among others the
dissemination of hostile propaganda.
The author of served as an observer at the criminal trial on behalf
of the International Human Rights Law Group IHRLG. His report contains
preliminary observations, background information on the case, a
description of the proceedings, interviews with Gotovac, the judge
and the prosecutor, an evaluation of the proceedings, references to
international human rights law. With conclusion.

CATALOGUE SIGNATURE: 0000/0966/-3=840000
TITLE: Trade union situation and labour relations in Yugoslavia: report
of a mission from the ILO
AUTHOR: Lagergren, Ian ; Schregle, Johannes ; Servais, Jean-Michel
(...et al)
PLACE OF PUBLICATION: Geneva
PUBLISHER: International Labour Office - ILO (D)
DATE OF PUBLICATION: 840000
NUMBER OF PAGES: 80 p.
LANGUAGE: ENG
STATISTICAL INFORMATION: Y
BIBLIOGRAPHIES: Y
INDEX: association (freedom of) / trade unions / fact-finding missions
GEOGRAPHICAL INDEX: Yugoslavia
GEOGRAPHICAL CODE: 8153
FREE TEXT: Report of a fact-finding mission in October 1983, to study
the trade union situation and the industrial relations system. Contacts
were established with authorities, representatives of trade unions,
jurists and researchers, and several undertakings were visited. The
report contains background information on the country, the trade union
movement, the organizations which represent the self-managed
enterprises, the Yugoslav system of self-management and its application
(self-management within the enterprise, the enterprise in the economy,
collective agreements), determination of income, the self-managed
public and social services, and disputes. With final remarks.

CATALOGUE SIGNATURE: 0000/0035/-3=840000
TITLE: Proès de messieurs Haroutioun Levonian et Raffi Elbekian:
Belgrade - février 1984: rapport de mission d'observation
judiciaire...
AUTHOR: Katz, Claude
PLACE OF PUBLICATION: Paris
PUBLISHER: Fédération Internationale des Droits de l'Homme - FIDH (D)
DATE OF PUBLICATION: 840000
NUMBER OF PAGES: 7 p.
LANGUAGE: FRE
INDEX: trials / fact-finding missions
GEOGRAPHICAL INDEX: Yugoslavia
GEOGRAPHICAL CODE: 8153
FREE TEXT: The report is based on the observation of a trial against
two Armenians, who were arrested after the assassination of the
Turkish ambassador. The aim of the mission was to investigate alleged
violations of the rights of the defence. The delegate was limited in
his attempts to fulfil the mission; in the report, serious doubts
concerning the fairness of the trial are expressed.

CATALOGUE SIGNATURE: 0000/1245/-3=840900
TITLE: Report on Yugoslavia: a Helsinki Watch report
AUTHOR: Beckman, Eric
PLACE OF PUBLICATION: New York
PUBLISHER: Helsinki Watch - HW (D)
DATE OF PUBLICATION: 840900
NUMBER OF PAGES: 24 p.
LANGUAGE: ENG
INDEX: expression (freedom of) / trials / fact-finding missions
GEOGRAPHICAL INDEX: Yugoslavia
GEOGRAPHICAL CODE: 8153
FREE TEXT: The report provides background information on the charges
against seven members of a free discussion group known as the "flying
university" and the current human rights situation. With: introduction
by Adrian DeWind; background: recent violations of the Helsinki accords
in Yugoslavia, with attention to legal and extralegal punishment,
freedom of expression, freedom of the press, prison conditions and
torture, unrest in Kosovo, nationalism in Bosnia-Herzegovina, emigrès
and workers abroad; report from sources in Yugoslavia with information
on the trial of the seven intellectuals; suggestions for action.

CATALOGUE SIGNATURE: 0000/0134/-0=850127
TITLE: Five days of the Belgrade trial against six intellectuals: 14
to 18 January, 1985: a report
AUTHOR: Drion, H.
PLACE OF PUBLICATION: Utrecht
PUBLISHER: International Humanist and Ethical Union - IHEU (D)
DATE OF PUBLICATION: 850127
NUMBER OF PAGES: 3 p.
LANGUAGE: ENG
INDEX: trials / fact-finding missions
GEOGRAPHICAL INDEX: Yugoslavia
GEOGRAPHICAL CODE: 8153
FREE TEXT: Short report on the Belgrade trial against six
intellectuals, with observations and impressions of the hearings and
conclusions with regard to the shortcomings of the proceedings.

TURKEY / IRAN

CATALOGUE SIGNATURE: 0000/0088/-4
TITLE: Trial of 27 Iranian students in Istanbul: report to the
International Commission of Jurists
AUTHOR: Meingast, Konrad
TITLE OF GENERIC ITEM: ICJ Newsletter
EDITION: no. 19
PLACE OF PUBLICATION: Geneva
PUBLISHER: International Commission of Jurists - ICJ (D)
DATE OF PUBLICATION: 831200
NUMBER OF PAGES: p. 61-63
LANGUAGE: ENG
INDEX: trials / fact-finding missions
GEOGRAPHICAL INDEX: Turkey / Iran
GEOGRAPHICAL CODE: 8248 / 7327
FREE TEXT: Report on the trial of 27 Iranian students who occupied
the General Consulate of Iran on 6 October 1981 in protest against
the mass executions in their country. The sentence does eliminate
the immediate danger of extradition, and gives time for diplomatic
interventions with a view to finding a country or countries willing
to accept the students as political refugees.

ARGENTINA

CATALOGUE SIGNATURE: 0000/0088/-3=750000
TITLE: Report ... on the situation of defence lawyers in Argentina,
March 1975
AUTHOR: Fragoso, Heleno Claudio
PLACE OF PUBLICATION: Geneva
PUBLISHER: International Commission of Jurists - ICJ (D)
DATE OF PUBLICATION: 750000
NUMBER OF PAGES: 21 p.
LANGUAGE: FRE
BIBLIOGRAPHIES: Y
INDEX: lawyers / political violence / fact-finding missions
GEOGRAPHICAL INDEX: Argentina
GEOGRAPHICAL CODE: 6414
FREE TEXT: The report is divided into two parts. The first part is on
the position in which lawyers who engage in the defence of political
detainees find themselves. They have been victims of extensive
violence, ranging from material damage and threats of murder to actual
physical elimination. With information on specific cases, mainly based
on written sources. In the second part, certain data are published on
the process of political violence. Attention is paid to the state of
siege, the subversive organizations, the activities of the para-police
groups, attacks on the judiciary, arrests, torture, freedom of the
press. With appendix: penal legislation.

CATALOGUE SIGNATURE: 0000/0035/-3=750500
TITLE: Rapport ... sur la situation des droits de l'homme en Argentine
AUTHOR: Aisenstein, Léopold ; Jacoby, Daniel ; Jaudel, Etienne
(...et al)
PLACE OF PUBLICATION: Paris
PUBLISHER: Fédération Internationale des Droits de l'Homme - FIDH
(D) ; Mouvement International des Juristes Catholiques Pax Romana - IMCL
(D)
DATE OF PUBLICATION: 750500
NUMBER OF PAGES: 92 p.
LANGUAGE: FRE
INDEX: political prisoners / fact-finding missions
GEOGRAPHICAL INDEX: Argentina
GEOGRAPHICAL CODE: 6414
FREE TEXT: The purposes of the four member mission to Argentina from
18 to 24 May 1975 were to collect information on the situation of
political prisoners, and on the human rights situation in general. The
report contains information on the mission, introductory conclusions,
and chapters on: democratic institutions and their degradation (with
attention to laws on associations of workers and trade unions, reform
of the penal code, law of national security, the state of siege);
principal violations of fundamental rights (trade unions, freedom of
information and the press, due process, political refugees from
countries like Chile and Uruguay, the universities and academic
freedom); the situation of political prisoners (legal, the period from
arrest to detention, detention conditions). With conclusions.

CATALOGUE SIGNATURE: 0000/0249/-3=770000
TITLE: Report of an Amnesty International mission to Argentina: 1-15 November 1976
AUTHOR: (Lord Avebury) ; (Drinan, Robert) ; (Feeney, Patricia)
PLACE OF PUBLICATION: London
PUBLISHER: Amnesty International - AI (D)
DATE OF PUBLICATION: 770000
NUMBER OF PAGES: 92 p.
ISBN: 0 900058 47 1
DOCUMENT SYMBOL: AI Index: PUB 68/00/77
LANGUAGE: ENG
STATISTICAL INFORMATION: Y
INDEX: civil and political rights / dictatorship / fact-finding missions
GEOGRAPHICAL INDEX: Argentina
GEOGRAPHICAL CODE: 6414
FREE TEXT: In March 1976, the government of Maria Estela de Peron was overthrown by a military coup, following which all violence increased. The aim of the mission was to discuss with members of the government the number and identity of political prisoners; the allegations of torture; the alleged complicity of the police and military in illegal and violent abductions; the status and security of Latin American refugees; the nature and effects of the legislation enacted since the coup.
The report contains an introduction, and chapters on legislation, prisons and prisoners, disappearances, torture and refugees. With conclusions and recommendations, and appendices: testimony concerning military tribunals; Lord Avebury's account of his visit to Villa Devoto prison; testimony concerning the operation of Uruguayan security forces in Argentina; cases of refoulement of Uruguayan refugees; representative case histories; list of disappearances since 24 March 1976; resolution 3452 (XXX) adopted by the United Nations.

CATALOGUE SIGNATURE: 0000/0035/-0=780100
TITLE: Rapport de la mission en Argentine effectuée du 18 au 25
janvier 1978
AUTHOR: Sanguinetti, Antoine ; Lépany, Franceline ; Semmel, Herbert
(et al...)
PLACE OF PUBLICATION: Paris
PUBLISHER: Fédération Internationale des Droits de l'Homme - FIDH (D)
DATE OF PUBLICATION: 780100
NUMBER OF PAGES: 29 p. in v.p.
LANGUAGE: FRE
INDEX: disappearances / detention / civil and political rights /
fact-finding missions
GEOGRAPHICAL INDEX: Argentina
GEOGRAPHICAL CODE: 6414
FREE TEXT: The aim of the mission was to investigate the situation of
a number of disappeared and detained persons. The report begins with a
description of the general situation in Argentina (regime, human rights
violations, prisoners, arrests and disappearances), followed by parts
on: legal procedures (habeas corpus, right to leave the country);
estimation of the quantity of human rights violations (disappearances,
prisoners, lists of prisoners, affirmations by the government);
perspectives for changes (legal resistance, the role of the church,
disagreement among the armed forces); the need for international
solidarity and possible actions.
With appendices: description of nongovernmental human rights
organizations, list of detained or disappeared lawyers, habeas corpus
in the case of Alfredo Bravo, worsening of the repression.

CATALOGUE SIGNATURE: 0000/0966/-0=780000
TITLE: Interim conclusions in the case relating to Argentina: case no.
842: complaints presented by the World Federation of Trade Unions, the
World Confederation of Labour, the National Confederation of Workers
of Peru and other workers' organisations against the government of
Argentina: complaint concerning the observance by Argentina of the
Freedom of Association and Protection of the Right to Organise
Convention (No. 87), presented by a number of delegates to the 63rd
(1977) session of the International Labour Conference under article 26
of the Constitution of the ILO
AUTHOR: International Labour Office - ILO - Committee on Freedom of
Association
TITLE OF GENERIC ITEM: Official Bulletin: reports of the Governing Body
Committee on Freedom of Association (187th, 188th and 189th)
EDITION: vol. LXI, series B no. 3
PLACE OF PUBLICATION: Geneva
PUBLISHER: International Labour Office - ILO (D)
DATE OF PUBLICATION: 780000
NUMBER OF PAGES: p. 155-180
LANGUAGE: ENG
INDEX: trade unions / association (freedom of) / disappearances /
fact-finding missions
GEOGRAPHICAL INDEX: Argentina
GEOGRAPHICAL CODE: 6414
FREE TEXT: The issues raised in this case have two aspects, one
relating to the arrest or disappearance of serving and former trade
unionists and the other to the taking over by the government of the
General Confederation of Labour (CGT) and other trade union
organizations, and to the restrictions imposed on trade union
activities. The report contains information on the treatment of the
cases and the mission to Argentina by Antonio Malintoppi, as
representative of the Director-General, and Luis Segovia from 27
August to 3 September 1978.
The Committee decided to examine the various outstanding issues in
the light of the mission report. Attention is given to: the arrest
or disappearance of serving and former trade unionists; the taking
over of trade union organizations and restrictions on trade union
activities; information gathered by the representative, and the
latest communication from the government. With conclusions and
recommendations, and annex: latest information communicated by the
government on persons mentioned in the complaints.

CATALOGUE SIGNATURE: 6414/-0=790522
TITLE: Report of the mission of lawyers to Argentina: April 1-7, 1979
AUTHOR: Schell, Orville H. ; Frankel, Marvin E. ; Healy, Harold H.
(et al...)
PLACE OF PUBLICATION: New York
PUBLISHER: Association of the Bar of the City of New York - ABNY (D)
DATE OF PUBLICATION: 790522
NUMBER OF PAGES: 48 p.
LANGUAGE: ENG
BIBLIOGRAPHIES: Y
INDEX: emergency legislation / justice (right to) / judicial systems /
civil and political rights / fact-finding missions
GEOGRAPHICAL INDEX: Argentina
GEOGRAPHICAL CODE: 6414
FREE TEXT: The aim of the five-member mission was to inquire into the
independence of lawyers and the administration of justice in Argentina,
in response to reports of widespread imprisonment, disappearance and
torture of lawyers and others. The delegates were mandated to express
the concern of the Association both for the ability of lawyers to carry
out their professional duties free of governmental intimidation, and
for the right of all incarcerated persons to humane treatment and fair
trials.
In the report, attention is paid to the state of siege (the
constitution, the military junta), detained persons (the grounds for
detention, the right of option and other limits on the executive power,
future perspectives), disappearances, prison conditions and the role of
the bar and the judiciary.

CATALOGUE SIGNATURE: 6000/1011/-3=800411
TITLE: Report on the situation of human rights in Argentina
AUTHOR: Inter-American Commission on Human Rights - IACHR
PLACE OF PUBLICATION: Washington DC
PUBLISHER: Organization of American States - OAS (D) ; Inter-American
Commission on Human Rights - IACHR
DATE OF PUBLICATION: 800411
NUMBER OF PAGES: 269 p. in v.p.
ISBN: 0 8270 1099 0
DOCUMENT SYMBOL: OEA/Ser.L/V/II.49 doc.19 corr.1
LANGUAGE: ENG
INDEX: civil and political rights / disappearances /
fact-finding missions
GEOGRAPHICAL INDEX: Argentina
GEOGRAPHICAL CODE: 6414
FREE TEXT: The report is largely based on the findings of a mission in
September 1979. After an introduction with the background, activities
of the Commission during its on-site observation, and the methodology,
the report is divided into the following chapters:
I) The political and legal system in Argentina, with attention to
restrictions on human rights under the legal system; the international
legal order; human rights, subversion and terrorism;
II) The right to life, with attention to deaths attributed by claimants
to government agents; deaths in prison; and the NN: unidentified dead;
III) The problem of "the disappeared", with some cases; testimonies;
the laws on disappeared;
IV) The right to liberty, with attention to preventive detention at the
disposal of the Executive and the right of option to leave the country;
V) Right to personal security, with attention to the prison system;
inspections is prisons and other detention centres; unlawful use of
force and torture; sanctions against those responsible for torture and
other unlawfull uses of force;
VI) The right to a fair trial and due process; VII) Freedom of opinion,
expression and information; VIII) Labour rights, and trade unions;
IX) Political rights; X) Religious freedom and worship; XI) Status of
human rights organizations. With conclusions and recommendations.

CATALOGUE SIGNATURE: 0000/1246/-3=831201
TITLE: "The elections in Argentina: one step toward democracy": a
mission report on the October 30 Argentine elections
AUTHOR: Claude, Richard ; Crotty, William ; Griesgraber, Jo Marie
(...et al)
PLACE OF PUBLICATION: Washington DC
PUBLISHER: International Human Rights Law Group - IHRLG (D) ;
Washington Office on Latin America - WOLA (D)
DATE OF PUBLICATION: 831201
NUMBER OF PAGES: 26 p.
LANGUAGE: ENG
INDEX: democracy / elections / fact-finding missions
GEOGRAPHICAL INDEX: Argentina
GEOGRAPHICAL CODE: 6414
FREE TEXT: On 30 October 1983 Argentina held its first elections in
ten years, ending seven years of extremely repressive military rule.
Convinced that elections are only one element in the democratic
process, a six member mission visited Argentina from 23 October until
2 November to observe the elections, and to learn whether the entire
electoral process was open, fair and just. In addition, the delegation
proposed to examine the challenges to the long-term survival of
democracy in Argentina, and to see what lessons might apply for other
countries moving form military authoritarianism to civilian democracy.
The report contains a summary, general conclusions, an analysis of
the electoral process, and prospects for democracy. With appendices:
participation in the elections by political parties and individuals;
the amnesty law; list of contacts in Argentina.

CATALOGUE SIGNATURE: 0000/1193/-0=840700
TITLE: The medical and scientific investigation of the human remains
of the "disappeared" and the identification of "disappeared" children
in Argentina: a preliminary report of a AAAS scientific delegation
AUTHOR: Levine, Lowell J. ; Lukash, Leslie ; King, Marie-Claire
(et al...)
PLACE OF PUBLICATION: Washington DC
PUBLISHER: American Association for the Advancement of Science - AAAS -
Committee on Scientific Freedom and Responsibility (D)
DATE OF PUBLICATION: 840700
NUMBER OF PAGES: 14 p.
LANGUAGE: ENG
INDEX: disappearances / torture / fact-finding missions
GEOGRAPHICAL INDEX: Argentina
GEOGRAPHICAL CODE: 6414
FREE TEXT: In June 1984, in response to a request from the Argentine
National Commission on Disappeared Persons, the AAAS sent a five member
scientific delegation to Argentina to observe and assist in the medical
and scientific investigation of the human remains of the "disappeared"
and the identification of "disappeared" children. The term disappeared
refers to the thousands of people killed or missing during Argentina's
period of military rule from 1976 to 1983. The delegation visited
individual and mass grave sites, morgues and forensic facilities, as
well as a former secret detention centre outside of Buenos Aires. The
team participated in symposia on the application of forensic techniques
and procedures designed to aid in the exhumation, identification, and
determination of probable cause of death of individuals interred in
mass and single, unmarked graves.
With summary of findings and recommendations regarding disappearance
and torture, the medical and scientific investigation and the
identification of "disappeared" children. With press release.

214

BOLIVIA

CATALOGUE SIGNATURE: 0000/0966/-0=770000
TITLE: Interim conclusions in the cases relating to Bolivia: complaints presented by a number of trade union organisations against the government of Bolivia (cases no. 685, 781, 806 and 814): complaint concerning the observance by Bolivia of the Freedom of Association and Protection of the Right to Organise Convention, 1948 (no. 87), made by a number of delegates to the 60th (1975) session of the International Labour Conference under article 26 of the Constitution of the ILO
AUTHOR: International Labour Office - ILO - Committee on Freedom of Association
TITLE OF GENERIC ITEM: Official Bulletin: reports of the Governing Body Committee on Freedom of Association (160th, 161st, 162nd, 163rd)
EDITION: vol. LX, series B no. 1
PLACE OF PUBLICATION: Geneva
PUBLISHER: International Labour Office - ILO (D)
DATE OF PUBLICATION: 770000
NUMBER OF PAGES: p. 128-172
LANGUAGE: ENG
INDEX: association (freedom of) / trade unions / legislation / fact-finding missions
GEOGRAPHICAL INDEX: Bolivia
GEOGRAPHICAL CODE: 6419
FREE TEXT: The Committee has been examining various complaints concerning infringement of trade union rights in Bolivia; the Director-General appointed Geraldo von Potobsky to undertake missions to Bolivia in March-April and in June-July 1976. Following, the Committee examined the complaints, taking into account the reports of the missions.
The report of the Committee contains background information on the country, allegations relating to the first phase (21 August 1971 - 9 November 1974); allegations regarding the second phase (from 9 November 1974): legal provisions in respect of trade unions; the closing down of radio stations belonging to miners' unions; the arrests at Agua de Castilla in Oruro; the dismissal of workers and trade union officials at the "Manaco" footwear factory; trade union legislation in general (with comments referring to freedom of association sent by the government: provisions of the draft Labour Code and Rules of Procedure dealing with workers' and employers' organizations and collective labour disputes); events in the mining sector in June and July 1976; the arrest of Marcel Pepin, president of the WCL. With conclusions and recommendations.

Bolivia

CATALOGUE SIGNATURE: 0000/0138/-3=800000
TITLE: Mission d'enquête en Bolivie: 11 au 16 août 1980
AUTHOR: Nordmann, Joë
PLACE OF PUBLICATION: Brussels
PUBLISHER: Association Internationale des Juristes Démocrates - IADL (D)
DATE OF PUBLICATION: 800000
NUMBER OF PAGES: 33 p. in v.p.
LANGUAGE: FRE
INDEX: dictatorship / fact-finding missions
GEOGRAPHICAL INDEX: Bolivia
GEOGRAPHICAL CODE: 6419
FREE TEXT: The aims of the mission were to express solidarity with
the Bolivian people and to inform the public opinion and international
institutions on the situation in the country. The delegate reports on
the background of the country and the military putsch of 17 July 1980,
which halted a process of democratization. Many people were arrested,
tortured or murdered. The severe and systematic violations of human
rights are listed. With annexes: resolution of the Sub-Commission on
Prevention of Discrimination and Protection of Minorities of the
United Nations; correspondence between IADL and UNESCO; resolution of
the Inter-Parliamentary Union; interview with a leader of the miners'
trade union; correspondence between wives of miners and the Archbishop
of La Paz; declaration of Episcopal Conference of Bolivia.

CATALOGUE SIGNATURE: 0000/0966/-0=800000
TITLE: Case no. 983: complaints presented by the International
Confederation of Free Trade Unions, the World Confederation of Labour,
the World Federation of Trade Unions and other workers' organisations
against the government of Bolivia
AUTHOR: International Labour Office - ILO - Committee on Freedom of
Association
TITLE OF GENERIC ITEM: Official Bulletin: reports of the Governing Body
Committee on Freedom of Association (204rd, 205th, 206th)
EDITION: vol. LXIII, series B no. 3
PLACE OF PUBLICATION: Geneva
PUBLISHER: International Labour Office - ILO (D)
DATE OF PUBLICATION: 800000
NUMBER OF PAGES: p. 86-96
LANGUAGE: ENG
INDEX: association (freedom of) / trade unions / detention /
fact-finding missions
GEOGRAPHICAL INDEX: Bolivia
GEOGRAPHICAL CODE: 6419
FREE TEXT: In view of the seriousness of the allegations and on request
of the Director-General, a direct contacts mission to Bolivia was
carried out in October 1980 by his representative Ian Lagergren and by
Daniel de Patoul. The case was examined by the Committee in the light
of the information obtained during the mission and a communication
received by the government.
The report of the Committee contains the allegations of the
complainants, information obtained during the mission, the reply of
the government, and conclusions and recommendations of the Committee.
With appendix: information obtained concerning persons referred to by
the complainants.

CATALOGUE SIGNATURE: 0000/0249/-3=810200
TITLE: Memorandum from Amnesty International to His Excellency General
Luis García Meza President of the Republic of Bolivia
AUTHOR: (Sanguinetti, Antoine) ; (Klein, Michael) ; (Feeney, Patricia)
PLACE OF PUBLICATION: London
PUBLISHER: Amnesty International - AI (D)
DATE OF PUBLICATION: 810200
NUMBER OF PAGES: 13 p.
DOCUMENT SYMBOL: AI Index: AMR 18/05/81
LANGUAGE: ENG
INDEX: civil and political rights / fact-finding missions
GEOGRAPHICAL INDEX: Bolivia
GEOGRAPHICAL CODE: 6419
FREE TEXT: The mission visited La Paz, Bolivia, on 16-25 November 1980
to discuss reports of persistent human rights violations since the coup
of July 1980. The report contains information on the protection of
human rights in Bolivia; arbitrary arrest, detention and exile; torture
and cruel, inhuman or degrading treatment or punishment; disappearances
and political killings, with references to specific cases. With
recommendations.
It is concluded that widespread, serious human rights violations have
occurred in Bolivia; reports received since the mission indicate that
these abuses are continuing.

CATALOGUE SIGNATURE: 0000/1079/-3=811231
TITLE: Study by the Special Envoy of the Commission on Human Rights,
Professor Héctor Gros Espiell, appointed pursuant to resolution 34
(XXXVII) of the Commission on Human Rights of 11 March 1981, on the
human rights situation in Bolivia
AUTHOR: Gros Espiell, Héctor
PLACE OF PUBLICATION: Geneva
PUBLISHER: Commission on Human Rights of the United Nations Economic
and Social Council - UNCHR (D)
DATE OF PUBLICATION: 811231
NUMBER OF PAGES: 57 p. in v.p.
SERIES TITLE: Commission on Human Rights: thirty-eight session: item 12
of the provisional agenda: question of the violation of human rights
and fundamental freedoms in any part of the world, with particular
reference to colonial and other dependent countries and territories
DOCUMENT SYMBOL: E/CN.4/1500
AVAILABILITY: F
LANGUAGE: ENG / SPA
BIBLIOGRAPHIES: Y
INDEX: legislation / fact-finding missions
GEOGRAPHICAL INDEX: Bolivia
GEOGRAPHICAL CODE: 6419
FREE TEXT: The report deals with the general situation of human rights
in Bolivia. It contains: an introduction and background information
on the mission; the international and domestic legal framework;
a classification of alleged violations; the purpose of the study;
sources; other studies or reports on the situation of human rights
in Bolivia; the period covered by the study; political developments
between 17 July 1980 and 27 October 1981; criteria for the evaluation
of information and documentation; classification and analysis of the
principal alleged or reported violations of human rights; the visit
to Bolivia in October 1981. With conclusions.

CATALOGUE SIGNATURE: 0000/1079/-3=821213
TITLE: Study by the Special Envoy of the Commission on Human Rights,
Professor Héctor Gros Espiell, appointed pursuant to resolution 1982/33
of the Commission on Human Rights, of 11 March 1982, on the human
rights situation in Bolivia
AUTHOR: Gros Espiell, Héctor
PLACE OF PUBLICATION: Geneva
PUBLISHER: Commission on Human Rights of the United Nations Economic
and Social Council - UNCHR (D)
DATE OF PUBLICATION: 821213
NUMBER OF PAGES: 49 p. in v.p.
SERIES TITLE: Commission on Human Rights: thirty-ninth session: item 12
of the provisional agenda: question of the violation of human rights
and fundamental freedoms in any part of the world, with particular
reference to colonial and other dependent countries and territories
DOCUMENT SYMBOL: E/CN.4/1983/22
AVAILABILITY: F
LANGUAGE: ENG / SPA
INDEX: protection / legislation / fact-finding missions
GEOGRAPHICAL INDEX: Bolivia
GEOGRAPHICAL CODE: 6419
FREE TEXT: The study comprises an analysis of the implementation of the
government of Bolivia of practical measures to ensure full respect for
human rights and fundamental freedoms. The report contains: an
introduction; background information; a review of documents and
communications received; the international legal framework; alleged
violations of human rights and fundamental freedoms in Bolivia since
March 1982: classification and analysis; political developments between
March 1982 and February 1983; the visit to Bolivia in November 1982.
With conclusions.

CATALOGUE SIGNATURE: 0000/1079/-3=840118
TITLE: Assistance to Bolivia
AUTHOR: Gros Espiell, Hèctor
PLACE OF PUBLICATION: Geneva
PUBLISHER: Commission on Human Rights of the United Nations Economic
and Social Council - UNCHR (D)
DATE OF PUBLICATION: 840118
NUMBER OF PAGES: 16 p. in v.p.
SERIES TITLE: Commission on Human Rights: fortieth session: item 22 of
the provisional agenda: advisory services in the field of human
rights
DOCUMENT SYMBOL: E/CN.4/1984/46
AVAILABILITY: F
LANGUAGE: ENG / SPA
INDEX: protection / legislation / development / fact-finding missions
GEOGRAPHICAL INDEX: Bolivia
GEOGRAPHICAL CODE: 6419
FREE TEXT: Pursuant to resolution 1983/33 of the Commission on Human
Rights, Gros Espiell was appointed as expert to provide advisory
services and other forms of appropriate human rights assistance as may
be requested by the government of Bolivia. His report contains an
introduction with background information on the mission, and sections
on: the meaning and object of the report; human rights advisory
services and assistance in Bolivia; the impact of the adverse economic
and social conditions in Bolivia on the effective enjoyment of human
rights, and action by the United Nations. With conclusions and
recommendations.

CATALOGUE SIGNATURE: 0000/0249/-0=840900
TITLE: Human rights in Bolivia: findings of an Amnesty International
mission February - March 1984
AUTHOR: (Banos, Jorge)
PLACE OF PUBLICATION: London
PUBLISHER: Amnesty International - AI (D)
DATE OF PUBLICATION: 840900
NUMBER OF PAGES: 36 p.
DOCUMENT SYMBOL: AI Index: AMR 18/04/84
LANGUAGE: ENG
INDEX: disappearances / detention / fact-finding missions
GEOGRAPHICAL INDEX: Bolivia
GEOGRAPHICAL CODE: 6419
FREE TEXT: The aim of the mission was to discuss with government
representatives and national organizations the progress made both
in promoting and protecting human rights and in investigating past
abuses, particularly "disappearances" and extrajudicial executions.
The delegation also investigated the situation of seven prisoners.
With attention to the background of the country, disappearances in
general and a number of specific cases, judicial investigations into
disappearances and extrajudicial executions and cases, the killing of
the leaders of the revolutionary movement MIR, torture of prisoners
in military custody and cases, the legal situation of the seven
prisoners and death in military custody.

BRAZIL

CATALOGUE SIGNATURE: 0000/0138/-3=760301
TITLE: Brazil 76: political prisoners and the state of emergency =
Brésil 76: prisonniers politiques et état d'exception
AUTHOR: Weil, Jean-Louis
PLACE OF PUBLICATION: Brussels
PUBLISHER: International Association of Democratic Lawyers - IADL (D)
DATE OF PUBLICATION: 760301
NUMBER OF PAGES: 25 p.
LANGUAGE: ENG / FRE
STATISTICAL INFORMATION: Y
INDEX: political prisoners / emergency legislation /
fact-finding missions
GEOGRAPHICAL INDEX: Brazil
GEOGRAPHICAL CODE: 6420
FREE TEXT: The report is divided in three parts. The first is on the
historical background of exceptional legislation and the state of
emergency since the coup d'état of April 1964, including legislative
texts. The second part is on the economic and social structure of
Brazil. The third part, "Repression in 1976", is based on documentary
material collected during a fact-finding mission in December 1975.
Important is a document from Brazilian prisoners establishing a
synthesis and general picture of repression.
With annexes: declaration by the bishops of the state of Sao Paulo;
two documents from the federal police.

CATALOGUE SIGNATURE: 0000/0249/-3=820900
TITLE: A report of the trial of Father Aristides Camio and Father
François Gouriou, Belém, 21-22 June 1982
AUTHOR: Amnesty International - AI
PLACE OF PUBLICATION: London
PUBLISHER: Amnesty International - AI (D)
DATE OF PUBLICATION: 820900
NUMBER OF PAGES: (13 p.)
DOCUMENT SYMBOL: AI Index: AMR 19/07/82
LANGUAGE: ENG
INDEX: judicial systems / expression (freedom of) / trials /
fact-finding missions
GEOGRAPHICAL INDEX: Brazil
GEOGRAPHICAL CODE: 6420
FREE TEXT: On 22 June 1982, a military court in Belém found two French
priests, Aristides Camio and François Gouriou, guilty of inciting
"violent struggle between social classes". The co-defendants, a group
of 13 peasants, were found guilty of using "violence for reasons of
dissidence or socio-political non-conformity against those in
authority."
The document contains a description of the trial proceedings by an AI
observer, as well as information on the competence of the military
court, flaws in the criminal investigation, the lack of precision in
the formal charges, irregularities in the judicial hearing, and the
aftermath. With assessment (conclusions), glossary and map.

CATALOGUE SIGNATURE: 0000/0249/-3=830800
TITLE: Brazil: a report on the appeal to the Supreme Military Tribunal
by Father Aristides Camio and Father François Gouriou and thirteen
posseiros: Brasilia 2-3 December 1982
AUTHOR: (Klein, Peter)
PLACE OF PUBLICATION: London
PUBLISHER: Amnesty International - AI (D)
DATE OF PUBLICATION: 830800
NUMBER OF PAGES: 14 p. in v.p.
DOCUMENT SYMBOL: AI Index: AMR 19/02/83
LANGUAGE: ENG
INDEX: judicial systems / trials / fact-finding missions
GEOGRAPHICAL INDEX: Brazil
GEOGRAPHICAL CODE: 6420
FREE TEXT: The Supreme Military Tribunal found the two french priests
guilty of inciting "violent struggle between social classes" and of
"collective disobedience of the laws". Also the convictions against
the co-defendants, 13 peasant squatters (posseiros), were upheld.
The report contains information on the proceedings at the appeal
(including presentations by the prosecutor and defence lawyers, the
vote of the ministers and the formal pronouncement of the decision)
and AI's assessment of the case. With appendix: information on the
aftermath of the appeal.

CANADA

CATALOGUE SIGNATURE: 0000/1246/-3=820923
TITLE: The riot and deaths at Archambault Penitentiary,
Sainte-Anne-des-Plaines, Canada, on July 25, 1982: a report to the
International Human Rights Law Group
AUTHOR: Kolb, Charles E.M.
PLACE OF PUBLICATION: Washington DC
PUBLISHER: International Human Rights Law Group - IHRLG (D)
DATE OF PUBLICATION: 820923
NUMBER OF PAGES: 67 p.
LANGUAGE: ENG
INDEX: prison conditions / legislation / fact-finding missions
GEOGRAPHICAL INDEX: Canada
GEOGRAPHICAL CODE: 6322
FREE TEXT: During the night from July 25 to 26, 1982, tragic events
occurred in the prison of Archambault, Quebec, during which three
guards and two detainees died. The purpose of the mission was to
inspect the prison and to meet with people involved in order to
prepare a detailed report on the reported violations of the civil
and human rights of the prisoners. With description of events, based
on on-site visits and interviews with staff, prisoners, correctional
officers and attorneys. The findings are appraised in the framework
of Canadian constitutional law and other applicable statutes,
declarations, rules and judicial decisions. With conclusions and
recommendations.

CATALOGUE SIGNATURE: 0000/0035/-3=820000
TITLE: Rapport de mission sur la situation au pénitencier Archambault
à Saint-Anne des Plaines, Québec, Canada
AUTHOR: Maleville, Thierry
PLACE OF PUBLICATION: Paris
PUBLISHER: Fédération Internationale des Droits de l'Homme - FIDH (D)
DATE OF PUBLICATION: 820000
NUMBER OF PAGES: 20 p.
LANGUAGE: FRE
INDEX: prison conditions / fact-finding missions
GEOGRAPHICAL INDEX: Canada
GEOGRAPHICAL CODE: 6322
FREE TEXT: During the night from 25 to 26 July 1982, tragic events
occurred in the prison of Archambault, Quebec, during which three
guards and two detainees died. The purpose of the mission was to
investigate causes of the incidents, detention conditions before and
after the riot of the prisoners and the rights of the defence, and to
assist at an investigation.
With description of events, observation of a trial against three
detainees, interviews with family members of detainees, defence
lawyers, detainees, the director of the prison and others.
With conclusions and recommendations, and guidelines for legal
observers of the FIDH.

CATALOGUE SIGNATURE: 0000/0249/-3=830000
TITLE: Amnesty International report on allegations of ill-treatment of
prisoners at Archambault institution, Quebec, Canada (including a
memorandum to the government of Canada following a mission from 10 to
15 April 1983)
AUTHOR: (Weissbrodt, David) ; (Jaffé, Helen)
PLACE OF PUBLICATION: London
PUBLISHER: Amnesty International - AI (D)
DATE OF PUBLICATION: 830000
NUMBER OF PAGES: 46 p. in v.p.
ISBN: 0 86210 062 3
DOCUMENT SYMBOL: AI Index: AMR 20/03/83
LANGUAGE: ENG
BIBLIOGRAPHIES: Y
INDEX: detention / prison conditions / fact-finding missions
GEOGRAPHICAL INDEX: Canada
GEOGRAPHICAL CODE: 6322
FREE TEXT: The mission went to Quebec to collect information on the
treatment of inmates of Archambault Institution following a riot in the
prison on 25 July 1982. The mission was undertaken because of AI's
opposition to torture and other cruel, inhuman or degrading treatment
or punishment of all prisoners without reservation. The delegates
interviewed prisoners, the families of prisoners, prison officials, and
those who have conducted official and unofficial investigations of the
situation at the prison following the riot. The mission included a
visit to the prison.
The report contains chapters on the riot and its aftermath, allegations
of ill-treatment, an assessment of the credibility of the testimony by
prisoners, official investigations, previous outside inquiries (other
fact-finding missions), and the lack of complaints to the authorities.
With conclusions, recommendations and appendices: correspondence
between AI and Canadian authorities.

CHILE

CATALOGUE SIGNATURE: 0000/0249/-3=730000
TITLE: Report of a mission to Santiago, Chile: 1st-8th November, 1973
AUTHOR: Newman, Frank C. ; Sumner, Bruce W. ; Plant, Roger
PLACE OF PUBLICATION: London
PUBLISHER: Amnesty International - AI (D)
DATE OF PUBLICATION: 730000
NUMBER OF PAGES: 17 p. in v.p.
LANGUAGE: ENG
INDEX: political prisoners / fact-finding missions
GEOGRAPHICAL INDEX: Chile
GEOGRAPHICAL CODE: 6424
FREE TEXT: The main aims of the mission were to make representations
to the government concerning the executions being carried out; to
enquire into and report upon the procedures of interrogation,
detention, charge and trial of those who are in custody; to enquire
into allegations of torture; to meet with those responsible for
representation of prisoners before the courts and tribunals; and to
advise on financial and other assistance which can be given to
prisoners and their families. The report contains the findings of the
mission, conclusions and appendices: letters by Newman and by a group
of lawyers to the Colegio de Abogados.

CATALOGUE SIGNATURE: 6424/-0=740000
TITLE: Report of the Chicago commission of inquiry into the status of
human rights in Chile
AUTHOR: DeMaio, Ernest ; Feinglass, Abraham ; Fox, Geoffrey (et al...)
PLACE OF PUBLICATION: (Chicago)
PUBLISHER: (Chicago Citizens' Committee to Save Lives in Chile) (D)
DATE OF PUBLICATION: 740000
NUMBER OF PAGES: 35 p. in v.p.
LANGUAGE: ENG
INDEX: dictatorship / political violence / fact-finding missions
GEOGRAPHICAL INDEX: Chile
GEOGRAPHICAL CODE: 6424
FREE TEXT: The mission consisted of twelve inhabitants of Chicago from
different walks of life. The purpose of the mission was to investigate
the situation of human rights after the military took over power on 11
September 1973. The report contains a summary of findings, a
description of the work of the mission and the organization of the
report and the evidence, and an analysis of the situation in Chile.
Attention is paid to the general atmosphere of "state of war",
detentions and executions, the economic situation, trade unions, health
and social services, education, mass media, the treatment of minority
groups and the investigation of the murder of Frank Teruggi, Jr. With
list of persons interviewed.

CATALOGUE SIGNATURE: 0000/0088/-3=740000
TITLE: Final report of mission to Chile, April 1974, to study the
legal system and the protection of human rights
AUTHOR: MacDermot, Niall ; Madlener, Kurt ; Covey, Oliver
PLACE OF PUBLICATION: Geneva
PUBLISHER: International Commission of Jurists - ICJ (D)
DATE OF PUBLICATION: 740000
NUMBER OF PAGES: 39 p.
LANGUAGE: ENG
INDEX: judicial systems / civil and political rights /
fact-finding missions
GEOGRAPHICAL INDEX: Chile
GEOGRAPHICAL CODE: 6424
FREE TEXT: The mission was established to inquire into the situation
concerning human rights and the rule of law. The report deals with
the political background and the reasons given in justification of
the military coup of 1973; the Junta and the constitution; the legal
basis of the state of siege and suspension of civil rights and
fundamental freedoms; the system of military justice in time of war;
the arrest, interrogation and detention of political suspects and the
treatment of foreigners. With elaborate comments and conclusions, and
appendix: case at the Supreme Court of Justice.

CATALOGUE SIGNATURE: 0000/0138/-3=740600
TITLE: Mission internationale de juristes au Chili: rapport de René de
Schutter (Belgique) et Mauricio Birgin (Argentine) sur leur mission à
Santiago: 14-21 avril 1974
AUTHOR: Schutter, René de ; Birgin, Mauricio
PLACE OF PUBLICATION: Brussels
PUBLISHER: Association Internationale des Juristes Démocrates - IADL (D)
DATE OF PUBLICATION: 740600
NUMBER OF PAGES: (36 p.)
LANGUAGE: FRE / SPA
INDEX: dictatorship / trials / fact-finding missions
GEOGRAPHICAL INDEX: Chile
GEOGRAPHICAL CODE: 6424
FREE TEXT: The aims of the mission were to obtain information on the
general situation in Chile and the actual forms of repression, and more
specifically on the violations of social and trade union rights by the
military Junta.
The first part of the report, by René de Schutter, is in french. It
contains information on the conduct of the mission, the repression in
Chile; observations made at hearings of the trial of the Chilean Air
Force; the situation of refugees and asylum; the situation of trade
unions; and the social and economic situation. With conclusions, and
annexes: press release on the trial by a US-based NGO; some figures on
the social-economic situation.
The second part of the report, by Mauricio Birgin, is in spanish. It
deals with the general situation of repression in Chile, the powers of
the military Junta, the judicial powers, the situation of civil and
political rights, and the trial of the Chilean Air Force.

CATALOGUE SIGNATURE: 0000/0249/-3=740900
TITLE: Chile: an Amnesty International report = Chile: ein Bericht von
Amnesty International
AUTHOR: Amnesty International - AI
PLACE OF PUBLICATION: London
PUBLISHER: Amnesty International - AI (D)
DATE OF PUBLICATION: 740900
NUMBER OF PAGES: 80 p.
ISBN: 0 900058 01 3
DOCUMENT SYMBOL: AI Index: PUB 31/00/74
LANGUAGE: ENG
INDEX: political prisoners / judicial systems / fact-finding missions
GEOGRAPHICAL INDEX: Chile
GEOGRAPHICAL CODE: 6424
FREE TEXT: Since September 1973, when the democratically elected
government of President Allende was overthrown in a military coup of
astonishing savagery, the infringement and repression of human rights
in Chile have continued unabated. The report is based on information
submitted to Amnesty International by organizations which have
conducted inquiries in Chile since September 1973, the findings of
a mission to Santiago in November 1973, and findings of lawyers who
recently visited Chile. It deals with the situation of political
prisoners, their identity, legal situation, treatment and conditions.
A major section of the report is devoted to the analysis of military
justice in Chile, and a description of the severe and almost
insurmountable problems facing lawyers who have attempted to give a
serious defence to political prisoners.
With appendices: information on specific cases of repression;
chronology of the activities of AI with regard to the situation of
human rights in Chile.

CATALOGUE SIGNATURE: 0000/0966/-3=750000
TITLE: The trade union situation in Chile: report of the Fact-Finding
and Conciliation Commission on Freedom of Association
AUTHOR: Bustamante i Rivero, Jose Luis ; Ducoux, Jacques ;
Kirkaldy, H.S.
PLACE OF PUBLICATION: Geneva
PUBLISHER: International Labour Office - ILO (D)
DATE OF PUBLICATION: 750000
NUMBER OF PAGES: 155 p. in v.p.
ISBN: 92 2 101345 6
LANGUAGE: ENG
BIBLIOGRAPHIES: Y
STATISTICAL INFORMATION: Y
INDEX: association (freedom of) / trade unions / legislation /
fact-finding missions
GEOGRAPHICAL INDEX: Chile
GEOGRAPHICAL CODE: 6424
FREE TEXT: The function of the Commission, established in 1950, is
to examine such cases of infringements or alleged infringements of
trade union rights as may be referred to it, to ascertain the facts,
and to discuss the situation with the government concerned with a
view to securing the adjustment of difficulties by agreement.
The report of the Commission consists of six parts:
-introduction; referral of the case of Chile and appointment of a
panel; summary of the case brought before the Commission;
-procedure adopted by the Commission (two sessions in Geneva;
communications received; the visit to Chile from 28 November to 19
December 1974);
-Chilean legislation respecting trade unions;
-examination of the case by the Commission (dissolution of trade
union; death and execution of trade union leaders; detention of trade
union leaders; dismissal and resignation of trade union leaders;
situation with regard to the executive organs of trade union
organizations; trade union meetings; collective bargaining, the right
to strike and claims within the undertaking; relations between trade
unions and the authorities; the new draft legislation on trade union
organizations; further communications and comments received by the
Commission);
-conclusions and recommendations.
With appendices: lists of trade union leaders or former leaders;
Draft Bill on trade union organizations; Draft Labour Code (extracts).

CATALOGUE SIGNATURE: 0000/0966/-3=750000
TITLE: Report of the Commission appointed under article 26 of the
Constitution of the International Labour Organisation to examine the
observance by Chile of the Hours of Work (Industry) Convention, 1919
(no. 1), and the Discrimination (Employment and Occupation) Convention,
1958 (no. 111)
AUTHOR: Bustamante i Rivero, Jose Luis ; Ducoux, Jacques ;
Kirkaldy, H.S.
PLACE OF PUBLICATION: Geneva
PUBLISHER: International Labour Office - ILO (D)
DATE OF PUBLICATION: 750000
NUMBER OF PAGES: 54 p.
ISBN: 92 2 101346 4
LANGUAGE: ENG
BIBLIOGRAPHIES: Y
INDEX: social and economic rights / legislation / fact-finding missions
GEOGRAPHICAL INDEX: Chile
GEOGRAPHICAL CODE: 6424
FREE TEXT: In view of a resolution of the International Labour
Conference at its 59th session, the Governing Body appointed a three
member commission under article 26 of the Constitution. The report of
the commission consists of four parts:
-the appointment of the Commission;
-procedures followed by the Commission (sessions in Geneva, evidence
received, the visit to Chile from 28 November to 19 December 1974);
-the question concerning the observance by Chile of the Hours of Work
(Industry) Convention (increase in hours of work; written statements
of international organizations of workers and of the government of
Chile; statements of witnesses and information gathered in Chile;
conclusions);
-the question concerning the observance by Chile of the Discrimination
(Employment and Occupation) Convention: dismissals carried out since
11 September 1973; written statements of the international workers'
organizations and the government of Chile; statements of witnesses and
information gathered in Chile; supplementary communication from the
government of Chile; conclusions and recommendations).

CATALOGUE SIGNATURE: 0000/0035/-3=750000
TITLE: Mission à Santiago du Chili du 6 au 14 mai 1975...
AUTHOR: Gaillac, Henry ; De Givry, Emmanuel
PLACE OF PUBLICATION: Paris
PUBLISHER: Fédération Internationale des Droits de l'Homme - FIDH
(D) ; Mouvement International des Juristes Catholiques Pax Romana -
IMCL (D)
DATE OF PUBLICATION: 750000
NUMBER OF PAGES: 34 p.
LANGUAGE: FRE
INDEX: judicial systems / legislation / fact-finding missions
GEOGRAPHICAL INDEX: Chile
GEOGRAPHICAL CODE: 6424
FREE TEXT: The report, based on a mission in May 1975, deals with the
judicial system in Chile, the conditions under which the rights of the
defence are exercised and the functioning of habeas corpus procedures.
Attention is given to the conduct of the mission, the normative system,
the imperfections in the judicial system (repression, and demission of
the Supreme Court), the Decrees 1008 and 1009, the rights of the
defence, repression (with reference to specific cases) and general
economic developments.

CATALOGUE SIGNATURE: 0000/2121/-3=760200
DATE OF ENTRY: 840501
TITLE: Rapport de mission au Chili (décembre 1975)
AUTHOR: Cuvelliez, Marie-Thérèse
PLACE OF PUBLICATION: Brussels
PUBLISHER: Ligue Belge pour la Défense des Droits de l'Homme - LBDDH
(D)
DATE OF PUBLICATION: 760200
NUMBER OF PAGES: 7 p.
LANGUAGE: FRE
INDEX: political prisoners / dictatorship / fact-finding missions
GEOGRAPHICAL INDEX: Chile
GEOGRAPHICAL CODE: 6424
FREE TEXT: The purpose of the mission was to receive information on the
situation of a number of political prisoners. The report contains a
description of general economic situation in Santiago, the repression,
problems faced by defence lawyers, the arrest of two lawyers with whom
the delegate spoke. With recommendations and conclusions, and analysis
of the "habeas corpus" procedure according to Chilean law.

CATALOGUE SIGNATURE: 0000/0138/-0=770301
TITLE: Rapport de la mission au Chile ... concernant la situation des
personnes disparues
AUTHOR: Bourgaux, Jacques
PLACE OF PUBLICATION: Brussels
PUBLISHER: Association Internationale des Juristes Démocrates - IADL (D)
DATE OF PUBLICATION: 770301
NUMBER OF PAGES: 8 p.
LANGUAGE: FRE
INDEX: disappearances / fact-finding missions
GEOGRAPHICAL INDEX: Chile
GEOGRAPHICAL CODE: 6424
FREE TEXT: Text delivered at a press conference on 1 March 1977 in
Brussels after a fact-finding mission to Chile. The report deals with
the situation of prisoners and the state of repression in Chile, and
the general situation with regard to disappearances. It also contains
a description of findings with regard to specific cases and an analysis
of the attitude of the government of Belgium with regard to the
situation in Chile. With conclusions.

CATALOGUE SIGNATURE: 0000/1068/-3=781025
TITLE: Protection of human rights in Chile
AUTHOR: Ad Hoc Working Group on the Situation of Human Rights in Chile
PLACE OF PUBLICATION: Geneva
PUBLISHER: United Nations General Assembly (D)
DATE OF PUBLICATION: 781025
NUMBER OF PAGES: 560 p. in v.p.
SERIES TITLE: General Assembly: thirty-third session: agenda item 12:
report of the Social and Economic Council
DOCUMENT SYMBOL: A/33/331
AVAILABILITY: F
LANGUAGE: ENG / FRE / SPA
STATISTICAL INFORMATION: Y
BIBLIOGRAPHIES: Y
INDEX: dictatorship / legislation / civil and political rights /
fact-finding missions
GEOGRAPHICAL INDEX: Chile
GEOGRAPHICAL CODE: 6424
FREE TEXT: The report of the Ad Hoc Working Group was prepared in
accordance with paragraph 8 of Assembly resolution 32/118 of 16
December 1977. The group consisted of G.A. Allana of Pakistan
(Chairman-Rapporteur), Leopoldo Benites of Ecuador, A. Dièye of
Senegal, F. Ermacora of Austria and M.J.T. Kamara of Sierra Leone.
Three members of the group visited Chile from 12 to 27 July 1978.
The report contains an introduction, information on the visit, and
chapters on: constitutional and legal aspects with a bearing on
human rights; decree law No. 2,191 of 19 April 1978 granting amnesty;
the rights to life, liberty and security of the person; missing
persons; exile and return; freedom of expression and information;
the right to education; freedom of association and right of assembly;
economic and social rights. With concluding observations and
recommendations, the adoption of the report, and eighty-two annexes:
resolutions; contacts between the UN and the government; press
statements; legislation; information supplied by the government and
nongovernmental organizations; notes, lists and statements.

CATALOGUE SIGNATURE: 6424/0298/-3=790000
TITLE: Report of a visit to Chile from 23 June - 1 July 1979
AUTHOR: Dijk, P. van ; Hoof, G.J.H van
PLACE OF PUBLICATION: Utrecht
PUBLISHER: Foundation for Legal Aid in Chile = Stichting Rechtshulp
Chili- SRC (D)
DATE OF PUBLICATION: 790000
NUMBER OF PAGES: 25 p.
LANGUAGE: ENG
INDEX: legal protection / civil and political rights /
fact-finding missions
GEOGRAPHICAL INDEX: Chile
GEOGRAPHICAL CODE: 6424
FREE TEXT: The purpose of the visit was to evaluate the impact which
the Foundations' activities have, and to investigate the most
pressing legal questions relating to the protection of human rights
in Chile for treatment in its future reports. To that end,
consultations and discussions were held with governmental officials,
private institutions, and individuals, so as to establish contact
with as broad a section of the Chilean society as possible.
The report contains an introduction on the Foundation, the programme
of the mission, summary reports of several of the meetings held, of
the follow-up meeting with the Chilean Ambassador in The Hague and
of the evaluation meeting with representatives of the Dutch Ministry
of Foreign Affairs.

CATALOGUE SIGNATURE: 0000/0035/-3=800000
TITLE: Chili: un cas parmi d'autres
AUTHOR: Otto, Maxim
PLACE OF PUBLICATION: Paris
PUBLISHER: Fédération Internationale des Droits de l'Homme - FIDH (D)
DATE OF PUBLICATION: 800000
NUMBER OF PAGES: 5 p.
LANGUAGE: FRE
INDEX: prison conditions / political prisoners / fact-finding missions
GEOGRAPHICAL INDEX: Chile
GEOGRAPHICAL CODE: 6424
FREE TEXT: The purpose of the mission in July 1980 was to collect
information on the situation of José Benado Medvinsky, recently
arrested by the political police. The delegate received information
from a witness and contacted the "Vicaría de la Solidaridad" of the
Archiepiscopate of Santiago de Chile, different embassies of Western
countries, Chilean authorities and lawyers. He visited Medvinski in
Santiago prison; Medvinsky declared that he was treated badly.

CATALOGUE SIGNATURE: 6424/0298/-3=800000
TITLE: Report of a visit to Chile from 9 September 1980 on the
occasion of the plebiscite of 11 September 1980
AUTHOR: Dijk, P. van
PLACE OF PUBLICATION: Utrecht
PUBLISHER: Foundation for Legal Aïd in Chile = Stichting Rechtshulp
Chili - SRC (D)
DATE OF PUBLICATION: 800000
NUMBER OF PAGES: 16 p.
LANGUAGE: ENG
INDEX: legislation / elections / fact-finding missions
GEOGRAPHICAL INDEX: Chile
GEOGRAPHICAL CODE: 6424
FREE TEXT: The delegate was sent as an observer on the occasion of
the plebiscite of 11 September 1980, concerning a new constitution.
He discussed with government officials, private institutions and
individuals on the preparation and the contents of the proposal for
a new constitution, and the circumstances under which the plebiscite
was taking place. In the conclusions, points of criticism on the
procedure, the way of counting and the circumstances are mentioned.
It is stated that the Chilean government has abused its power to
influence the outcome of the plebiscite.

CATALOGUE SIGNATURE: 0000/0035/-3=800000
TITLE: (Rapport du mission au Chili: 31 octobre - 10 novembre 1980)
AUTHOR: (Lépany, Franceline)
PLACE OF PUBLICATION: Paris
PUBLISHER: Fédération Internationale des Droits de l'Homme - FIDH (D)
DATE OF PUBLICATION: 800000
NUMBER OF PAGES: 33 p.
LANGUAGE: FRE
INDEX: political prisoners / disappearances / fact-finding missions
GEOGRAPHICAL INDEX: Chile
GEOGRAPHICAL CODE: 6424
FREE TEXT: The purpose of the mission was to receive information on
the situation of political prisoners and disappeared persons, and
especially on Carlos Eduardo Gonzales. The report consists of a
chronological description of events and impressions, and interviews
with government representatives, representatives of human rights
organizations, lawyers, witnesses, and Carlos Eduardo Gonzales
himself. With examples of torture practices.

CATALOGUE SIGNATURE: 0000/0966/-0=810000
TITLE: Cases in which the Committee has reached interim conclusions:
case no. 823: complaints presented by the International Confederation
of Free Trade Unions, the World Confederation of Labour, the World
Federation of Trade Unions and several other trade union organisations
against the government of Chile
AUTHOR: International Labour Office - ILO - Committee on Freedom of
Association
TITLE OF GENERIC ITEM: Official Bulletin: reports of the Committee
on Freedom of Association (208th, 209th and 210th)
EDITION: vol. LXIV, series B no. 1
PLACE OF PUBLICATION: Geneva
PUBLISHER: International Labour Office - ILO (D)
DATE OF PUBLICATION: 810000
NUMBER OF PAGES: p. 33-43
LANGUAGE: ENG
INDEX: association (freedom of) / trade unions / fact-finding missions
GEOGRAPHICAL INDEX: Chile
GEOGRAPHICAL CODE: 6424
FREE TEXT: Since its May 1980, the Committee received additional
complaints and observations by the government. Following contacts and
correspondence exchanged with the government, the Director-General
appointed Nicolas Valticos, Manuel Araoz and Bernard Gernigon to carry
out a mission to Chile, which took place in December 1980. All the
information collected on the spot was the subject of a detailed mission
(report, which the Committee fully took into account when examining the
allegations before it.
The report of the Committee deals with legislation on trade union
organizations and collective bargaining, the dissolution of trade
union organizations, the dismissal of trade unionists, and arrest and
disappearance of trade unionists. With recommendations.

CATALOGUE SIGNATURE: 6424/-0=810600
TITLE: Human rights in Chile today: report of a mission of inquiry
AUTHOR: Fine, Jonathan ; Koopman, James S.
PLACE OF PUBLICATION: Washington DC
PUBLISHER: American Public Health Association - APHA (D)
DATE OF PUBLICATION: 810600
NUMBER OF PAGES: (15 p.)
LANGUAGE: ENG
INDEX: health / fact-finding missions
GEOGRAPHICAL INDEX: Chile
GEOGRAPHICAL CODE: 6424
FREE TEXT: The report of the medical fact-finding mission highlights
the arrests of three prominent Chilean doctors who are defenders of
human rights in Chile and have provided medical care to victims of
torture. It also contains information on the general situation of
human rights in Chile, paying attention to arrests and torture, some
case histories, repression at universities, suppression of the freedom
of speech and freedom of assembly. With suggestions for action and
press release.

CATALOGUE SIGNATURE: 0000/0138/-3=810900
TITLE: Misión en Chile: septiembre de 1981
AUTHOR: Stuby, Gerhard
PLACE OF PUBLICATION: Brussels
PUBLISHER: Association Internationale des Juristes Démocrates - IADL (D)
DATE OF PUBLICATION: 810900
NUMBER OF PAGES: 28 p.
LANGUAGE: SPA
INDEX: dictatorship / association (freedom of) / trade unions /
fact-finding missions
GEOGRAPHICAL INDEX: Chile
GEOGRAPHICAL CODE: 6424
FREE TEXT: Report on a fact-finding mission to Chile in September 1981.
The reason for sending the mission were massive arrests following the
presentation of a document by the federation of trade unions CNS to the
government. The report contains information on the legal basis of the
trial against the leaders of the CNS, the programme of the government
(liquidation of the trade union movement, the situation of the Chilean
opposition, the economic programme), the general concept of fascism,
the formation of a social movement and the meaning of the activities of
the CNS. With summary of findings and analysis.

CATALOGUE SIGNATURE: 0000/2955/-3=820200
TITLE: On human rights in Chile
AUTHOR: Neier, Aryeh
PLACE OF PUBLICATION: New York
PUBLISHER: American Watch - AW (D)
DATE OF PUBLICATION: 820200
NUMBER OF PAGES: 13 p.
LANGUAGE: ENG
INDEX: civil and political rights / human rights and foreign policy /
fact-finding missions
GEOGRAPHICAL INDEX: Chile
GEOGRAPHICAL CODE: 6424
FREE TEXT: The report on the current state of human rights is based on
information of domestic nongovernmental organizations and a mission in
December 1981. Attention is given to political arrests, torture,
intimidation, internal banishment, expulsions, persecution of human
rights monitors, the state of exception and the Letelier-Moffitt
murders. With text of provisions of the United States International
Security and Development Act of 1981 respecting assistance for Chile,
and recommendation to President Reagan.

CATALOGUE SIGNATURE: 0000/2955/-3=821200
TITLE: Human rights in Chile: notes on a sentence of exile
AUTHOR: Trias, José E.
PLACE OF PUBLICATION: New York
PUBLISHER: Americas Watch - AW (D)
DATE OF PUBLICATION: 821200
NUMBER OF PAGES: 22 p.
LANGUAGE: ENG
INDEX: association (freedom of) / trials / fact-finding missions
GEOGRAPHICAL INDEX: Chile
GEOGRAPHICAL CODE: 6424
FREE TEXT: The author visited Chile in September 1982 to observe
criminal proceedings against nine defendants accused of organizing
the Christian Left Party, banned by the Pinochet government in 1973.
In the report, attention is paid to the crime, the criminal procedures,
the arrests, the charges, the defence and the hearings, conviction and
appeal. With comment: the cour convicted the defendants in this case
solely or primarily on the basis of out-of-court confessions that had
been repudiated in court as the product of threats and torture.

CATALOGUE SIGNATURE: 0000/0249/-3=830000
TITLE: Chile: evidence of torture: an Amnesty International report
AUTHOR: (Wallach, Marianne) ; (Rasmussen, Ole Vedel)
PLACE OF PUBLICATION: London
PUBLISHER: Amnesty International - AI (D)
DATE OF PUBLICATION: 830000
NUMBER OF PAGES: 75 p.
ISBN: 0 86210 053 4
DOCUMENT SYMBOL: AI Index: AMR 22/35/83
LANGUAGE: ENG
STATISTICAL INFORMATION: Y
BIBLIOGRAPHIES: Y
INDEX: torture / detention / fact-finding missions
GEOGRAPHICAL INDEX: Chile
GEOGRAPHICAL CODE: 6424
FREE TEXT: The report presents findings of a delegation which examined
people who said they had been tortured while in the custody of the
Chilean security forces between March 1980 and April 1982.
The first part provides the background, with information on current and
past allegations of torture. The role of the Secret Police (CNI) is
examined, and an account is given of secret CNI premises in central
Santiago and the procedures followed there. The evidence is based on
testimonies received.
The current legal and institutional background is summarised next,
followed by a section dealing with the judicial protection which, in
theory, the law provides against torture and ill-treatment of detained
persons. The bulk of the report consists of the findings of the medical
delegation: analysis of findings, details of 19 examinations.
With conclusions and recommendations.

CATALOGUE SIGNATURE: 0000/0035/-3=830000
TITLE: Chili: rapport de mission: 29 mai - 4 juin 1983
AUTHOR: Laburthe, Patrick ; Rostoker, Christian
PLACE OF PUBLICATION: Paris
PUBLISHER: Fédération Internationale des Droits de l'Homme - FIDH (D)
DATE OF PUBLICATION: 830000
NUMBER OF PAGES: 27 p.
LANGUAGE: FRE
INDEX: peaceful assembly (right to) / fact-finding missions
GEOGRAPHICAL INDEX: Chile
GEOGRAPHICAL CODE: 6424
FREE TEXT: The reason for sending the mission was the manifestation
of 11 May, and the mass arrests following. With a chronological list
of events 1970-1973, and chapters on arrests, detention conditions,
torture (with figures and detailed testimony of victim), and the
situation in the poor quarters ("poblaciones"). With conclusions:
grave violations of human rights were committed in Chile, and
appendices: registration forms of the secret police, illustrations.

CATALOGUE SIGNATURE: 0000/0138/-0=850600
TITLE: Rapport de mission au Chili
AUTHOR: Bourgaux, Jacques
PLACE OF PUBLICATION: Brussels
PUBLISHER: Association Internationale des Juristes Démocrates - IADL (D)
DATE OF PUBLICATION: 850600
NUMBER OF PAGES: 17 p. in v.p.
LANGUAGE: FRE
INDEX: civil and political rights / state of emergency /
fact-finding missions
GEOGRAPHICAL INDEX: Chile
GEOGRAPHICAL CODE: 6424
FREE TEXT: The aims of the mission were to investigate the general
human-rights situation, in order to draw a balance eight months after
the proclamation of the state of siege, to collect information on the
socio-economic repression and on the situation of certain political
prisoners and persons assassinated. With report on findings and
annexes in Spanish: information on the state of emergency (or siege);
assassinations; legal background to the arrest and assassination of
three persons.

CATALOGUE SIGNATURE: 0000/0035/-4
TITLE: Chili: relation d'une mission a Santiago du Chili, suite au
décès du père André Jarlan
AUTHOR: Stasi, Mario
TITLE OF GENERIC ITEM: La Lettre de la FIDH
EDITION: no. 121-122
PLACE OF PUBLICATION: Paris
PUBLISHER: Fédération Internationale des Droits de l'Homme - FIDH (D)
DATE OF PUBLICATION: 850827
NUMBER OF PAGES: p. 9-11
LANGUAGE: FRE
INDEX: trials / fact-finding missions
GEOGRAPHICAL INDEX: Chili
GEOGRAPHICAL CODE: 6424
FREE TEXT: Short report on a mission undertaken from 19 to 22 June 1985.
The aim of the mission was to investigate the circumstances of the
murder of the french father Andre Jarlan, killed on 4 September 1985,
and the ongoing trial: the soldier who was accused of homicide made an
appeal.

CATALOGUE SIGNATURE: 0000/0035/-3=860000
TITLE: Rapport de la mission accomplie à Santiago du Chili, en novembre
1985...
AUTHOR: Julien-Laferriere, Francois; Tayon, Bernard
PLACE OF PUBLICATION: Paris
PUBLISHER: Fédération Internationale des Droits de l'Homme - FIDH (D)
DATE OF PUBLICATION: 860000
NUMBER OF PAGES: 63 p.
LANGUAGE: FRE
INDEX: detention / political prisoners / fact-finding missions
GEOGRAPHICAL INDEX: Chile
GEOGRAPHICAL CODE: 6424
FREE TEXT: On 18 October 1985, an attempt to escape of prisoners from
the Penitenciaria in Santiago de Chile resulted in violence between
prisoners and guards, eight deaths and twenty injured persons. The aim
of the mission was to investigate the circumstances of this incident,
the health situation of the injured persons and the fate of the
detainees involved in the attempt to escape. The authors place the
problem of political prisoners in the context of the general situation
in Chile. Attention is given to developments in Chile at the end of
1985, the events of 18 October, the situation of political prisoners,
the demands of the prisoners and the work of organizations providing
them aid, and the follow up of the mission. With conclusions and
annexes: scheme of the Penitenciaria; list of contacts of the mission.

CATALOGUE SIGNATURE: 0000/1079/-3=860212
TITLE: Question of human rights in Chile: final report...
AUTHOR: Volio Jiménez, Fernando
PLACE OF PUBLICATION: Geneva
PUBLISHER: Commission on Human Rights of the United Nations Economic
and Social Council - UNCHR (D)
DATE OF PUBLICATION: 860212
NUMBER OF PAGES: 121 p. in v.p.
SERIES TITLE: Commission on Human Rights: forty-second session: agenda
item 5
DOCUMENT SYMBOL: E/CN.4/1986/2
AVAILABILITY: F
LANGUAGE: SPA / ENG
INDEX: civil and political rights / dictatorship /
fact-finding missions
GEOGRAPHICAL INDEX: Chile
GEOGRAPHICAL CODE: 6424
FREE TEXT: Volio Jiménez is Special Rapporteur on the question of
human rights in Chile, pursuant to the mandate conferred under
resolution 1985/47 of the Commission on Human Rights. His report is
based on a visit to Chile in December 1985, during which he
interviewed a large number of senior officials of the government and
the judiciary, senior representatives of the Catholic church,
representatives of numerous human rights, social and trade-union
organizations, and many private individuals.
The report begins with a detailed description of the visit. Next,
there is information on complaints of violations of human rights in
the second half of 1985 (with specific cases relating to the right
to life, right to physical integrity of persons, right to liberty,
disappearances, right to security, the situation of persons under
investigation by the Military Prosecutor, the right to enter and leave
the country freely, right to freedom of movement, the right to freedom
of expression and information). With conclusions, recommendations and
appendix: General Assembly resolution 40/145 of 13 December 1985.

CATALOGUE SIGNATURE: 0000/0138/-0=860400
TITLE: Rapport de mission au Chili: Santiago, 15-20 mars 1986
AUTHOR: Schaller, Rudolf
PLACE OF PUBLICATION: Brussels
PUBLISHER: Association Internationale des Juristes Démocrates - IADL (D)
DATE OF PUBLICATION: 860400
NUMBER OF PAGES: 15 p.
LANGUAGE: FRE
BIBLIOGRAPHIES: Y
INDEX: dictatorship / judicial systems / fact-finding missions
GEOGRAPHICAL INDEX: Chile
GEOGRAPHICAL CODE: 6424
FREE TEXT: The aim of the mission was to obtain information on recent
developments with regard to the situation of human rights in Chile, and
to express the solidarity of the IADL with the courageous struggle of
democratic forces in Chile. In Santiago, the delegate met with lawyers,
oppositionary politicians, and representatives of human rights
organizations. In his report, attention is paid to recent reports on
the situation in Chile, the absolute power of the President and the
absence of the rule of law, the lack of independence of the judicial
powers, the economic policy and the repression of the poor, and
education. With conclusions.

CATALOGUE SIGNATURE: 6003/1226/-3=860700
TITLE: Chile, the multilateral development banks and U.S. human rights
law: a delegation report
AUTHOR: Morrison, Bruce A. ; Shinpoch, Jan ; Bouvier, Virginia M.
PLACE OF PUBLICATION: Washington
PUBLISHER: Washington Office on Latin America - WOLA (D)
DATE OF PUBLICATION: 860700
NUMBER OF PAGES: 45 p. in v.p.
ISBN: 0 9613249 5 3
LANGUAGE: ENG
STATISTICAL INFORMATION: Y
INDEX: development cooperation / fact-finding missions
GEOGRAPHICAL INDEX: Chile
GEOGRAPHICAL CODE: 6424
FREE TEXT: The document contains a report on a WOLA delegation to Chile
from 27 March to 2 April 1986. The aim of the mission was to examine
whether continued US support for multilateral development bank loans to
Chile is consistent with US law, and to explore the options for US
policymakers toward Chile.
After an introduction and a summary of conclusions, the report is
divided into the following parts:
I) Delegation activities in Chile;
II) Chile and section 701: with attention to:
- Human rights violations and the lack of basic protection;
- The use of States of exception to limit basic rights;
- Incommunicado detention, torture and detention without charge;
- Political prisoners and treats to their relatives;
- Lack of an independent judiciary;
- Political parties banned and freedom of assembly restricted;
- Freedom of expression curtailed;
- Random violence in poor neighbourhoods;
III) Other section 701 considerations: with attention to:
- Consultations with Congress; - Disregarding Congressional intent;
- Other US foreign assistance programs; - Access of international
  organizations;
IV) US policy considerations: with attention to:
- US leverage: MDBs and the Chilean economy; - Loans as political
  support; - encouraging a return to full democracy;
V) Conclusions. With notes and appendices.

COLOMBIA

CATALOGUE SIGNATURE: 0000/0249/-3=800000
TITLE: Informe de una misión de Amnistia Internacional a la República
de Colombia: 15 de enero - 21 de enero de 1980
AUTHOR: (Carretero Pérez, Antonio) ; (Allodi, Federico) ;
(García, Edmundo)
PLACE OF PUBLICATION: London
PUBLISHER: Amnesty International - AI (D)
DATE OF PUBLICATION: 800000
NUMBER OF PAGES: 248 p.
DOCUMENT SYMBOL: AI Index: AMR 23/06/80
LANGUAGE: SPA
INDEX: political prisoners / torture / legislation /
fact-finding missions
GEOGRAPHICAL INDEX: Colombia
GEOGRAPHICAL CODE: 6425
FREE TEXT: The aim of the mission was to investigate the protection
of human rights in a situation where extraordinary measures are in
force, such as the state of siege, the State of Security, and a number
of decrees which enlarge the jurisdiction of the military over the
administration of justice. The report contains background information,
conclusions and recommendations, and chapters on the state of siege in
a historical context; indigenous peoples; farmers; labourers and trade
unions; other professionals; torture (medical enquiry; the principal
methods of torture and torture centres); political killings.
With appendices: relevant international instruments; comments and
analysis by the government of Colombia on the conclusions and
recommendations in the AI report.

CATALOGUE SIGNATURE: 6000/1011/-3=810630
TITLE: Report on the situation of human rights in the Republic of
Colombia
AUTHOR: Inter-American Commission on Human Rights - IACHR
PLACE OF PUBLICATION: Washington DC
PUBLISHER: Organization of American States - OAS (D) ; Inter-American
Commission on Human Rights - IACHR
DATE OF PUBLICATION: 810630
NUMBER OF PAGES: 225 p. in v.p.
ISBN: 0 8270 1374 4
DOCUMENT SYMBOL: OEA/Ser.L/V/II.53 doc.22
LANGUAGE: ENG
INDEX: civil and political rights / trials / fact-finding missions
GEOGRAPHICAL INDEX: Colombia
GEOGRAPHICAL CODE: 6425
FREE TEXT: The report is largely based on a mission undertaken by the
Commission in April 1980. It contains an introduction on the activities
of the delegation and contacts with the authorities, and chapters on:
I) the political and legal system in Colombia; II) the right to life
(with information on specific cases); III) the right to personal
liberty; IV) the right to personal security and humane treatment
(detention; mistreatment and torture); V) the right to a fair trial
and due process (with reference to specific cases); VI) other rights;
VII) military operations in rural areas. With conclusions and
recommendations.

CATALOGUE SIGNATURE: 0000/2955/-3=821000
TITLE: Human rights in the two Colombias: functioning democracy,
militarized society
AUTHOR: Neier, Aryeh
PLACE OF PUBLICATION: New York
PUBLISHER: Americas Watch - AW (D)
DATE OF PUBLICATION: 821000
NUMBER OF PAGES: 35 p.
LANGUAGE: ENG
INDEX: democracy / military / civil and political rights /
fact-finding missions
GEOGRAPHICAL INDEX: Colombia
GEOGRAPHICAL CODE: 6425
FREE TEXT: Much of the research for this report was conducted during
a visit to Colombia in late September 1982. The author interviewed
government representatives and people concerned with the human rights
situation. He describes the ambiguous character of Colombian society:
though officially it is a democracy, large parts of the country are in
hands of the armed forces. Their rule is harsh and marked by torture,
massacres and disappearances. A number of murderous vigilante
organizations, e.g. the MAS, seem to be connected with the armed
forces. Attention is paid to the United States Department of State
Country Report on human rights in Colombia. With recommendations.

CATALOGUE SIGNATURE: 0000/0035/-3=820000
TITLE: Rapport de mission ... Colombie - décembre 1982
AUTHOR: Katz, Claude
PLACE OF PUBLICATION: Paris
PUBLISHER: Fédération Internationale des Droits de l'Homme - FIDH (D)
DATE OF PUBLICATION: 820000
NUMBER OF PAGES: 10 p.
LANGUAGE: FRE
INDEX: amnesty / judicial systems / fact-finding missions
GEOGRAPHICAL INDEX: Colombia
GEOGRAPHICAL CODE: 6425
FREE TEXT: The delegate participated in an international mission of
nine members. He was mandated to obtain information on the amnesty
law, and more in particular on the conditions in which the law is
applied and on activities of para-military groups against prisoners
who were set free. Some of the articles of the law are contrary to
its character, and reflect the influence of military authorities.
With conclusion: in general, the law is a positive factor for the
improvement of the situation of human rights, though it has negative
effects as well.
With annex: text of the amnesty law (translated into french).

CATALOGUE SIGNATURE: 0000/2955/-3=830700
TITLE: The "MAS Case" in Colombia: taking on the death squads
AUTHOR: Brown, Cynthia
PLACE OF PUBLICATION: New York
PUBLISHER: Americas Watch - AW (D)
DATE OF PUBLICATION: 830700
NUMBER OF PAGES: 25 p.
LANGUAGE: ENG
INDEX: disappearances / democracy / political violence /
fact-finding missions
GEOGRAPHICAL INDEX: Colombia
GEOGRAPHICAL CODE: 6425
FREE TEXT: "MAS" is Colombia's most active death squad. The "MAS case"
is an attempt to bring military and civilian death squads to justice.
The report, based on a mission in April 1983, examines the unfolding
of the MAS case and the struggle it has provoked between an abusive
military establishment and a reformist president. With analysis of the
general human rights situation and of kidnapping, the relation between
MAS and the military, the reports of the attorney general and the
military response, the legal issues.
With prospects for the future and the role of the United States policy.

CATALOGUE SIGNATURE: 0000/2955/-3=860900
TITLE: Human rights in Colombia as President Barco begins
AUTHOR: Fellner, Jamie ; Goldman, Robert K.
PLACE OF PUBLICATION : New York ; Washington
PUBLISHER: Americas Watch - AW (D)
DATE OF PUBLICATION: 860900
NUMBER OF PAGES: 70 p. in v.p.
ISBN: 0 938579 26 6
LANGUAGE: ENG
INDEX: military / peace / fact-finding missions
GEOGRAPHICAL INDEX: Colombia
GEOGRAPHICAL CODE: 6425
FREE TEXT: This report, an update of "The Central Americanization of
Colombia? Human rights and the peace process", is based on information
gathered between January and mid-July 1986, and a visit to Colombia in
May 1986.
The report is divided into three parts:
I) Developments in the peace process: the M-19; the FARC: 1) New peace
accord; 2) The Union Patriotica; 3) Post-election developments;
II) Investigations into the siege of the palace of justice;
III) Human rights developments: disappearences; extra-judicial
executions; military jurisdiction over civilians; an occupation army;
human rights abuses by the guerrillas; response to human rights
violations by the Colombian military.
In the appendix: the laws of war (international humanitarian law as
codified in the Geneva Conventions).

CUBA

CATALOGUE SIGNATURE: 0000/2230/-0=770300
TITLE: An eleven-day journey into Cuba
AUTHOR: McCloud, J. Oscar
PLACE OF PUBLICATION: (New York)
PUBLISHER: (National Council of Churches of Christ in the USA -
NCCCUSA) (D)
DATE OF PUBLICATION: 770300
NUMBER OF PAGES: 10 p.
LANGUAGE: ENG
INDEX: social and economic rights / church and state /
fact-finding missions
GEOGRAPHICAL INDEX: Cuba
GEOGRAPHICAL CODE: 6127
FREE TEXT: The author of the report was member of a group of eight
religious leaders who went to Cuba in March 1977 at the invitation of
the Ecumenical Christian Church of Cuba, and at the request of the
National Council of the Churches of Christ and the Cuba Resource
Center. The primary reason that the group was invited was to show it
developments in the country and to provide an occasion for contact
between Cuban and American Christians. The author describes his
experiences under the topics: food and clothing, housing, education,
health, solidarity, and Christianity and the Church in Cuba.

CATALOGUE SIGNATURE: 0000/0249/-3=781109
TITLE: Memorandum submitted to the government of the Republic of Cuba
by Mr Thomas Hammarberg, chairperson of the International Executive
Committee and Mr Roger Plant of the International Secretariat of
Amnesty International
AUTHOR: Hammarberg, Thomas ; Plant, Roger
PLACE OF PUBLICATION: London
PUBLISHER: Amnesty International - AI (D)
DATE OF PUBLICATION: 781109
NUMBER OF PAGES: 8 p.
DOCUMENT SYMBOL: AI Index: AMR 25/01/78
LANGUAGE: ENG
INDEX: political prisoners / fact-finding missions
GEOGRAPHICAL INDEX: Cuba
GEOGRAPHICAL CODE: 6127
FREE TEXT: The authors paid a visit to Cuba from 28 November to 6
December 1977, and were received by the government in their personal
capacity. The memorandum contains issues of concern to Amnesty
International: long-term political prisoners, the prison regime
(detention conditions), the situation of released prisoners, and the
legal situation concerning political prisoners.

ECUADOR

CATALOGUE SIGNATURE: 0000/0088/-4
TITLE: A case report from Ecuador: the trial of Professor Galarza and others
AUTHOR: Martinez, Lisandro
TITLE OF GENERIC ITEM: ICJ Review
EDITION: no. 13
PLACE OF PUBLICATION: Geneva
PUBLISHER: International Commission of Jurists - ICJ (D)
DATE OF PUBLICATION: 741200
NUMBER OF PAGES: p. 60-62
LANGUAGE: ENG
INDEX: judicial systems / trials / fact-finding missions
GEOGRAPHICAL INDEX: Ecuador
GEOGRAPHICAL CODE: 6430
FREE TEXT: The observer was requested by the ICJ and Amnesty International to enquire into certain criminal proceedings against the writer Jaime Galarza and other Ecuadorian citizens held in Quito, Ecuador, in September 1974. His report is on the background of the case and the proceedings, including comments.

EL SALVADOR

CATALOGUE SIGNATURE: 0000/1295/-0=780000
TITLE: Human rights in El Salvador - 1978: report of findings of an investigatory mission
AUTHOR: Drinan, Robert F. ; McAward, John J. ; Anderson, Thomas P.
PLACE OF PUBLICATION: Boston
PUBLISHER: Unitarian Universalist Service Committee - UUSC (D)
DATE OF PUBLICATION: 780000
NUMBER OF PAGES: 87 p.
LANGUAGE: ENG
STATISTICAL INFORMATION: Y
INDEX: civil and political rights / human rights and foreign policy / fact-finding missions
GEOGRAPHICAL INDEX: El Salvador
GEOGRAPHICAL CODE: 6231
FREE TEXT: The purpose of the fact-finding mission was to investigate the often-made charges that the government of El Salvador is violating the basic human rights of its citizens, and to make public the findings of the investigators. The report provides background information on the country, and contains descriptions of meetings on human rights issues with the clergy, families of the disappeared, the ambassador of the United States, the political opposition, farmers, the President and Vice-President, union leaders, the publisher of La Cronica, and the Ministers of Justice of the Interior.
In the third chapter, the policy of the United States towards El Salvador is analyzed; it is stated that the "carrot and stick" policy has been ineffective. Suggestions for improvement are made.
With glossary and appendices: lists of victims of human rights violations and of persecuted priests; the Law for the Defense and Guarantee of the Public Order (Ley de Orden); sermon delivered by Robert F. Drinan SJ at the cathedral of San Salvador; memorandum of conversation with President Carlos Humberto Romero; letter of John McAward to Vice-President Julio Ernesto Astacio; information on USIS and the American embassy; statement on the mission.

CATALOGUE SIGNATURE: 0000/0088/-3=780900
TITLE: Report ... mission to El Salvador in July 1978 to study the application of the November 1977 "Law of Defence and Guarantee of Public Order"
AUTHOR: Fox, Donald T.
PLACE OF PUBLICATION: Geneva
PUBLISHER: International Commission of Jurists - ICJ (D)
DATE OF PUBLICATION: 780900
NUMBER OF PAGES: 14 p.
LANGUAGE: ENG
INDEX: legislation / fact-finding missions
GEOGRAPHICAL INDEX: El Salvador
GEOGRAPHICAL CODE: 6231
FREE TEXT: The report begins with an outline of the geopolitical situation in El Salvador. The institutions involved in the implementation of the Law (Ley de Defensa y Garantía del Orden Público) are described. Much attention is paid to the constitutional and legal framework. The Law is analyzed, and its implementation is described. With conclusions.

CATALOGUE SIGNATURE: 6000/1011/-3=781117
TITLE: Report on the situation of human rights in El Salvador
AUTHOR: Inter-American Commission on Human Rights - IACHR
PLACE OF PUBLICATION: Washington DC
PUBLISHER: Organization of American States - OAS (D) - Inter-American
Commission on Human Rights - IACHR
DATE OF PUBLICATION: 781117
NUMBER OF PAGES: 188 p.
DOCUMENT SYMBOL: OEA/Ser.L/V/II.46 doc.23 rev.1
LANGUAGE: ENG
INDEX: political violence / fact-finding missions
GEOGRAPHICAL INDEX: El Salvador
GEOGRAPHICAL CODE: 6231
FREE TEXT: The report is based on a fact-finding mission in January
1978. It contains an introduction, and the following chapters:
I) legal norms relating to human rights; II) right to life; III) right
to humane treatment; IV) right to physical liberty; V) right to a fair
trial and due process of law; VI) right of residence and movement;
VII) right of assembly and of association; VIII) right to freedom of
thought and expression; IX) right to vote and to participate in
government; X) right to equality before the law and non discrimination;
XI) economic and social rights. With conclusions and recommendations.

CATALOGUE SIGNATURE: 0000/0035/-3=790000
TITLE: Rapport sur le Salvador
AUTHOR: Lévy, Jean-Paul ; Barth, Maurice ; Rosenbaum, Willy
PLACE OF PUBLICATION: Paris
PUBLISHER: Fédération Internationale des Droits de l'Homme - FIDH
(D) ; Mouvement International des Juristes Catholiques Pax Romana -
IMCL
DATE OF PUBLICATION: 790000
NUMBER OF PAGES: 28 p.
LANGUAGE: FRE
INDEX: political prisoners / fact-finding missions
GEOGRAPHICAL INDEX: El Salvador
GEOGRAPHICAL CODE: 6231
FREE TEXT: The purpose of the mission was to investigate human
rights violations in general, and especially to favorise the release
of persons held against their will in some embassies.
The report gives a description of the background of the country,
violations of the right to physical integrity and the right to life,
the rights of the defence, political rights, trade union rights,
freedom of expression and demonstration. With description of action
undertaken on behalf of the political detainees in the embassies.

CATALOGUE SIGNATURE: 0000/1192/-0=800300
TITLE: Ecumenical visit to El Salvador: March 22-25, 1980
AUTHOR: McCoy, Alan ; Nute, Betty ; Wipfler, William (et al...)
PLACE OF PUBLICATION: Philadelphia
PUBLISHER: American Friends Service Committee - AFSC (D)
DATE OF PUBLICATION: 800300
NUMBER OF PAGES: 6 p.
LANGUAGE: ENG
INDEX: armed conflict / church and state / fact-finding missions
GEOGRAPHICAL INDEX: El Salvador
GEOGRAPHICAL CODE: 6231
FREE TEXT: The aim of the five-member mission was to express support
and solidarity for Archbishop Romero and the suffering people and
church of El Salvador, to investigate the situation, and to present
their findings to the United States government, churches, NGOs and
the concerned public. The delegation visited refugee camps and met
with human rights organizations, popular organizations, the US
Ambassador, government representatives and others. On the third day
of the mission Archbishop Romero was assassinated.
The report contains a list of findings, recommendations and
conclusions.

CATALOGUE SIGNATURE: 6231/-0=800700
TITLE: Abuses of medical neutrality: report of the public health
commission to El Salvador: July 1980
AUTHOR: Guttmacher, Sally ; Hubbard, Frances ; Lear, Walter (et al...)
PLACE OF PUBLICATION: New York
PUBLISHER: Committee for Health Rights in El Salvador (D)
DATE OF PUBLICATION: 800700
NUMBER OF PAGES: (13 p.)
LANGUAGE: ENG
INDEX: health / fact-finding missions
GEOGRAPHICAL INDEX: El Salvador
GEOGRAPHICAL CODE: 6231
FREE TEXT: The aim of the five-member mission was to investigate reports
of violations of the neutrality of medical institutions and of the
rights of health workers, including the killing of doctors and patients.
The team interviewed almost 50 individuals in the health and relief
fields, representing many organizations and a spectrum of political
beliefs.
The report contains conclusions and recommendations, and findings with
regard to violence to health workers, violations of the neutrality of
health institutions, the stoppage on the medical work, medical supplies
and blood, the closing of the medical school, health in rural areas and
refugees. With chronological lists of armed incursions in medical
centres and of physicians assaulted.

CATALOGUE SIGNATURE: 0000/0035/-3=800908
TITLE: Rapport de mission: Salvador
AUTHOR: Lévy, Jean-Paul
PLACE OF PUBLICATION: Paris
PUBLISHER: Fédération Internationale des Droits de l'Homme - FIDH (D)
DATE OF PUBLICATION: 800908
NUMBER OF PAGES: 8 p.
LANGUAGE: FRE
INDEX: civil and political rights / fact-finding missions
GEOGRAPHICAL INDEX: El Salvador
GEOGRAPHICAL CODE: 6231
FREE TEXT: The mission, consisting of Charles Josselin, Jacques Lebas
and the author, investigated the general human rights situation. The
description of facts established is divided according to articles of
the Universal Declaration of Human Rights (right to life, liberty and
security; prohibition of torture; equality before the law and justice;
guarantee of individual freedoms etc.) The report is based on contacts
with the government, nongovernmental organizations, witnesses and
guerilla sources, and visits to a village and a prison.

CATALOGUE SIGNATURE: 0000/0138/-3=800000
TITLE: Mission de l'AIJD au Salvador: 16-19 septembre 1980
AUTHOR: Stuby, Gerhard ; Quinteros-Yanez, Luis ; Kroes, Jacques
PLACE OF PUBLICATION: Brussels
PUBLISHER: Association Internationale des Juristes Démocrates - IADL (D)
DATE OF PUBLICATION: 800000
NUMBER OF PAGES: 13 p.
LANGUAGE: FRE / SPA
STATISTICAL INFORMATION: Y
INDEX: trials / fact-finding missions
GEOGRAPHICAL INDEX: El Salvador
GEOGRAPHICAL CODE: 6231
FREE TEXT: The members of the mission observed the trial of 17 trade
union activists, with the aim of drawing international attention to
their case. They received oral information from various sources on the
circumstances which lead to the arrestment and the state of judicial
inquiry in the procedure. The members also obtained information from
nongovernmental organizations, Church delegates and victims on the
general situation of human rights in El Salvador, and investigated the
position of organizations for the protection and promotion of human
rights. The members visited a refugee centre established by the Church.
With conclusions and annex: figures of persons killed, list of persons
disappeared.

CATALOGUE SIGNATURE: 0000/0035/-3=810000
TITLE: Rapport de mission au Salvador
AUTHOR: Texier, Philippe
PLACE OF PUBLICATION: Paris
PUBLISHER: Fédération Internationale des Droits de l'Homme - FIDH (D)
DATE OF PUBLICATION: 810000
NUMBER OF PAGES: 19 p.
LANGUAGE: FRE
INDEX: civil and political rights / fact-finding missions
GEOGRAPHICAL INDEX: El Salvador
GEOGRAPHICAL CODE: 6231
FREE TEXT: The mission of Texier took place in the framework of a
mission by Pax Christi to Central America. The purpose of the mission
to El Salvador was to investigate the general human rights situation.
With description of the background of the country: decrees create a
situation of exception and permit repression. With attention to
massacres, the work of nongovernmental organizations, disappearances
and torture, political refugees, political prisoners, the situation
of civil and political liberties and the situation of the church.
With suggestions for solutions of the conflict and conclusions.

CATALOGUE SIGNATURE: 0000/2230/-0=811000
TITLE: Report of El Salvador trip
AUTHOR: Andrews, James ; Cole, Kara ; Reed, David (...et al)
PLACE OF PUBLICATION: New York
PUBLISHER: National Council of Churches of Christ in the USA - NCCCUSA
(D)
DATE OF PUBLICATION: 811000
NUMBER OF PAGES: 6 p.
LANGUAGE: ENG
INDEX: church and state / fact-finding missions
GEOGRAPHICAL INDEX: El Salvador
GEOGRAPHICAL CODE: 6231
FREE TEXT: A nine-member delegation sponsored by the NCCCUSA visited
El Salvador in October 1981. The visit was a "pastoral visit to the
churches of El Salvador, intended to convey our identification with
them in the current tragic suffering they and their nation were
facing." The visit was also intended to obtain a deeper insight into
the current reality of El Salvador, in order to respond more adequately
to the needs of the churches and population. The report contains
information on the situation in El Salvador, the position of the
Christian churches, and the future of the country. With recommendations
to the churches in the United States and the government of the United
States.

CATALOGUE SIGNATURE: 0000/1079/-3=820118
TITLE: Final report on the situation of human rights in El Salvador...
AUTHOR: Pastor Ridruejo, José Antonio
PLACE OF PUBLICATION: Geneva
PUBLISHER: Commission on Human Rights of the United Nations Economic
and Social Council - UNCHR (D)
DATE OF PUBLICATION: 820118
NUMBER OF PAGES: 45 p.
SERIES TITLE: Commission on Human Rights: thirty-eight session: item 12
of the provisional agenda: question of the violation of human rights
and fundamental freedoms in any part of the world, with particular
reference to colonial and other dependent countries and territories
DOCUMENT SYMBOL: E/CN.4/1502
AVAILABILITY: F
LANGUAGE: ENG / SPA
BIBLIOGRAPHIES: Y
INDEX: civil and political rights / fact-finding missions
GEOGRAPHICAL INDEX: El Salvador
GEOGRAPHICAL CODE: 6231
FREE TEXT: Pastor Ridruejo submitted his final report in fulfilment
of the mandate conferred under Commission resolution 32 (XXXVII). He
visited El Salvador in September 1981, and established contacts with
the authorities, private citizens and prisoners. He visited a refugee
center. His report contains an introduction, and chapters on:
international and national legal rules applicable; the current
political situation; economic, social and cultural rights; civil and
political rights; refugees and displaced persons; the compliance with
international rules of humanitarian law applicable in armed conflicts.
With conclusions and recommendations.

CATALOGUE SIGNATURE: 0000/0491/-3=820000
TITLE: El Salvador
AUTHOR: Bettazzi, L. ; Benoit, André ; Bijnen, Toon van (...et al)
PLACE OF PUBLICATION: Antwerpen
PUBLISHER: Pax Christi International - PAXCI (D) ; OMEGA Books (D)
DATE OF PUBLICATION: 820000
NUMBER OF PAGES: 87 p.
SERIES TITLE: Pax Christi International Human Rights Reports
VOLUME: no. 3
ISBN: 90 70316 19 2
LANGUAGE: ENG
INDEX: church and state / fact-finding missions
GEOGRAPHICAL INDEX: El Salvador
GEOGRAPHICAL CODE: 6231
FREE TEXT: The report is one in a series of four, published after a
fact-finding mission of seven members to Central America in 1981.
The report analyses the violations of human rights and the situation
of the Catholic Church in El Salvador, as well as the socio-political
background of the violations. The report denounces the "deliberate
policy of genocide" of the Junta. It is stated that the Church is
severely persecuted; the position of the Christian Democrats towards
the Junta is analyzed. With conclusions and recommendations.

251

CATALOGUE SIGNATURE: 0000/1079/-3=830120
TITLE: Final report on the situation of human rights in El Salvador...
AUTHOR: Pastor Ridruejo, José Antonio
PLACE OF PUBLICATION: Geneva
PUBLISHER: Commission on Human Rights of the United Nations Economic
and Social Council - UNCHR (D)
DATE OF PUBLICATION: 830120
NUMBER OF PAGES: 47 p.
SERIES TITLE: Commission on Human Rights: thirty-ninth session: item 12
of the provisional agenda: question of the violation of human rights
and fundamental freedoms in any part of the world, with particular
reference to colonial and other dependent countries and territories
DOCUMENT SYMBOL: E/CN.4/1983/20
AVAILABILITY: F
LANGUAGE: ENG / SPA
BIBLIOGRAPHIES: Y
INDEX: civil and political rights / fact-finding missions
GEOGRAPHICAL INDEX: El Salvador
GEOGRAPHICAL CODE: 6231
FREE TEXT: Pastor Ridruejo submitted his final report in fulfilment
of the mandate conferred under Commission resolution 1982/28. He
visited El Salvador in September 1982, and established contacts with
the authorities, representatives of the Church and of nongovernmental
organizations. He visited prisons, and interviewed political prisoners.
His report contains an introduction, and chapters on: international
and national legal rules applicable; the current political situation;
economic, social and cultural rights; civil and political rights;
refugees and displaced persons; the compliance with international rules
of humanitarian law applicable in armed conflicts. With conclusions and
recommendations.

CATALOGUE SIGNATURE: 6231/-0=830100
TITLE: Human rights in El Salvador, January 1983 report of the public
health delegation of inquiry
AUTHOR: Eisenberg, Carola ; Halperin, David ; Hargraves, Anne
(...et al.)
PLACE OF PUBLICATION: Washington DC
PUBLISHER: American Public Health Association - APHA (D)
DATE OF PUBLICATION: 830100
NUMBER OF PAGES: 11 p. in v.p.
LANGUAGE: ENG
INDEX: health / disappearances / fact-finding missions
GEOGRAPHICAL INDEX: El Salvador
GEOGRAPHICAL CODE: 6231
FREE TEXT: The aim of the mission to El Salvador from 15 to 19 January
1983 of seven US health professionals was to study the disappearances
of health workers and reported abuses of medical neutrality. The
delegation found that human rights violations run so deep in the
society that there is an overall debasement of human rights; people are
stripped of the basic elements essential for physical and psychological
survival by a government which appears to have no other rationale than
maintaining power by military force, political repression and terror.
The report contains findings based on several contacts and visits to a
refugee camp, several hospitals, and the Mariona and Ilopango prisons.
With appendices: press release; information on the delegates.

CATALOGUE SIGNATURE: 0000/2915/-0=830000
TITLE: El Salvador's armed conflict and the Geneva Conventions
AUTHOR: Parker, Karen
PLACE OF PUBLICATION: (Berkeley)
PUBLISHER: Human Rights Advocates - HRA (D)
DATE OF PUBLICATION: 830000
NUMBER OF PAGES: 22 p.
LANGUAGE: ENG
BIBLIOGRAPHIES: Y
INDEX: armed conflict / refugees / humanitarian law /
fact-finding missions
GEOGRAPHICAL INDEX: El Salvador
GEOGRAPHICAL CODE: 6231
FREE TEXT: The author visited El Salvador in January 1983 as a member
of a delegation of the Faculty Committee on Human Rights in El Salvador
and Central America. Her report deals with violations of Protocol II
and Article 3 Common to the Geneva Conventions in the armed conflict in
El Salvador. It is stated that serious violations of Protocol II take
place. The report is concluded with questions on the role of the United
States in El Salvador's internal armed conflict and on whether the US
policy regarding refugees is consistent with its treaty obligations.

CATALOGUE SIGNATURE: 6231/-0=830300
TITLE: Justice in El Salvador: a report of a mission of inquiry of
the Association of the Bar of the City in New York
AUTHOR: DeWind, Adrian W. ; Kass, Stephen L.
PLACE OF PUBLICATION: New York
PUBLISHER: Association of the Bar of the City of New York - ABNY (D)
DATE OF PUBLICATION: 830300
NUMBER OF PAGES: 28 p.
LANGUAGE: ENG
INDEX: judicial systems / fact-finding missions
GEOGRAPHICAL INDEX: El Salvador
GEOGRAPHICAL CODE: 6231
FREE TEXT: The mission was appointed by the Association to visit El
Salvador and inquire into the independence of lawyers and the
administration of justice in that country. Emphasis was put on the
effects of the dominant role played by the military and security
forces in El Salvador's criminal justice system, the legal system's
capacity to discipline military personnel for human rights abuses,
and the judicial process effecting persons held for alleged political
offences. With findings and recommendations. The delegation concludes
that the collapse of the criminal justice system is general and
pervasive. Only a strong civilian government and a new social
consensus can implement the reforms needed. Among the defaults are
intimidation in law cases, inadequate training, inadequate access to
the counsel; abduction, torture and murder by security forces,
detention without trial, the inadequate judicial review of security
actions. The US State Department Certification is criticized.

CATALOGUE SIGNATURE: 0000/1212/-3=830400
TITLE: Medical fact-finding mission to El Salvador: 11-15 January
1983
AUTHOR: Gellhorn, Alfred ; Lawrence, Robert ; McCleskey, Kathie
(...et al)
PLACE OF PUBLICATION: New York
PUBLISHER: International League for Human Rights - ILHR (D) ;
American Association for the Advancement of Science - AAAS ;
Institute of Medicine of the National Academy of Sciences ;
National Academy of Sciences ; New York Academy of Sciences
DATE OF PUBLICATION: 830400
NUMBER OF PAGES: 16 p.
LANGUAGE: ENG
STATISTICAL INFORMATION: Y
INDEX: health / political prisoners / fact-finding missions
GEOGRAPHICAL INDEX: El Salvador
GEOGRAPHICAL CODE: 6231
FREE TEXT: One of the purposes of the mission was to investigate
sixteen cases of "disappeared" health workers. Five of them were
found in government custody.
The mission team also found evidence that health professionals have
been singled out for harassment, arrest and disappearance because
of their duties and that torture and other forms of cruel treatment
are carried out on a routine basis by security forces during
interrogation. The report also contains information on health
conditions and medical care for political prisoners, university and
medical education, the state of public health and human services.
With appendices: status of 16 health workers, and additional cases;
suggestions for implementation of recommendations.
(This is the April 1983 issue of the Clearinghouse Report on Science
and Human Rights, v.5(1), and the winter 1983 issue of the Human
Rights Bulletin of the ILHR)

CATALOGUE SIGNATURE: 0000/2171/-3=830000
TITLE: El Salvador: de moord op Marianella Garcia Villas: een
onderzoeksrapport door Adrien Claude Zöller
AUTHOR: Zöller, Adrien-Claude
PLACE OF PUBLICATION: The Hague
PUBLISHER: Pax Christi Nederland - PAXCI-NL (D)
DATE OF PUBLICATION: 830000
NUMBER OF PAGES: 76 p.
SERIES TITLE: Pax Christi Boekenreeks
VOLUME: no. 9
ISBN: 907044 322 8
LANGUAGE: DUT / FRE
BIBLIOGRAPHIES: Y
INDEX: homicide / nongovernmental organizations / fact-finding missions
GEOGRAPHICAL INDEX: El Salvador
GEOGRAPHICAL CODE: 6231
FREE TEXT: The purpose of the mission in April 1983 was to investigate
the circumstances under which Marianella Garcia Villas died, the work
she has done, the accusations of the military authorities, the
government policy in relation to human rights organizations, and the
consequences of Marianellas death. With conclusions: Marianella was
taken prisoner, tortured and murdered; and recommendations.
The report contains chapters on the work of Marianella and the Comisión
de Derechos Humanos de El Salvador (CDHES), her last mission, the
official versions of her death, a reconstruction of the murder and the
situation of human rights in El Salvador.
With appendices: press release, letter of Marianella, newspaper
reports, correspondence between Dutch non-govermental organizations and
the Dutch Ministry of Foreign Affairs.

CATALOGUE SIGNATURE: 0000/2955/-3=830719
TITLE: July 19, 1983 third supplement to the Report on human rights in
El Salvador
AUTHOR: Neier, Aryeh ; Mendez, Juan
PLACE OF PUBLICATION: New York
PUBLISHER: Americas Watch - AW (D) ; American Civil Liberties Union -
ACLU (D)
DATE OF PUBLICATION: 830719
NUMBER OF PAGES: 91 p.
LANGUAGE: ENG
STATISTICAL INFORMATION: Y
INDEX: armed conflict / political violence / fact-finding missions
GEOGRAPHICAL INDEX: El Salvador
GEOGRAPHICAL CODE: 6231
FREE TEXT: The third supplement is partly based on a fact-finding
mission to El Salvador in June 1983. Attention is paid to the murder
of civilians by government forces, disappearances, torture, repression
against professional groups, the Amnesty Law, the emergency Decree
507, aerial attacks on the civilian population, human rights violations
by the guerillas, the government-sponsored Human Rights Commission,
statistical methodology, disciplining of members of the armed forces,
and the judiciary system. With summary and conclusions.

El Salvador

CATALOGUE SIGNATURE: 0000/1079/-3=840119
TITLE: Final report on the situation of human rights in El Salvador...
AUTHOR: Pastor Ridruejo, José Antonio
PLACE OF PUBLICATION: Geneva
PUBLISHER: Commission on Human Rights of the United Nations Economic
and Social Council - UNCHR (D)
DATE OF PUBLICATION: 840119
NUMBER OF PAGES: 47 p.
SERIES TITLE: Commission on Human Rights: fortieth session: item 12
of the provisional agenda: question of the violation of human rights
and fundamental freedoms in any part of the world, with particular
reference to colonial and other dependent countries and territories
DOCUMENT SYMBOL: E/CN.4/1984/25
AVAILABILITY: F
LANGUAGE: ENG / SPA
BIBLIOGRAPHIES: Y
INDEX: civil and political rights / fact-finding missions
GEOGRAPHICAL INDEX: El Salvador
GEOGRAPHICAL CODE: 6231
FREE TEXT: Pastor Ridruejo submitted his final report in fulfilment
of the mandate conferred under Commission resolution 1983/29. He
visited the country in September 1983, and received information from
the government, the Church, human rights organizations, private
associations and individuals, and left-wing opposition forces. He
visited prisons and camps for displaced persons. The report contains
an introduction, and chapters on: the general political situation;
the situation of civil and political rights; the situation of refugees
and displaced persons; respect for human rights in the course of armed
conflicts; concern of the government for human rights. With conclusions
and recommendations.

CATALOGUE SIGNATURE: 0000/2955/-3=840131
TITLE: As bad as ever: a report on human rights in El Salvador:
January 31, 1984: fourth supplement
AUTHOR: Arnson, Cynthia ; Neier, Aryeh ; Benda, Susan
PLACE OF PUBLICATION: New York
PUBLISHER: Americas Watch - AW (D) ; American Civil Liberties Union -
ACLU (D)
DATE OF PUBLICATION: 840131
NUMBER OF PAGES: 74 p.
LANGUAGE: ENG
STATISTICAL INFORMATION: Y
INDEX: civil and political rights / fact-finding missions
GEOGRAPHICAL INDEX: El Salvador
GEOGRAPHICAL CODE: 6231
FREE TEXT: This Fourth Supplement is partly based on a fact-finding
mission to El Salvador in January 1984. Attention is paid to: murder
of civilians by government forces, disappearances, attacks on civilian
non-combatants, torture, political prisoners, repression against
particular sectors, human rights violations by guerillas, the
government-sponsored Human Rights Commission, elections, prosecution
of members of the armed forces, U.S. human rights policy towards El
Salvador, analysis of a State Department's report. With appendix:
examples of death squad communiqués.

CATALOGUE SIGNATURE: 0000/1582/-3=840400
TITLE: El Salvador's other victims: the war on the displaced
AUTHOR: Helton, Arthur C. ; Borton, Nan ; Rone, Jemera (...et al)
PLACE OF PUBLICATION: New York
PUBLISHER: Lawyers Committee for International Human Rights - LCIHR
(D) ; Americas Watch - AW (D)
DATE OF PUBLICATION: 840400
NUMBER OF PAGES: 257 p.
LANGUAGE: ENG
STATISTICAL INFORMATION: Y
INDEX: refugees / armed conflict / fact-finding missions
GEOGRAPHICAL INDEX: El Salvador
GEOGRAPHICAL CODE: 6231
FREE TEXT: The report deals with the situation of about half a
million Salvadorans who have left their homes but remained within
their country's border, the so called displaced persons. Special
attention is paid to their need for legal protection. They, and
persons assisting them, are subject to deliberate attacks by the
Salvadoran armed forces.
With conclusions and recommendations, description of the background
of the problem and chapters on problems of protection in zones
controlled by the oppositionary FMLN and by the government, the
registration programme, current conditions of displaced people,
the role of the United States, health conditions and the legal
framework. With various appendices.

CATALOGUE SIGNATURE: 0000/0249/-3=840500
TITLE: Extrajudicial executions in El Salvador: report of an Amnesty
International mission to examine post-mortem and investigative
procedures in political killings: 1-6 July 1983
AUTHOR: (Vidarte, Juan María) ; (Allen, Terence)
PLACE OF PUBLICATION: London
PUBLISHER: Amnesty International - AI (D)
DATE OF PUBLICATION: 840500
NUMBER OF PAGES: 48 p.
ISBN: 0 86210 070 4
LANGUAGE: ENG
BIBLIOGRAPHIES: Y
INDEX: extrajudicial executions / armed conflict /
fact-finding missions
GEOGRAPHICAL INDEX: El Salvador
GEOGRAPHICAL CODE: 6231
FREE TEXT: The purpose of the mission was to observe at first hand how
data on individual deaths are recorded, and medical and legal evidence
are pursued by the relevant official agencies. The mission also sought
to examine the methodology employed by the various human rights groups
in the country, which attempt to record and investigate violent deaths.
Finally, it intended to investigate the difficulties faced by the
various monitoring and reporting groups in their work. The report
contains a summary of findings, information on the scale of and
responsibility for extrajudicial executions and case studies which
illustrate the difficulties involved in the forensic, medical and
legal investigation of extrajudicial executions (four US churchwomen,
Marianella García Villas) and recommendations.

El Salvador

CATALOGUE SIGNATURE: 0000/2210/-3=840000
TITLE: A university survives: report of a Dutch inter-university
mission to El Salvador, June, 1984 = Een universiteit overleeft:
rapport van een Nederlandse universitaire missie naar El Salvador,
juni 1984
AUTHOR: Veldhoven, G.M. van ; Adriaanse, H.P. ; Kroon, J.W.
PLACE OF PUBLICATION: The Hague
PUBLISHER: Netherlands Universities Foundation For International
Cooperation - NUFFIC (D)
DATE OF PUBLICATION: 840000
NUMBER OF PAGES: (41 p.)
LANGUAGE: ENG
STATISTICAL INFORMATION: Y
BIBLIOGRAPHIES: Y
INDEX: academic freedom / education / fact-finding missions
GEOGRAPHICAL INDEX: El Salvador
GEOGRAPHICAL CODE: 6231
FREE TEXT: Report of a five-member mission, meant to take a first-
hand look at the situation of the University of El Salvador, and to
consider how a contribution could perhaps be made to solving the
problems of this institute. The emphasis was to lie on the problem of
the repression of professors and students. With: composition of the
delegation and agenda; background of the country, including the human
rights situation; information on the University; the findings of the
mission; conclusions and points of action.
With appendix: letter to Dutch universities, statistical material and
cases of violations, article from Index on Censorship, declaration of
the universities and the members of the mission, ideas for projects.

CATALOGUE SIGNATURE: 0000/2955/-3=840800
TITLE: Free fire: a report on human rights in El Salvador: August 1984
5th supplement
AUTHOR: Guest, Iain ; Orentlicher, Diane ; Rone, Jemera
PLACE OF PUBLICATION: New York
PUBLISHER: Americas Watch - AW (D) ; Lawyers Committee for
International Human Rights - LCIHR (D)
DATE OF PUBLICATION: 840800
NUMBER OF PAGES: 153 p. in v.p.
LANGUAGE: ENG
STATISTICAL INFORMATION: Y
INDEX: armed conflict / refugees / fact-finding missions
GEOGRAPHICAL INDEX: El Salvador
GEOGRAPHICAL CODE: 6231
FREE TEXT: This report, based on two fact-finding missions in June and
July 1984, is intended to serve both as the fifth supplement to the
"Report on human rights in El Salvador, January 1982" and as the first
supplement to "El Salvador's other victims: the war on the displaced,
April 1984". Attention is paid to:
1) Killings of civilian noncombatants by government forces (death
squads, indiscriminate attacks, bombardment, shelling, group sweeps,
displacement, the Singlaub report) 2) Disappearances; 3) Human rights
violations by the guerillas (murder of civilian noncombatants,
treatment of captured soldiers, forced recruitment) 4) Arrests and
abductions by the air force; 5) Decree 50; 6) Discipline for human
rights abuses; 7) El Salvador's displaced (protection problems,
registration, administration, pacification and living conditions)
8) The government's Human Rights Commission; 9) The 1984 elections
and the inauguration of president Duarte. With appendices.

CATALOGUE SIGNATURE: 0000/2764/-4
TITLE: Observing El Salvador: the 1984 elections
AUTHOR: Chitnis, Pratap C.
TITLE OF GENERIC ITEM: Third World Quarterly
EDITION: v.6(4).
PLACE OF PUBLICATION: London
PUBLISHER: Third World Foundation - TWF (D)
DATE OF PUBLICATION: 841000
NUMBER OF PAGES: p. 963-980
LANGUAGE: ENG
STATISTICAL INFORMATION: Y
INDEX: elections / fact-finding missions
GEOGRAPHICAL INDEX: El Salvador
GEOGRAPHICAL CODE: 6231
FREE TEXT: The author states that a free and fair election is a
process of political debate and education over many weeks, months
or, in the case of the most self-regarding democracy, years, which
culminates in the act of voting for defined choices. Chitnis, who
visited El Salvador twice during the campaign, describes the election
in its wider social, human rights, military and political context,
and his findings on the way in which the elections were held.
Attention is given to the early campaign, the first round and the
second round, and the aftermath of the elections. With appendix:
results.

CATALOGUE SIGNATURE: 0000/1234/-2=850000
TITLE: The 1982 and 1984 elections in El Salvador
AUTHOR: Gastil, Raymond ; McColm, Bruce ; Rustin, Bayard (...et al)
TITLE OF GENERIC ITEM: Freedom in the world: political rights and civil
liberties 1984-1985 / Gastil, Raymond
EDITION: 1st.
PLACE OF PUBLICATION: Westport ; London ; New York
PUBLISHER: Westwood Press (D) ; Freedom House (D)
DATE OF PUBLICATION: 850000
NUMBER OF PAGES: p.87-114
LANGUAGE: ENG
STATISTICAL INFORMATION: Y
BIBLIOGRAPHIES: Y
INDEX: elections / fact-finding missions
GEOGRAPHICAL INDEX: El Salvador
GEOGRAPHICAL CODE: 6231
FREE TEXT: This chapter includes:
-part I: report of the Freedom House mission to observe the election in
El Salvador, 28 March 1982. The aim of the mission was to examine in so
far as possible the election and its context in order to make a judgment
as to whether this election represented democratic progress. With
background information, findings of the mission, analysis of the
election results, summary and conclusions. With appendices: results in
figures and information on the participating parties; presumed
misunderstandings and errors in the discussion on El Salvador.
-part II: the 1984 presidential elections in El Salvador. Attention is
paid to the election process, the first 1984 campaign, the results,
the presidential run-off, assessment and perspectives for the future.

CATALOGUE SIGNATURE: 0000/1079/-3=850201
TITLE: Final report on the situation of human rights in El Salvador...
AUTHOR: Pastor Ridruejo, José Antonio
PLACE OF PUBLICATION: Geneva
PUBLISHER: Commission on Human Rights of the United Nations Economic
and Social Council - UNCHR (D)
DATE OF PUBLICATION: 850201
NUMBER OF PAGES: 52 p.
SERIES TITLE: Commission on Human Rights: forty-first session: item 12
of the provisional agenda: question of the violation of human rights
and fundamental freedoms in any part of the world, with particular
reference to colonial and other dependent countries and territories
DOCUMENT SYMBOL: E/CN.4/1985/18
AVAILABILITY: F
LANGUAGE: ENG / SPA
BIBLIOGRAPHIES: Y
INDEX: civil and political rights / fact-finding missions
GEOGRAPHICAL INDEX: El Salvador
GEOGRAPHICAL CODE: 6231
FREE TEXT: Pastor Ridruejo submitted his final report in fulfilment
of the mandate conferred under Commission resolution 1984/52. He
visited El Salvador in September 1984, and established contacts with
the authorities, representatives of nongovernmental organizations,
and individuals. He also visited prisons, and talked with political
prisoners. The report contains an introduction, and chapters on: the
general political situation; the situation of economic, social and
cultural rights; the situation of civil and political rights (murders;
abductions and disappearances; political prisoners; criminal justice;
human rights violations attributed to the guerilla forces); the
situation of refugees and displaced persons; human rights in armed
conflicts; and the concern of the government for human rights. With
conclusions and recommendations.

El Salvador

CATALOGUE SIGNATURE: 0000/2955/-3=850300
TITLE: Draining the sea...: sixth supplement to the Report on
human rights in El Salvador
AUTHOR: Neier, Aryeh
PLACE OF PUBLICATION: New York
PUBLISHER: Americas Watch - AW (D)
DATE OF PUBLICATION: 850300
NUMBER OF PAGES: 77 p.
LANGUAGE: ENG
BIBLIOGRAPHIES: Y
INDEX: armed violence / military / human rights and foreign policy /
fact-finding missions
GEOGRAPHICAL INDEX: El Salvador
GEOGRAPHICAL CODE: 6231
FREE TEXT: Some of the information for this report was gathered during
a visit to El Salvador by Aryeh Neier, Jemera Rone and Cynthia Arnson
in January 1985. In the introduction, it is stated that the Salvadoran
armed forces are draining the sea in order to deny the fish sustenance.
The sea is the civilian population in guerrilla-controlled zones; the
fish are the guerrillas. This strategy involves the use of terror
tactics (bombings, strafings, shellings, and, occasionally, massacres
of civilians), as a consequence of which approximately one quarter of
the population of El Salvador have fled their homes.
The report contains chapters on: indiscriminate attacks by the armed
forces on the civilian population; killings by death squads;
disappearances; forced displacement; human rights violations by the
guerrillas; the administration of justice; the Duarte government.

CATALOGUE SIGNATURE: 6231/-0=850300
TITLE: In a war-torn country, the people seek peace and justice: report
of an ecumenical visit to El Salvador organized by the Inter-Church
Committee on Human Rights in Latin America, March 22-30, 1985
AUTHOR: O'Mara, John ; Pfrimmer, David
PLACE OF PUBLICATION: Toronto
PUBLISHER: Inter-Church Committee on Human Rights in Latin America -
ICCHRLA (D)
DATE OF PUBLICATION: 850300
NUMBER OF PAGES: 8 p.
LANGUAGE: ENG
INDEX: refugees / religion (freedom of) / fact-finding missions
GEOGRAPHICAL INDEX: El Salvador
GEOGRAPHICAL CODE: 6231
FREE TEXT: The principal aim of the visit was to participate in a
number of events organized to mark the fifth anniversary of the
martyrdom of Archbishop Oscar Arnulfo Romero. Other purposes were to
assess the current situation of the war and human rights violations;
to assess the need for humanitarian aid and the type of aid required
for displaced persons; and to express the solidarity and support of
the Canadian churches for the churches and the people of El Salvador.
In the report, attention is paid to the position of the churches, the
reality of the war, the situation of human rights, humanitarian
assistance and the preference for political instead of military
solutions. With recommendations.

262

CATALOGUE SIGNATURE: 0000/1079/-3=860203
TITLE: Final report on the situation of human rights in El Salvador...
AUTHOR: Pastor Ridruejo, José Antonio
PLACE OF PUBLICATION: Geneva
PUBLISHER: Commission on Human Rights of the United Nations Economic
and Social Council - UNCHR (D)
DATE OF PUBLICATION: 860203
NUMBER OF PAGES: 52 p.
SERIES TITLE: Commission on Human Rights: forty-second session: item 12
of the provisional agenda: question of the violation of human rights
and fundamental freedoms in any part of the world, with particular
reference to colonial and other dependent countries and territories
DOCUMENT SYMBOL: E/CN.4/1986/22
AVAILABILITY: F
LANGUAGE: ENG / SPA
BIBLIOGRAPHIES: Y
INDEX: civil and political rights / fact-finding missions
GEOGRAPHICAL INDEX: El Salvador
GEOGRAPHICAL CODE: 6231
FREE TEXT: Pastor Ridruejo submitted his final report in fulfilment
of the mandate conferred under Commission resolution 1985/53. He
visited El Salvador in September 1985, and established contacts with
the authorities, representatives of nongovernmental organizations,
and individuals. He also visited prisons, and talked with political
prisoners. The report contains an introduction, and chapters on: the
general political situation; the situation of economic, social and
cultural rights; the situation of civil and political rights (murders;
abductions and disappearances; political prisoners; criminal justice;
human rights violations attributed to the guerilla forces); the
situation of refugees and displaced persons; human rights in armed
conflicts; and the concern of the government for human rights. With
conclusions and recommendations.

GRENADA

CATALOGUE SIGNATURE: 0000/1246/-3=850000
TITLE: Elections in Grenada: return to parliamentary democracy: a
report on the December 3, 1984 Grenadian election
AUTHOR: Garber, Larry
PLACE OF PUBLICATION: Washington DC
PUBLISHER: International Human Rights Law Group - IHRLG (D)
DATE OF PUBLICATION: 850000
NUMBER OF PAGES: 46 p. in v.p.
LANGUAGE: ENG
STATISTICAL INFORMATION: Y
INDEX: elections / fact-finding missions
GEOGRAPHICAL INDEX: Grenada
GEOGRAPHICAL CODE: 6134
FREE TEXT: Report on the elections in Grenada, with a summary and
sections on the background of the country and the elections, the
evaluation of the Grenadian electoral system, conclusions and
appendices: terms of reference of the mission, press release,
results of the election. It is stated that the election provided
the opportunity for the reopening of a political process; parties
organized and campaigned freely, Grenadian citizens had the
opportunity to cast a free and secret vote, and the integrity of
the ballot was respected.

GUATEMALA

CATALOGUE SIGNATURE: 0000/0088/-3=790000
TITLE: Human rights in Guatemala: report of a mission to Guatemala in
June 1979 on behalf of the International Commission of Jurists =
Derechos humanos en Guatemala: informe de la misión enviada por la
Comisión Internacional de Juristas a Guatemala, en junio de 1979
AUTHOR: Fox, Donald T.
PLACE OF PUBLICATION: Geneva
PUBLISHER: International Commission of Jurists - ICJ (D)
DATE OF PUBLICATION: 790000
NUMBER OF PAGES: 58 p.
LANGUAGE: ENG / SPA
STATISTICAL INFORMATION: Y
INDEX: political violence / social and economic rights /
fact-finding missions
GEOGRAPHICAL INDEX: Guatemala
GEOGRAPHICAL CODE: 6236
FREE TEXT: The report begins with a general introduction to Guatemala.
The main part of the report, "the violence of Guatemala", is a general
description of human rights violations and their background, based on
written sources. With attention to socio-economic violence, nature of
the forces of repression, the Guerilla Army of the Poor, consequences
and effects on principal institutions like the church, the labour
movement, political parties and the educational system.
The last part is on opportunities for democratizing Guatemala; parts
of the Constitution are included. With conclusions.

CATALOGUE SIGNATURE: 0000/0249/-3=790000
TITLE: Memorandum presented to the government of the Republic of
Guatemala following a mission to the country from 10 to 15 August 1979
AUTHOR: (Gallin, Dan) ; (Álvarez de Miranda, Fernando) ;
(Ulltveit-Moe, Tracy)
PLACE OF PUBLICATION: London
PUBLISHER: Amnesty International - AI (D)
DATE OF PUBLICATION: 790000
NUMBER OF PAGES: 16 p. in v.p.
DOCUMENT SYMBOL: AI Index: AMR 34/45/79
LANGUAGE: ENG
INDEX: political violence / association (freedom of) /
fact-finding missions
GEOGRAPHICAL INDEX: Guatemala
GEOGRAPHICAL CODE: 6236
FREE TEXT: The objectives of the mission were to investigate at first
hand reports of political violence received from Guatemala, and to
press the government for information about the steps being taken to
control such violence. AI was particularly concerned about widespread
reports of violence directed against trade unions and their leaders
during the term of office of the present government.
The report deals with disappearances, political killings and repression
of trade unionists and politicians.
With observations and recommendations, and appendices: selection of
human rights violations in recent months; covering letter to President
Romeo Lucas García.

265

CATALOGUE SIGNATURE: 0000/1291/-0=800000
TITLE: Guatemala: repression and resistance: report of the National
Lawyers Guild and La Raza Legal Alliance joint Guatemala delegation
1979
AUTHOR: Handschu, Barbara Ellen ; Hilliard, Bob ; Kaplan, Harvey
(...et al)
PLACE OF PUBLICATION: (New York)
PUBLISHER: National Lawyers Guild - NLG (D)
DATE OF PUBLICATION: 800000
NUMBER OF PAGES: 33 p.
LANGUAGE: ENG
BIBLIOGRAPHIES: Y
INDEX: political violence / military / fact-finding missions
GEOGRAPHICAL INDEX: Guatemala
GEOGRAPHICAL CODE: 6236
FREE TEXT: In March 1979, a six person mission went to Guatemala to
investigate charges that the Guatemalan government had intensified
its repressive practices against many sectors of Guatemalan society.
The mission was invited by the National Committee for Trade Union
Unity CNUS. It met with factory workers, farm workers, students,
trade unionists, clergy, peasants, press, street vendors, urban slum
dwellers, progressive political leaders and lawyers. The members
concluded that: "... there is an extremely high level of systematic
repression which is characterized by brutal tortures of thousands of
people and the murders of six to eight people daily throughout the
country. The current reign of terror has permeated every level of
Guatemalan society." The report includes as an appendix a submission
to the Inter-American Commission on Human Rights, which contains
documentation, interviews and testimonies of Guatemalans with which
the mission met.

CATALOGUE SIGNATURE: 6236/-0=810000
TITLE: From Guatemala: an epistle to the believing communities in the
Unites States
AUTHOR: Howard, William ; Wee, Paul ; Nicholson, Beverly (...et al)
PLACE OF PUBLICATION: New York
PUBLISHER: Agricultural Missions ; National Council of Churches of
Christ in the USA - NCCCUSA (D)
DATE OF PUBLICATION: 810000
NUMBER OF PAGES: 9 p.
LANGUAGE: ENG
INDEX: church and state / fact-finding missions
GEOGRAPHICAL INDEX: Guatemala
GEOGRAPHICAL CODE: 6236
FREE TEXT: The report contains the impressions and findings of a
mission of six delegates to Guatemala in April 1981, to obtain
information on the general human rights situation. It is based on
various sources, including victims, government and church people.
With conclusions and recommendations, and proposals for action.

CATALOGUE SIGNATURE: 0000/0035/-3=810000
TITLE: Rapport de mission: Guatemala 22-28 juin 1981
AUTHOR: Texier, Philippe
PLACE OF PUBLICATION: Paris
PUBLISHER: Fédération Internationale des Droits de l'Homme - FIDH (D)
DATE OF PUBLICATION: 810000
NUMBER OF PAGES: 15 p.
LANGUAGE: FRE
INDEX: civil and political rights / fact-finding missions
GEOGRAPHICAL INDEX: Guatemala
GEOGRAPHICAL CODE: 6236
FREE TEXT: The mission of Texier took place in the framework of a
mission by Pax Christi to Central America. The report contains
information on the background of the country, massacres, torture,
disappearances, the absence of legal aid in case of human rights
violations, the problem of the Indians and forced displacements of
the population, and the situation of civil and political liberties.
With conclusions.

CATALOGUE SIGNATURE: 0000/0491/-3=820000
TITLE: Guatemala
AUTHOR: Texier, Philippe ; Novello, Gianni ; Bettazzi, Luigi (...et al)
PLACE OF PUBLICATION: Antwerpen
PUBLISHER: Pax Christi International - PAXCI (D) ; OMEGA Books (D)
DATE OF PUBLICATION: 820000
NUMBER OF PAGES: 77 p.
SERIES TITLE: Pax Christi International Human Rights Reports
VOLUME: no. 4
ISBN: 90 70316 12 9
LANGUAGE: ENG
INDEX: church and state / fact-finding missions
GEOGRAPHICAL INDEX: Guatemala
GEOGRAPHICAL CODE: 6236
FREE TEXT: The report, based on a fact-finding mission in 1981, is an
attempt to analyze the social and political background of the current
repression in the country. It describes the economic and strategic
interests concerned, as well as the conditions of extreme poverty in
which the majority of the Guatemalans, especially the Indians, live.
It concludes that economic, social and cultural rights are notions
that do not yet exist in Guatemala. Human rights are systematically
violated. A separate chapter is devoted to the persecuted catholic
Church.

Guatemala

CATALOGUE SIGNATURE: 0000/1193/-0=820727
TITLE: Human rights in Guatemala today: the case of Dr. Juan José
Hurtado: a report of a mission of inquiry to Guatemala...
AUTHOR: Fine, Jonathan ; Hinshaw, Robert ; Mendez, Juan
PLACE OF PUBLICATION: (Washington DC)
PUBLISHER: American Association for the Advancement of Science - AAAS
(D)
DATE OF PUBLICATION: 820727
NUMBER OF PAGES: (17 p.)
LANGUAGE: ENG
INDEX: detention / military / fact-finding missions
GEOGRAPHICAL INDEX: Guatemala
GEOGRAPHICAL CODE: 6236
FREE TEXT: Report of a mission in July 1982, prepared for the American
Association for the Advancement of Science, the American Public Health
Association, the American Anthropological Association, the National
Association of Social Workers, the Public Health Association of New
York City and the Institute of Medicine of the National Academy of
Sciences.
The mission was undertaken to investigate the seizure and detention of
Dr Hurtado, a prominent pediatrician, anthropologist and medical
educator. Attention is paid to the background of his arrest and
detention, and legal aspects; possible motives are analyzed. His case
is placed in the context of the more general status of human rights in
Guatemala.
With conclusions and recommendations, text of a statement made during
the mission and list of officials and other persons interviewed.

CATALOGUE SIGNATURE: 0000/2955/-3=820000
TITLE: Human rights in Guatemala: no neutrals allowed: an Americas
Watch report
AUTHOR: Schell, Orville H. ; Karp, Russell ; Goldman, Robert Kogod
(...et al)
PLACE OF PUBLICATION: New York
PUBLISHER: Americas Watch - AW (D)
DATE OF PUBLICATION: 820000
NUMBER OF PAGES: 133 p.
LANGUAGE: ENG
BIBLIOGRAPHIES: Y
INDEX: dictatorship / human rights and foreign policy /
fact-finding missions
GEOGRAPHICAL INDEX: Guatemala
GEOGRAPHICAL CODE: 6236
FREE TEXT: The purpose of the four member mission in October 1982 was
to assess the veracity of persistent reports of human rights violations
under the Guatemalan government headed by president Rios Montt. The
report combines the delegation's findings and experience with material
from other organizations and missions.
The report is divided in three parts. The first deals with human rights
practices (the right to life; civil and political rights); the second
is on the legislation (the Constitution of 1965; legal measures of the
Rios Montt government that violate the constitution and Guatemala's
international legal obligations), the third is on human rights
reporting by the United States embassy and the State Department.
With appendices: letter of Assistant Secretary of State Enders to
Amnesty International USA; State Department critique of AI report.

268

CATALOGUE SIGNATURE: 6236/-0=820000
TITLE: Report of an inquiry team to Guatemala organized by the
National (Council) of Churches of Christ in the USA
AUTHOR: Sinclair, John H. ; Johnson, Corinne B. ; MacDonald, J.
Lorne (...et al)
PLACE OF PUBLICATION: New York
PUBLISHER: Division of Overseas Ministries ; National Council of
Churches of Christ in the USA - NCCCUSA (D)
DATE OF PUBLICATION: 820000
NUMBER OF PAGES: 14 p.
LANGUAGE: ENG
INDEX: military / fact-finding missions
GEOGRAPHICAL INDEX: Guatemala
GEOGRAPHICAL CODE: 6236
FREE TEXT: The purpose of the mission of four members in November
1982 was to investigate into alleged violations of human rights, in
response to a government invitation. In the report, attention is paid
to specific violations of human rights, including a description of
cases and response of the military authorities. With description of
plans for economic development and findings of on-site visits,
conclusions and recommendations.

CATALOGUE SIGNATURE: 0000/1037/-3-830000
TITLE: Witness to genocide: the present situation of Indians in
Guatemala
AUTHOR: Nelson, Craig W. ; Taylor, Kenneth I. ; Kruger, Janice
PLACE OF PUBLICATION: London
PUBLISHER: Survival International - SI (D)
DATE OF PUBLICATION: 830000
NUMBER OF PAGES: 44 p.
ISBN: 0 946592 00 4
LANGUAGE: ENG
INDEX: minorities / refugees / fact-finding missions
GEOGRAPHICAL INDEX: Guatemala
GEOGRAPHICAL CODE: 6236
FREE TEXT: In Guatemala, whole sections of the rural, largely Indian
population have been indiscriminately and ruthlessly destroyed. The
report is based on testimonies by twenty-three Guatemalan refugees,
interviewed in southern Mexico by representatives of Survival
International (USA). The events described took place in the districts
Huehuetenango and El Quiche, Guatemala, between December 1981 and
August 1982. Attention is paid to the background of the country, the
government policy and recent developments. The report contains the
complete texts of the testimonies.
With update: events between September 1982 and February 1983, legal
commentary and appendices.

CATALOGUE SIGNATURE: 6000/1011/-3=831005
TITLE: Report on the situation of human rights in the Republic of
Guatemala
AUTHOR: Inter-American Commission on Human Rights - IACHR
PLACE OF PUBLICATION: Washington DC
PUBLISHER: Organization of American States - OAS (D) ; Inter-American
Commission on Human Rights - IACHR
DATE OF PUBLICATION: 831005
NUMBER OF PAGES: 134 p.
ISBN: 0 8270 1863 0
DOCUMENT SYMBOL: OEA/Ser.L/V/II.61 doc.47 rev.1
LANGUAGE: ENG
INDEX: legislation / civil and political rights /
fact-finding missions
GEOGRAPHICAL INDEX: Guatemala
GEOGRAPHICAL CODE: 6236
FREE TEXT: Report of a fact-finding mission undertaken by the
Commission from 21 to 26 September 1983. The report contains an
introduction on the activities of the delegation and the relation
with the authorities, and chapters dealing with different aspects
of the human rights situation: the political and normative system
(legislation); the right to life (political violence); the right to
personal liberty, security and integrity (including disappearances);
the right to justice and due process; freedom of thought and
expression; freedom of conscience and religion; political rights;
freedom of movement and residence (refugees and displaced persons);
and the coup d'état of 8 August 1983. With conclusions and
recommendations.

CATALOGUE SIGNATURE: 0000/0035/-3=831100
TITLE: Rapport: mission spéciale au Guatemala pour enquêter sur les
droits de l'homme et en particulier sur les disparitions forcées:
octobre 1983
AUTHOR: Garcia Borrajo, Antonio
PLACE OF PUBLICATION: Paris
PUBLISHER: Fédération Internationale des Droits de l'Homme - FIDH (D)
DATE OF PUBLICATION: 831100
NUMBER OF PAGES: (80 p.)
LANGUAGE: FRE
STATISTICAL INFORMATION: Y
INDEX: disappearances / fact-finding missions
GEOGRAPHICAL INDEX: Guatemala
GEOGRAPHICAL CODE: 6236
FREE TEXT: The general aim of the mission was to investigate the human
rights situation in Guatemala, and more in particular the forced or
unvoluntary disappearance of persons. The author states that the human
rights and fundamental liberties of the Guatemalan people are strongly
violated by the illegitimate government of General Mejia Victores. More
than 35.000 persons have disappeared. The specific purpose of the
mission was to intercede with the authorities for the transference of
the bodies of fourteen disappeared persons carried off by the army.
Garcia Borrajo was threatened and almost kidnapped, and had to leave
the country prematurely.
Detailed report, with appendices: witness report, lists of disappeared
persons and copies of newspaper and periodical articles.

CATALOGUE SIGNATURE: 0000/2955/-3=840100
TITLE: Guatemala: a nation of prisoners: an Americas Watch report
AUTHOR: Brown, Cynthia (ed.) ; Manz, Beatriz ; Nelson, Anne
PLACE OF PUBLICATION: New York
PUBLISHER: Americas Watch - AW (D)
DATE OF PUBLICATION: 840100
NUMBER OF PAGES: 260 p.
LANGUAGE: ENG
INDEX: political violence / dictatorship / fact-finding missions
GEOGRAPHICAL INDEX: Guatemala
GEOGRAPHICAL CODE: 6236
FREE TEXT: The detailed third AW report on human rights violations in
Guatemala is partly based on a fact finding mission in November 1983.
Special chapters are devoted to individual rights (political killings,
torture, disappearances); rights to free conscience, association and
expression (the situation of the Church, the press and human rights
monitors); the social and economic consequences of repression;
counterinsurgency as a means of control (the civil patrol system;
specific cases; urban repression); the role of the United States.
With appendices: chronology of violence, 10 August - 8 December 1983,
based on newspaper articles; testimonies of victims and witnesses;
letter of Americas Watch to Guatemalan authorities.

CATALOGUE SIGNATURE: 0000/1079/-3=840208
TITLE: Report on the situation of human rights in Guatemala...
AUTHOR: Viscount Colville of Culross
PLACE OF PUBLICATION: Geneva
PUBLISHER: Commission on Human Rights of the United Nations Economic
and Social Council - UNCHR (D)
DATE OF PUBLICATION: 840208
NUMBER OF PAGES: 57 p. in v.p.
SERIES TITLE: Commission on Human Rights: fortieth session: item 12 of
the provisional agenda: question of the violation of human rights and
fundamental freedoms in any part of the world, with particular
reference to colonial and other dependent countries and territories
DOCUMENT SYMBOL: E/CN.4/1984/30
AVAILABILITY: F
LANGUAGE: ENG
STATISTICAL INFORMATION: Y
INDEX: civil and political rights / refugees / fact-finding missions
GEOGRAPHICAL INDEX: Guatemala
GEOGRAPHICAL CODE: 6236
FREE TEXT: Viscount Colville of Culross is Special Rapporteur in
accordance with paragraph 9 of Commission on Human Rights resolution
1983/37 of 8 March 1983. He visited Guatemala in June-July 1983 and
in November 1983. His report contains an introduction, and sections on
relevant international instruments, the historical background of the
country, the current conflict, introduction of reforms (elections, the
Council of State, social and economic reforms), unresolved indications
of abuses (Special Tribunals, disappearances, killings, the role of
the army and civil patrons, religious freedom), general concerns about
alleged violations of human rights (refugees in Mexico, protected or
model villages), conclusions and recommendations. With annexes: General
Assembly resolution 1983/100; historical background 1954-1982;
itineraries; progress chart of rural projects.

CATALOGUE SIGNATURE: 6326/-0=840000
TITLE: "We will neither go nor be driven out": a special report by the
IUF trade union delegation on the occupation of the Coca-Cola bottling
plant in Guatemala
AUTHOR: Plumb, Richard ; Hernandez, Luis ; Gacek, Stanley (et al...)
PLACE OF PUBLICATION: Geneva ; Washington DC
PUBLISHER: International Union of Food and Allied Workers Association -
IUF (D) ; North American Regional Organization of the IUF (D)
DATE OF PUBLICATION: 840000
NUMBER OF PAGES: 19 p.
LANGUAGE: ENG
BIBLIOGRAPHIES: Y
INDEX: trade unions / TNCs (transnational corporations) /
fact-finding missions
GEOGRAPHICAL INDEX: Guatemala
GEOGRAPHICAL CODE: 6236
FREE TEXT: When the plant owners of a Coca-Cola bottling plant in
Guatemala informed the workers that the business was closing down they
refused to accept the loss of their jobs and their trade union, and
occupied the plant peacefully. A North American trade union delegation
went to Guatemala in March 1984 to lend support to the workers and
their union. The report provides information on the background of the
conflict: the response of North American trade unions, meetings with
government officials, the organization of the trade union, security
problems, the bankruptcy, occupation and life inside the plant. With
conclusions, recommendations and appendices: impact of the plant
closing on the wives and families of slain and missing Coca-Cola
workers; investigation into the financial situation of the plant.

CATALOGUE SIGNATURE: 0000/0138/-3=850000
TITLE: Mission to Guatemala: 22-29 January 1985 = Mission au Guatemala:
22-29 janvier 1985 = Misión en Guatemala: 22-29 de enero de 1985
AUTHOR: Chemillier-Gendreau, Monique ; Rubman, David ; Steinberg, Kip
PLACE OF PUBLICATION: Brussels
PUBLISHER: International Association of Democratic Lawyers - IADL (D) ;
National Lawyers Guild - NLG - Central American Task Force (D)
DATE OF PUBLICATION: 850000
NUMBER OF PAGES: (52 p.)
LANGUAGE: ENG / FRE / SPA
BIBLIOGRAPHIES: Y
INDEX: civil and political rights / fact-finding missions
GEOGRAPHICAL INDEX: Guatemala
GEOGRAPHICAL CODE: 6236
FREE TEXT: The aim of the mission was to investigate the general human
rights situation, including forced disappearances, extrajudicial
executions, arbitrary detentions, torture, different liberties; the
application of humanitarian law, the independence of jurisdiction and
the rule of law. The report consists of a description of activities
undertaken by the mission, background information on the country, the
possibilities for international action, the situation of specific
civil and political rights in Guatemala (the right to life, the right
to bodily integrity and the prohibition of torture, guarantees when
on trial and rights of the defence, freedom of expression, freedom of
association, freedom of movement, treatment of political prisoners),
the independence of the judiciary, conclusions and perspectives. With
annexes: interviews with witnesses, final note, letter, newspaper
articles.

CATALOGUE SIGNATURE: 0000/1079/-3=850208
TITLE: Report on the situation of human rights in Guatemala...
AUTHOR: Viscount Colville of Culross
PLACE OF PUBLICATION: Geneva
PUBLISHER: Commission on Human Rights of the United Nations Economic
and Social Council - UNCHR (D)
DATE OF PUBLICATION: 850208
NUMBER OF PAGES: 57 p. in v.p.
SERIES TITLE: Commission on Human Rights: forty-first session: agenda
item 12: question of the violation of human rights and fundamental
freedoms in any part of the world, with particular reference to
colonial and other dependent countries and territories
DOCUMENT SYMBOL: E/CN.4/1985/19
AVAILABILITY: F
LANGUAGE: ENG
STATISTICAL INFORMATION: Y
INDEX: civil and political rights / refugees / fact-finding missions
GEOGRAPHICAL INDEX: Guatemala
GEOGRAPHICAL CODE: 6236
FREE TEXT: Viscount Colville of Culross is Special Rapporteur in
accordance with paragraph 14 of Commission on Human Rights resolution
1984/53 of 14 March 1984. He visited Guatemala in August 1984 and in
January 1985. His report contains an introduction, and sections on
civil rights (right to life and personal integrity; right to personal
liberty; freedom of movement and residence); political rights (right
of assembly and freedom of association; freedom of expression and
religious freedom); and economic, social and cultural rights (standard
of living; refugees in Mexico, Honduras and Belize). With conclusions
and recommendations, and annexes: General Assembly resolution 39/120;
map of the itinerary of the Special Rapporteur in Guatemala.

CATALOGUE SIGNATURE: 6003/1226/-0=850600
TITLE: Security and development conditions in the Guatemalan highlands
AUTHOR: Krueger, Chris ; Enge, Kjell
PLACE OF PUBLICATION: Washington DC
PUBLISHER: Washington Office on Latin America - WOLA (D)
DATE OF PUBLICATION: 850600
NUMBER OF PAGES: 78 p. in v.p.
LANGUAGE: ENG
INDEX: armed conflict / political violence / development (right to) /
military / fact-finding missions
GEOGRAPHICAL INDEX: Guatemala
GEOGRAPHICAL CODE: 6236
FREE TEXT: The report is the result of three weeks of documentation
review and personal interviews carried out in Washington DC and of
three weeks of interviews and a field investigation in Guatemala in
March 1985. The authors conclude that there is political violence on
a large scale in Guatemala. The military government has undertaken a
highly publicized security and development program based on civil
patrols, model villages and development poles, and an
Inter-Institutional Coordination System which directs public sector
institutions and resources towards priority projects. To date, such
projects have centered on minimum shelter and infrastructure
construction and reconstruction in areas heavily affected by violence
and mostly for families relocated into high security "model" villages.
The program has virtually all security with little development content.
The army is in a position to maintain real if not formal control of
development institutions and processes even after a civilian government
is installed. With summary of findings, conclusions and
recommendations.

CATALOGUE SIGNATURE: 0000/1246/-3=851200
TITLE: The 1985 Guatemalan elections: will the military relinquish
power?
AUTHOR: Booth, John A. ; Howard, Anne L. ; Lord Kennet (...et al)
PLACE OF PUBLICATION: Washington DC
PUBLISHER: International Human Rights Law Group - IHRLG (D) ;
Washington Office on Latin America - WOLA (D)
DATE OF PUBLICATION: 851200
NUMBER OF PAGES: 131 p. in v.p.
LANGUAGE: ENG
INDEX: democracy / elections / fact-finding missions
GEOGRAPHICAL INDEX: Guatemala
GEOGRAPHICAL CODE: 6236
FREE TEXT: The report of an observer mission to the 1985 elections
contains a thorough analysis of the entire electoral process and its
significance for Guatemala. The report contains an executive summary,
and chapters on different aspects of the elections. With appendices:
correspondence with authorities of Guatemala, terms of reference of
the mission, itinerary, statements, letter from Guatemalan bishops.
It is stated that the elections were procedurally correct and signify
important progress towards the goal of civilian rule. Nonetheless, the
elections were far from perfect, as they occurred in a climate where
parties and voters were subject to various forms of intimidation and
human rights abuses. Moreover, whether the military intend to cede
real power remains questionable.

CATALOGUE SIGNATURE: 0000/0035/-4
TITLE: Rapport de mission: Guatemala: 9-14 décembre 1985: sur la
situation générale et notamment celle des droits de l'homme
AUTHOR: Rouquette, R. ; Breton, A. ; Garapon, A.
PLACE OF PUBLICATION: Paris
PUBLISHER: Fédération Internationale des Droits de l'Homme - FIDH (D)
DATE OF PUBLICATION: 851200
NUMBER OF PAGES: (55 p.)
LANGUAGE: FRE
INDEX: military / nongovernmental organizations / fact-finding missions
GEOGRAPHICAL INDEX: Guatemala
GEOGRAPHICAL CODE: 6236
FREE TEXT: The aim of the mission was to collect all useful information
on the way in which the Universal Declaration is applied in Guatemala.
The report contains a list of contacts, and sections on the general
situation in Guatemala, the transition of power and the policy against
insurrections, violations of human rights (assassinations,
disappearances, clandestine prisons), the work of the Group for Mutual
Assistance (GAM), and the legal and political powers of the new regime.
With conclusions and appendices which provide background information on
the mission, such as correspondence with the Ambassador of Guatemala in
France, articles in Guatemalan newspapers, background information on
the country, information sheets of the Group for Mutual Assistance.

CATALOGUE SIGNATURE: 0000/0249/-0=860100
TITLE: Memorandum presented to the government of Guatemala following a
mission to the country in April 1985
AUTHOR: (Amnesty International - AI)
PLACE OF PUBLICATION: London
PUBLISHER: Amnesty International - AI (D)
DATE OF PUBLICATION: 860100
NUMBER OF PAGES: 46 p. in v.p.
DOCUMENT SYMBOL: AI Index: AMR 34/01/86
LANGUAGE: ENG
INDEX: political violence / military / civil and political rights /
fact-finding missions
GEOGRAPHICAL INDEX: Guatemala
GEOGRAPHICAL CODE: 6236
FREE TEXT: The document is divided into seven parts: 1) AI's long-
term human rights concern in Guatemala: torture, disappearance and
extrajudicial executions; 2) categories of victims; 3) clandestine
cemeteries and secret detention centres; 4) the forces responsible;
5) domestic efforts to investigate human rights abuses: failure of
the Guatemalan judicial system to investigate and punish human rights
violations; failure to prosecute police or military personnel; human
rights violations directed at journalists who attempt to accurately
investigate and report on human rights violations; domestic human
rights groups; 6) human rights education of Guatemala's security
forces; 7) recommendations.
With appendices: representative incidents of human rights violations;
information on disappearances and extrajudicial executions.

CATALOGUE SIGNATURE: 0000/1079/-3=860213
TITLE: Report on the situation of human rights in Guatemala...
AUTHOR: Viscount Colville of Culross
PLACE OF PUBLICATION: Geneva
PUBLISHER: Commission on Human Rights of the United Nations Economic
and Social Council - UNCHR (D)
DATE OF PUBLICATION: 860213
NUMBER OF PAGES: 20 p. in v.p.
SERIES TITLE: Commission on Human Rights: forty-second session: agenda
item 12: question of the violation of human rights and fundamental
freedoms in any part of the world, with particular reference to
colonial and other dependent countries and territories
DOCUMENT SYMBOL: E/CN.4/1986/23
AVAILABILITY: F
LANGUAGE: ENG
STATISTICAL INFORMATION: Y
INDEX: civil and political rights / elections / refugees /
fact-finding missions
GEOGRAPHICAL INDEX: Guatemala
GEOGRAPHICAL CODE: 6236
FREE TEXT: Viscount Colville of Culross is Special Rapporteur in
accordance with paragraph 14 of Commission on Human Rights resolution
1985/36 of 13 March 1985. He visited Guatemala from 28 January to 2
February 1986. His report contains an introduction, and sections on:
the elections for President and Vice-President, Congress and municipal
authorities in November-December 1985; particular violations of human
rights; liability for past violations; freedom of association; recent
information on the rule of law, disappearances, clandestine prisons,
civil patrols, development poles and model villages, and the
distribution of titles to land. With conclusions and recommendations,
and annex: General Assembly resolution 40/140.

CATALOGUE SIGNATURE: 0000/2955/-3=860800
TITLE: Civil patrols in Guatemala
AUTHOR: Simon, Jean-Marie ; Brown, Cynthia (ed.)
PLACE OF PUBLICATION: New York
PUBLISHER: Americas Watch - AW (D)
DATE OF PUBLICATION: 860800
NUMBER OF PAGES: 105 p.
ISBN: 0 938579 24 X
LANGUAGE: ENG
INDEX: military / political violence / fact-finding missions
GEOGRAPHICAL INDEX: Guatemala
GEOGRAPHICAL CODE: 6236
FREE TEXT: This is the seventh AW report on Guatemala, based on a three
member fact-finding mission in May 1985. Sources include interviews
recorded on tape, the Guatemalan and US press, and official Guatemalan
publications gathered since 1982. The report contains an introduction
on political violence, economic conditions and civilian versus military
power, and chapters on the development of self-defence civil patrols
(Patrullas de Autodefensa Civil PAC), the patrollers and their bosses,
the effects of PAC and the functioning of PAC in two communities. With
appendix: Civil Patrol Code of Conduct, and notes.

GUYANA

CATALOGUE SIGNATURE: 0000/2955/-3=851100
TITLE: Political freedom in Guyana
AUTHOR: Lord Chitnis ; Greenberg, Jack ; Rosenblum, Daniel
PLACE OF PUBLICATION: New York ; London
PUBLISHER: Americas Watch - AW (D) ; Parliamentary Human Rights Group
- PHRG (D)
DATE OF PUBLICATION: 851100
NUMBER OF PAGES: 60 p.
LANGUAGE: ENG
INDEX: legislation / elections / fact-finding missions
GEOGRAPHICAL INDEX: Guyana
GEOGRAPHICAL CODE: 6437
FREE TEXT: The mission was mounted in response to an invitation from
fourteen civic, religious and political organizations in Guyana.
However, the government refused to cooperate with the delegation, and
the members were refused visa. In order to respond in some measure to
the request from Guyana, AW and the PHRG decided to send delegates to
Trinidad, where a number of people from Guyana were able to join them
to discuss conditions in their country. The report examines, in some
detail, the background to many of the abuses and manipulations of the
electoral system in recent years. Attention is paid to elections
before the independence, changes in the electoral law in 1967-68, the
elections of 1968 and 1973, the institutionalization of electoral
fraud in the period 1974-1980, amendments in the constitution, the
referendum of 1978, the 1980 elections, the media and access to them,
and freedom of assembly.
Conclusion: since 1964, the electoral system has been undermined and
brought under the control of the ruling party. The process by which
an electoral system that worked has been destroyed by a combination
of changes in the law and changes in the way in which the law was
applied has been particularly stressed. The evidence for massive
rigging and widespread abuse before, during and after elections is
enormous.

HAITI

CATALOGUE SIGNATURE: 6000/1011/-3=791213
TITLE: Report on the situation of human rights in Haiti: approved by
the Commission at its 644th session, held December 13, 1979
AUTHOR: Inter-American Commission on Human Rights - IACHR
PLACE OF PUBLICATION: Washington DC
PUBLISHER: Organization of American States - OAS (D) ; Inter-American
Commission on Human Rights - IACHR
DATE OF PUBLICATION: 791213
NUMBER OF PAGES: 83 p. in v.p.
ISBN: 0 8270 1094 X
DOCUMENT SYMBOL: OEA/Ser.L/V/II.46 doc.66 rev.1
LANGUAGE: ENG
INDEX: legislation / civil and political rights / fact-finding missions
GEOGRAPHICAL INDEX: Haiti
GEOGRAPHICAL CODE: 6138
FREE TEXT: The report is based on a fact-finding mission in August
1978. It begins with an introduction, and a chapter on the legal
framework (international obligations, the 1964 Constitution, emergency
legislation).
Subsequent chapters discuss those rights that the Commission feels are
particular pertinent to the situation of human rights in Haiti: the
right to life, liberty, and personal security; the right of protection
from arbitrary arrest and to due process of law; the right to freedom
of investigation, opinion, expression and dissemination of ideas, and
to religious freedom and freedom of worship; the right of assembly and
of association; the right to residence and movement and to nationality;
the right to vote and to participate in the government; the right to
education and the right to the preservation of health and well-being;
the right to work and to fair wage.
With conclusions and recommendations.

CATALOGUE SIGNATURE: 6138/2147/-3=820600
TITLE: La situation des droits de l'homme en Haïti: communication
presentée à la Division des Droits de l'Homme des Nations Unies
AUTHOR: Buss, Théo ; Martin, Claude
PLACE OF PUBLICATION: Geneva
PUBLISHER: Centre Haïtien de Recherches et de Documentation - CHRD
(D); Commission Tiers-Monde de l'Eglise catholique de Geneve - COTMEC
(D) ; Commission Tiers-Monde de l'Eglise nationale protestante (D)
DATE OF PUBLICATION: 820600
NUMBER OF PAGES: 57 p.
LANGUAGE: FRE
INDEX: dictatorship / civil and political rights /
fact-finding missions
GEOGRAPHICAL INDEX: Haiti
GEOGRAPHICAL CODE: 6138
FREE TEXT: The report gives account on various forms of violations
of human rights in present day Haiti, based on on-site visits and
testimonies of witnesses. The report contains descriptions of the
violations and the present repression; special attention is given
to the actors of the repression, the places of detention, treatment
of prisoners, torture, the situation of the churches, control over
development agencies and the slaughtering of pigs. With conclusions
and annexes: map, newspaper articles, list of political prisoners,
extract of court proceedings.

CATALOGUE SIGNATURE: 0000/0035/-3=820911
TITLE: Rapport de mission dans les Caraïbes et en Amérique Centrale:
août 1982
AUTHOR: Melet, Christian ; Macabies, Pierre
PLACE OF PUBLICATION: Paris
PUBLISHER: Fédération Internationale des Droits de l'Homme - FIDH (D)
DATE OF PUBLICATION: 820911
NUMBER OF PAGES: 28 p.
LANGUAGE: FRE
INDEX: trials / fact-finding missions
GEOGRAPHICAL INDEX: Haiti
GEOGRAPHICAL CODE: 6138
FREE TEXT: The report deals mainly with the human rights situation in
Haiti, with attention to background of the country, an account of an
interview with the Minister of Foreign Affairs and a government
consultant, and a description of specific cases. With annexes: the
second trial of opposition leader Sylvio Claude on 27 August; the
situation of Haitian sugar workers in the Dominican Republic; Haitian
refugees in Florida; law establishing a National Human Rights
Commission.

CATALOGUE SIGNATURE: 0000/1582/-3=830800
TITLE: Haiti: report of a human rights mission: June 26-29, 1983
AUTHOR: Days, Drew ; Hooper, Michael ; Leiman, Elizabeth
PLACE OF PUBLICATION: New York
PUBLISHER: Lawyers Committee for International Human Rights - LCIHR
(D) ; Americas Watch - AW (D) ; International League for Human
Rights - ILHR (D)
DATE OF PUBLICATION: 830800
NUMBER OF PAGES: 24 p.
LANGUAGE: ENG
INDEX: association (freedom of) / detention / fact-finding missions
GEOGRAPHICAL INDEX: Haiti
GEOGRAPHICAL CODE: 6138
FREE TEXT: In May 1983, a number of human rights activists were
arrested. The aim of the mission was to investigate the circumstances
surrounding the detention, the physical conditions and legal actions
of the government against five of them. The members had contacts with
government representatives and the detainees. The detentions are the
most recent in a series of harsh actions by Haitian authorities
against critics of the Duvalier regime, and against members of the
Haitian League for Human Rights. With conclusions and recommendations.

CATALOGUE SIGNATURE: 0000/2955/-3=840300
TITLE: Elections 1984: Duvalier style: a report on human rights in
Haiti: based on a mission of inquiry
AUTHOR: Hooper, Michael
PLACE OF PUBLICATION: New York
PUBLISHER: Americas Watch - AW (D) ; Lawyers Committee for
International Human Rights - LCIHR (D)
DATE OF PUBLICATION: 840300
NUMBER OF PAGES: 17 p.
LANGUAGE: ENG
INDEX: elections / fact-finding missions
GEOGRAPHICAL INDEX: Haiti
GEOGRAPHICAL CODE: 6138
FREE TEXT: The report, based on a mission of the author and Brenda
Pillors, examines the environment in which the legislative elections
held on 12 February 1984 took place. The circumstances in which the
elections occurred are described: there was no free participance, no
press freedom and freedom of expression. The election procedures
were not fair. With description of findings, and information on the
background of the country, recent human rights violations and the
position of the oppositionary Christian Democratic Party. With
conclusions.

CATALOGUE SIGNATURE: 0000/1582/-0=840600
TITLE: Violations of human rights in Haiti: a report to the United
Nations Commission on Human Rights by the Lawyers Committee for
International Human Rights
AUTHOR: Hooper, Michael
PLACE OF PUBLICATION: New York
PUBLISHER: Lawyers Committee for International Human Rights - LCIHR
(D)
DATE OF PUBLICATION: 840600
NUMBER OF PAGES: 22 p. in v.p.
LANGUAGE: ENG
INDEX: military / civil and political rights / fact-finding missions
GEOGRAPHICAL INDEX: Haiti
GEOGRAPHICAL CODE: 6138
FREE TEXT: The report on recent violations of human rights in Haiti is
based on two fact-finding missions by the LCIHR and Americas Watch in
June 1983 and January 1984. The delegates met with Haitian government
officials, journalists, trade unionists, church officials and victims
and families of those who have been tortured and detained by the
Haitian government. The report includes chapters on the background of
violations of human rights in Haiti, the role of the Haitian security
forces, persecution of human rights monitors, activities of the
political opposition and especially the Haitian Christian Democratic
Party, the elections of Febuary 1984 and denials of the freedom of
expression and the freedom of the press.

Haiti

CATALOGUE SIGNATURE: 0000/1582/-0=850300
TITLE: Haiti: rights denied: a report on human rights in Haiti in 1984
to the United Nations Commission on Human Rights
AUTHOR: Hooper, Michael S.
PLACE OF PUBLICATION: New York
PUBLISHER: National Coalition for Haitian Refugees (D) ; Americas Watch
- AW (D) ; Lawyers Committee for International Human Rights - LCIHR (D)
DATE OF PUBLICATION: 850300
NUMBER OF PAGES: 25 p.
LANGUAGE: ENG
INDEX: dictatorship / association (freedom of) / fact-finding missions
GEOGRAPHICAL INDEX: Haiti
GEOGRAPHICAL CODE: 6138
FREE TEXT: The report, based on information collected during three
fact-finding missions, examines the situation of human rights in Haiti
in 1984. Attention is paid to the denial of the right to engage in
political activity (freedom of assembly and association), denials of
freedom of expression and press, the persecution of human rights
monitors like the Haitian League for Human Rights, the governmental
National Commission of Human Rights, and the structure and functioning
of the Haitian security forces. With conclusions.

CATALOGUE SIGNATURE: 0000/0035/-4
TITLE: Special Haïti: rapport sur la situation des droits de l'homme
en Haïti: la FIDH demande qu'il soit procedé à une large amnistie
le 22 avril 85
AUTHOR: Rostoker, Christian
TITLE OF GENERIC ITEM: La Lettre de la FIDH
EDITION: no. 103
PLACE OF PUBLICATION: Paris
PUBLISHER: Fédération Internationale des Droits de l'Homme - FIDH (D)
DATE OF PUBLICATION: 850412
NUMBER OF PAGES: 16 p.
LANGUAGE: FRE
INDEX: legislation / detention / judicial systems /
fact-finding missions
GEOGRAPHICAL INDEX: Haiti
GEOGRAPHICAL CODE: 6138
FREE TEXT: Report of a fact-finding mission carried out from 4 to 11
March 1985. The aim of the mission was to investigate how certain
presidential decrees were put into practice, by examining four
specific cases. The report consists of a report on the proceedings of
the mission, and sections on: legal texts and their application in
practice, preventive detention, and free choice of defence lawyers;
description of a visit to the National Penitentiary; the legal
situation of 51 persons probably held in detention.

CATALOGUE SIGNATURE: 0000/2955/-3=851000
TITLE: Haiti: human rights under hereditary dictatorship
AUTHOR: Hooper, Michael ; Neier, Aryeh ; Pillors, Brenda
PLACE OF PUBLICATION: New York
PUBLISHER: Americas Watch - AW (D) ; National Coalition for Haitian
Refugees (D)
DATE OF PUBLICATION: 851000
NUMBER OF PAGES: 33 p.
LANGUAGE: ENG
INDEX: dictatorship / elections / fact-finding missions
GEOGRAPHICAL INDEX: Haiti
GEOGRAPHICAL CODE: 6138
FREE TEXT: The report, based on a fact-finding mission to Haiti in late
July 1985, consists of an introduction on the national referendum of 22
July, and chapters on: the June 1985 law on political parties; freedom
of the press; the situation of the church and of intellectuals;
disappearances and the National Commission for Human Rights; and the
role of the United States, in general and with regard to the expulsion
of three Belgian priests. With appendix: newspaper article.

CATALOGUE SIGNATURE: 0000/0018/-3=860200
DATE OF ENTRY: 860701
TITLE: Report of a WCC delegation to Haiti: 13-18 February 1986
AUTHOR: Fischer, Jan ; Kirton, Allan ; Maury, Jacques (...et al)
PLACE OF PUBLICATION: Geneva
PUBLISHER: World Council of Churches - WCC (D)
DATE OF PUBLICATION: 860200
NUMBER OF PAGES: 31 p.
LANGUAGE: ENG
INDEX: dictatorship / fact-finding missions
GEOGRAPHICAL INDEX: Haiti
GEOGRAPHICAL CODE: 6138
FREE TEXT: Within the context of the national political upheaval after
the departure of dictator Duvalier, the Methodist Church in Haiti and
the Caribbean Conference of Churches invited the WCC to send a mission
to Haiti. The aims of the five-member mission were to render a pastoral
visit to the churches, to observe the evolving situation in the
country, and to report to the ecumenical community worldwide on steps
to take for the strenghtening of the churches' witness and service.
The report contains a review of interviews and encounters, and
information on the historical background of the country, recent
political developments, the role of the churches, the fall of Duvalier,
and events following (kleptocracy in relation to poverty), popular
hopes and obstacles, and the "diaspora". With recommendations, and
appendices: text of press conference, statements by churches in Haiti.

CATALOGUE SIGNATURE: 0000/2955/-3=861000
TITLE: Haiti: Duvalierism since Duvalier
AUTHOR: Hooper, Michael S.
PLACE OF PUBLICATION: New York
PUBLISHER: Americas Watch - AW (D) ; National Coalition for Haitian
Refugees (D)
NUMBER OF PAGES: 79 p. in v.p.
ISBN: 0 938579 28 2
LANGUAGE: ENG
INDEX: democracy / trials / fact-finding missions
GEOGRAPHICAL INDEX: Haiti
GEOGRAPHICAL CODE: 6138
FREE TEXT: The report is based on three fact-finding missions conducted
in March, May and mid-July 1986. It analyzes the situation of human
rights in Haiti and the human rights policy of the government of the
United States toward Haiti.
After an introduction with conclusions and recommendations, the report
is divided into the following parts:
I) The economic context; II) Lack of progress in halting abuses by the
security forces; III) Lack of investigation and prosecution of past
human rights abuses; IV) The trials of Luc Desyr and Col. Samuel
Jeremie: exceptions thet prove the rule; V) Lack of progress in
establishing democratic structures: civil rights in jeopardy (the press;
political parties); VI) Political developments regarding the established
Haitian churches and allegations of persecution of Voodoo "practicants";
VII) Violations of trade union rights in Haiti; VIII) The role of the
United States policy.

HONDURAS

CATALOGUE SIGNATURE: 6003/1226/-3=810000
TITLE: Elections in Honduras: a report by an international observer
delegation to the Honduran national elections: November 29, 1981...
AUTHOR: Barbieri, Leyda ; Girling, Robert ; Wilson, David
PLACE OF PUBLICATION: Washington DC
PUBLISHER: Washington Office on Latin America - WOLA (D)
DATE OF PUBLICATION: 810000
NUMBER OF PAGES: 28 p.
LANGUAGE: ENG
INDEX: elections / fact-finding missions
GEOGRAPHICAL INDEX: Honduras
GEOGRAPHICAL CODE: 6239
FREE TEXT: A seven member international team was present to observe
the elections at the invitation of the Honduran National Electoral
Tribunal and the Honduran government. The delegation concluded that
the election constituted a definite step towards a more democratic
society, though the electoral process is not without problems. With:
background of country and region; criteria for evaluation; parties and
candidates; treatment of minor parties and independent candidates;
role of the military; electoral law and proceedings. With summary and
conclusions, and appendix: programme of the delegation.

CATALOGUE SIGNATURE: 0000/2955/-3=821200
TITLE: Human rights in Honduras: signs of "the Argentine method"
AUTHOR: Mendez, Juan E. ; Arnson, Cynthia
PLACE OF PUBLICATION: New York
PUBLISHER: Americas Watch - AW (D)
DATE OF PUBLICATION: 821200
NUMBER OF PAGES: 39 p.
LANGUAGE: ENG
STATISTICAL INFORMATION: Y
INDEX: refugees / disappearances / fact-finding missions
GEOGRAPHICAL INDEX: Honduras
GEOGRAPHICAL CODE: 6239
FREE TEXT: Report on the general human rights situation in Honduras,
based on a fact-finding mission in October 1982 and other information.
Attention is paid to: the political background of the country;
disappearances (responsibility, targets); extrajudicial executions;
freedom of expression; the Honduran policy with regard to refugees
from El Salvador, Guatemala and Nicaragua; and other human rights
problems.
With conclusions and recommendations, and annexes: list of disappeared
persons; list of Salvadorean refugees reported as murdered or
disappeared on Honduran territory.

CATALOGUE SIGNATURE: 0000/0084-0=831124
TITLE: Ecumenical visit to Honduras: 26 September - 4 October 1983
AUTHOR: World Council of Churches - WCC ; National Council of Churches
of Christ in the USA - NCCCUSA ; Latin American Council of Churches
PLACE OF PUBLICATION: Geneva
PUBLISHER: World Council of Churches - WCC (D)
DATE OF PUBLICATION: 831124
NUMBER OF PAGES: 22 p.
LANGUAGE: ENG
STATISTICAL INFORMATION: Y
INDEX: church and state / fact-finding missions
GEOGRAPHICAL INDEX: Honduras
GEOGRAPHICAL CODE: 6239
FREE TEXT: The aims of the visit of a five-person ecumenical team were
to gather information on the general situation in Honduras, on the
situation of the churches and on Honduran groups and/or agencies
through which churches and their agencies in other countries might
channel their support for programmes and local projects.
In the report, attention is given to the general situation in Honduras,
the church situation, institutions and churches visited involved in
service to the community and refugees and displaced persons. With
conclusions, recommendations and appendices.

CATALOGUE SIGNATURE: 0000/2955/-3=840200
TITLE: Honduras: on the brink: a report on human rights based on a
mission of inquiry
AUTHOR: Barbieri, Leyda ; Wilson, David ; Crotty, William (...et al)
PLACE OF PUBLICATION: New York
PUBLISHER: Americas Watch - AW (D) ; Lawyers Committee for
International Human Rights - LCIHR (D) ; Washington Office on Latin
America - WOLA (D)
DATE OF PUBLICATION: 840200
NUMBER OF PAGES: 71 p.
LANGUAGE: ENG
INDEX: democracy / civil and political rights / fact-finding missions
GEOGRAPHICAL INDEX: Honduras
GEOGRAPHICAL CODE: 6239
FREE TEXT: In October 1983, the three organizations sent a six-member
delegation to Honduras to examine the development of democratic
institutions and assess the human rights situation in that country.
After a preface, their report provides an introduction on the political
situation in the country, and conclusions and recommendations of the
mission.
The first chapter is on democratic institutions in Honduras; the second
deals with military abuses, with attention to disappearances, torture,
arbitrary arrests and political killings. The third chapter is on the
Olancho incident, an operation against a guerilla force. Following,
attention is paid to civilian militias, the criminal justice system,
freedom of expression, human rights organizations, refugees, and the
role of the United States.

CATALOGUE SIGNATURE: 6003/1226/-0=840510
TITLE: Crisis and continuity in Honduras: an analysis of recent
developments in Honduras based on a trip April 6-15, 1984
AUTHOR: Barbieri, Leyda
PLACE OF PUBLICATION: Washington DC
PUBLISHER: Washington Office on Latin America - WOLA (D)
DATE OF PUBLICATION: 840510
NUMBER OF PAGES: 15 p.
LANGUAGE: ENG
INDEX: military / fact-finding missions
GEOGRAPHICAL INDEX: Honduras
GEOGRAPHICAL CODE: 6239
FREE TEXT: The report contains information on recent developments in
Honduras: pressures within the military forces and popular pressure
leading to the removal of Alvarez, the chief of the armed forces;
the internal reorganization of the military institution; criticism
of nongovernmental organizations and the church on violations of
human rights and other abuses.
With conclusions: an official investigation of human rights abuses
and disappearances is unlikely; criticism on the involvement of the
United States with political developments in Honduras.

CATALOGUE SIGNATURE: 0000/2921/-0=841000
TITLE: Honduras: a journalism of silence
AUTHOR: Marash, David ; Marash, Kerry ; Koeppel, Barbara
PLACE OF PUBLICATION: (New York)
PUBLISHER: Committee to Protect Journalists - CPJ (D)
DATE OF PUBLICATION: 841000
NUMBER OF PAGES: 15 p.
LANGUAGE: ENG
INDEX: press (freedom of the) / censorship / military /
fact-finding missions
GEOGRAPHICAL INDEX: Honduras
GEOGRAPHICAL CODE: 6239
FREE TEXT: A three person delegation of the CPJ visited Honduras in
August 1984 to investigate conditions of the press in the light of
the recent military build-up in that country. The report briefly
describes the findings of the mission, based on interviews with 28
individuals, including reporters, broadcasters, editors, photographers,
publishers, foreign correspondents, economists, sociologists, students
and other observers. Attention is paid to censorship, working
conditions of journalists, expulsions and physical harassment.
Conclusion: the level of repression has been reduced under the elected,
civilian government, but most observers stress that only the style,
and not the substance, will ultimately change under military chief
General Walter Lopez.

CATALOGUE SIGNATURE: 0000/2955/-3=860200
TITLE: Human rights in Honduras after general Alvarez
AUTHOR: Nelson, Anne ; Rone, Jemera
PLACE OF PUBLICATION: New York
PUBLISHER: Americas Watch - AW (D)
DATE OF PUBLICATION: 860200
NUMBER OF PAGES: 60 p.
LANGUAGE: ENG
INDEX: democracy / fact-finding missions
GEOGRAPHICAL INDEX: Honduras
GEOGRAPHICAL CODE: 6239
FREE TEXT: The report is based on information collected by the two
authors during a visit to Hunduras in November 1985, and on previous
visits to Honduras in June and September 1985.
The report is divided into the following parts: I) introduction; II)
democratic forms; III) violations of political and religious freedoms:
the church; the press; trade unions; IV) detention and disappearances:
the investigation of the armed forces; political prisoners; abuse of
authority; V) refugees: relations with the Honduran armed forces;
living conditions: freedom of movement and enclosure; distance from
the border; presence of guerrillas in the camps and relocation; VI)
the United States and Honduras: impact of US military policy. With
appendix: an historical footnote.

JAMAICA

CATALOGUE SIGNATURE: 0000/1022/-3=810000
TITLE: Child labour in Jamaica: a general review
AUTHOR: Ennew, Judith ; Young, Pansy
PLACE OF PUBLICATION: London
PUBLISHER: Anti-Slavery Society for the Protection of Human Rights –
ASPHR (D)
DATE OF PUBLICATION: 810000
NUMBER OF PAGES: 75 p.
SERIES TITLE: Child labour series
VOLUME: no.6
LANGUAGE: ENG
STATISTICAL INFORMATION: Y
BIBLIOGRAPHIES: Y
INDEX: child labour / fact-finding missions
GEOGRAPHICAL INDEX: Jamaica
GEOGRAPHICAL CODE: 6140
FREE TEXT: Report on child labour in Jamaica, based on government
sources, principals, teachers, interviews with and drawings of pupils,
and a sample. With attention to the economic background, unemployment,
education, families, different types of work in the formal and informal
sectors. With conclusions, recommendations and appendices: methodology
of the research, tables, extracts of Juveniles Act, dissemination of
the report, publications by the Anti-Slavery Society.

CATALOGUE SIGNATURE: 0000/0249/-0=840000
TITLE: Jamaica: the death penalty: report of an Amnesty International
mission
AUTHOR: (Fattah, Ezzat A.); (Ennals, Martin)
PLACE OF PUBLICATION: London
PUBLISHER: Amnesty International – AI (D)
DATE OF PUBLICATION: 840000
NUMBER OF PAGES: 59 p.
DOCUMENT SYMBOL: AI Index: AMR 38/07/84
LANGUAGE: ENG
STATISTICAL INFORMATION: Y
INDEX: death penalty / fact-finding missions
GEOGRAPHICAL INDEX: Jamaica
GEOGRAPHICAL CODE: 6140
FREE TEXT: Amnesty International's major concern for sending a mission
in November 1983 was an increase in executions after 1980, following a
period of more than four years in which no executions had been carried
out. Twenty-four prisoners were executed between August 1980 and July
1984. Nearly all those executed had been sentenced to death either
before or during the period in which executions were held in abeyance
while parliament considered the issue. At the time of the mission
there were more than 150 prisoners under sentence of death in Jamaica.
The government expressed the view that public opinion and the high
rate of violent crime in Jamaica make total abolition of the death
penalty impossible at the present time, but it expressed a willingness
to consider moves toward limiting the offences for which the death
penalty could be imposed.
The report contains conclusions and recommendations, and appendices:
list of prisoners, statistics, correspondence between AI and the
government.

CATALOGUE SIGNATURE : 0000/2955/-3=860900
TITLE: Human rights in Jamaica
AUTHOR: Chevigny, Paul ; Whitman, Lois ; Chevigny, Bell
PLACE OF PUBLICATION: New York ; Washington
PUBLISHER: Americas Watch — AW (D)
NUMBER OF PAGES: 66 p. in v.p.
ISBN: 0 938579 27 4
LANGUAGE: ENG
INDEX: detention / prison conditions / fact-finding missions
GEOGRAPHICAL INDEX: Jamaica
GEOGRAPHICAL CODE: 6140
FREE TEXT: This report examines the human rights situation in Jamaica.
It is based on information gathered in the course of two trips to Jamaica
in 1986, from 24 February to 6 March, and from 26 June to 4 July.
The Americas Watch investigation came about at the request of the Jamaica
Council for Human Rights.
Despite the openness of Jamaica and its well-developed institutional
protections for its citizens, Americas Watch finds that a number of
serious abuses of human rights are prevalent in Jamaica:
- a practice of summary executions by the police;
- a practice of unlawful detentions by the police, at times accompanied
by police assaults on detainees;
- a practice of confining detainees in police station lock-ups under
squalid and degrading conditions.

MEXICO

CATALOGUE SIGNATURE: 0000/0035/-3=781200
TITLE: Report of the commission of enquiry to Mexico
AUTHOR: Goldman, Robert K. ; Jacoby, Daniel
PLACE OF PUBLICATION: Paris
PUBLISHER: International League for Human Rights - ILHR (D) ;
Fédération Internationale des Droits de l'Homme - FIDH (D) ;
International Movement of Catholic Lawyers Pax Romana - IMCL (D)
DATE OF PUBLICATION: 781200
NUMBER OF PAGES: 45 p. in v.p.
LANGUAGE: ENG
STATISTICAL INFORMATION: Y
INDEX: prison conditions / detention / civil and political rights /
fact-finding missions
GEOGRAPHICAL INDEX: Mexico
GEOGRAPHICAL CODE: 6243
FREE TEXT: The purposes of the mission were to enquire detention
conditions in certain prisons, to receive information on the
penitentiary regime with regard to international conventions, and
to verify allegations of human rights violations.
With attention to relevant individual rights and guarantees in the
Mexican Constitution, arbitrary arrests and detentions, torture and
other cruel punishment and treatment, violations of the right to a
fair trial, equal protection and due process of law, disappeared
persons, intimidation of relatives of political prisoners and the
situation in prisons.
With conclusions and appendices: letter to the Minister of the
Interior, list of prisoners interviewed; list of disappeared
persons detained in military camps.

CATALOGUE SIGNATURE: 0000/0035-3=850600
TITLE: Rapport de voyage au Mexique du 7 au 20 juin 1985
AUTHOR: Ferrari-Lopez, Carlos
PLACE OF PUBLICATION: Paris
PUBLISHER: Fédération Internationale des Droits de l'Homme - FIDH (D)
DATE OF PUBLICATION: 850800
NUMBER OF PAGES: (22 p.)
LANGUAGE: FRE
INDEX: fact-finding missions
GEOGRAPHICAL INDEX: Mexico
GEOGRAPHICAL CODE: 6243
FREE TEXT: The aim of the mission, which was held at the request of,
and in cooperation with the Mexican League for Human Rights, was to
investigate various aspects of the situation of human rights. In the
report, attention is paid to torture, territorial conflicts in peasant
communities, and the situation in several prisons visited. It is
concluded that serious violations of human rights occur in Mexico.
With annexes: newspaper articles, interview with Indian peasants,
statements by a non-governmental organization on violent acts and
repression.

CATALOGUE SIGNATURE: 0000/0249/-3=860000
TITLE: Mexico: human rights in rural areas: exchange of documents with
the Mexican government on human rights violations in Oaxaca and Chiapas
AUTHOR: (Amnesty International - AI)
PLACE OF PUBLICATION: London
PUBLISHER: Amnesty International - AI (D)
DATE OF PUBLICATION: 860000
NUMBER OF PAGES: 136 p.
DOCUMENT SYMBOL: AI Index: AMR 41/07/86
ISBN: 0 86210 98 4
LANGUAGE: ENG
INDEX: civil and political rights / fact-finding missions
GEOGRAPHICAL INDEX: Mexico
GEOGRAPHICAL CODE: 6243
FREE TEXT: Over many years AI has received reports of human rights
violations in rural Mexico. Peasants and Indians have reportedly been
victims of political killings and "disappearances", torture, and
imprisonment on false criminal charges. Most of such reports received
recently have come from rural regions in the southern part of the
country. AI sent fact-finding missions to Mexico in March 1984 and in
January 1985. This report comprises the full text of a memorandum
submitted on 22 November 1985 to the government of President Miguel de
la Madrid Hurtado, and the reply of the government.
The report contains information on human rights violations in rural
Mexico in general, and evidences of abuses in the states of Oaxaca and
Chiapas, including specific cases. Attention is paid to political
killings, torture and ill-treatment, political imprisonment and
trials.

CATALOGUE SIGNATURE: 0000/0035/-4
TITLE: Mexique: les droits de l'homme à l'heure du mundial
AUTHOR: Jacoby, Daniel; Froment, Blandine; Garapon, Antoine
TITLE OF GENERIC ITEM: La Lettre de la FIDH
EDITION: no. 158
PLACE OF PUBLICATION: Paris
PUBLISHER: Fédération Internationale des Droits de l'Homme - FIDH (D)
DATE OF PUBLICATION: 860603
NUMBER OF PAGES: p.5-10
LANGUAGE: FRE
INDEX: detention / fact-finding missions
GEOGRAPHICAL INDEX: Mexico
GEOGRAPHICAL CODE: 6243
FREE TEXT: The mission took place from 29 April until 10 May. The
delegation was received by authorities and visited ten prisons, two
communities of Indians and Mexico City (earthquake). It received
testimonies on human rights violations (torture, ill-treatment) of
a large number of persons involved in land struggles.

NICARAGUA

CATALOGUE SIGNATURE: 0000/0249/-3=770700
TITLE: The Republic of Nicaragua: an Amnesty International report
including the findings of a mission to Nicaragua: 10-15 May 1976
AUTHOR: (Madlener, Kurt) ; (McClintock, Michael)
PLACE OF PUBLICATION: London
PUBLISHER: Amnesty International - AI (D)
DATE OF PUBLICATION: 770700
NUMBER OF PAGES: 75 p.
ISBN: 0 900058 62 5
DOCUMENT SYMBOL: AI Index: PUB 74/00/77
LANGUAGE: ENG
STATISTICAL INFORMATION: Y
BIBLIOGRAPHIES: Y
INDEX: political prisoners / law enforcement / fact-finding missions
GEOGRAPHICAL INDEX: Nicaragua
GEOGRAPHICAL CODE: 6245
FREE TEXT: AI monitored the situation of human rights in Nicaragua with
increasing concern since the imposition of the decree of suspension of
constitutional guarantees on 28 December 1974. The mission was granted
but one official meeting, and was not allowed to visit places of
detention or to speak to prisoners. The authorities made no effort to
restrict the movements of the delegation, nor to hinder meetings.
The report contains chapters dealing with the suspension of guarantees;
the military courts; political prisoners under the military courts and
under police courts; death and disappearance in the countryside;
torture. With conclusions and recommendations, and appendices: meeting
between the delegates and the Minister of the Interior and Justice;
observation of a trial; lists of political prisoners; case studies and
detailed reports.

CATALOGUE SIGNATURE: 6000/1011/-3=781117
TITLE: Report on the situation of human rights in Nicaragua: findings
of the "on-site" observation in the Republic of Nicaragua: October
3-12, 1978
AUTHOR: Inter-American Commission on Human Rights - IACHR
PLACE OF PUBLICATION: Washington DC
PUBLISHER: Organization of American States - OAS (D) ; Inter-American
Commission on Human Rights - IACHR
DATE OF PUBLICATION: 781117
NUMBER OF PAGES: 78 p.
DOCUMENT SYMBOL: OEA/Ser.L/V/II.45 doc.16 rev.1
LANGUAGE: ENG
INDEX: civil and political rights / fact-finding missions
GEOGRAPHICAL INDEX: Nicaragua
GEOGRAPHICAL CODE: 6245
FREE TEXT: This report presents a basic narration of the on-site
observation undertaken by the Commission. It contains an extensive
introduction with information on the background, activities and
findings of the fact-finding mission. On basis of the information
thus obtained as well as on other sources, the report comments
briefly on the legal emergency status that is in force, and the
status of the observance in Nicaragua of the fundamental rights
of life, liberty and personal security; freedom of expression and
thought; freedom of conscience, belief and religion; the rights of
assembly and association. With conclusions.

CATALOGUE SIGNATURE: 0000/0088/-3=800000
TITLE: Human rights in Nicaragua: yesterday and today = Derechos
humanos en Nicaragua: ayer y hoy
AUTHOR: Fragoso, Heleno Claudio ; Artucio, Alejandro
PLACE OF PUBLICATION: Geneva
PUBLISHER: International Commission of Jurists - ICJ (D)
DATE OF PUBLICATION: 800000
NUMBER OF PAGES: 85 p.
ISBN: 92 9037 001 4
LANGUAGE: ENG / SPA
INDEX: political systems / fact-finding missions
GEOGRAPHICAL INDEX: Nicaragua
GEOGRAPHICAL CODE: 6245
FREE TEXT: The purpose of the mission was to study the present
situation of human rights, and to gather information about the
repression under the former regime of President Somoza.
The first part of the report is on the Somoza regime, with a
historical survey, an evaluation of the role of the National Guard,
the state of siege and martial law, and the human rights situation.
The second part is on the present regime, with attention to the
government institutions, the human rights situation, the programme
for alphabetization, and the position of supporters of the Somoza
regime. With conclusions and recommendations, and annexes: witness
statements on atrocities under Somoza; the Statute of the Rights of
Nicaraguans.

CATALOGUE SIGNATURE: 0000/0088/-4
TITLE: An unusual observer mission to Nicaragua
AUTHOR: Butler, William J.
TITLE OF GENERIC ITEM: ICJ Newsletter
EDITION: no. 8
PLACE OF PUBLICATION: Geneva
PUBLISHER: International Commission of Jurists - ICJ (D)
DATE OF PUBLICATION: 810300
NUMBER OF PAGES: p. 9-11
LANGUAGE: ENG
INDEX: legislation / trials / fact-finding missions
GEOGRAPHICAL INDEX: Nicaragua
GEOGRAPHICAL CODE: 6245
FREE TEXT: The observer attented the trial of José Esteban Gonzalez,
coordinator of the Permanent Commission of Human Rights CPDDH of
Nicaragua, for slandering the revolution. All charges were dismissed
after a "statement of clarification" made by the defendant after
consultations with the ICJ observer.

CATALOGUE SIGNATURE: 6000/1011/-3=810630
TITLE: Report on the situation of human rights in the Republic of
Nicaragua
AUTHOR: Inter-American Commission of Human Rights - IACHR
PLACE OF PUBLICATION: Washington DC
PUBLISHER: Organization of American States - OAS (D) ; Inter-American
Commission on Human Rights - IACHR
DATE OF PUBLICATION: 810630
NUMBER OF PAGES: 176 p. in v.p.
ISBN: 0 8270 1373
DOCUMENT SYMBOL: OEA/Ser.L/V/II.53 doc.25
LANGUAGE: ENG
INDEX: civil and political rights / fact-finding missions
GEOGRAPHICAL INDEX: Nicaragua
GEOGRAPHICAL CODE: 6245
FREE TEXT: This report is the result of various pieces of background
information and evidence on the situation of human rights in Nicaragua
which the Commission compiled before, during, and after a fact-finding
mission in October 1980. It contains an introduction on activities of
the IACHR with regard to the situation of human rights in Nicaragua and
the activities of the delegation.
The report is divided into the following chapters: I) the current
political and legal system in relation to human rights; II) the right
to life (including illegal executions); III) personal liberty; IV) the
right to a fair trial and to due process (on the judicial system);
V) the right to humane treatment (on detention); VI) freedom of thought
and expression; VII) political rights; VIII) the situation of local
human rights organizations; IX) economic and social rights. With
conclusions and recommendations.

CATALOGUE SIGNATURE: 0000/2171/-3=820000
TITLE: Mensenrechten in Nicaragua: een rapport aan Pax Christi Internationaal
AUTHOR: Benoit, André ; Bijnen, Toon van ; Sala, Enrico (...et al)
PLACE OF PUBLICATION: The Hague
PUBLISHER: Pax Christi Nederland - PAXCI-NL (D) ; OMEGA Books (D)
DATE OF PUBLICATION: 820000
NUMBER OF PAGES: 119 p.
SERIES TITLE: Pax Christi International Human Rights Reports
VOLUME: no. 2
ISBN: 90 79443 10 4
LANGUAGE: DUT / ENG / FRE
INDEX: church and state / fact-finding missions
GEOGRAPHICAL INDEX: Nicaragua
GEOGRAPHICAL CODE: 6245
FREE TEXT: The report is one in a series of four, published after a
fact-finding mission of seven members to Central America in June-July
1981.
In Nicaragua, the mission investigated the human rights situation,
especially after the revolution of 1979, and the role and position of
the Church. It is concluded that the new government is still working
towards her aim: the establishment of a just and human society.
With attention to the revolution, the building up of the institutions,
human rights under Somoza and after the revolution, and Church and
peace in Nicaragua. The section on human rights deals with social,
economic and cultural rights and with civil and political rights.
With conclusions.

CATALOGUE SIGNATURE: 0000/0966/-0=820000
TITLE: Complaint presented by the International Organisation of
Employers against Nicaragua
AUTHOR: International Labour Office - ILO - Committee on Freedom of
Association
TITLE OF GENERIC ITEM: Official Bulletin: reports of the Committee
on Freedom of Association (214th, 215th, and 216th)
EDITION: vol. LXV, series B no. 1
PLACE OF PUBLICATION: Geneva
PUBLISHER: International Labour Office - ILO (D)
DATE OF PUBLICATION: 820000
NUMBER OF PAGES: p. 222-235
LANGUAGE: ENG
INDEX: association (freedom of) / trade unions / detention /
fact-finding missions
GEOGRAPHICAL INDEX: Nicaragua
GEOGRAPHICAL CODE: 6245
FREE TEXT: The complaint is contained in a communication from the
International Organisation of Employers IOE dated 21 October 1981
alleging the detention of several employers leaders prominent in the
Nicaraguan employers' organisations. The report of the Committee
contains information on the allegations of the complainant, the reply
of the government and the findings of a direct contacts mission.
This mission was carried out from 29 November to 4 December 1981 by
Ian Lagergren as the representative of the Director-General, Manuel
Araoz and Daniel de Patoul. With conclusions and recommendations of
the Committee, and annex: letter by the Supreme Council of Private
Enterprises of Nicaragua to Daniel Ortega, coordinator of the
Government of National Reconstruction.

CATALOGUE SIGNATURE: 6245/-0=820227
TITLE: Mission to Nicaragua
AUTHOR: Manglapus, Raúl S.
PLACE OF PUBLICATION: Washington DC
PUBLISHER: Center for Development Policy (D)
DATE OF PUBLICATION: 820227
NUMBER OF PAGES: 13 p.
SERIES TITLE: Country notes
LANGUAGE: ENG
INDEX: civil and political rights / democracy / fact-finding missions
GEOGRAPHICAL INDEX: Nicaragua
GEOGRAPHICAL CODE: 6245
FREE TEXT: The author participated on behalf of the Center for
Development Policy in a fact-finding mission of twelve members to
Nicaragua from 8 to 11 February 1982, organized by Ramsey Clark under
the auspices of Disarm. The report contains background information on
the political situation in Nicaragua, and information on developments
since the revolution of 1979. The main question which the report deals
with is the extent to which there is democratic pluralism in Nicaragua.
Attention is paid to freedom of the press, the views of the government,
and the role of the Jesuits. At several instances, a comparison is made
between developments in the history of the United States and recent
developments in Nicaragua.

CATALOGUE SIGNATURE: 0000/0138/-3=820000
TITLE: Mission au Nicaragua: 18-24 février 1982 = Informe de misión en
Nicaragua: 18-24 de febrero de 1982
AUTHOR: Bentoumi, Amar; Chemillier-Gendreau, Monique
PLACE OF PUBLICATION: Brussels
PUBLISHER: Association Internationale des Juristes Démocrates - IADL (D)
DATE OF PUBLICATION: 820000
NUMBER OF PAGES: 43 p.
LANGUAGE: FRE / SPA
INDEX: judicial systems / fact-finding missions
GEOGRAPHICAL INDEX: Nicaragua.
GEOGRAPHICAL CODE: 6245
FREE TEXT: The aim of the mission was to investigate into the general
situation of human rights and liberties in contemporary Nicaragua.
In the introduction, general remarks are made on the importance of
fact-finding missions. A preliminary paragraph is on the institutions
of Nicaragua. The report is divided in sections on the judicial system
and the situation of human rights (legal protection; non-governmental
organizations; prisons, education, freedom of expression, minorities).
With conclusions and two annexes: decree no. 52 on the rights and
guarantees of Nicaraguans (in Spanish) and decree of 15 March 1982 of
the Nicaraguan government.

CATALOGUE SIGNATURE: 0000/2230/-0=820300
TITLE: Report: ecumenical visit to Nicaragua March 15-18, 1982
AUTHOR: Renfer, Rudolf ; Mahler, Kenneth ; Ramos, José Antonio
(...et al)
PLACE OF PUBLICATION: New York
PUBLISHER: National Council of Churches of Christ in the USA - NCCCUSA
(D)
DATE OF PUBLICATION: 820300
NUMBER OF PAGES: 12 p.
LANGUAGE: ENG
INDEX: indigenous peoples / fact-finding missions
GEOGRAPHICAL INDEX: Nicaragua
GEOGRAPHICAL CODE: 6245
FREE TEXT: The five member delegation representing the World Council of
Churches, the NCCCUSA and the Moravian Church were invited to Nicaragua
by the Moravian Church of Nicaragua and CEPAD, the Evangelical
Committee for Aid and Development. The reason for sending the mission
was the complex internal reality along the eastern coast of Nicaragua,
populated primarily by indigenous people (Miskitos, Sumos and Ramas)
and by English-speaking people of African descent. The report contains
a summary of activities of the mission, the situation in the Atlantic
Coast of Nicaragua and the situation of the Moravian Church. With
recommendations and letter of the delegation to the Christian
communities of Zelaya.

CATALOGUE SIGNATURE: 0000/2955/-3=820500
TITLE: On human rights in Nicaragua
AUTHOR: Kass, Stephen L. ; Mendez, Juan E.
PLACE OF PUBLICATION: New York
PUBLISHER: Americas Watch - AW (D)
DATE OF PUBLICATION: 820500
NUMBER OF PAGES: 87 p.
LANGUAGE: ENG
INDEX: civil and political rights / legislation / indigenous peoples /
fact-finding missions
GEOGRAPHICAL INDEX: Nicaragua
GEOGRAPHICAL CODE: 6245
FREE TEXT: The report is based on a fact finding mission in March 1982.
Three major areas of human rights concerns in Nicaragua are analyzed:
personal security and due process of law (torture, interrogation
practices, disappearances and extrajudicial executions, conditions in
prisons, detention of political prisoners), freedom of speech and of
political expression, and the treatment of the Miskito Indians.
Each part of the report consists of observations, interim findings and
recommendations to the Nicaraguan government and to other parties
involved. Attention is also paid to the reporting on the human rights
situation by the United States Department of State.

CATALOGUE SIGNATURE: 0000/0249/-0=820600
TITLE: Report of the Amnesty International missions to the Republic of
Nicaragua: August 1979, January 1980 and August 1980
AUTHOR: (Alvarez, Roberto) ; (Yrigoyen, Hipólito Solari)
PLACE OF PUBLICATION: London
PUBLISHER: Amnesty International - AI (D)
DATE OF PUBLICATION: 820600
NUMBER OF PAGES: 73 p.
ISBN: 0 86210 047 X
DOCUMENT SYMBOL: AI Index: AMR 43/02/82
LANGUAGE: ENG
INDEX: judicial systems / trials / fact-finding missions
GEOGRAPHICAL INDEX: Nicaragua
GEOGRAPHICAL CODE: 6245
FREE TEXT: This report is based primarily on the observations of three
missions to Nicaragua on behalf of Amnesty International. It deals
mainly with aspects of the new legal order established in Nicaragua
after July 1979, when the government of General Somoza was overthrown.
Special attention is paid to two distinct sets of trials: first, the
trials in Special Tribunals of former members of the Nicaraguan
National Guard and alleged collaborators with the previous government
who were charged with criminal offences; second, trials in ordinary
courts of people charged with crimes against public order or state
security committed since the formation of the new government.

CATALOGUE SIGNATURE: 0000/2787/-3=830000
TITLE: Declaration with reference to the visit of a Dutch delegation
to Nicaragua
AUTHOR: Goudzwaard, B. ; Fiolet, H.A.M. ; Legêne, J.J. (...et al)
PLACE OF PUBLICATION: Zeist (Netherlands)
PUBLISHER: Interchurch Coordination Committee Development Projects -
ICCO (D)
DATE OF PUBLICATION: 830000
NUMBER OF PAGES: 14 p.
LANGUAGE: ENG
INDEX: church and state / fact-finding missions
GEOGRAPHICAL INDEX: Nicaragua
GEOGRAPHICAL CODE: 6245
FREE TEXT: Report on the general situation in Nicaragua, based on
interviews with various sources made during a fact finding mission of
ten members in February 1983. The report contains the terms of
reference of the mission, its points of attention, conclusions and
findings with regard to: dynamics versus polarisation, political
organizations, trade unions, political rights and the position of the
churches. With list of institutions and persons interviewed.

CATALOGUE SIGNATURE: 0000/0084/-3=830400
TITLE: Report of a visit to churches in Nicaragua: a visit by a
delegation representing the Latin American Council of Churches and the
World Council of Churches = Imforme de visita a iglesias en Nicaragua:
visita realizada per delegación especial que representaba al Consejo
Latinoamericano de Iglesias y al Consejo Mundial de Iglesias
AUTHOR: Alvarez, Carmelo ; Borges, Eloah Mara P. ; Calvo, Samuel
(...et al)
PLACE OF PUBLICATION: San José (Costa Rica)
PUBLISHER: World Council of Churches - WCC (D) ; Latin American Council
of Churches (D)
DATE OF PUBLICATION: 830400
NUMBER OF PAGES: 18 p.
LANGUAGE: ENG / SPA
INDEX: church and state / fact-finding missions
GEOGRAPHICAL INDEX: Nicaragua
GEOGRAPHICAL CODE: 6245
FREE TEXT: At the invitation of the Nicaraguan Evangelical Churches, a
delegation of nine persons paid a visit to Nicaragua from 15-22 April
1983. The group's objectives were two-fold: to visit and be present
with the members and leadership of Nicaraguan churches during a
critical period, bringing them the full expression of warmth and
support of sister churches elsewhere; and to learn - through direct
encounters, testimonies, interviews and reports - as much as could be
known of the actual pressure confronting the Nicaraguan people and
government. The report reflects the group's impressions and contains
specific recommendations to its sponsoring bodies. With programme,
description of the general situation (economic, military and
religious), the participation of the churches in the revolution,
recommendations and press release.

CATALOGUE SIGNATURE: 0000/2179/-3=830500
TITLE: Verslag van de reis naar Nicaragua eind april, begin mei 1983
AUTHOR: Zumpolle, Liduin ; Bartels, Wim ; Jamarillo, Nelson
PLACE OF PUBLICATION: The Hague
PUBLISHER: Interkerkelijk Vredesberaad - IKV (D)
DATE OF PUBLICATION: 830500
NUMBER OF PAGES: 55 p.
LANGUAGE: DUT
INDEX: peace / solidarity / fact-finding missions
GEOGRAPHICAL INDEX: Nicaragua
GEOGRAPHICAL CODE: 6245
FREE TEXT: In April-May 1983, a delegation of fourteen members of
European and American peace movements visited Nicaragua. The purpose
of the mission was to get an impression of the present situation and
to discuss the relation between the peace movement and liberation
processes. The members participated in a conference for peace and
selfdetermination in Central America and the Caribbean, and had
contacts with the population and authorities.
With descripton of the general situation, report of the conference,
interviews, on-site visit.
With annexes: nongovernmental organizations in Nicaragua; press
release; large number of articles from Nicaraguan newspapers.

CATALOGUE SIGNATURE: 0000/0084/-3=830000
TITLE: Report on Nicaragua: report to the World Council of Churches of
its delegation sent to Nicaragua: September 4-10, 1983 = Informe sobre
Nicaragua: informe presentado al Consejo Mundial de Iglesias por su
delegación enviada a Nicaragua: 4 al 10 de septiembre de 1983
AUTHOR: Armistead, Robert ; Harper, Charles ; Keene, Beverly (...et al)
PLACE OF PUBLICATION: Geneva
PUBLISHER: World Council of Churches - WCC (D)
DATE OF PUBLICATION: 830000
NUMBER OF PAGES: 24 p. in v.p.
AVAILABILITY: X
LANGUAGE: ENG / FRE / SPA / GER
INDEX: church and state / fact-finding missions
GEOGRAPHICAL INDEX: Nicaragua
GEOGRAPHICAL CODE: 6245
FREE TEXT: The eight member delegation was sent by decision of the
Sixth Assembly of the World Council of Churches. The aims of the
mission were to render a pastoral visit to Nicaraguan churches, engage
in fact-finding as to the present situation in Nicaragua, and review
ways by which the WCC and its member churches might give future support
to the churches and people of Nicaragua.
The report contains the program of the delegation, and chapters on the
current national situation and the situation of the church. With
recommendations to the World Council of Churches, and annex: statement
of the World Council of Churches Sixth Assembly (Vancouver, July-August
1983) on Central America.

CATALOGUE SIGNATURE: 6245/-0=831100
TITLE: Face to face: an inside view of labor in Nicaragua
AUTHOR: Andrews, Barbara ; Arnodo, Glen ; Blake, Marshall (et al...)
PUBLISHER: (American Labor Education Center) (D)
DATE OF PUBLICATION: 831100
NUMBER OF PAGES: 7 p.
LANGUAGE: ENG
INDEX: trade unions / TNCs (transnational corporations) /
human rights and foreign policy / fact-finding missions
GEOGRAPHICAL INDEX: Nicaragua
GEOGRAPHICAL CODE: 6245
FREE TEXT: The aims of the eleven-member mission of trade unionists
was to investigate the activities of transnational corporations, wages
and working conditions in Nicaragua, as well as the impact of the
policy of the Reagan administration. The report deals with working
conditions and trade unions, opinions of opposition leaders, social
and economic developments, the role of United States corporations and
the US government.

CATALOGUE SIGNATURE: 6000/1011/-3=840000
TITLE: Report on the situation of human rights of a segment of the
Nicaraguan population of Miskito origin and resolution on the friendly
settlement procedure regarding the human rights situation of a segment
of the Nicaraguan population on Miskito origin
AUTHOR: Inter-American Commission on Human Rights - IACHR
PLACE OF PUBLICATION: Washington DC
PUBLISHER: Organization of American States - OAS (D) ; Inter-American
Commission on Human Rights - IACHR
DATE OF PUBLICATION: 840000
NUMBER OF PAGES: 142 p.
ISBN: 0 8270 1994 7
DOCUMENT SYMBOL: OEA/Ser.L/V/II.62 doc.10 rev.3 and doc.26
LANGUAGE: ENG
INDEX: indigenous peoples / fact-finding missions
GEOGRAPHICAL INDEX: Nicaragua
GEOGRAPHICAL CODE: 6245
FREE TEXT: The report consists of three parts. The first part, "Origin
and development of the controversy", describes the background of the
problem, the involvement of the IACHR, the collection of information
among others by fact-finding missions, treatment of the findings and
attempts to reach a friendly settlement. Part two is on the rights
which the government of Nicaragua is alleged to have violated (special
protection of the Miskitos as an ethnic group; the right to life; the
right to liberty, to personal security and to due process; right to
residence and movement; right to property). The third part contains
conclusions, proposals and recommendations.
With annex: resolution on the friendly settlement procedure.

CATALOGUE SIGNATURE: 6245/-0=840301
TITLE: Report on an investigatory visit to Kukra Hill on the Atlantic
Coast of Nicaragua: February 22-24, 1984
AUTHOR: Healy, Peggy
PLACE OF PUBLICATION: Managua
PUBLISHER: Maryknoll Sisters; Panama - Nicaragua region (D)
DATE OF PUBLICATION: 840301
NUMBER OF PAGES: 10 p. in v.p.
LANGUAGE: ENG
INDEX: indigenous peoples / fact-finding missions
GEOGRAPHICAL INDEX: Nicaragua
GEOGRAPHICAL CODE: 6245
FREE TEXT: The author visited the small river town on the Atlantic
Coast of Nicaragua after having read a report on a visit by Jim
Stieglitz, who stated to have discovered two concentration camps which
housed a total of 37.000 Miskitos Indians, in which he found forced
labour, gross violations of human rights including torture, tiger
cages and the withholding of food, diseases such as smallpox, cholera
and yellow fever.
It turned out that one of the places mentioned as a concentration camp
does not exist; in the other, Kukra Hill, there were no signs
indicating the existence of a concentration camp. The report deals
with employment, working conditions, health conditions, the
infrastructure, food supply and religions. The author concludes that
the majority of the claims made by Stieglitz are absolutely false.

CATALOGUE SIGNATURE: 0000/2955/-3=840400
TITLE: Human rights in Nicaragua: an Americas Watch report
AUTHOR: Mendez, Juan E. ; Neier, Aryeh ; Schwartz, Robert
PLACE OF PUBLICATION: New York
PUBLISHER: Americas Watch - AW (D)
DATE OF PUBLICATION: 840400
NUMBER OF PAGES: 51 p.
LANGUAGE: ENG
INDEX: indigenous peoples / civil and political rights /
fact-finding missions
GEOGRAPHICAL INDEX: Nicaragua
GEOGRAPHICAL CODE: 6245
FREE TEXT: The third AW report on human rights in Nicaragua is based
on the findings of two missions to Nicaragua. After an introduction
and conclusions, it contains chapters on: the situation of the
indigenous Miskito Indians: relocation, trials and arrests,
repatriation and negotiations; disappearances and arbitrary arrests;
prison conditions; jurisdiction and the Special Courts; freedom of
expression; elections; the attitudes of the government towards
human rights; human rights violations by oppositionary groups (the
contras), and difficulties of fact finding in Nicaragua.

CATALOGUE SIGNATURE: 0000/0153/-9=840500
TITLE: Los derechos humanos en Nicaragua: informe: informe realizado
por la Comisión de la APDH en sa visita a Nicaragua los días 13 al 23
de marzo del presente ano
AUTHOR: Alonso Andion, Luis Miguel ; Gimbernat Ordeig, José Antonio ;
Naval Garavilla, Milagros (...et al)
PLACE OF PUBLICATION: Madrid
PUBLISHER: Asociación pro Derechos Humanos de Espana - APDH (D)
DATE OF PUBLICATION: 840500
NUMBER OF PAGES: 27 p.
LANGUAGE: SPA
STATISTICAL INFORMATION: Y
INDEX: political conflict / fact-finding missions
GEOGRAPHICAL INDEX: Nicaragua
GEOGRAPHICAL CODE: 6245
FREE TEXT: Report of a fact-finding mission of four members, with
attention to: meetings and activities of the mission; the geopolitical
background of the country; the state of emergency; the militarization
of society; improvements in the human rights situation; the position of
the church; ethnic minorities, and elections. With annexes: historical
background of the Atlantic Coast; main aspects of the electoral law;
the role of the United States.

CATALOGUE SIGNATURE: 0000/2230/-0=840900
TITLE: Report of delegation to investigate "religious persecution" in
Nicaragua
AUTHOR: Taylor, Robert ; Henneberger, James ; Cogswell, James
(et al...)
PLACE OF PUBLICATION: (New York)
PUBLISHER: (National Council of Churches of Christ in the USA -
NCCCUSA) (D)
DATE OF PUBLICATION: 840900
NUMBER OF PAGES: 20 p.
LANGUAGE: ENG
INDEX: church and state / religion (freedom of) /
fact-finding missions
GEOGRAPHICAL INDEX: Nicaragua
GEOGRAPHICAL CODE: 6245
FREE TEXT: The six-member delegation visited Nicaragua from 29 August
to 2 September. Its aims were to gather information from different
sources regarding charges of religious persecution in Nicaragua, to
analyze these findings in relation to the present status of the
relation between church and state, to draw conclusions, to inform
member communions and congregations and to encourage appropriate
advocacy and action in relation to the policy of the United States.
The report contains an itinerary; a description of the issue of
religious persecution from Nicaraguan perspective: responses among
protestants, Moravians, within the Jewish community, and conflicting
Roman Catholic perspectives; political perspectives: the response of
the government, the embassy of the United States and the political
opposition.
With summary of findings: there is a strong feeling among many
Nicaraguans that the most serious instances of "religious persecution"
are those being perpetrated by the counter-revolutionary forces who
are invading the borders of Nicaragua with financial and legalistic
support of the United States. With regard to the charges of religious
persecution by the government of Nicaragua, the response varied widely.
The mission did not find a basis for the charge of systematic religious
persecution.

CATALOGUE SIGNATURE: 6245/-3=841100
TITLE: Nicaragua: labor, democracy, and the struggle for peace: report
of the West Coast trade union delegation to Nicaragua
AUTHOR: Auerbach, Roger ; Baeza, Ray ; Blue, Luisa (...et al)
PLACE OF PUBLICATION: Oakland
PUBLISHER: Labor Network on Central America (D)
DATE OF PUBLICATION: 841100
NUMBER OF PAGES: 32 p.
LANGUAGE: ENG
INDEX: trade unions / social and economic rights /
fact-finding missions
GEOGRAPHICAL INDEX: Nicaragua
GEOGRAPHICAL CODE: 6245
FREE TEXT: A sixteen member delegation of national, state and local
trade union leaders visited Nicaragua in September 1984, in order to
investigate the situation in that country at first hand. The mission
visited several factories, a state farm, the port of Corinto, a
hospital and other workplaces. The delegates spoke with industrial
workers, farmworkers, community and service workers, and people on
the street, and met with the leadership of trade union federations,
the women's organization, the Supreme Electoral Council, government
supporters and critics.
The report contains an introduction, and chapters on developments
after the revolution of 1979, the labour movement, democracy and
elections, and the struggle for peace. With conclusions and
recommendations.

CATALOGUE SIGNATURE: 0000/2955/-3=841100
TITLE: The Miskitos in Nicaragua: 1981-1984
AUTHOR: Mendez, Juan
PLACE OF PUBLICATION: New York
PUBLISHER: Americas Watch - AW (D)
DATE OF PUBLICATION: 841100
NUMBER OF PAGES: 60 p.
LANGUAGE: ENG
INDEX: indigenous peoples / fact-finding missions
GEOGRAPHICAL INDEX: Nicaragua
GEOGRAPHICAL CODE: 6245
FREE TEXT: Report on the situation of human rights of the Miskito
people in Nicaragua, based on previous AW reports and fact-finding
missions in May 1984 and October 1984. With: background of the country
and of the minority problem; forced relocation; the Miskitos outside
the settlements; the policy of the Nicaraguan government since 1982;
problems; human rights violations by opposition groups; the report of
the Inter-American Commission on Human Rights; the policy of the United
States with regard to human rights in Nicaragua. With conclusions and
recommendations.

CATALOGUE SIGNATURE: 6003/2268/-3=840000
TITLE: Nicaragua 1984: democracy, elections and war: the report of a
six-person Canadian Church and human rights delegation which observed
the 1984 Nicaraguan election
AUTHOR: Brownstone, Meyer; Czerny, Michael; Fournier, Francine
(... et al)
PLACE OF PUBLICATION: Toronto
PUBLISHER: Inter-Church Committee on Human Rights in Latin America -
ICCHRLA (D); La Ligue des Droits et Libertés; Canadian Council on
International Cooperation - CCIC
DATE OF PUBLICATION: 840000
NUMBER OF PAGES: 65 p. in v.p.
LANGUAGE: ENG
INDEX: democracy / elections / fact-finding missions
GEOGRAPHICAL INDEX: Nicaragua
GEOGRAPHICAL CODE: 6245
FREE TEXT: A six person Canadian Church and human rights delegation
was in Nicaragua from 28 October to 8 November 1984 to observe the
first national elections to be held in that country since the overthrow
of the Somoza dictatorship, more than five years ago.
The objectives of the mission included:
-to gain the on-the-ground experience necessary to interpret the entire
electoral process in Nicaragua within the broader framework of human
rights concerns;
-to evaluate the elections, and hopefully contribute to their
integrity, by assessing both the immediate technical features and the
broader socio-political context in which they occur;
-to unmask any flawed, fraudulent, or inadequate electoral procedures;
-to consider and evaluate any complaints or criticism of the electoral
system;
-to suggest improvements insofar as they may be required.
The report is divided into three parts. Part I, Democracy, treats some
of the factors which condition the exercise of democracy in Nicaragua
both positively and negatively. It concerns the position of the
Miskitos, freedom of religion, legal and judicial rights, prisoners,
women's rights, health and freedom of expression. With evaluation.
Part II, Election, gives the results of the study and observation of
the national elections on 4 November.
Part III, Conclusions, presents reflections and recommendations to the
government of Canada.
With appendices: itinerary; summary report.

CATALOGUE SIGNATURE: 0000/0084/-0=841100
TITLE: Report of World Council of Churches' pastoral delegation to
Nicaragua: November 3-7, 1984
AUTHOR: Altmann, Walter ; Liggett, Thomas J. ; Millard, Susan
(...et al)
PLACE OF PUBLICATION: (Geneva)
PUBLISHER: World Council of Churches - WCC (D)
DATE OF PUBLICATION: 841100
NUMBER OF PAGES: 10 p.
LANGUAGE: ENG
INDEX: elections / church and state / fact-finding missions
GEOGRAPHICAL INDEX: Nicaragua
GEOGRAPHICAL CODE: 6245
FREE TEXT: The purpose of the visit of the four member delegation
was to contact and support member churches of the World Council of
Churches in Nicaragua during the November 1984 elections. The
delegation was granted equivalent status to that of all official
observers invited by the government. The report contains descriptions
of the findings of the mission, conclusions with regard to the
political developments in Nicaragua and the relationship between
church and state, and personal impressions of mission member Susan
Millard.

CATALOGUE SIGNATURE: 6245/-0=841106
TITLE: Verklaring van de delegatie die op verzoek van een aantal
kerkelijke organisaties uit Nederland als waarnemer aanwezig is
geweest bij de verkiezingen in Nicaragua op 4 november 1984
AUTHOR: De Gaay Fortman, Bas ; Heuvel, Ien van den ; Spit, Wim
(...et al)
PLACE OF PUBLICATION: Panama
PUBLISHER: (Delegation to observe elections in Nicaragua) (D)
DATE OF PUBLICATION: 841106
NUMBER OF PAGES: 9 p in v.p.
LANGUAGE: DUT
INDEX: elections / fact-finding missions
GEOGRAPHICAL INDEX: Nicaragua
GEOGRAPHICAL CODE: 6245
FREE TEXT: The delegation of three members and a secretary was sent on
behalf of nine dutch church organizations to observe the elections in
Nicaragua on 4 November 1984. Their report contains conclusions, and
the findings of the delegation (contacts with churches and Christians;
contacts with social groups, especially the trade unions; information
on the elections in the light of the political situation). It is
concluded that the elections were a step in the direction of pluralist
democracy.
With appendices: list of Dutch church organizations which took the
initiative to send the delegation; list of contacts established during
the mission.

CATALOGUE SIGNATURE: 0000/2955/-3=841200
TITLE: Freedom of expression and assembly in Nicaragua during the
election period
AUTHOR: Schell, Orville H. ; Lang, Margaret ; Mendez, Juan E.
PLACE OF PUBLICATION: New York
PUBLISHER: Americas Watch - AW (D)
DATE OF PUBLICATION: 841200
NUMBER OF PAGES: 14 p.
LANGUAGE: ENG
INDEX: expression (freedom of) / assembly (freedom of) / elections /
fact-finding missions
GEOGRAPHICAL INDEX: Nicaragua
GEOGRAPHICAL CODE: 6245
FREE TEXT: The report is based on a fact-finding mission with the aim
to explore the conditions under which the electoral campaign was
taking place in Nicaragua, with a specific focus on the possibilities
to exercise the freedom of expression and the freedom of assembly.
Attention is paid to: the background of the country and the political
situation; freedom of expression; freedom of assembly; the attitude
of the Reagan administration. Conclusion: freedoms of elections and
assembly were restricted. Even so, opposition voices could be heard
and important issues could be discussed; further advances are needed.

CATALOGUE SIGNATURE: 0000/1246/-3=841200
TITLE: A political opening in Nicaragua: report on Nicaraguan
elections of November 4, 1984
AUTHOR: Shannon, James ; Stephansky, Ben ; Whalen, Charles
PLACE OF PUBLICATION: Washington DC
PUBLISHER: International Human Rights Law Group - IHRLG (D) ;
Washington Office on Latin America - WOLA (D)
DATE OF PUBLICATION: 841200
NUMBER OF PAGES: (83 p.)
LANGUAGE: ENG
STATISTICAL INFORMATION: Y
BIBLIOGRAPHIES: Y
INDEX: elections / fact-finding missions
GEOGRAPHICAL INDEX: Nicaragua
GEOGRAPHICAL CODE: 6245
FREE TEXT: Two delegations of the IHRLG and WOLA visited Nicaragua:
an advance mission took place in September 1984, and the second
delegation observed the November elections. The report consists of a
preface and four chapters: an introduction with information on the
missions; the political background of the country and the elections;
different aspects of the electoral process (reasons for holding
elections, development of electoral system, political parties, the
campaign, procedures, voter attitudes, the role of the United States);
summary, conclusions and recommendations.
With footnotes and annexes: terms of reference and lists of contacts,
places visited by the mission and statements issued; results of the
elections; comparison between elections in El Salvador and Nicaragua,
based on observer reports.

CATALOGUE SIGNATURE: 0000/2955/-3=850300
TITLE: Violations of the laws of the war by both sides in Nicaragua:
1981-1985
AUTHOR: Goldman, Robert K. ; Mendez, Juan E. ; Neier, Aryeh (...et al)
PLACE OF PUBLICATION: New York
PUBLISHER: Americas Watch - AW (D)
DATE OF PUBLICATION: 850300
NUMBER OF PAGES: 97 p.
LANGUAGE: ENG
BIBLIOGRAPHIES: Y
INDEX: humanitarian law / armed conflict / fact-finding missions
GEOGRAPHICAL INDEX: Nicaragua
GEOGRAPHICAL CODE: 6245
FREE TEXT: The report is largely based on information collected during
several fact-finding missions. It consists of a summary of findings, a
review of international humanitarian law applicable to the conflict in
Nicaragua, a review of violations of the applicable laws (violence to
life and person, kidnapping and taking of hostages, outrages against
personnel dignity, violations of the rights of the wounded and sick
and medical neutrality, displacement - by the government of Nicaragua
and by the contras) and the role of the United States.

CATALOGUE SIGNATURE: 0000/1582/-3=850400
TITLE: Nicaragua: revolutionary justice: a report on human rights
and the judicial system
AUTHOR: Orentlicher, Diane ; Rone, Jemera ; Cook, Helena
PLACE OF PUBLICATION: New York
PUBLISHER: Lawyers Committee for International Human Rights - LCIHR
(D)
DATE OF PUBLICATION: 850400
NUMBER OF PAGES: 166 p. in v.p.
LANGUAGE: ENG
BIBLIOGRAPHIES: Y
INDEX: judicial systems / fact-finding missions
GEOGRAPHICAL INDEX: Nicaragua
GEOGRAPHICAL CODE: 6245
FREE TEXT: In 1984 and the first months of 1985, four LCIHR missions
visited Nicaragua to investigate aspects of the government's human
rights performance. These delegations have examined the state of
the judiciary in Nicaragua, focusing on the Popular Anti-Somocista
Tribunals. Meetings were held with Justices of the Supreme Court,
government representatives, defense attorneys, representatives of
human rights organizations and representatives of the US Embassy.
The report consists of an introduction, a summary of findings, and
chapters on: the judiciary; the Popular Anti-Somocista Tribunals;
pilot projects for popular tribunals; police courts; the right to
personal security; arrest and detention; discipline for military
abuses; the Bar, human rights organizations; and the role of the
United States.
The first of thirteen conclusions is that despite various sources of
pressure, the regular judiciary is generally independent, with some
notable exceptions. But several developments have placed tremendous
strains on Nicaragua's fledgling court system, undercutting both its
independence and the rights it is charged to uphold.

CATALOGUE SIGNATURE: 6003/1226/-3=850400
TITLE: Report ... concerning abuses against civilians by
counter-revolutionaries operating in Nicaragua
AUTHOR: Fox, Donald T. ; Glennon, Michael J.
PLACE OF PUBLICATION: Washington DC
PUBLISHER: International Human Rights Law Group - IHRLG (D) ;
Washington Office on Latin America - WOLA (D)
DATE OF PUBLICATION: 850400
NUMBER OF PAGES: 84 p. in v.p.
LANGUAGE: ENG
INDEX: armed conflict / humanitarian law / fact-finding missions
GEOGRAPHICAL INDEX: Nicaragua
GEOGRAPHICAL CODE: 6245
FREE TEXT: The aim of the fact-finding mission upon which this report
is based was to investigate allegations of abuses against the civilian
population by the counter-revolutionary forces (contras) fighting the
Nicaraguan government. The report consists of: an introduction;
background information on the country and case investigated;
methodology of the fact-finding mission; findings with regard to the
Sandinistas, the contras and the government of the United States;
conclusions; recommendations; final thoughts. With appendices: terms
of reference and biographies of the delegates; itinerary; twenty-five
statements of selected individuals; Common Article III of the Geneva
Conventions of 1949.

CATALOGUE SIGNATURE: 0000/2827/-0=850900
TITLE: A nation is coming: new realities in Miskitu-Sandinista
relations
AUTHOR: Dunbar Ortiz, Roxanne
PLACE OF PUBLICATION: San Francisco
PUBLISHER: Indigenous World Association - El Mundo Indigena (D)
DATE OF PUBLICATION: 850900
NUMBER OF PAGES: 5 p.
LANGUAGE: ENG
INDEX: indigenous peoples / fact-finding missions
GEOGRAPHICAL INDEX: Nicaragua
GEOGRAPHICAL CODE: 6245
FREE TEXT: The aim of the visit was to investigate the situation of
indigenous peoples in Nicaragua. The author concludes that it is most
important that the Miskitu and Sumu people return to their territories.
The government of Nicaragua is quite limited in the economic support it
can give for the reconstruction of the villages that have been totally
destroyed by warfare. Support for this return should be the top
priority for all who seek an end to crisis in Central America.

CATALOGUE SIGNATURE: 0000/0138/-3=860000
TITLE: Mission au Nicaragua: 14-24 janvier 1986
AUTHOR: Chemillier-Gendreau, Monique ; Bright, Teresa
PLACE OF PUBLICATION: Brussels
PUBLISHER: International Association of Democratic Lawyers - IADL (D)
DATE OF PUBLICATION: 860000
NUMBER OF PAGES: 52 p. in v.p.
LANGUAGE: FRE
INDEX: judicial systems / democracy / fact-finding missions
GEOGRAPHICAL INDEX: Nicaragua
GEOGRAPHICAL CODE: 6245
FREE TEXT: Report of a fact-finding mission which visited Nicaragua
from 14 to 21 January 1986. Included is information on the conduct of
the mission; the political institutions, constitutional mechanisms and
the maintenance of democracy during a state of war; the judicial system
and proposals for its reform; the state of emergency declared in October
1985, public freedoms and human rights.
With annexes: proposals for a new constitution of Nicaragua; information
provided by the Comisión Permanente de Derechos Humanos de Nicaragua;
declaration of the IADL with regard to human rights in Nicaragua.

CATALOGUE SIGNATURE: 0000/2955/-3=860300
TITLE: Human rights in Nicaragua: 1985-1986
AUTHOR: Mendez, Juan ; Neier, Aryeh ; Rone, Jemera
PLACE OF PUBLICATION: New York
PUBLISHER: Americas Watch - AW (D)
DATE OF PUBLICATION: 860300
NUMBER OF PAGES: 57 p. in v.p.
LANGUAGE: ENG
INDEX: civil and political rights / armed conflict /
fact-finding missions
GEOGRAPHICAL INDEX: Nicaragua
GEOGRAPHICAL CODE: 6245
FREE TEXT: From May 1982 to July 1985, Americas Watch published eight
reports on human rights in Nicaragua. This ninth report includes
information gathered after the July 1985 report, during visits to
Nicaragua in August 1985, November 1985, January 1986 and the first
week of February 1986. After an introduction, the summary, and
conclusions, the report is divided into the following parts:
A) The state of emergency; B) Personal freedom and due process:
treatment of detainees; disappearances; extrajudicial executions;
access to pre-trial detention centres; limitations on habeas corpus;
penitentiary system; the Tribunales Populares Antisomocistas (TPAs);
C) Freedom of expression, association, and worship: association and
assembly; freedom of worship; CPDH publications; D) The Miskitos;
E) Violations of the laws of war by the government of Nicaragua and
by the insurgents; F) Cuapa, UNO, and the Reagan administration;
G) The Reagan administration and reports of Contra abuses; H) José
Alvaro Baldizon (a defector from the government who made statements
about human rights violations allegedly committed by the Nicaraguan
government).

PANAMA

CATALOGUE SIGNATURE: 0000/1234/-2=850000
TITLE: The presidential and legislative elections in Panama
AUTHOR: Drinan, Robert F. ; Gastil, Raymond D. ; Hood Vaughan, Jack
TITLE OF GENERIC ITEM: Freedom in the world: political rights and civil
liberties 1984-1985 / Gastil, Raymond
EDITION: 1st.
PLACE OF PUBLICATION: Westport ; London ; New York
PUBLISHER: Westwood Press (D) ; Freedom House (D)
DATE OF PUBLICATION: 850000
NUMBER OF PAGES: p.115-126
LANGUAGE: ENG
INDEX: democracy / elections / fact-finding missions
GEOGRAPHICAL INDEX: Panama
GEOGRAPHICAL CODE: 6246
FREE TEXT: The report contains background information on Panama, the
political context in which the elections of 6 May 1984 took place, the
campaign, the election process, counting and authenticating the tallies
and an analysis of the elections. It is concluded that the elections
represented another attempt to reestablish democratic institutions
after a long period of interruption. They represented the fulfillment
of a promise made by the country's rulers to return the country to
democracy. Yet, as in most attempts of this kind, the election also
represented a threat to the established government and the interests
that had developed around it over sixteen years of largely military
rule.

PARAGUAY

CATALOGUE SIGNATURE: 0000/0138/-3=760600
TITLE: Mission d'observation au Paraguay: 13-24 juin 1976
AUTHOR: Chartrain, François ; Cornevaux, Alain
PLACE OF PUBLICATION: Brussels
PUBLISHER: Association Internationale des Juristes Democrates - IADL (D)
DATE OF PUBLICATION: 760600
NUMBER OF PAGES: 13 p.
LANGUAGE: FRE
INDEX: judicial systems / political prisoners/ fact-finding missions
GEOGRAPHICAL INDEX: Paraguay
GEOGRAPHICAL CODE: 6447
FREE TEXT: The aim of the mission was to obtain information on the
actual judicial problems in Paraguay, the functioning of institutions
and the application of legal norms relating to human rights.
The first part of the report is on the functioning of institutions:
legal, tolerated and clandestine political parties; the military; the
church; trade unions. In "The game of the institutions", attention is
paid to the division of power. In practice, the Executive (which is
the President) has all the power.
The second part is on the political prisoners and the judicial system,
with reference to specific cases.

CATALOGUE SIGNATURE: 0000/1212/-3=800500
TITLE: Mbaretè: the higher law of Paraguay: report on the denial
of human rights in Paraguay by the Third Commission of Enquiry of
the International League for Human Rights
AUTHOR: Helfeld, David M. ; Wipfler, William L.
PLACE OF PUBLICATION: New York
PUBLISHER: International League for Human Rights - ILHR (D)
DATE OF PUBLICATION: 800500
NUMBER OF PAGES: 237 p. in v.p.
LANGUAGE: ENG
STATISTICAL INFORMATION: Y
INDEX: dictatorship / fact-finding missions
GEOGRAPHICAL INDEX: Paraguay
GEOGRAPHICAL CODE: 6447
FREE TEXT: The aim of the mission in October 1979 was to obtain
information on a number of questions dealing with the situation of
human rights in Paraguay. The first part of the report is on scope,
method and findings of the mission. The second part contains the texts
of interviews with government representatives. The following parts are
on the state of siege and the administration of the legal system under
Law 209, with references to specific cases. Part six deals with human
rights violations like restrictions on the freedom of the press,
freedom of religion and the rights of political parties and voluntary
associations. Part seven is on prospects for political democracy and
human rights. With conclusions and recommendations.
With appendices: figures on repression, list of "political delinquents"
released, correspondence of the mission, and a government resolution
suspending newspapers.

CATALOGUE SIGNATURE: 0000/0035/-3=830600
TITLE: Mission d'ètude au Paraguay: juin 1983
AUTHOR: Cheron, François
PLACE OF PUBLICATION: Paris
PUBLISHER: Fédération Internationale des Droits de l'Homme - FIDH (D)
DATE OF PUBLICATION: 830600
NUMBER OF PAGES: 14 p.
LANGUAGE: FRE
INDEX: civil and political rights / nongovernmental organizations /
judicial systems / fact-finding missions
GEOGRAPHICAL INDEX: Paraguay
GEOGRAPHICAL CODE: 6447
FREE TEXT: The aim of the mission was to investigate the judicial
system and the general human rights situation in Paraguay. The
delegate met with representatives of human rights organizations;
contacts with government representatives were cancelled by the
authorities without motivation. In the first part of the report,
the judicial mechanisms of Paraguay, the institutional system and
the political structure are described.
The second part is on the consequences these mechanisms have on the
human rights situation, especially on the right to life, of respect
for physical integrity, fair hearing, freedom of movement, and
freedom of the press. With conclusion.

CATALOGUE SIGNATURE: 0000/0088/-4
TITLE: Judicial independence in Paraguay: report of a mission on
behalf of the Association of Latin American Lawyers for Human Rights,
the Centre for the Independence of Judges and Lawyers, and the
International Commission of Jurists
AUTHOR: O'Donnell, Daniel
TITLE OF GENERIC ITEM: CIJL Bulletin
EDITION: no. 14
PLACE OF PUBLICATION: Geneva
PUBLISHER: Centre for the Independence of Judges and Lawyers - CIJL
(D)
DATE OF PUBLICATION: 841000
NUMBER OF PAGES: p. 14-40
LANGUAGE: ENG / FRE / SPA
BIBLIOGRAPHIES: Y
INDEX: judicial systems / fact-finding missions
GEOGRAPHICAL INDEX: Paraguay
GEOGRAPHICAL CODE: 6447
FREE TEXT: Report of a mission undertaken in February 1984, to
investigate the independence of the judiciary in Paraguay. The report
contains information on the background of the country, the absolute
authority of General Stroessner, elections, the state of siege, the
constitution as guarantor of executive control, the extent of judicial
subordination, the system of justice and torture, criminal justice,
the appointment of a new Supreme Court, and the Ovando case (an officer
convicted of homicide was finally released after completing his 15-year
sentence).

CATALOGUE SIGNATURE: 0000/2955/-3=850100
TITLE: Rule by fear: Paraguay after thirty years under Stroessner
AUTHOR: Bell, Peter D. ; Greathead, Scott ; Pittman, Patricia
PLACE OF PUBLICATION: New York
PUBLISHER: Americas Watch - AW (D)
DATE OF PUBLICATION: 850100
NUMBER OF PAGES: 105 p.
LANGUAGE: ENG
STATISTICAL INFORMATION: Y
BIBLIOGRAPHIES: Y
INDEX: civil and political rights / legislation / fact-finding missions
GEOGRAPHICAL INDEX: Paraguay
GEOGRAPHICAL CODE: 6447
FREE TEXT: The report is based on a fact-finding mission undertaken in
June 1984 at the invitation of the government. The members had a broad
range of contacts, visited prisons and interviewed prisoners.
The report consists of an introduction with background information on
the country, and sections on freedom of the press, political parties,
the administration of justice, trade unions, land disputes and the
repression of peasant rights. With appendices: list of disappeared
persons, list of persons expelled, extracts from the Constitution.

CATALOGUE SIGNATURE: 0000/2955/-3=860800
DATE OF ENTRY: 860915
TITLE: Paraguay: Latin America's oldest dictatorship under pressure
AUTHOR: Nelson, Anne
PLACE OF PUBLICATION: New York
PUBLISHER: Americas Watch - AW (D)
DATE OF PUBLICATION: 860800
NUMBER OF PAGES: 71 p.
ISBN: 0 938579 23 1
LANGUAGE: ENG
INDEX: association (freedom of) / civil and political rights /
fact-finding missions
GEOGRAPHICAL INDEX : Paraguay
GEOGRAPHICAL CODE: 6447
FREE TEXT: The report is an outgrowth of a three member mission sent
to Paraguay in March 1986. The report contains information on the
general political situation in Paraguay, and chapters dealing with
the freedom of association (restrictions on peasant organizations,
trade unions, student organizations and political parties); and the
relationship between law and reality (arbitrary arrests; Bogado
Nunez, a personal prisoner of General Duarte, and other prisoners;
torture); abuses of the rights of indigenous peoples (Indians); and
government control over the press - censorship.

PERU

CATALOGUE SIGNATURE: 0000/2955/-3=841000
TITLE: Abdicating democratic authority: human rights in Peru
PLACE OF PUBLICATION: New York
PUBLISHER: Americas Watch - AW (D)
DATE OF PUBLICATION: 841000
NUMBER OF PAGES: 164 p. in v.p.
LANGUAGE: ENG
INDEX: political violence / armed conflict / fact-finding missions
GEOGRAPHICAL INDEX: Peru
GEOGRAPHICAL CODE: 6448
FREE TEXT: Information for this report was collected during a visit
to Peru in December 1983. Firstly, background information on Peru is
provided: the judicial system; the prisons; the police; the state of
emergency measures; the anti-terrorist law and beyond; trade union
and peasant oranizations; the press; the climate of intolerance;
monitoring human rights.
The second chapter is on Ayacucho: the guerillas and the armed forces;
the military zone and counter-insurgency; the counter-insurgency plan;
paramilitary patrols; detained and disappeared persons; extrajudicial
executions and massacres and torture.
The third chapter is on the role of the United States in Peru.

CATALOGUE SIGNATURE: 0000/0035-3=850200
TITLE: Perou: rapport de mission
AUTHOR: García, Antonio; Feder, Alain
PLACE OF PUBLICATION: Paris
PUBLISHER: Fédération Internationale des Droits de l'Homme - FIDH (D)
DATE OF PUBLICATION: 850200
NUMBER OF PAGES: 36 p. in v.p.
LANGUAGE: FRE
INDEX: disappearances / fact-finding missions
GEOGRAPHICAL INDEX: Peru
GEOGRAPHICAL CODE: 6448
FREE TEXT: The aim of the fact-finding mission, held from 17 to 27
February 1985, was to investigate the situation of Mrs Argumedo, as
well as that of eight disappeared journalists and their guides. The
report consists of two parts: the preliminary report of the mission,
with general information on the political situation in Peru and the
conduct of the army in the zone where there is a state of emergency;
and the final report, with general information and a description of
four cases of abduction and assassination.

CATALOGUE SIGNATURE: 0000/2955/-3=850900
TITLE: A new opportunity for democratic authority: human rights in
Peru
AUTHOR: Mendez, Juan
PLACE OF PUBLICATION: New York
PUBLISHER: Americas Watch - AW (D)
DATE OF PUBLICATION: 850900
NUMBER OF PAGES: 44 p.
LANGUAGE: ENG / SPA
BIBLIOGRAPHIES: Y
INDEX: democracy / fact-finding missions
GEOGRAPHICAL INDEX: Peru
GEOGRAPHICAL CODE: 6448
FREE TEXT: The information in this report was compiled by the author
during fact-finding missions in December 1984 and June 1985. The
report consists of an introduction on recent political developments;
an outline of recent developments in the situation of human rights
(disappearances and political murders, political imprisonment), the
Rondas Campesinas, legislative and judicial developments, Sendero
Luminoso, attitudes towards human rights; recommendations to the new
administration of President Alan García Perez.

CATALOGUE SIGNATURE: 0000/1079/-3=860108
TITLE: Report on the visit to Peru by two members of the Working
Group on Enforced or Involuntary Disappearances (17-22 June 1985)
AUTHOR: Working Group on Enforced or Involuntary Disappearances
PLACE OF PUBLICATION: Geneva
PUBLISHER: Commission on Human Rights of the United Nations Economic
and Social Council - UNCHR (D)
DATE OF PUBLICATION: 860108
NUMBER OF PAGES: 35 p.
SERIES TITLE: Commission on Human Rights: forty-second session: item
10(c) of the agenda: question of the human rights of all persons
subjected to any form of detention or imprisonment, in particular:
question of enforced or involuntary disappearances: report of the
Working Group on Enforced or Involuntary Disappearances
DOCUMENT SYMBOL: E/CN.4/1986/18/Add.1
AVAILABILITY: F
LANGUAGE: ENG
STATISTICAL INFORMATION: Y
INDEX: disappearances / political violence / fact-finding missions
GEOGRAPHICAL INDEX: Peru
GEOGRAPHICAL CODE: 6448
FREE TEXT: Upon the invitation of the government, two members of the
Working Group, Toine van Dongen and Luis Valera Quirós, visited Peru.
The report contains an analysis of the situation of disappearances.
After an introduction, attention is given to: the background of the
violence in Peru; the legal and institutional framework; reports on
disappearances received from non-governmental sources and steps
taken by the relatives of missing persons before the authorities;
the position of the government and information provided by official
sources; human rights organizations, relatives and their associations
and other sources of reports on disappearances, and the role of the
press; economic and social consequences. With concluding observations.

CATALOGUE SIGNATURE: 0000/2955/-3=860900
TITLE: Human rights in Peru after president Garcia's first year
AUTHOR: Mendez, Juan E. ; Nelson, Anne (ed.)
PLACE OF PUBLICATION: New York ; Washington
PUBLISHER: Americas Watch - AW (D)
DATE OF PUBLICATION: 860900
NUMBER OF PAGES: 121 p. in v.p.
ISBN: 0 938579 25 8
LANGUAGE: ENG
INDEX: extra-judicial executions / dissappearences /
political prisoners / expression, freedom of / fact-finding missions
GEOGRAPHICAL INDEX: Peru
GEOGRAPHICAL CODE: 6448
FREE TEXT: This report is largely based on the observations gathered by
Juan Mendez during his trip to Peru in June 1986.
According to Americas Watch:
"The 1984 America Watch report on Peru documented the cruel measures the
insurgency known as Sendero Luminoso practiced against civilians, as
well as severe abuses commited by the government in the course of its
counter-insurgency campaign, condemning the violations on both sides.
When President Alan Garcia took office on June 29, 1985, his inaugural
message offered hope for change. It included specific references to a
new policy that proposed to instill a scrupulous respect for
internationally recognized standards of human rights within the conduct
of the counter-insurgency campaign.
Peru has indeed experienced dramatic changes regarding human rights
over the past year.
At the end of Garcia's first year in office, the gains that have been
made in battle for human rights are in serious jeopardy. It is not,
however, too late for President Garcia to gove momentum to his peace
and human rights initiatives."
The report is divided into six parts: I) Introduction;
II) Extra-judicial executions, disappearances and political prisoners;
III) Couter-insurgency; IV) Sendero Luminoso; V) The state of
emergency; VI) Freedom of expression.

SURINAME

CATALOGUE SIGNATURE: 0000/0088/-3=810000
TITLE: Suriname: recent developments relating to human rights: report
by a mission to Suriname in February 1981
AUTHOR: Griffiths, J.
PLACE OF PUBLICATION: Geneva
PUBLISHER: International Commission of Jurists - ICJ (D)
DATE OF PUBLICATION: 810000
NUMBER OF PAGES: 34 p.
LANGUAGE: ENG
INDEX: detention / press (freedom of the) / trials /
fact-finding missions
GEOGRAPHICAL INDEX: Suriname
GEOGRAPHICAL CODE: 6454
FREE TEXT: The aim of the mission was to investigate the general
situation of human rights in Suriname. The report contains information
on the background, purpose and limitations of the mission and the
sources of information used. The author recognizes three problem areas
of current importance: the unsatisfactory position of the press; the
occurrence of arbitrary arrest and detention, and of mistreatment of
detainees; substantive and procedural unfairness involved in the
anti-corruption proceedings before the Special Tribunals and in the
trial of the "left coup" case. He concludes that the situation with
respect to most of the problems seems to be developing in a positive
direction, many violations of basic human rights belong to the past.
With summary and appendix: text of decree on Special Tribunals (in
Dutch).

CATALOGUE SIGNATURE: 0000/0088/-3=830000
TITLE: Human rights in Suriname: report of a mission to Suriname in
February/March 1983
AUTHOR: Bossuyt, M. ; Griffiths, J.
PLACE OF PUBLICATION: Geneva
PUBLISHER: International Commission of Jurists - ICJ (D)
DATE OF PUBLICATION: 830000
NUMBER OF PAGES: 11 p.
LANGUAGE: ENG
INDEX: judicial systems / fact-finding missions
GEOGRAPHICAL INDEX: Suriname
GEOGRAPHICAL CODE: 6454
FREE TEXT: The purpose of the mission was to enquire into the
present situation concerning the rule of law and the system of
justice, including legal guarantees for ensuring the fair trial of
suspects with an independent judiciary and legal profession. In
the report, attention is paid to the background of the country,
recent developments, the conduct and findings of the mission,
events subsequent to the mission and the suspension of development
assistance from the Netherlands. With conclusions.

CATALOGUE SIGNATURE: 6000/1011/-3=831005
TITLE: Report on the situation of human rights in Suriname
AUTHOR: Inter-American Commission on Human Rights - IACHR
PLACE OF PUBLICATION: Washington DC
PUBLISHER: Organization of American States - OAS (D) ; Inter-American
Commission on Human Rights - IACHR
DATE OF PUBLICATION: 831005
NUMBER OF PAGES: 46 p.
ISBN: 0 8270 1848 7
DOCUMENT SYMBOL: OAS/Ser.L/II.61 doc.6 rev.1
LANGUAGE: ENG
INDEX: judicial systems / extrajudicial executions /
fact-finding missions
GEOGRAPHICAL INDEX: Suriname
GEOGRAPHICAL CODE: 6454
FREE TEXT: The report is based upon a fact-finding mission by a Special
Commission to Paramaribo from 20 to 24 June 1983. The members met with
principal government officials and private citizens. Serious doubts
were raised about the intention of the government to construct new
institutions for the expression of the popular will. Also, it seemed
that no effort has been made to insulate the State radio and television
from direct political supervision. Concerning the killings in December
1982 officials declared that they must be placed in the context of
attempted coups against the present government, while claiming that the
deaths were excesses.
After an introduction the report is divided into three chapters:
I) the regulatory and political system of Suriname, with attention to:
the constitution of 1975; the interruption of the constitutional order
beginning February 25th, 1980; the institutional evolution since then;
the organization of the state under the present political system; the
suspension of constitutional guarantees; international law and human
rights in Suriname;
II) the right to life and the right to personal integrity;
III) other human rights: the right to personal integrity; right to
justice and due process; freedom of opinion, expression and
dissemination of thoughts; freedom of association and freedom of trade
unions; political rights. With conclusions.

CATALOGUE SIGNATURE: 0000/0966/-3=831100
TITLE: Case No. 1160: complaints presented by the International
Confederation of Free Trade Unions and the World Confederation of
Labour against the government of Suriname
AUTHOR: International Labour Office - ILO - Committee on Freedom of
Association ; Simpson, W.R.
TITLE OF GENERIC ITEM: Official Bulletin: reports of the
Committee on Freedom of Association (230th, 231st and 232nd)
EDITION: v. LXVI, series B no. 3
PLACE OF PUBLICATION: Geneva
PUBLISHER: International Labour Office - ILO (D)
DATE OF PUBLICATION: 831100
NUMBER OF PAGES: p. 139-170
LANGUAGE: ENG
INDEX: association (freedom of) / trade unions / fact-finding missions
GEOGRAPHICAL INDEX: Suriname
GEOGRAPHICAL CODE: 6454
FREE TEXT: The report contains information on previous examination of
the case, further communications from the government and the direct
contacts mission undertaken by W.R. Simpson, as representative of the
Director-General.
The analysis of the mission report deals with questions related to the
attack of the premises of the trade union Moederbond on 17 September
1982, events leading up to 8 December 1982, the arrests and deaths on
7 and 8 December, the destruction of the Moederbond premises and the
statement of the Acting Permanent Secretary of Labour to the Committee.
With conclusions and recommendations of the Committee.
With annex: text of the report of the direct contacts mission, with
introduction on the conduct of the mission, background information
on the country, the allegations (see above), future perspectives and
concluding remarks.

CATALOGUE SIGNATURE: 0000/1079/-0=850212
TITLE: Visit by the special rapporteur to Suriname
AUTHOR: Wako, Amos S.
PLACE OF PUBLICATION: Geneva
PUBLISHER: Commission on Human Rights of the United Nations Economic
and Social Council - UNCHR (D)
DATE OF PUBLICATION: 850212
NUMBER OF PAGES: 16 p.
SERIES TITLE: Commission on Human Rights: forty-first session: agenda
item 12: question of the violation of human rights and fundamental
freedoms in any part of the world, with particular reference to
colonial and other territories
DOCUMENT SYMBOL: E/CN.4/1985/17/Annex5
AVAILABILITY: F
LANGUAGE: ENG / FRE / SPA
INDEX: extrajudicial executions / fact-finding missions
GEOGRAPHICAL INDEX: Suriname
GEOGRAPHICAL CODE: 6454
FREE TEXT: S. Amos Wako is Special Rapporteur on summary or arbitrary
executions, appointed pursuant to resolution 1984/35 of 24 May 1984
of the Economic and Social Council. He was invited by the government
of Suriname to investigate an allegation of the summary or arbitrary
execution of a number of persons on or about 9 December 1982.
His visit took place from 22 to 27 July 1984, and was followed by a
visit to the Netherlands on 30 and 31 July 1984. The subjects for
examination during the visit were a)the alleged occurrence of summary
or arbitrary executions in December 1982 and the official measures
taken to determine the facts of those incidents; b) the safeguards
adopted or envisaged to enhance the protection of the right to life.
The report is divided into the following parts:
I) introduction; II) allegations; III) reports by other international
organizations; IV) information obtained during the visit: developments
leading up to the December killings; events of December 1982; the
military's version and other versions of the events of December 1982;
questions whether any measures were taken to determine the facts;
information concerning the safeguards adopting or envisaged to enhance
the protection of the right to life; assurances given that the events
of December 1982 would not recur; concluding remarks.

CATALOGUE SIGNATURE: 6000/1011/-3=851002
TITLE: Second report on the human rights situation in Suriname =
Tweede verslag over de mensenrechtensituatie in Suriname
AUTHOR: Inter-American Commission on Human Rights - IACHR
PLACE OF PUBLICATION: Washington DC
PUBLISHER: Organization of American States - OAS (D) ; Inter-American
Commission on Human Rights - IACHR
DATE OF PUBLICATION: 851002
NUMBER OF PAGES: 69 p.
ISBN: 0 8270 2257 3
DOCUMENT SYMBOL: OAS/Ser.L/V/II.66 doc.21 rev.1
LANGUAGE: ENG / DUT
INDEX: legislation / fact-finding missions
GEOGRAPHICAL INDEX: Suriname
GEOGRAPHICAL CODE: 6454
FREE TEXT: This report is a follow-up on the study published by the
Commission in October 1983; it is based on a fact-finding mission in
January 1985.
It contains an introduction and the following chapters: I) political
and legal developments in Suriname; II) the right to life; III) right
to a fair trial and due process of law; IV) right to humane treatment;
V) freedom of movement and residence; VI) freedom of association and
trade unions; VII) freedom of thought and expression; VIII) economic,
social and cultural situation. Most chapters contain information on
applicable international and domestic law, and on the practice.
With conclusions: the general situation is still serious.

URUGUAY

CATALOGUE SIGNATURE: 0000/0088/-3=740000
TITLE: Report of mission to Uruguay in April/May 1974
AUTHOR: MacDermot, Niall ; Fahlander, Inger
PLACE OF PUBLICATION: Geneva
PUBLISHER: International Commission of Jurists - ICJ (D) ; Amnesty International - AI (D)
DATE OF PUBLICATION: 740000
NUMBER OF PAGES: 8 p.
LANGUAGE: ENG
INDEX: political prisoners / judicial systems / fact-finding missions
GEOGRAPHICAL INDEX: Uruguay
GEOGRAPHICAL CODE: 6459
FREE TEXT: The members of the mission had interviews with government representatives and with lawyers. They discussed the emergency legislation and legal procedures relating to the arrest and detention of political suspects. The report deals as well with torture and ill-treatment, and the military justice procedure. With conclusions and recommendations.
With appendix: report of visit to "Libertad" prison where political suspects subject to trial are being held (the delegates were refused permission to visit any of the military baracks where interrogations are carried out).

CATALOGUE SIGNATURE: 0000/0035/-3=750000
TITLE: Rapport a monsieur le sécretaire général de la Fédération Internationale des Droits de l'Homme
AUTHOR: Choucq, Yann
PLACE OF PUBLICATION: Paris
PUBLISHER: Fédération Internationale des Droits de l'Homme - FIDH (D)
DATE OF PUBLICATION: 750000
NUMBER OF PAGES: 11 p.
LANGUAGE: FRE
INDEX: political prisoners / prison conditions / fact-finding missions
GEOGRAPHICAL INDEX: Uruguay
GEOGRAPHICAL CODE: 6459
FREE TEXT: The purpose of the mission was to investigate detention conditions and legal guarantees for political prisoners. The delegate met with jurists involved in the case of mr. Raul Sendik, both judges and defence lawyers. He was not allowed to visit prisons; the part of the report on detention conditions is based on information received from former detainees. With attention to the institutional and legal framework: law of state security, and detention conditions. With conclusions.

324

CATALOGUE SIGNATURE: 0000/0966/-0=760000
TITLE: Cases Nos. 763, 786 and 801: complaints by the World Federation
of Trade Unions, the World Confederation of Labour and various other
trade union organisations against the government of Uruguay
AUTHOR: International Labour Office - ILO - Committee on Freedom of
Association
TITLE OF GENERIC ITEM: Official Bulletin: reports of the Governing Body
Committee on Freedom of Association (153rd, 154th, 155th)
EDITION: vol. LIX, series B no. 1
PLACE OF PUBLICATION: Geneva
PUBLISHER: International Labour Office - ILO (D)
DATE OF PUBLICATION: 760000
NUMBER OF PAGES: p. 43-75
LANGUAGE: ENG
INDEX: association (freedom of) / trade unions / fact-finding missions
GEOGRAPHICAL INDEX: Uruguay
GEOGRAPHICAL CODE: 6459
FREE TEXT: The Committee on Freedom of Association has been examining
various complaints alleging breaches of trade union rights in Uruguay;
the Director-General of the ILO appointed Philippe Cahier to examine
the facts relating to complaint No. 763, and to report thereon to the
Committee. The mission took place from 20 June to 1 July 1975.
The report of the Committee is based on information obtained during
the mission. It contains background information on the country and the
case, allegations relating to: restrictions on trade union rights; the
arrest and orders for arrest of trade union leaders and militants, the
dissolution of other trade union organizations; the searching of trade
union premises; acts of anti-trade union discrimination; new
allegations. With conclusions and recommendations.

Uruguay

CATALOGUE SIGNATURE: 0000/0966/-0=810000
TITLE: Case No. 763: complaints presented by the World Federation of
Trade Unions, the World Confederation of Labour, International
Confederation of Free Trade Unions, and various other trade union
organisations against the government of Uruguay: complaint concerning
the observance by Uruguay of the Freedom of Association and Protection
of the Right to Organise Convention, 1948 (no. 87), and the Right to
Organise and Collective Bargaining Convention, 1949 (no. 98), presented
by a number of delegates to the 61st session of the International
Labour Conference (1976) under article 26 of the Constitution of the
ILO
AUTHOR: International Labour Office - ILO - Committee on Freedom of
Association
TITLE OF GENERIC ITEM: Official Bulletin: reports of the Committee
on Freedom of Association (208th, 209th and 210th)
EDITION: vol. LXIV, series B no. 2
PLACE OF PUBLICATION: Geneva
PUBLISHER: International Labour Office - ILO (D)
DATE OF PUBLICATION: 810000
NUMBER OF PAGES: p. 99-115
LANGUAGE: ENG
INDEX: association (freedom of) / trade unions / legislation
fact-finding missions
GEOGRAPHICAL INDEX: Uruguay
GEOGRAPHICAL CODE: 6459
FREE TEXT: The Committee has examined this case on several occasions.
Its Chairman held discussions with representatives of the government
of Uruguay, which requested the establishment of direct contacts "so
as to consider in a broader manner the different subjects of common
interest that are being examined." Philippe Cahier, as representative
of the Director-General, and Manuel Araoz undertook the mission in
January 1981.
The report of the Committee contains information on the conduct of
the mission, and matters discussed: the Occupational Associations Act,
arrests and detentions, and other allegations. With recommendations.

CATALOGUE SIGNATURE: 0000/2921/-3=830600
TITLE: Uruguay: does democracy include freedom of the press?: a report
by the Committee to Protect Journalists and the PEN American Center
AUTHOR: Uriarte, Mercedes Lynn de ; Komisar, Lucy
PLACE OF PUBLICATION: New York
PUBLISHER: Committee to Protect Journalists - CPJ (D) ; PEN American
Center (D)
DATE OF PUBLICATION: 830600
NUMBER OF PAGES: 35 p.
LANGUAGE: ENG
INDEX: journalists (protection of) / censorship
fact-finding missions
GEOGRAPHICAL INDEX: Uruguay
GEOGRAPHICAL CODE: 6459
FREE TEXT: The CPJ and PEN decided to send a delegation to Uruguay
because of their concern with the increasing threats to press freedom
in that country; the delegation went to see what the role of the press
was in the announced transition to a civilian, democratic government,
to discover whether democratic rights would be extended to the press
and to find out about conditions and prospects of the journalists in
prison. The delegation met with a broad spectrum of Uruguayans working
in or concerned with the media, and others.
The report contains an introduction, summary and recommendations, and
chapters on the political background of the country (prior to 1980; the
transition); the press prior to 1980; recent government actions against
the press (chronology; case studies); detentions; government actions
against cultural expression; and the role of the United States.
With appendix: statement by US Ambassador Thomas Aranda, Jr. to the
delegation.

CATALOGUE SIGNATURE: 0000/0249/-3=831100
TITLE: Amnesty International report on human rights violations in
Uruguay (including a memorandum sent to the government on 26 July
1983)
AUTHOR: (Fragoso, Heleno Claudio) ; (Brett, Sebastian)
PLACE OF PUBLICATION: London
PUBLISHER: Amnesty International - AI (D)
DATE OF PUBLICATION: 831100
NUMBER OF PAGES: 42 p. in v.p.
ISBN: 0 86210 064 X
DOCUMENT SYMBOL: AI Index: AMR 52/35/83
LANGUAGE: ENG
INDEX: civil and political rights / political prisoners
judicial systems / fact-finding missions
GEOGRAPHICAL INDEX: Uruguay
GEOGRAPHICAL CODE: 6459
FREE TEXT: During the first two weeks of April 1983, the delegation
visited Montevideo to gather additional information regarding AI's
concerns: political prisoners, torture and the judicial system, and
to discuss them directly with governmental authorities.
The report contains information on abuses since the mission and on
the political background of the country, and chapters on detention
procedures, "disappearances", torture and cruel, inhuman or degrading
treatment, prisoners of conscience, the treatment of prisoners in
military prisons, trial procedures and legal concerns.
With recommendations.

CATALOGUE SIGNATURE: 0000/1582/-3=840500
TITLE: Uruguay: the end of a nightmare?: a report on human rights
based on a mission of enquiry
AUTHOR: Posner, Michael ; Derian, Patricia
PLACE OF PUBLICATION: New York
PUBLISHER: Lawyers Committee for International Human Rights - LCIHR (D)
DATE OF PUBLICATION: 840500
NUMBER OF PAGES: 85 p.
LANGUAGE: ENG
INDEX: civil and political rights / dictatorship
fact-finding missions
GEOGRAPHICAL INDEX: Uruguay
GEOGRAPHICAL CODE: 6459
FREE TEXT: The report examines Urguay's human rights situation with a
particular focus on events of 1983, and is partly based on a visit to
Uruguay on 11 and 12 December 1983 by Michael Posner and Patricia
Derian. After an introduction, conclusions, and background information
on the country, attention is paid to prison conditions (including
torture and disappearances); restrictions on the legal system under
military rule; the freedom of association and trade unions; freedom of
the press; human rights organizations; the return to democracy; and
the role of the United States.

CATALOGUE SIGNATURE: 0000/2231/-3=850000
TITLE: Report on a mission to Uruguay: August 1984
AUTHOR: Breslin, Patrick ; Kennedy, David ; Goldstein, Richard
PLACE OF PUBLICATION: New York
PUBLISHER: New York Academy of Sciences (D)
DATE OF PUBLICATION: 850000
NUMBER OF PAGES: 31 p.
LANGUAGE: ENG
BIBLIOGRAPHIES: Y
INDEX: political prisoners / detention / fact-finding missions
GEOGRAPHICAL INDEX: Uruguay
GEOGRAPHICAL CODE: 6459
FREE TEXT: The delegation visited Uruguay and entered the men's and
women's political prisons in March 1984 to see four medical students
imprisoned since June 1983, and a number of political prisoners
reported to be in ill health. The students, when arrested, were held
incommuncando, and tortured. At the time of the visit, none of them
complained of ill health; three of them were released in September
1984. The report provides background information on the country,
preparations for the visit, the visit itself (including description
of interviews with prisoners and prison authorities held at Punta
Rieles and Libertad prisons, and final meetings). With postcript of
July 1984, notes and appendices: press release; Principles of Medical
Ethics adopted in resolution 37/194 of the General Assembly of the
United Nations, March 1983.

CATALOGUE SIGNATURE: 6003/1226/-3=850000
TITLE: From shadow into sunlight: a report on the 1984 Uruguayan
electoral process
AUTHOR: Young, Amy ; Eldridge, Joseph
PLACE OF PUBLICATION: Washington DC
PUBLISHER: Washington Office on Latin America - WOLA (D) ;
International Human Rights Law Group - IHRLG (D)
DATE OF PUBLICATION: 850000
NUMBER OF PAGES: 73 p. in v.p.
LANGUAGE: ENG
STATISTICAL INFORMATION: Y
BIBLIOGRAPHIES: Y
INDEX: elections / fact-finding missions
GEOGRAPHICAL INDEX: Uruguay
GEOGRAPHICAL CODE: 6459
FREE TEXT: WOLA and the IHRLG send two delegations to Uruguay to
report on the electoral process. The first mission (pre-election
mission) visited Uruguay between 24 August and 2 September 1984.
The purpose of this mission was to gather factual information on
the November elections, including the electoral procedures,
registration laws, and the political and human rights context of
the elections.
The second delegation visited Uruguay from 18 to 27 November 1984,
during the elections. The purpose of this mission was to produce a
report evaluating the extent to which democratic freedoms and
procedures were respected in Uruguay during the campaign and at
the time of the elections themselves.
The report is divided into the following parts: I) introduction;
II) historical background; III) electoral laws; IV) political
parties; V) conduct of the campaign; VI) the role of the military
in the campaign; VII) the role of the United States; VIII) election
day procedures; IX) election results; X) prognosis.
With appendices: terms of reference; incidents of repression of the
press; results of the election.

CATALOGUE SIGNATURE: 0000/1582/-3=850200
TITLE: The generals give back Uruguay: a report on human rights
AUTHOR: Estlund, Cynthia ; Issacharoff, Samuel
PLACE OF PUBLICATION: New York ; Washington DC
PUBLISHER: Lawyers Committee for International Human Rights - LCIHR (D)
DATE OF PUBLICATION: 850200
NUMBER OF PAGES: 67 p. in v.p.
LANGUAGE: ENG
INDEX: democracy / political prisoners / fact-finding missions
GEOGRAPHICAL INDEX: Uruguay
GEOGRAPHICAL CODE: 6459
FREE TEXT: The report is based primarily on visits to Uruguay from 15
to 18 October 1984 and from 29 November to 1 December 1984. The authors
examine the human rights situation in Uruguay during a period of
significant transition, just before a newly elected civilian president,
Julio Sanguinetti, will take office. His coming to power marks the end
of more than a decade of military rule in Uruguay. Attention is paid to:
political detainees and prisoners (detention conditions, rights of the
defence, releases, the disappeared); politically-based proscriptions and
classifications; trade unions; human rights organizations; transition
to civilian rule; future perspectives and the role of the United States.

CATALOGUE SIGNATURE: 6357/-0=790800
TITLE: Report of international jurists visit with human rights
petitioners in the United States: August 3-20, 1979: report and
findings
AUTHOR: Chandra, Harish ; Eklund, Per ; Harvey, Richard (et al...)
DATE OF PUBLICATION: 790800
NUMBER OF PAGES: 45 p.
LANGUAGE: ENG
INDEX: international machinery / detention / fact-finding missions
GEOGRAPHICAL INDEX: United States
GEOGRAPHICAL CODE: 6357
FREE TEXT: In December 1978, a petition was filed with the United
Nations Sub-Commission on Prevention of Discrimination and Protection
of Minorities, pursuant to ECOSOC Resolution 1503 "Procedure for
dealing with communications relating to violations of human rights
and fundamental freedoms" by attorney Lennox S. Hinds, on behalf of
the National Conference of Black Lawyers, the National Alliance
against Racist and Political Repression and the Commission for Racial
Justice of the United Church of Christ.
These organizations invited an international delegation of jurists
and lawyers to review the allegations of the petition, the
documentation of those allegations, and the relevancy of the United
Nations resolutions. Personal interviews with named prisoners were
arranged, and observations were made on conditions complained of, so
that the independent observers could determine if it concerned a
consistent pattern of gross and reliably attested violations of human
rights and fundamental freedoms, including policies of racial
discrimination.
The report contains information on the mission and its findings, with
attention to criteria for inquiring, categories of prisoners, abuse of
criminal processes, sentencing, prison conditions, appellate remedies,
native Americans and the so-called Olympic prison. With conclusions
after each chapter.

ANTIGUA AND BARBUDA / UNITED KINGDOM

CATALOGUE SIGNATURE: 0000/0966/-0=780000
TITLE: Case no. 857: complaint presented by the Antigua Workers' Union
against the government of the United Kingdom / Antigua
AUTHOR: International Labour Office - ILO - Committee on Freedom of
Association
TITLE OF GENERIC ITEM: Official Bulletin: reports of the Governing Body
Committee on Freedom of Association (187th, 188th, 189th)
EDITION: vol. LXI, series B no. 3
PLACE OF PUBLICATION: Geneva
PUBLISHER: International Labour Office - ILO (D)
DATE OF PUBLICATION: 780000
NUMBER OF PAGES: p. 41-64
LANGUAGE: ENG
INDEX: association (freedom of) / trade unions / legislation /
fact-finding missions
GEOGRAPHICAL INDEX: Antigua and Barbuda / United Kingdom
GEOGRAPHICAL CODE: 6112 / 8251
FREE TEXT: The complaint of the Antigua Workers Union AWU was contained
in a communication dated 1 July 1976; additional information was
provided by the complainant and the government. The Director-General
appointed William R. Simpson to carry out a mission in Antigua from 25
July to 2 August 1978.
The report of the Committee contains a summary of the complaints and
reports of the Committee; background information on the country and the
trade union situation; the general situation; allegations relating to:
dismissals in the civil service and other public bodies, and the hotel
industry; the Labour Commissioner and the processing of labour disputes;
the Antigua Labour Code (Amendment) Act of 1976; the Industrial Court;
the Public Order Act of 1972. With conclusions and recommendations.

ARGENTINA / CHILE

CATALOGUE SIGNATURE: 0000/0035/-3=810000
TITLE: Rapport de mission en Argentine et au Chili du 13 au 18/7/1981
AUTHOR: Lévy, Jean-Paul
PLACE OF PUBLICATION: Paris
PUBLISHER: Fédération Internationale des Droits de l'Homme - FIDH (D)
DATE OF PUBLICATION: 810000
NUMBER OF PAGES: 10 p.
LANGUAGE: FRE
INDEX: disappearances / fact-finding missions
GEOGRAPHICAL INDEX: Argentina / Chile
GEOGRAPHICAL CODE: 6414 / 6424
FREE TEXT: The purpose of the mission was to investigate the case of
two disappeared Chileans. They were condemned as political criminals
and banned from their country, and attempted to return illegally to
Chile. They were arrested while still in Argentina. The delegate
visited Argentina and Chile. He concludes that the disappeared probably
have been transferred to the Chilean government, which is violating
fundamental human rights.

333

ARGENTINA / URUGUAY

CATALOGUE SIGNATURE: 0000/0138/-3=760000
TITLE: La répression en Argentine et plus particulièrement la
situation des réfugiés uruguayens dans ce pays
AUTHOR: Albala, Nuri
PLACE OF PUBLICATION: Brussels
PUBLISHER: Association Internationale des Juristes Démocrates - IADL (D)
DATE OF PUBLICATION: 760000
NUMBER OF PAGES: 7 p.
LANGUAGE: FRE
INDEX: refugees / fact-finding missions
GEOGRAPHICAL INDEX: Argentina / Uruguay
GEOGRAPHICAL CODE: 6414 / 6459
FREE TEXT: The aim of the mission in June 1976 was to investigate the
situation of political refugees from Uruguay. The delegate also
received information on the transformation of the nature of repression
in Argentina. During his stay, the former president of Bolivia, general
Torres, was murdered. The author tried to get information on five
disappeared persons. The authorities involved refused to receive him.
He provides general information on the situation of Uruguayan refugees,
on laws by which certain organizations are forbidden, and on human
rights violations in general. Annex: declaration of the Argentine
League for Human Rights on political detainees.

CATALOGUE SIGNATURE: 6003/2268/-3=761100
TITLE: One gigantic prison: the report of the fact-finding mission to
Chile, Argentina and Uruguay
AUTHOR: Brewin, Andrew; Duclos, Louis; MacDonald, David (... et al)
EDITION: repr.
PLACE OF PUBLICATION: Toronto
PUBLISHER: Inter-Church Committee on Chile - ICCC
DISTRIBUTOR: Inter-Church Committee on Human Rights in Latin America -
ICCHRLA
DATE OF PUBLICATION: 761100
NUMBER OF PAGES: 84 p.
LANGUAGE: ENG
INDEX: refugees / fact-finding missions
GEOGRAPHICAL INDEX: Argentina / Uruguay
GEOGRAPHICAL CODE: 6414 / 6459
FREE TEXT: Three members of the Canadian Parliament undertook a mission
from 30 September to 10 October 1976. The aims of the delegation were
to undertake an observation and evaluation of the situation of refugees
and the Canadian response to their needs, and to observe the general
situation of human rights in the countries visited. The mission was not
allowed to visit Chile.
The report contains the findings of the mission in Argentina and
Uruguay, a summary and statements made by the delegates during a press
conference in Ottawa.
It also contains a report by George Cram, a representative of the ICCC
who accompanied the members of Parliament. His report deals with the
advance work undertaken by the sending NGO in order to facilitate the
taking place of the actual mission, and the contacts established in the
countries visited.
The third section of the report contains documentation received by the
mission in Argentina and Uruguay. It concerns information on the
Permanent Assembly for Human Rights, the penitentiary jail in Cordoba,
personal testimonies and information on violence against church people.
With appendices: lists of Uruguayans tortured or disappeared, excerpts
from a United Nations report on Chile, statements, letters and
suggestions for action.

CATALOGUE SIGNATURE: 0000/0138/-3=780000
TITLE: Mission d'enquête en Argentine et en Uruguay: 10-20 mai 1978
AUTHOR: Vermeylen, Pierre ; Morchena Navarro, Julia ; Rijckmans,
Geneviève (...et al)
PLACE OF PUBLICATION: Brussels
PUBLISHER: Association Internationale des Juristes Démocrates - IADL (D)
DATE OF PUBLICATION: 780000
NUMBER OF PAGES: 15 p.
LANGUAGE: FRE
INDEX: civil and political rights / political prisoners /
fact-finding missions
GEOGRAPHICAL INDEX: Argentina / Uruguay
GEOGRAPHICAL CODE: 6414 / 6459
FREE TEXT: The report on the four member mission to Uruguay is
published in full; the report on the mission to Argentina is an
abstract. In Uruguay, the mission tried to get information on the
general situation of human rights. Meetings with officials and a
journalist could not take place. The background of the country and
the evolution of repression are described, with examples. The
situation of political prisoners is described more in detail. The
Church seems the only institution which has some possibilities to
protest.
Extract of the report on Argentine: attention is paid to detentions
and disappearances, habeas corpus and the attitude of the
government.

CATALOGUE SIGNATURE: 0000/0138/-0=851200
TITLE: Rapport d'organisation: voyage du secrétaire général en
Argentine et en Uruguay: 1-13 décembre 1985 = Informe de organizacion:
viaje del secretario general a Argentina y Uruguay: 1-13 de diciembre
de 1985
AUTHOR: (Bentoumi, Amar)
PLACE OF PUBLICATION: Brussels
PUBLISHER: Association Internationale des Juristes Démocrates - IADL (D)
DATE OF PUBLICATION: 851200
NUMBER OF PAGES: 12 p.
LANGUAGE: FRE / SPA
INDEX: judicial systems / fact-finding missions
GEOGRAPHICAL INDEX: Argentina / Uruguay
GEOGRAPHICAL CODE: 6414 / 6459
FREE TEXT: The Secretary General of the IADL visited Argentina and
Uruguay in December 1985. His report contains a description of his
visits, participation in meetings and contacts established with lawyers
and representatives of nongovernmental organizations, mainly lawyers
associations, in these countries and in Brazil. During the meetings,
issues relating to the situation of human rights and the rule of law
were discussed.

CANADA / ALGERIA

CATALOGUE SIGNATURE: 0000/0035/-0=780000
TITLE: Situation de Dalila Maschino
AUTHOR: Zavrian, Michel
PLACE OF PUBLICATION: Paris
PUBLISHER: Fédération Internationale des Droits de l'Homme - FIDH (D)
DATE OF PUBLICATION: 780000
NUMBER OF PAGES: 9 p.
LANGUAGE: FRE
INDEX: disappearances / international law / fact-finding missions
GEOGRAPHICAL INDEX: Canada / Algeria
GEOGRAPHICAL CODE: 6322 / 5311
FREE TEXT: After being abducted in Montreal, Dalila Maschino was
transported to Alger, where she was kidnapped by her brother. The
report contains background information on this case collected by
the author, who states that Dalila Maschino was brought to Algeria
against her will.

CARIBBEAN COUNTRIES / GRENADA

CATALOGUE SIGNATURE: 0000/1192/-0=840100
TITLE: Grenada and the Eastern Caribbean: a report of a delegation
visit between December 27, 1983 and January 9, 1984
AUTHOR: Brown, J. Kaisha ; Colom, Bartolomé ; Colon, Awilda (et al...)
PLACE OF PUBLICATION: Philadelphia
PUBLISHER: American Friends Service Committee - AFSC - Latin America
Programme (D)
DATE OF PUBLICATION: 840100
NUMBER OF PAGES: 33 p.
LANGUAGE: ENG
INDEX: human rights and foreign policy / fact-finding missions
GEOGRAPHICAL INDEX: Caribbean countries / Grenada
GEOGRAPHICAL CODE: 6100 / 6134
FREE TEXT: The mission took place after the US-led invasion of Grenada.
The aims of the five member delegation to Grenada and neighbouring
islands (Barbados, Dominica, Trinidad and Puerto Rico) were to assess
the needs for humanitarian aid; to investigate conditions and treatment
of military and political detainees, to look broadly at the US role in
what had happened and the impact on Grenada, and to examine the impact
on the rest of the Caribbean. The group was able to interview more than
80 people, including heads of state, government officials, ordinary
citizens, church, trade unions, business professionals, and military
people.
With conclusions, recommendations for the policy of the United States
and a description of findings with regard to the overthrow of Maurice
Bishop in October 1983, perceptions of the necessity and legality of
the invasion, alternatives to invasion, Grenada and the foreseeable
future (the war; the government; civil liberties; the economy;
political parties, trade unions and churches), the role of the United
States in Grenada, the impact of the invasion on Grenada and the
region.

CENTRAL AMERICA

CATALOGUE SIGNATURE: 0000/1295/-0=820500
TITLE: Central America 1982: report of two factfinding missions
sponsored by the Unitarian Universalist Service Committee
AUTHOR: McAward, John
PLACE OF PUBLICATION: Boston
PUBLISHER: Unitarian Universalist Service Committee - UUSC (D)
DATE OF PUBLICATION: 820500
NUMBER OF PAGES: 7 p.
LANGUAGE: ENG
INDEX: human rights and foreign policy / democracy / development /
fact-finding missions
GEOGRAPHICAL INDEX: Central America
GEOGRAPHICAL CODE: 6200
FREE TEXT: Reports of two fact-finding missions with members of
Congress which took place in August 1981 and February 1982. The
reports contain descriptions of the findings with regards to the
general situation of human rights. The 1981 mission visited Mexico,
Guatemala, El Salvador, Honduras, Nicaragua and Costa Rica. The
second mission went to El Salvador and Nicaragua.
The general conclusion on the missions drawn by the UUSC is that the
socio-economic conditions in El Salvador, Guatemala and Honduras are
the cause of the region's problems. Only social and economic reforms
will alleviate the conflict; military solutions will bring neither
peace nor justice. With recommendations.

CATALOGUE SIGNATURE: 0000/2168/-3=840600
TITLE: HOM report Central America: report on a visit of a Dutch
delegation to Central America and the USA: February 11-25, 1984 =
HOM rapport Midden-Amerika: naar aanleiding van het bezoek van een
Nederlandse delegatie aan Midden-Amerika en de VS van 11 tot 25
februari 1984
AUTHOR: Veenen, Pieter van ; Thoolen, Hans
PLACE OF PUBLICATION: Utrecht
PUBLISHER: Humanistic Committee on Human Rights - HOM (D)
DATE OF PUBLICATION: 840600
NUMBER OF PAGES: 80 p. in v.p.
LANGUAGE: ENG / DUT
STATISTICAL INFORMATION: Y
INDEX: human rights and foreign policy / political and civil rights /
social and economic rights / fact-finding missions
GEOGRAPHICAL INDEX: Central America
GEOGRAPHICAL CODE: 6200
FREE TEXT: The report is based on a mission of three members of
parliament and two human rights specialists to Central America in
February 1984. The report is divided into separate chapters on
Nicaragua, Honduras, and El Salvador. In each chapter, attention is
paid to political and civil rights, social and economic rights, the
political situation, the role of the United States, conclusions and
recommendations.
With annexes: list of people with whom the delegation had contacts;
letter of the Minister of Interior Affairs of Nicaragua on political
prisoners; itinerary.

CATALOGUE SIGNATURE: 0000/1295/-0=840911
TITLE: Out of step, out of line: U.S. military policy in Central
America
AUTHOR: King, Edward L.
PLACE OF PUBLICATION: Boston
PUBLISHER: Unitarian Universalist Service Committee - UUSC (D)
DATE OF PUBLICATION: 840911
NUMBER OF PAGES: 53 p. in v.p.
LANGUAGE: ENG
INDEX: military / human rights and foreign policy /
fact-finding missions
GEOGRAPHICAL INDEX: Central America
GEOGRAPHICAL CODE: 6200
FREE TEXT: The report is based on fact-finding missions to different
countries and deals with the situation of the military forces in El
Salvador, Nicaragua, Honduras and Costa Rica.
With executive summary, conclusions and description of findings on
the different countries based on many contacts with the military.
The author concludes that the United States military policy with
regard to these countries is parochial and does not adequately serve
the needs, desires or capabilities of local military forces. The US
doctrine of counterinsurgency is not working. US military advisors
seem more interested in superimposing US military organization,
doctrine and tactics upon local forces than working with them to
exploit their traditional infantry strengths and correct their
organizational weaknesses. US military advisors have misread and
misunderstood the true internal positions of the Salvadoran and
Honduran armed forces. US military pressure against Nicaragua is
counterproductive because it has not been followed up with timely
diplomatic efforts.

CATALOGUE SIGNATURE: 0000/0018/-0=850800
TITLE: Pastoral letter to the people of the churches of Central
America
AUTHOR: Buhrig, Marga ; Paulos mar Gregorios ; Thompson, William P.
(...et al)
PLACE OF PUBLICATION: Buenos Aires
PUBLISHER: World Council of Churches - WCC - Central Committee (D)
DATE OF PUBLICATION: 850800
NUMBER OF PAGES: 4 p.
DOCUMENT SYMBOL: Document No.2.10
LANGUAGE: ENG
INDEX: church and state / fact-finding missions
GEOGRAPHICAL INDEX: Central America
GEOGRAPHICAL CODE: 6200
FREE TEXT: A four member delegation of the WCC visited Costa Rica,
El Salvador, Honduras and Nicaragua in July 1985. The report of the
mission contains findings with regard to the general situation in
these countries, and the position of the church.

CATALOGUE SIGNATURE: 0000/2168/-3=860000
TITLE: Politiek en mensenrechten in Midden-Amerika: rapportage van
een HOM-delegatie naar Nicaragua, Honduras, El Salvador en de
Verenigde Staten
AUTHOR: Veenen, Pieter van (ed.)
PLACE OF PUBLICATION: Amsterdam ; Utrecht
PUBLISHER: Uitgeverij Jan Mets ; Humanistisch Overleg Mensenrechten -
HOM (D)
DATE OF PUBLICATION: 860000
NUMBER OF PAGES: 110 p.
ISBN: 90 70509 57 1
LANGUAGE: DUT
STATISTICAL INFORMATION: Y
BIBLIOGRAPHIES: Y
INDEX: civil and political rights / social and economic rights /
human rights and foreign policy / fact-finding missions
GEOGRAPHICAL INDEX: Central America
GEOGRAPHICAL CODE: 6200
FREE TEXT: From 1 to 14 March 1986, a three member delegation of the
HOM (Humanistic Committee on Human Rights), consisting of Relus ter
Beek, Ab Eikenaar and Pieter van Veenen, visited Central America and
the United States. Their report provides a balance of regional
developments with regard to the political situation and human rights.
The delegation paid attention to both civil and political rights and
to social and economic rights.
The report contains sections on Nicaragua, Honduras and El Salvador.
Each section consists of impressions; findings on the situation of
both categories of human rights and the role of the United States,
conclusions and recommendations.
With appendices: investigation into the violent death of four dutch
journalists in 1982; list of contacts of the delegation.

CENTRAL AMERICA / CARIBBEAN COUNTRIES

CATALOGUE SIGNATURE: 0000/1192/-0=801200
TITLE: Countries in crisis: report of an AFSC study tour to Central
America and the Caribbean: Nov./Dec. 1980
PLACE OF PUBLICATION: Philadelphia
PUBLISHER: American Friends Service Committee - AFSC (D)
DATE OF PUBLICATION: 801200
NUMBER OF PAGES: 19 p.
LANGUAGE: ENG
INDEX: human rights and foreign policy / fact-finding missions
GEOGRAPHICAL INDEX: Central America / Caribbean countries
GEOGRAPHICAL CODE: 6200 / 6100
FREE TEXT: The countries visited by the delegation of seventeen
persons were Guatemala, El Salvador, Nicaragua, Costa Rica, Panama,
Jamaica, Haiti (briefly), the Dominican Republic and Puerto Rico.
Contacts were made with local government authorities, United States
diplomats, Protestant and Catholic religious workers including many
priests and nuns, and leaders of peasant, labour union and political
movements, students and faculty people, journalists and others.
The aims of the mission were to deepen AFSC understanding of the
nature and causes of current crisis in the Caribbean and Central
America, to study the impact of US policy and private sector
interests in the region, and to provide a basis for focused public
education and advocacy work.
The report contains general observations and summaries of the
situation in the countries visited.

CATALOGUE SIGNATURE: 0000/0018/-0=810700
TITLE: Travel report: Central America and Caribbean: 23 May - 15 June,
1981
AUTHOR: Weingaertner, Erich
TITLE OF GENERIC UNIT: Commisioners only
EDITION: no. 8; special issue
PLACE OF PUBLICATION: Geneva
PUBLISHER: Commission of the Churches on International Affairs of the
World Council of Churches - CCIA / WCC (D)
DATE OF PUBLICATION: 810700
NUMBER OF PAGES: 39 p.
LANGUAGE: ENG
INDEX: church and state / fact-finding missions
GEOGRAPHICAL INDEX: Central America / Caribbean countries
GEOGRAPHICAL CODE: 6200 / 6100
FREE TEXT: Charles Harper and Erich Weingaertner travelled to Guyana,
Puerto Rico, Haiti, Costa Rica, Nicaragua, Mexico and Cuba. The travel
was meant to investigate the latest analyses of the church partners of
the WCC, as well as secular experts and people in political
responsibility. Their findings are presented as a contribution to the
ongoing concern of the ecumenical fellowship of churches for this
critical area.
The report starts with a general analysis of geo-political developments,
especially the growing influence of the United States in the region.
In the country reports, attention is paid to the political and economic
situation of the countries visited, international attention to the
country and the role and position of the churches.
With recommendations and appendices.

CENTRAL AMERICA / EL SALVADOR

CATALOGUE SIGNATURE: 0000/1295/-0=810700
TITLE: Central America 1981: El Salvador, Guatemala, Nicaragua,
Honduras, Costa Rica: report of a fact-finding mission with analyses
and recommendations...
AUTHOR: Edgar, Robert ; Mikulski, Barbara ; Studds, Gerry (...et al)
PLACE OF PUBLICATION: Boston
PUBLISHER: Unitarian Universalist Service Committee - UUSC (D)
DATE OF PUBLICATION: 810700
NUMBER OF PAGES: 27 p.
LANGUAGE: ENG
INDEX: human rights and foreign policy / fact-finding missions
GEOGRAPHICAL INDEX: Central America / El Salvador
GEOGRAPHICAL CODE: 6200 / 6231
FREE TEXT: Report of a fact-finding mission undertaken in January 1981,
in which three Members of Congress participated. The report contains a
summary of findings and recommendations, and background information on
developments in El Salvador (military rule, assassinations, popular
organizations, the political situation, the role of the church, the
coup of 1979, repression and reform, American targets, the character of
the regime, the core of the problems), Guatemala, Honduras, Nicaragua
and Costa Rica.

CATALOGUE SIGNATURE: 8000/2251/3=840402
TITLE: Verslag namens de Politieke Commissie over de situatie in Midden
Amerika = Report drawn up on behalf of the Political Affairs Committee
on the situation in Central America
AUTHOR: Lenz, M.
PLACE OF PUBLICATION: (Brussels)
PUBLISHER: European Parliament - EP (D)
DATE OF PUBLICATION: 840402
NUMBER OF PAGES: 94 p.
SERIES TITLE: Zittingsdocumenten = Working Documents
DOCUMENT SYMBOL: 1-56/84/B; PE 89/121/def./B
LANGUAGE: DUT / ENG
INDEX: human rights and foreign policy / development cooperation /
peace / fact-finding missions
GEOGRAPHICAL INDEX: Central America / El Salvador
GEOGRAPHICAL CODE: 6200 / 6231
FREE TEXT: The report contains a motion for a resolution, and an
explanatory statement. The rapporteur visited Venezuela, El Salvador
and Mexico from 26 October to 4 November 1982 to obtain information
on facts, opinions and perspectives with regard to the situation in
El Salvador. A delegation of the European Parliament visited the
governments of Nicaragua, Honduras, Costa Rica and El Salvador.
The report deals with peaceful and political solutions for the
existings tensions and conflicts, the situation of human rights,
humanitarian aid, the development of pluralistic and democratic
societies through free elections, and the role of the European
Communities in Central America with regard to a more intensive
economic and development cooperation.
With: introduction; the role of El Salvador in the conflict; new
conflicts (in Cuba, Nicaragua, Costa Rica, Honduras, Guatemala);
the role of the United States; the Contadora peace initiative; the
European Communities and Central America; final remark.
With appendices: seventeen motions for a resolution on aspects of
the situation in Central America.

CENTRAL AMERICA / HONDURAS

CATALOGUE SIGNATURE: 6003/1226/-0=820921
TITLE: Honduras trip report...
AUTHOR: Barbieri, Leyda
PLACE OF PUBLICATION: (Washington DC)
PUBLISHER: Washington Office on Latin America - WOLA (D)
DATE OF PUBLICATION: 820921
NUMBER OF PAGES: 5 p.
LANGUAGE: ENG
INDEX: military / refugees / fact-finding missions
GEOGRAPHICAL INDEX: Central America / Honduras
GEOGRAPHICAL CODE: 6200 / 6239
FREE TEXT: The author traveled to Honduras to visit refugee camps,
and had contacts with Honduran government officials, representatives of
the four major political parties, national and international refugee
relief workers, personnel of the embassy of the United States, and
nongovernmental organizations. Her report deals with the presence of
the military in the Honduran democracy, the situation of human rights,
refugees from El Salvador, Guatemala and Nicaragua and relations with
Nicaragua.
Conclusion: "After ten months of democratic rule in Honduras, the
military is stronger, the economy is weaker and the threat of unwanted
war is greater than ever."

CATALOGUE SIGNATURE: 6003/2268/-0=851000
TITLE: Report: Canadian church task force on Salvadorean and indigenous
Nicaraguan refugees in Honduras: August 29th to September 5th 1985
AUTHOR: Eek, Arie Van; Fugere, Robert; Ryan, Tim (...et al)
PLACE OF PUBLICATION: Toronto
PUBLISHER: Inter-Church Committee for Refugees - ICCR (D);
Inter-Church Committee on Human Rights in Latin America - ICCHRLA (D)
DATE OF PUBLICATION: 851000
NUMBER OF PAGES: 38 p. in v.p.
LANGUAGE: ENG
INDEX: refugees / fact-finding missions
GEOGRAPHICAL INDEX: Central America / Honduras
GEOGRAPHICAL CODE: 6200 / 6239
FREE TEXT: The Canadian church task force of five delegates was sent to
Honduras in response to reports received from church partners in the
late Spring of 1985 on the deteriorating situation of Salvadoran and
Nicaraguan refugees in Honduras. The report contains an itinerary of
the mission; findings with regard to the Miskitu and Sumo refugees in
the Honduran Moskitia; findings with regard to the Salvadorean refugees
in the Mesa Grande camp in Colomoncagua; interviews held in Tegucigalpa;
conclusions and recommendations.
With appendices: maps and photographs, testimonies on a military attack
and testimonies of new arrivals.

COLOMBIA / USA

CATALOGUE SIGNATURE: 0000/2955/-3=860100
TITLE: The Central-Americanization of Colombia?: human rights and the
peace process
AUTHOR: Fellner, Jamie ; Brown, Cynthia (ed.)
PLACE OF PUBLICATION: New York
PUBLISHER: Americas Watch - AW (D)
DATE OF PUBLICATION: 860100
NUMBER OF PAGES: 149 p. in v.p.
LANGUAGE: ENG
INDEX: peace / democracy / fact-finding missions
GEOGRAPHICAL INDEX: Colombia / USA
GEOGRAPHICAL CODE: 6425 / 6357
FREE TEXT: The information in this report has been obtained from
various sources, including interviews conducted in Colombia during
two visits in August and December 1985. The authors examine the peace
process, the forces that have undermined it, and its relationship
to human rights violations in Colombia during the past three years.
The report is divided into six parts:
I) Introduction;
II) Colombia: social and political context, with attention to: social
conditions; the political system; the military; the guerrillas;
III) The peace process, with attention to: the election of President
Belisario Betancur; amnesty; negotiations with the guerrillas;
acuerdos de paz; post-accord politics and development; information
and disinformation; an overview of the military's role in the peace
process; national dialogue; beyond a cease-fire: political, social
and economic reforms; crime; restructuring the peace process;
IV) Human rights and the peace process: with attention to: major
initiatives and events affecting human rights; reports by Amnesty
International; militarization; paramilitary activity; torture;
extrajudicial executions; disappearances; military jurisdiction over
civilians; military justice; human rights violations by guerrillas;
V) The role of the United States;
VI) Epilogue.

DOMINICAN REPUBLIC / HAITI

CATALOGUE SIGNATURE: 0000/1022/-0=820000
TITLE: Haitian migrant labour in the Dominican Republic
PLACE OF PUBLICATION: London
PUBLISHER: Anti-Slavery Society for the Protection of Human Rights -
ASSPHR (D)
DATE OF PUBLICATION: 820000
NUMBER OF PAGES: 44 p.
LANGUAGE: ENG
BIBLIOGRAPHIES: Y
INDEX: migration / labour / slavery / fact-finding missions
GEOGRAPHICAL INDEX: Dominican Republic / Haiti
GEOGRAPHICAL CODE: 6129 / 6138
FREE TEXT: Between April and June 1982 a representative of the Anti-
Slavery Society paid two visits to the Dominican Republic and Haiti.
The purpose of these visits was to investigate and report upon
innumerable reports which had reached the ASSPHR in recent years
concerning allegations of slavery or slavery-like conditions to which
Haitian migrant workers have been subjected in the Dominican Republic,
above all in the Dominican sugar industry. The representative visited
sugar mills and plantations and rural living quarters where the vast
majority of the inhabitants during the harvest season are Haitian
migrant workers. He also talked with Dominican and Haitian trade
unionists, administrators, field managers, and other arrangement
personnel; with Dominican and Haitian labour inspectors, and with
health and social security personnel. He also spoke with high-level
officials and other, nongovernmental sources of information. In the
report, attention is paid to the nature of the allegations of slavery,
the evolution of the Dominican sugar industry (historical survey on
the structure of ownership and production; the role of the Haitian
workers) and the working and living conditions of the Haitian migrants
in the period 1979-1982 (recruitment, wages and remuneration, hours of
work, living conditions, health and social security, labour inspection,
freedom of organization and trade union rights). With conclusions and
recommendations.

CATALOGUE SIGNATURE: 0000/0966/-3=830000
TITLE: Report of the Commission of Enquiry appointed under article 26
of the Constitution of the International Labour Organisation to examine
the observance of certain international labour Conventions by the
Dominican Republic and Haiti with respect to the employment of Haitian
workers on the sugar plantations in the Dominican Republic
AUTHOR: International Labour Office - ILO
PLACE OF PUBLICATION: Geneva
PUBLISHER: International Labour Office - ILO (D)
DATE OF PUBLICATION: 830000
NUMBER OF PAGES: 176 p. in v.p.
LANGUAGE: ENG
INDEX: forced labour / fact-finding missions
GEOGRAPHICAL INDEX: Dominican Republic / Haiti
GEOGRAPHICAL CODE: 6129 / 6138
FREE TEXT: On 23 June 1981, the ILO received complaints of violations
of the Conventions on Forced Labour, Freedom of Association and
Protection of the Right to Organise and Collective Bargaining by the
governments of the Dominican Republic and Haiti; the complaints were
investigated by a Commission of Enquiry.
The report contains chapters on: the filing of the complaints and
establishment of the Commission; the procedure followed by the
Commission (sessions in Geneva and visits to the countries concerned
in January 1983); an analysis of relevant legislation; the structure
of the sugar industry in the Dominican Republic and the construction
of its labour force; the agreements for recruitment of workers in
Haiti for employment in the sugar harvest in the Dominican Republic;
analysis of the allegations, replies, evidence and information gathered
on the spot; findings and recommendations.
With appendices: texts of complaints and of comments by the governments
concerned, texts of the substantive provisions of the relevant
international labour Conventions, text of the contract between the
State Sugar Board of the Dominican Republic and the government of Haiti
(1982-1983 and 1983-1984).

EL SALVADOR / GUATEMALA

CATALOGUE SIGNATURE: 0000/0028/-0=801000
TITLE: Compte rendu de la délégation oecuménique européenne au
Guatemala et au Salvador: 3-10 septembre 1980
AUTHOR: Toulat, Pierre ; Metzger, Ludwig ; Cochet, Pierre (...et al)
PLACE OF PUBLICATION: Paris
PUBLISHER: Commission Française Justice et Pax - CFJP (D) ; Commission
Sociale, Economique et Internationale de la Fédération protestante de
France (D)
DATE OF PUBLICATION: 801000
NUMBER OF PAGES: 12 p.
LANGUAGE: FRE
INDEX: church and state / fact-finding missions
GEOGRAPHICAL INDEX: El Salvador / Guatemala
GEOGRAPHICAL CODE: 6231 / 6236
FREE TEXT: The aim of the mission was to express the sympathy and
fraternal solidarity to the Church which in Guatemala and El Salvador
is victim of persecution because of its actions in favour of the
people, and to publish the testimonies and information received. The
report contains a description of the working methods and findings of
the misssion; special attention is paid to the situation of the Church
in Guatemala.

EL SALVADOR / HONDURAS

CATALOGUE SIGNATURE: 0000/0491/-3=810000
TITLE: Honduras: Salvadorean refugees
AUTHOR: Novello, Gianni ; Zöller, Adrien-Claude ; Bettazzi, Luigi
(...et al)
PLACE OF PUBLICATION: Antwerpen
PUBLISHER: Pax Christi International - PAXCI (D) ; OMEGA Books (D)
DATE OF PUBLICATION: 810000
NUMBER OF PAGES: 64 p.
SERIES TITLE: Pax Christi International Human Rights Reports
VOLUME: no. 1
ISBN: 90 70316 05 6
LANGUAGE: ENG
INDEX: refugees / fact-finding missions
GEOGRAPHICAL INDEX: El Salvador / Honduras
GEOGRAPHICAL CODE: 6231 / 6239
FREE TEXT: The aims of the July 1981 mission were to gather information
about the situation of the Salvadorean refugees in Honduras, to check
allegations about their ill-treatment, and to formulate recommendations
concerning initiatives to be undertaken by solidarity organizations, in
order to contribute to the improvement of the situation of these
refugees. The delegation concentrated its attention on the border area
with El Salvador. Several refugee camps were visited. There is a
coordination of military activities between Honduras and El Salvador.
With attention to the background of the country. With conclusions and
recommendations.

CATALOGUE SIGNATURE: 6239/-0=810831
TITLE: Statement by representatives of U.S. religious community
regarding visit to and findings at Salvadorean refugee camp, La Virtud,
Honduras
AUTHOR: McDonough Fitzpatrick, Ruth ; Shaw, Patty
PLACE OF PUBLICATION: Washington DC ; Detroit
PUBLISHER: Religious Task Force on El Salvador (D) ; Michigan
Inter-Church Committee on Central American Human Rights - MICAH (D)
DATE OF PUBLICATION: 810831
NUMBER OF PAGES: 7 p.
LANGUAGE: ENG
INDEX: refugees / armed conflict / fact-finding missions
GEOGRAPHICAL INDEX: El Salvador / Honduras
GEOGRAPHICAL CODE: 6231 / 6239
FREE TEXT: Report of a visit to the refugee camp La Virtud, where there
are 3.000 Salvadoran peasant refugees, mainly women and children.
Attention is paid to the situation of the refugees, the work of relief
organizations and military activities of Salvadoran and Honduran troups
in the region.

CATALOGUE SIGNATURE: 6231/0391/-0=811000
TITLE: Report on a visit from 30 September to 5 October 1981 to
Salvadorean refugee camps in Honduras by a representative of the
El Salvador Committee for Human Rights
AUTHOR: El Salvador Committee for Human Rights - ESCHR
PLACE OF PUBLICATION: London
PUBLISHER: El Salvador Committee for Human Rights - ESCHR (D)
DATE OF PUBLICATION: 811000
NUMBER OF PAGES: 15 p.
LANGUAGE: ENG
INDEX: refugees / fact-finding missions
GEOGRAPHICAL INDEX: El Salvador / Honduras
GEOGRAPHICAL CODE: 6231 / 6239
FREE TEXT: Fact-finding report on the situation of refugees from El
Salvador in camps in the Lempira and Intibuca departments in Honduras,
with attention to origins of the refugees, organizations assisting
them, living conditions in the camps, the health situation, harassment
of refugees and agency personnel by the Honduran army and security
forces, and relocation. With excerpts from interviews with refugees.

CATALOGUE SIGNATURE: 6239/-0=811000
TITLE: Refugees and human rights in Honduras: report of a U.S.
ecumenical delegation to Honduras: October 17-23, 1981
AUTHOR: Wipfler, William L. ; Gold, Eva ; Wheaton, Phillip E.
PLACE OF PUBLICATION: (Washington DC)
PUBLISHER: (US Committee in Solidarity with the People of El
Salvador - CISPES) (D)
DATE OF PUBLICATION: 811000
NUMBER OF PAGES: 9 p.
LANGUAGE: ENG
INDEX: refugees / disappearances / fact-finding missions
GEOGRAPHICAL INDEX: El Salvador / Honduras
GEOGRAPHICAL CODE: 6231 / 6239
FREE TEXT: The main purpose of the mission was to investigate the human
rights conditions of Salvadoran refugees who have fled to Honduras, and
particularly to seek information regarding 11 Salvadorans who were
legally resident in Honduras and have disappeared. In the report,
attention is paid to the political and economic background, the impact
of the regional crisis on Honduras, refugee conditions and harassment,
relocation of the refugees and the situation in the present camps,
political prisoners and the disappeared. With conclusions.

CATALOGUE SIGNATURE: 0000/0084/-0=820100
TITLE: Rapport de la mission effectuée au Honduras dans les camps de
réfugiés Salvadoriens situés dans la zone frontalière: 10-21
décembre 1981
AUTHOR: Camus, Geneviève
PLACE OF PUBLICATION: Geneva
PUBLISHER: Refugee Service ; Commission on Inter-Church Aid, Refugee
and World Service ; World Council of Churches - WCC (D)
DATE OF PUBLICATION: 820100
NUMBER OF PAGES: 14 p.
LANGUAGE: ENG
INDEX: refugees / fact-finding missions
GEOGRAPHICAL INDEX: El Salvador / Honduras
GEOGRAPHICAL CODE: 6231 / 6239
FREE TEXT: An international delegation was witness to an attack on a
refugee camp by the Salvadoran army. In order to witness and help
preventing such actions, an international commission of observers is
installed in the border zone. Attention is paid to the background of
the countries involved, and the role of the U.S. foreign policy in the
conflict. The situation of the refugees is described: poverty, terror
and fear; the work of aid agencies. With conclusions and
recommendations.

CATALOGUE SIGNATURE: 6239/-0=830200
TITLE: Des réfugiés en otage: les réfugiés salvadoriens au Honduras:
rapport de la délégation québécoise de solidarité internationale du
7 au 14 février 1983
AUTHOR: Gagné, Louise ; Gervais, Lizette ; Valois, Charles
PLACE OF PUBLICATION: (Quebec)
PUBLISHER: Société Québécoise de Solidarité Internationale (D)
DATE OF PUBLICATION: 830200
NUMBER OF PAGES: 23 p.
LANGUAGE: FRE
INDEX: refugees / fact-finding missions
GEOGRAPHICAL INDEX: El Salvador / Honduras
GEOGRAPHICAL CODE: 6231 / 6239
FREE TEXT: The aim of the mission was to investigate how the situation
of the Salvadoran refugees in Honduras was according to their own
opinion. In the refugee camps, the delegation also met representatives
of local and international humanitarian organizations working in this
field, as well as political authorities of the country. The report
provides information on the political situation in Honduras in the
context of Central America, the situation of the refugees, the attitude
of the population of Honduras. Background information is provided on
the origins of the refugees, the life in the camps Mesa Grande and
Colomoncagua, and the two main problems: the security of the refugees
and their deplacement. With recommendations.

CATALOGUE SIGNATURE: 0000/1582/-3=850100
TITLE: Honduras: a crisis on the border: a report on Salvadoran
refugees in Honduras
AUTHOR: Guest, Iain ; Orentlicher, Diane
PLACE OF PUBLICATION: New York ; Washington DC
PUBLISHER: Lawyers Committee for International Human Rights - LCIHR (D)
DATE OF PUBLICATION: 850100
NUMBER OF PAGES: 120 p. in v.p.
LANGUAGE: ENG
STATISTICAL INFORMATION: Y
INDEX: refugees / fact-finding missions
GEOGRAPHICAL INDEX: El Salvador / Honduras
GEOGRAPHICAL CODE: 6231 / 6239
FREE TEXT: The report is based on a visit to Honduras in June 1984. The
two delegates visited camps for Salvadoran refugees at Colomoncagua,
Buenos Aires, and Mesa Grande. The report is divided into the following
parts: I) Introduction and conclusions; II) Overview: recent history
and current conditions of Salvadoran refugees; III) Repatriation; IV)
The UNHCR (United Nations High Commissioner for Refugees): a limited
mandate; V) Relocation; VI) The border incidents; VII) Lessons for the
future; VIII) Behind the scenes: the United States.
Conclusions are drawn with regard to repatriation, public denigration
of refugees, the role of the Honduran military and of the UNHCR.

CATALOGUE SIGNATURE: 6200/-0=850614
TITLE: CCIC observer mission to El Salvador and Honduras: April 21-
May 14, 1985
AUTHOR: Altrows, Lawrence
PLACE OF PUBLICATION: Ottawa
PUBLISHER: Canadian Council for International Co-operation - CCIC (D)
DATE OF PUBLICATION: 850614
NUMBER OF PAGES: 53 p. in v.p.
LANGUAGE: ENG / FRE
INDEX: refugees / development cooperation / fact-finding missions
GEOGRAPHICAL INDEX: El Salvador / Honduras
GEOGRAPHICAL CODE: 6231 / 6239
FREE TEXT: The aims of the mission were to study the question of
repatriation of Salvadoran refugees in Honduras in the light of
increasing pressures from the Honduran government and the situation of
human rights in El Salvador, and to look at the renewal of Canadian
bilateral aid to the government of El Salvador.
The report begins with recommendations. In the following section on
Honduras, attention is paid to repatriation, the perspectives of the
refugees, the position of the United States and recent events. With
comments by the delegation on repatriation, security problems and the
question of the dependency of the refugees.
The part on El Salvador presents an analysis of chances for a safe
voluntary repatriation. With an overview of meetings and interviews,
the question of human rights in a war situation, displaced people and
the approaches of the government of El Salvador and international
agencies. With conclusions.
With appendices: partial list of contacts established by the mission;
brief history of Salvadoran refugees in Honduras, a request for
voluntary repatriation, United States policy, minimum standards of
treatment of the refugees.

CATALOGUE SIGNATURE: 0000/0035/-3=860200
TITLE: Rapport de mission sur la situation des réfugiés salvadoriens
au Honduras
AUTHOR: Barth, Maurice ; Katz, Claude ; Hartikainen, Anto
PLACE OF PUBLICATION: Paris
PUBLISHER: Fédération Internationale des Droits de l'Homme - FIDH (D)
DATE OF PUBLICATION: 860200
NUMBER OF PAGES: 9 p.
LANGUAGE: FRE
INDEX: refugees / fact-finding missions
GEOGRAPHICAL INDEX: El Salvador / Honduras
GEOGRAPHICAL CODE: 6231 / 6239
FREE TEXT: The aim of the mission in February 1986 was to obtain
information on the situation of refugees from El Salvador in Honduras.
The specific reason for sending it were events on 29 August 1985 at
Colomoncagua, where three refugees were killed and 55 others wounded
after Honduran military forces entered the refugee camp. The mission
visited three refugee camps; in the report, attention is paid to the
security of refugees, their living conditions, the transfer of
refugees to the interior of Honduras and repatriation of refugees to
El Salvador. With conclusions.

EL SALVADOR / NICARAGUA

CATALOGUE SIGNATURE: 6200/-0=830300
TITLE: Report by a delegation from Swedish churches after a visit to
Nicaragua and El Salvador: 20-27 February 1983
AUTHOR: Albertsson, Eskil ; Elmquist, Karl-Axel ; Nylund, Bo
PLACE OF PUBLICATION: Älvsjö ; Uppsala
PUBLISHER: Free Church Council of Sweden (D) ; Church of Sweden
Mission (D)
DATE OF PUBLICATION: 830300
NUMBER OF PAGES: 17 p. in v.p.
LANGUAGE: ENG
INDEX: church and state / fact-finding missions
GEOGRAPHICAL INDEX: El Salvador / Nicaragua
GEOGRAPHICAL CODE: 6239 / 6245
FREE TEXT: The aim of the mission was to study the work of the churches
in relation to the political situation in the region. The report deals
mainly with questions of human rights and with the way the churches
work. In the section on Nicaragua, attention is also paid to the
situation of the Miskito Indians; the section on El Salvador contains
also a description of the economy. With conclusions and recommendations,
and descision made by the Free Church Council of Sweden on basis of the
report.

CATALOGUE SIGNATURE: 0000/1295/-0=830000
TITLE: American principles sacrificed: U.S. foreign policy in Central
America: report of a fact-finding mission to El Salvador and Nicaragua
sponsored by the Unitarian Universalist Service Committee
AUTHOR: Burkhalter, Holly J.
PLACE OF PUBLICATION: Boston
PUBLISHER: Unitarian Universalist Service Committee - UUSC (D)
DATE OF PUBLICATION: 830000
NUMBER OF PAGES: 16 p.
LANGUAGE: ENG
INDEX: human rights and foreign policy / fact-finding missions
GEOGRAPHICAL INDEX: El Salvador / Nicaragua
GEOGRAPHICAL CODE: 6231 / 6245
FREE TEXT: A delegation of distinguished New England and New York
residents took part in a nineteen-member fact-finding mission to El
Salvador, Costa Rica and Nicaragua in August 1983.
The first section of the report deals with El Salvador: political and
military situation, violations of human rights, the role of the
military and perspectives for a political solution. The second section
is on Nicaragua, and contains information on the position of the
revolutionary government, the counterrevolution and the indigenous
peoples, and violations of human rights. With recommendations.

EL SALVADOR / USA

CATALOGUE SIGNATURE: 0000/1582/-3=830201
TITLE: Justice in El Salvador: a case study: a report on the
investigation into the killing of four US churchwomen in El Salvador:
update
AUTHOR: Ford, William ; Greathead, R. Scott ; Posner, Michael
PLACE OF PUBLICATION: New York
PUBLISHER: Lawyers Committee for International Human Rights - LCIHR
(D)
DATE OF PUBLICATION: 830201
NUMBER OF PAGES: 54 p.
LANGUAGE: ENG
INDEX: homicide / political violence / fact-finding missions
GEOGRAPHICAL INDEX: El Salvador / USA
GEOGRAPHICAL CODE: 6231 / 6357
FREE TEXT: Four US churchwomen were murdered on 2 December 1980. In
the period since their death, the treatment of the case has become
symbolic of the brutalities that mark the daily life in El Salvador.
The report examines the current status of the examination and
prosecution of the individuals responsible for the murder. It is
concluded that there is mounting evidence that both the responsible
officials of El Salvador and United States officials are studiously
avoiding measures that might expose the truth.
With reconstruction of the crime in short; investigation of the
Salvadoran government; the question of higher involvement; the role
of the United States government. With summary and conclusions. With
appendices: declaration and letter of William P. Ford.

CATALOGUE SIGNATURE: 0000/1295/-0=830400
TITLE: El Salvador 1983: report of a fact-finding mission sponsored by the Unitarian Universalist Service Committee
AUTHOR: Woodward, Bill
PLACE OF PUBLICATION: Boston
PUBLISHER: Unitarian Universalist Service Committee - UUSC (D)
DATE OF PUBLICATION: 830400
NUMBER OF PAGES: (14 p.)
LANGUAGE: ENG
INDEX: political violence / human rights and foreign policy / fact-finding missions
GEOGRAPHICAL INDEX: El Salvador / USA
GEOGRAPHICAL CODE: 6231 / 6357
FREE TEXT: From March 18 to 23, a delegation from the United States House of Representatives, sponsored by the UUSC, travelled to Mexico and El Salvador to examine future US policy options in El Salvador at first hand. Representatives Oberstar, Jeffords and Richardson were accompanied by eight persons.
In the report, attention is paid to the military situation; the situation of human rights (massacre at Las Hojas, institutional problems and human rights, explanations of the military); the agrarian reform; the political left and the FDR-FMLN; elections, reconciliation, and the problem of power; the role of the United States. With recommendations.
The report represents the UUSC's own findings; however, the three members have approved and endorsed the conclusions drawn on the mission, and the report has been entered into the Congressional Record.

CATALOGUE SIGNATURE: 0000/1212/-0-840120
TITLE: Humanitarian assistance to El Salvador: health related issues
AUTHOR: Goldstein, Richard ; Gellhorn, Alfred ; Lawrence, Robert
PLACE OF PUBLICATION: New York
PUBLISHER: International League for Human Rights - ILHR ; Aesculapius
International Medicine (D)
DATE OF PUBLICATION: 840120
NUMBER OF PAGES: 17 p. in v.p.
LANGUAGE: ENG
INDEX: health / development cooperation / fact-finding missions
GEOGRAPHICAL INDEX: El Salvador / USA
GEOGRAPHICAL CODE: 6231 / 6357
FREE TEXT: Report based on four fact-finding missions conducted in the
period January 1983 - January 1984. In addition to substantiating the
gross violations of human rights by the government of El Salvador
against the health community, the missions found that health
professionals have been singled out for harassment, arrest and
"disappearance" for performing their professional duties, notably, for
providing medical assistance to all those who request it. Health and
health care have suffered since 1979 over and above that expected in a
poor, developing country. The report criticizes the financing by the
United States Agency for International Development USAID of programmes
by the Salvadoran Ministry of Health, especially the "Health Systems
Vitalization" project. It is stated that the program fails to address
the problems in their totality.

CATALOGUE SIGNATURE: 0000/2955/-3=840200
TITLE: Protection of the week and unarmed: the dispute over counting
human rights violations in El Salvador
AUTHOR: Mendez, Juan ; Neier, Aryeh
PLACE OF PUBLICATION: New York
PUBLISHER: Americas Watch - AW (D)
DATE OF PUBLICATION: 840200
NUMBER OF PAGES: 51 p.
LANGUAGE: ENG
STATISTICAL INFORMATION: Y
INDEX: human rights and foreign policy / fact-finding missions
GEOGRAPHICAL INDEX: El Salvador / USA
GEOGRAPHICAL CODE: 6231 / 6357
FREE TEXT: Report on the methods of investigation and reporting on
human rights used by two principal sources: the Office for Legal
Protection of the Archdiocese Commission on Justice and Peace (Tutela
Legal) and the United States government. It throws light on the
controversy existing as to the credibility and impartiality of human
rights information. The report is partly based on a cable from the
United States Embassy in San Salvador, which is commented upon in
detail. With reference to relevant humanitarian law and information
of Tutela Legal.

GUATEMALA / MEXICO

CATALOGUE SIGNATURE: 0000/1295/-0=830300
TITLE: Guatemala 1983: report of a fact finding mission by the
Unitarian Universalist Service Committee
AUTHOR: AuCoin, Les ; Miller, George ; Sensenbrenner, James F.
PLACE OF PUBLICATION: Boston
PUBLISHER: Unitarian Universalist Service Committee - UUSC (D)
DATE OF PUBLICATION: 830300
NUMBER OF PAGES: 13 p.
LANGUAGE: ENG
INDEX: human rights and foreign policy / refugees /
fact-finding missions
GEOGRAPHICAL INDEX: Guatemala / Mexico
GEOGRAPHICAL CODE: 6236 / 6243
FREE TEXT: In January 1983, a delegation from the United States House
of Representatives, the UUSC and independent experts on Latin America
traveled to Mexico and Guatemala. The purpose of the trip, which was
originally intended to include a visit to El Salvador, was to gain
first hand exposure to the broadest possible spectrum of information
about United States relations with Central America.
In Guatemala, the mission met with leaders of the ORPA (Revolutionary
Organization of the Armed People), the second most powerful guerilla
organization. The group also visited Guatemala's president, Efrain
Rios Montt, and participated in a helicopter trip to three locations
in rural Guatemala, courtesy of the army. They travelled to the state
of Chiapas in southern Mexico to talk to Guatemalan refugees, while
also conferring with church, business, government and professional
leaders. The visit to El Salvador was cancelled because of security
concerns expressed by the State Department in Mexico.
The report contains conclusions and recommendations, and personal
impressions of the participating Congressmen.

CATALOGUE SIGNATURE: 0000/2955/-3=830500
TITLE: Creating a desolation and calling it peace: May 1983 supplement
to the Report on Human Rights in Guatemala
AUTHOR: Goldman, Robert Kogod ; Kass, Stephen L. ; Burkhalter, Holly
(...et al)
PLACE OF PUBLICATION: New York
PUBLISHER: Americas Watch - AW (D)
DATE OF PUBLICATION: 830500
NUMBER OF PAGES: 47 p.
LANGUAGE: ENG
INDEX: refugees / armed violence / fact-finding missions
GEOGRAPHICAL INDEX: Guatemala / Mexico
GEOGRAPHICAL CODE: 6236 / 6243
FREE TEXT: The purpose of the mission to southern Mexico in March 1983
was to determine whether refugees from Guatemala were continuing to
cross the border and, if so, to find out why they had fled their homes.
The delegates conclude that the human rights situation in Guatemala has
deteriorated since November 1982.
With summary and findings (conclusion) and recommendation. The report
contains a large number of direct testimonies and an outline of the
judicial system (secret courts). With appendices: notes on evidence;
map of Guatemalan-Mexican border region.

CATALOGUE SIGNATURE: 0000/1291/-3=830900
TITLE: Counterinsurgency as terrorism: human rights violations in
Guatemala: a report of the National Lawyers Guild and Lawyers
Committee Against U.S. Intervention in Central America
AUTHOR: Grey Postero, Nancy ; Smith, James F. ; Bartels, Angela
(...et al)
PLACE OF PUBLICATION: Boston
PUBLISHER: National Immigration Project of the National Lawyers Guild
- NLG (D)
DATE OF PUBLICATION: 830900
NUMBER OF PAGES: 41 p.
LANGUAGE: ENG
BIBLIOGRAPHIES: Y
INDEX: refugees / fact-finding missions
GEOGRAPHICAL INDEX: Guatemala / Mexico
GEOGRAPHICAL CODE: 6236 / 6243
FREE TEXT: The aim of the mission of eight delegates was to examine
human rights violations in Guatemala, the reasons for the increased
exodus of Guatemalan refugees and the propriety of continued US
military and economic aid to the Rios Montt regime. The mission was
hosted by the Guatemalan Commission on Human Rights, which arranged
meetings with exiled organizations in Mexico City. The delegation
visited refugee camps and a hospital in southern Mexico, and spoke
with numerous refugees.
The report contains conclusions and recommendations, and chapters on
the history of the country, the violence, the situation in refugee
camps, the policy of the Mexican government towards the refugees,
the involvement of the United States in Guatemala.
With appendices: excerpts of interviews with refugees and map.

CATALOGUE SIGNATURE: 6003/2268/-3=830000
TITLE: Why don't they hear us?: report of a Canadian inter-church
fact-finding mission to Guatemala and Mexico: August 22, 1983 to
September 8, 1983
AUTHOR: Proulx, Adolphe ; Bothwell, John C. ; Moffat, M. Jeanne
(... et al)
PLACE OF PUBLICATION: Toronto
PUBLISHER: Inter-Church Committee on Human Rights in Latin America -
ICCHRLA (D) ; Inter-Church Committee on Refugees - ICCR (D)
DATE OF PUBLICATION: 830000
NUMBER OF PAGES: 29 p. in v.p.
LANGUAGE: ENG
INDEX: refugees / fact-finding missions
GEOGRAPHICAL INDEX: Guatemala / Mexico
GEOGRAPHICAL CODE: 6236 / 6243
FREE TEXT: The ICCHRLA and ICCR organized a joint fact-finding
mission of Canadian church leaders to Guatemala and Mexico. The
eight member delegation worked in two teams: five delegation members
visited Guatemala and Mexico City and four (including one member of
the first team) visited Mexico City and several camps for Guatemalan
refugees in Southern Mexico. The major objective was to acquire first
hand information on the present state of human rights in Guatemala
and the situation of the tens of thousands of Guatemalan refugees in
Mexico, in order to orient and reinforce Canadian church response.
The first part of the report contains information on the political
and economic situation, violations of social and economic rights, the
situation of internal refugees, the growing militarization, the
persecution of Christians and the situation of the churches.
The second part is on the Guatemalan refugees in Mexico, with reasons
for their flight, protection and material assistance, repatriation.
With conclusions and recommendations, and press release.

CATALOGUE SIGNATURE: 0000/2955/-3-840900
TITLE: Guatemalan refugees in Mexico: 1980-1984
AUTHOR: Valencia, Eliecer
PLACE OF PUBLICATION: New York
PUBLISHER: Americas Watch - AW (D)
DATE OF PUBLICATION: 840900
NUMBER OF PAGES: 104 p.
LANGUAGE: ENG
STATISTICAL INFORMATION: Y
BIBLIOGRAPHIES: Y
INDEX: refugees / political violence / fact-finding missions
GEOGRAPHICAL INDEX: Guatemala / Mexico
GEOGRAPHICAL CODE: 6236 / 6243
FREE TEXT: About 400.000 Central Americans have poured into Mexico in
the last few years as a result of the current political crisis in the
region. The report, based on visits to refugee camps in southern
Mexico, is critical of the government of Mexico for violating the
rights of Guatemalan refugees. It is stated that some actions of the
government reflect insensitivity to the desparate situation of the
refugees; authorities have attempted to shield some of their activities
from the press and public, which has made matters worse. Attention is
paid to the background of the situation, the conditions of Guatemalan
refugees, international relations between Mexico and Guatemala, refugee
policy, and repatriation and relocation of the refugees. With
appendices.

CATALOGUE SIGNATURE: 0000/0035/-4
TITLE: Mexique: mission d'enquête sur la situation des réfugiés
guatémaltèques: 1ère partie
AUTHOR: Chaine, Rose-Marie ; Grolleaud, Michel ; Katz, Claude
TITLE OF GENERIC ITEM: La Lettre de la FIDH
EDITION: no. 87
PLACE OF PUBLICATION: Paris
PUBLISHER: Fédération Internationale des Droits de l'Homme - FIDH (D)
DATE OF PUBLICATION: 841221
NUMBER OF PAGES: p. 4-8
LANGUAGE: FRE
INDEX: refugees / fact-finding missions
GEOGRAPHICAL INDEX: Guatemala / Mexico
GEOGRAPHICAL CODE: 6236 / 6243
FREE TEXT: The aim of the mission in November-December 1984 was to
obtain information on the situation of refugees from Guatemala on
Mexican territory. The first part of the report contains descriptions
of the conduct of the mission and contacts established, and of the
situation in the refugee camps Chajul, Tienguitas and Gloria de San
Caralampio in the region Chiapas and in the camp Quetzal-Edzna in the
region Campeche in southern Mexico.
(The second part of the report is published in La Lettre 88)

CATALOGUE SIGNATURE: 0000/0035/-4
TITLE: Mexique: mission d'enquête sur la situation des réfugiés
guatémaltèques: 2ème partie
AUTHOR: Chaine, Rose-Marie ; Grolleaud, Michel ; Katz, Claude
TITLE OF GENERIC ITEM: La Lettre de la FIDH
EDITION: no. 88
PLACE OF PUBLICATION: Paris
PUBLISHER: Fédération Internationale des Droits de l'Homme - FIDH (D)
DATE OF PUBLICATION: 841228
NUMBER OF PAGES: p. 2-5
LANGUAGE: FRE
INDEX: refugees / fact-finding missions
GEOGRAPHICAL INDEX: Guatemala / Mexico
GEOGRAPHICAL CODE: 6236 / 6243
FREE TEXT: The aim of the mission in November-December 1984 was to
obtain information on the situation of refugees from Guatemala on
Mexican territory. The second part of the report deals with the
decision of the Mexican government to transfer the refugees from
Guatemala in the regions Campeche and Quintana-Roo (with motives
of external and of internal policy), the refusal of the refugees
to leave the region Chiapas and the development of the government
policy with regard to the problem.
(The first part of the report is published in La Lettre 87)

LATIN AMERICA

CATALOGUE SIGNATURE: 0000/0039/-3=770400
TITLE: Voyage d'information sur la situation des droits de l'homme au
Chili, en Argentine, en Uruguay, au Paraguay et au Brésil
PLACE OF PUBLICATION: Geneva
PUBLISHER: Fédération Internationale des Femmes des Carrières
Juridiques - FIFCJ (D)
DATE OF PUBLICATION: 770400
NUMBER OF PAGES: 114 p.
LANGUAGE: FRE
INDEX: judicial systems / nongovernmental organizations / women /
fact-finding missions
GEOGRAPHICAL INDEX: Latin America
GEOGRAPHICAL CODE: 6003
FREE TEXT: The report consists of a description of a large number of
unofficial meetings which the three members of the mission had with
representatives of non-governmental organizations, witnesses and
victims of human rights violations and lawyers, and of on-site visits.
The mission was not official, and the meetings had a spontaneous,
improvised character. They are presented in a chronological order,
without comment. There is special attention for the position of women
in prison, and for women in general. With conclusions and appendices:
documents of nongovernmental organizations; newspaper articles.

367

CATALOGUE SIGNATURE: 6003/-0=790000
TITLE: Refugees and political prisoners in Latin America...
PLACE OF PUBLICATION: London
PUBLISHER: Joint Working Group for Refugees from Latin America - JWG
(D)
DATE OF PUBLICATION: 790000
NUMBER OF PAGES: 42 p.
LANGUAGE: ENG
BIBLIOGRAPHIES: Y
INDEX: refugees / political prisoners / fact-finding missions
GEOGRAPHICAL INDEX: Latin America
GEOGRAPHICAL CODE: 6003
FREE TEXT: The aim of the visit by a member of the JWG to countries of
the Southern Cone (Argentina, Uruguay, Brazil, Chile, Bolivia), Peru
and Costa Rica was to make an up-to-date assessment of the situation in
these countries with the purpose of reviewing the assistance programme
of the Joint Working Group and determining priorities.
The report outlines the situation of refugees in Latin America in
general, and in particular in Argentina and Brazil, and recommends
further assistance for their resettlement in third countries and for
local resettlement programmes.
The situation of political prisoners in Argentina, Uruguay and Chile
is described (they are potential refugees since their only possibility
to be released under the existing emergency legislation is by asking
for their sentences to be commuted to exile). Also the prospects for
returning to Chile and Brazil are examined. With conclusions and
recommendations aimed at improving and extending British and
international aid to refugees.

NICARAGUA / USA

CATALOGUE SIGNATURE: 0000/0018/-0=781100
TITLE: Report and recommendations of an ecumenical delegation to
Nicaragua: 8 November 1978
AUTHOR: Collett, Wallace ; McCoy, Alan ; Epps, Dwain C. (...et al)
PLACE OF PUBLICATION: (Geneva)
PUBLISHER: Commission of the Churches on International Affairs of the
World Council of Churches - CCIA-WCC (D)
DATE OF PUBLICATION: 781100
NUMBER OF PAGES: (6 p.)
AVAILABILITY: X
LANGUAGE: ENG
INDEX: peace / human rights and foreign policy / fact-finding missions
GEOGRAPHICAL INDEX: Nicaragua / USA
GEOGRAPHICAL CODE: 6245 / 6357
FREE TEXT: Concerned about the grave state of affairs in Nicaragua,
four North American church organizations sent their representatives,
in order to determine how they might contribute to a just, peaceful
and lasting solution to the present conflict. The mission established
contacts with a very broad spectrum of people in Nicaragua, and with
groups and persons aiding refugees in Costa Rica. The report contains
their opinions on the situation in Nicaragua, and recommendations.
With appendix: telexes with information on involvement of the
government of the United States in Nicaragua.

SOUTH AMERICA

CATALOGUE SIGNATURE: 0000/2762/-0=810000
TITLE: Youth for freedom and democracy in Brasil, Argentina, Uruguay, Paraguay
PLACE OF PUBLICATION: Budapest
PUBLISHER: World Federation of Democratic Youth - WFDY (D)
DATE OF PUBLICATION: 810000
NUMBER OF PAGES: 23 p.
LANGUAGE: ENG
INDEX: youth / nongovernmental organizations / dictatorship / fact-finding missions
GEOGRAPHICAL INDEX: South America
GEOGRAPHICAL CODE: 6400
FREE TEXT: Report of a visit to Brazil, Argentina, Uruguay and Paraguay in May-June 1980. The report contains chapters on each country visited, with general information on the political and socio-economic situation, the situation of human rights and a description of the work of social organizations, political parties and personalities with which contacts were established.

AUSTRALIA

CATALOGUE SIGNATURE: 0000/0084/-3=810000
TITLE: Justice for Aboriginal Australians: report of the World Council
of Churches team visit to the Aborigines: June 15 to July 3, 1981
AUTHOR: Adler, Elisabeth ; Barkat, Anwar ; Bena-Silu (...et al)
PLACE OF PUBLICATION: Sydney
PUBLISHER: Programme to Combat Racism ; World Council of Churches - WCC
DISTRIBUTOR: Australian Council of Churches
DATE OF PUBLICATION: 810000
NUMBER OF PAGES: 90 p.
ISBN: 2 8254 0693 7
LANGUAGE: ENG
STATISTICAL INFORMATION: Y
BIBLIOGRAPHIES: Y
INDEX: indigenous peoples   social and economic rights
  discrimination   fact-finding missions
GEOGRAPHICAL INDEX: Australia
GEOGRAPHICAL CODE: 9012
FREE TEXT: The purpose of the mission was to assess the situation of
Australian Aborigines. The five delegates received most of their
information from Aborigines themselves. The report contains sections
on social and economic problems: land rights, mining, equality before
the law, health, housing, education, employment. With attention to
the responsibility of the government, political participation,
spirituality and culture. With summary of recommendations and
appendices: itinerary of the mission, materials examined, letters to
Aboriginals and to churches.

NEW CALEDONIA

CATALOGUE SIGNATURE: 0000/0018/-4=840000
TITLE: New Caledonia: towards Kanak independence: reports of an
ecumenical visit to New Caledonia: 27 April - 11 May 1984
AUTHOR: Weingaertner, Erich ; Trautmann, Frederic
PLACE OF PUBLICATION: Geneva
PUBLISHER: Commission of the Churches on International Affairs of the
World Council of Churches - CCIA-WCC (D)
DATE OF PUBLICATION: 840000
NUMBER OF PAGES: 51 p.
SERIES TITLE: Background information
VOLUME: v. 1984/2
LANGUAGE: ENG
INDEX: self-determination   indigenous peoples
  non-self governing territories   fact-finding missions
GEOGRAPHICAL INDEX: New Caledonia
GEOGRAPHICAL CODE: 9020
FREE TEXT: The report examines the current stage of the problem of the
self-determination and independence of the Melanesian people of New
Caledonia, the "Kanaks". The first part contains an analysis of the
political developments which have led to the current deadlock between
the French government and the inhabitants of New Caledonia. The second
is in the form of an interview and contains more details regarding the
church's position, actions and witness. With appendices: chronology of
events; standpoint, statements and resolutions of churches and the WCC;
discussion in French National Assembly.

PAPUA NEW GUINEA - PNG / INDONESIA

CATALOGUE SIGNATURE: 0000/0902/-3=850100
TITLE: The status of border crossers from Irian Jaya to Papua New
Guinea: report on mission to Papua New Guinea 2 to 16 September 1984
concerning the refugee status of "border crossers" from Irian Jaya
PLACE OF PUBLICATION: Sydney (Australia)
PUBLISHER: International Commission of Jurists, Australian section -
ICJ-AU (D)
DATE OF PUBLICATION: 850100
NUMBER OF PAGES: 68 p.
ISBN: 0 909738 04 1
LANGUAGE: ENG
BIBLIOGRAPHIES: Y
INDEX: refugees   fact-finding missions
GEOGRAPHICAL INDEX: Papua New Guinea - PNG / Indonesia
GEOGRAPHICAL CODE: 9024 / 7526
FREE TEXT: The mission to Papua New Guinea was sent by the Executive
Committee of the International Commission of Jurists (Australian
section). It consisted of six members (five members of the Australian
section of the ICJ and one representative of the Netherlands Institute
of Human Rights (SIM)).
The report contains: I) introduction (background and summary of the
mission) II) historical background; III) repatriation and the
constitution of Papua New Guinea; IV)international law concerning
refugees; V) attitudes of governments involved; VI) report on visits
to the camps; VII) the humanitarian issues of aid and assistance;
VIII) conclusions; appendix I) meetings, discussions and interviews;
appendix II) bibliography.

TRUST TERRITORY OF THE PACIFIC ISLANDS / USA

CATALOGUE SIGNATURE: 0000/0018/-4
TITLE: Marshall Islands: 37 years after: report of a World Council of
Churches delegation to the Marshall Islands, 20 May - 4 June, 1983
AUTHOR: Cole, Kara L. ; Cochran, Thomas B. ; Nabetari, Baiteke
(...et al)
PLACE OF PUBLICATION: Geneva
PUBLISHER: Commission of the Churches on International Affairs of the
World Council of Churches - CCIA-WCC (D)
DATE OF PUBLICATION: 831200
NUMBER OF PAGES: 45 p.
SERIES TITLE: Background information
VOLUME: v. 1983/5
LANGUAGE: ENG
INDEX: weapons of mass destruction   peace   fact-finding misssions
GEOGRAPHICAL INDEX: Trust Territory of the Pacific Islands /
USA
GEOGRAPHICAL CODE: 9030 / 6357
FREE TEXT: Report of four member delegation of the World Council of
Churches to the Marshall Islands. In 1946, the USA tested an atomic
bomb on Bikini island; the inhabitants were relocated and not allowed
to return. Since then, the US tested large atomic and hydrogen bombs
and numerous other weapons, such as the MX Missile, at the Marshall
Islands. During the fifties, the tests contaminated hundreds of
islanders with radioactive fallout. There are many health problems.
The education, medical treatment and compensation offered by the US
government are considered inadequate. There is a growing resentment,
especially against the US military presence at Kwajalein island. With:
WCC Sixth Assembly resolution on the Pacific, critical correspondence
between US government representative and the WCC.

CATALOGUE SIGNATURE: 0000/0018/-0=860300
TITLE: Report of visit to Belau: 4-11 March 1986
AUTHOR: Hsu, Victor; Quass, Susan
PLACE OF PUBLICATION: (Geneva)
PUBLISHER: Commission of the Churches on International Affairs of the
World Council of Churches - CCIA-WCC (D)
DATE OF PUBLICATION: 860300
NUMBER OF PAGES: 15 p.
LANGUAGE: ENG
INDEX: elections / self-determination / fact-finding missions
GEOGRAPHICAL INDEX: Trust Territory of the Pacific Islands /
USA
GEOGRAPHICAL CODE: 9030 / 6357
FREE TEXT: The aim of the mission of the CCIA / WCC and the Pacific
Conference of Churches was to observe the plebiscite on the "Improved"
Compact of Free Association with the United States of America, to be
held on 21 February 1986. This treaty is being negotiated between
Belau and the US to define their future political, economic and
security relationship. Free Association is to be an interim status
of self-government for Belau, which is less than independence.
The report deals with the socio-economic and political situation
of Belau, and the role of the churches. With conclusions and maps.

INDICES

377

COUNTRY INDEX

Country Index

PUBLISHERS INDEX

Publishers Index

KEYWORD INDEX